GASLIGHT NEW YORK REVISITED

Edited by Frank Oppel

CASTLE

Contents

The New York Police Department (1887)

HARPER'S
NEW MONTHLY MAGAZINE.

VOL. LXXIV.   MARCH, 1887.   No. CCCCXLII.

THE NEW YORK POLICE DEPARTMENT.

BY RICHARD WHEATLEY.

NEW-YORKERS religiously believe that they have the best police system and the finest police force in existence. As represented by the Board of Aldermen—August 11, 1886—they hold that "the Police Department has reached a standard of efficiency hitherto unattained, and superior to that of any force in the world." This opinion, expressed after the funeral of ex-President Grant, may only be that of a majority; but, nevertheless, exceptions prove the rule.

What is the number of the metropolitan police force? what are its duties? how is it organized? and in what manner are its duties performed? are questions whose answers determine the soundness or unsoundness of the popular faith.

The number of the police force, of all ranks and grades, on the last day of A.D. 1885, was 2933, including 35 probationers. The Legislature of the State of New York, on May 12, 1886, unanimously authorized the addition of 500, in deference to the general conviction that it was numerically too small to cope with the possible emergencies of the times. The city of New York, estimating its population at 1,650,000, then had, exclusive of the Central Park force, one police-officer to every 562 of the inhabitants. This, in view of the heterogeneous character of the people, and the peculiar relation of the city to the continent, was really an insufficient supply. In 1883 Philadelphia had one policeman to every 636 of its citizens; Baltimore, one to 525; Boston, one to 487; the metropolitan district of London, one to 342; and the ancient city of London, one to every 100.

The Police Department of New York, established and organized under the law of 1870, consists of the Board of Police—which is composed of four Commissioners, appointed by the Mayor—of the police force, and of officials appointed by the Commissioners. The term of each Commissioner extends over six years, during which his labors are lightened by the aid of a secretary. His salary is fixed at $5000 per annum. Stephen B. French, President of the Board of Police, is of French and Dutch ancestry, and is a native of Long Island. Fitness for his post was largely received through the early discipline of a sperm-whaler's adventurous experience, followed by nearly five years of changeful fortune in California. Mercantile life next sharpened his faculties, and prepared him for the conspicuous career in politics and public affairs upon which he entered in 1865. Appointed Police Commissioner in May, 1879, he was elected to the presidency of the Board in 1880, and still retains that office.

Fitz-John Porter, appointed October 28, 1884, is a native of New Hampshire, a graduate of West Point Military Academy, and a distinguished officer of the Mexican and civil wars.

John McClave, appointed November 24, 1884, was born in New York, graduated at the College of the City of New York, is a lumber merchant by occupation, and a successful politician.

John R. Voorhis, appointed May 9, 1885, was born in New Jersey, is a builder by trade, and is now serving for the third time as Commissioner of Police. Like all his colleagues, he is credited with rare intuition, quick perception, concentrated thought, remarkable tact, endurance, and executive ability. Courteous, prompt, positive, and efficient, the members of the Board of Police exemplify some of the best qualities of the American body-politic.

Each member of the Board of Police has specific duties. The President must examine and approve charges against officers of all grades before they are tried,

THE NEW YORK POLICE HEAD-QUARTERS, MULBERRY STREET.

and also answer communications on police subjects from all parts of the world. Commissioner Voorhis, as chairman of the Committee on Repairs and Supplies, is the purchaser of all required materials, and carefully scrutinizes the bills therefor rendered. He also visits all station-houses, and inspects their conditions and requirements. Commissioner Porter is chairman of the Board of Trustees of the Police Pension Fund, and as such spends much time in examining the applications of widows for pensions, petitions for retirement by old members of the force, and other matters of similar nature. Commissioner McClave is treasurer of the Police Board and also of the Pension Fund. In the first capacity he disbursed, during the year 1886, the sum of $3,853,272, appropriated by the Board of Estimate and Apportionment for the maintenance of the Police Department, and in the second, more than $250,000, collected from different sources, and paid over to pension-

ers. The office of Commissioner is not a sinecure, and when worthily filled absorbs most of the business time and energy of the incumbent.

Every Wednesday at 10 A.M. one of the number must preside at the trial of members of the force against whom written specific charges have been preferred. Pertinent testimony, sometimes given under subpœna, for or against the accused, is reduced to writing by an official stenographer, and must be examined by three at least of the Commissioners. Their proceedings are subject to review in the civil courts. All judgments must be in writing, entered in the department records, and notice thereof read to the force of the precinct to which the inculpated member belongs. During the year 1885 no less than 2570 charges were preferred against officers of all grades for violation of the rules. Some were accused of being off their posts, some of talking while on duty, and others of weightier offences. Sixteen dismissals, mainly for intoxication, followed, 1620 were fined to the amount of $9487 86, 317 reprimanded, and 517 exculpated. The remaining cases were still pending at the close of the year. All orders to the Superintendent of Police issue from the Board, and all expenditures of the Secret Service Fund for procuring useful information and for the arrest of criminals and suspects are at their discretion. Experience, observation, and inquiry combined have thus organized the Board of Police. They have **also** dictated the Superintendent's practice of frequently summoning each of the thirty-four captains to head-quarters, instructing them in the wishes of the Commissioners, and thus infusing fresh vigor and effectiveness into the entire force. The lax enforcement of excise laws, of the statutes in relation to gambling-houses and prostitutes, and the imminence of riot in labor strikes, are among the occasions of these personal interviews. Through this administration New York may justly claim that it affords as much of safety to life, liberty, and property as any city on the globe. Pugnacious ruffians, "sp'ilin' for a fight," can always be accommodated. The elements of violence and crime are never absent, but every outbreak is tolerably certain to leave the transgressor in the iron hands of justice. Political "pulls" have lost much of their ancient power, and should be totally paralyzed.

Under the instructions of the Board of Police, the members of the force exercise all the common-law and statutory powers of constables, except for the service of civil process; execute warrants for search or arrest issued by magistrates of the State in any part of it, and convey prisoners to the districts where they are made returnable; summarily arrest persons reasonably suspected of felony when found in the streets at night, or when visibly guilty of felony or misdemeanor; and may enter any house or building to suppress an affray or to execute plain duty. But they are prohibited from doing more than is necessary to the safe custody of prisoners in charge, from the use of pro-

STEPHEN B. FRENCH.

voking language, taking offence at harsh or abusive talk, or making arrests in personal quarrels, unless justified by the necessity of self-defence.

Ranking in the following order, 1, Superintendent, 2, Inspector, 3, Captain, 4, Sergeant, 5, Roundsman, 6, Patrolman, 7, Doorman, each division of the police force is charged with definite duties.

JOHN McCLAVE.

FITZ-JOHN PORTER.

JOHN R. VOORHIS.

watch-makers and jewellers, shows the estimation in which he is held by the mercantile community. The Socialists, whom he dispersed during the labor riots of 1877, respect his vigorous bravery. He divides with Inspector Byrnes the credit of unmasking more crime and convicting more criminals than any other man in the department. When raised from the rank of Inspector to that of Superintendent, he at once centralized the management, diminished the cost, and increased the efficiency of the force. He assigns the Inspectors in rotation to duty, issues orders received from the Board of Police, and supplements them with others in harmony with the originals and with the laws of the

William Murray, appointed Superintendent of Police on the 9th of June, 1885, is the chief executive officer. For the occupancy of this arduous and responsible position he has been qualified by long years of excellent service. Born in New York, wounded at Bull Run while serving in the Ellsworth Zouaves, and joining the police force in 1866, he signalized himself by some very skilful arrests. To thieves, burglars, and gamblers his name is one of terror. A thousand-dollar watch and chain, presented by forty prominent

WILLIAM MURRAY.

THOMAS BYRNES.

commonwealth. Exercising direct authority over detached companies, making and reporting details, inspecting prisons and station-houses, and the books and business of the latter; enforcing the laws against gambling-houses, lotteries, lewd resorts, and racing in the streets; assuming command at riots and great fires, reporting to the Board all diseases and nuisances that threaten the health or comfort of the citizens, providing for emergencies by suggestion, as in the establishment of the Bellevue Hospital ward for sick prisoners; keeping record of all orders, expenses, suspicious persons and places, reported crimes and misdemeanors for which no arrests have been made, houses of pros-

titution, assignation, and gambling—
his life is necessarily a busy one. Office-
work is abundant. The daily returns
from the various precincts must be examined and noted, grievances and complaints of visitors disposed of, Inspectors' reports scrutinized and the Inspectors instructed, the daily consolidated
report to the Board of Police prepared,
and the names of those arrested and
detained, and the reasons therefor, reported. Duty does not cease with daylight, but requires frequent nocturnal
visitation of precincts and station-
houses, in order to certainty that the
condition of all is agreeable to law.
The Superintendent is also obliged to
report quarterly upon the state of the
force, and to incorporate such statistics
and suggestions for its improvement as
to him may seem advisable. Besides
this, his duty is to forward all sworn
and formal charges against subordinates to the Committee on Rules and
Discipline for action. His salary of
$6000 appears to be well earned.

The four Inspectors are no less busily
employed. At present there are only
three, viz., Thomas Byrnes, George W.
Dilks, and Henry V. Steers. The last
joined the force in 1857, rose through all
the grades to his present position, while
patrolman saved seven persons from
drowning, and distinguished himself by
singly thrashing a desperate bully who
led a gang of desperadoes in their nightly
depredations. His knowledge of "crooks"
is exhaustive, and his respect for their
courage exceedingly small. Driven to
desperation, they often fight like cornered
rats, but will not add murder to lesser
crime unless certain of escape. To effect
the latter the most dangerous chances are
recklessly accepted. On the approach of
every storm Inspector Steers's barometric
ankle painfully recalls the memory of a
leap that nearly shook the teeth out of
his head, from the top of a high house to
that of one much lower, while in hot pursuit of a burglar, whom he triumphantly
captured.

George W. Dilks, who entered the force
as assistant captain in 1848, was made Inspector in 1860. In the tragic Astor Place
riot, incited by jealousy between the actors Forrest and Macready, he judiciously
commanded a body of police; and in the
terrible longshoremen's riots of 1857 conquered the disturbers, who fought with

GEORGE W. DILKS.

hay-sticks, cart-rungs. clubs, etc., after a
four days' conflict. In the draft riots of
1863 his gallantry was no less manifest.

Each Inspector is responsible for the
preservation of the peace and protection
of life and limb in his own district. His
daily and quarterly reports of duty, discipline, and police circumstance, together
with his books of record, contain much of
the matter on which the action of his official superiors is based. The long experience and excellent judgment of the three
Inspectors induced the Commissioners to

HENRY V. STEERS.

ALEXANDER S. WILLIAMS.

constitute them a Board of Examiners, whose duty it is to examine all applicants for promotion in the force before permitting them to appear before the Civil Service Examining Board.

The Board of Police Surgeons, which consists of eighteen professional men, including the president and secretary, is a constituent part of the force. Its members are not allowed to receive compensation for medical services to police-officers, nor to prefer private practice to the performance of official duty. It is also part of their task to take medical and surgical charge, gratuitously, of pensioners upon the Police Life-Insurance Fund and of their families whenever requested.

During the year 1885 the number of visits made by surgeons to police-officers was 22,863, and of visits to station-houses 816. More than 175 different diseases or injuries received treatment, and 2.48 per cent. of the corps were perpetually sick. Seven hundred and thirty-four applicants for appointment as patrolmen were examined, and 460 passed. Only three were found to be men of bad character and reputation.

Each of the thirty-four captains is vested with the power, subject to regulations, of posting the men under his command in such portions of his precinct, and of assigning to them such duties, as he may

think expedient. He must further make known the special merit or demerit of his inferiors, divide them into two platoons of two sections each, assign a sergeant to the command of each section, and one to the charge of the station-house.

The police captain is held strictly responsible for the preservation of the public peace in his own precinct, the safe custody of prisoners, the order and hygienic condition of his official quarters, and the due preservation of the library. Civility and due attention to all who call upon business affairs are to be exhibited, and all discussions of party politics by the men rigidly suppressed. He is required to journalize the times of his entering and leaving the building, to make requisitions for needful supplies, keep special record of all arrests and for what crimes, of the results of judicial proceedings, of the term of sentence and place of imprisonment of the convicted, and to report quarterly in detail. Every item of police duty, and of civil or criminal occurrence, is inscribed on the "blotter," which thus becomes a photographic exhibit of daily events affecting the peace and welfare of the city.

Many of the captains richly merit description of their services to the community. Space permits but the briefest allusions. Captain J. J. Mount and other officers of the same rank covered themselves with credit and renown by efficient gallantry in the draft and other riots. Captain Alexander S. Williams is one of the most prominent of his class. Perfectly fearless and resolute, he has made himself the dread and scourge of the worst criminals coming within reach of his arm. The Florence saloon and "Mulligan's Hell" were closed by his prowess. Very large amounts of property have been recovered by his ingenuity. His precinct is known as the "Tenderloin," because of its social characteristics. But none of its celebrities are allowed to infract the laws with impunity. One of the most eminent of newspaper proprietors is said to have been arrested and locked up on two different occasions for furious driving in the streets. Captain Williams's club enjoys the reputation among the roughs of being as hard, ready, and rough as themselves, and is certainly a notable instrument. Its owner is one of the most venomously hated, frequently tried, and most valuable of police-officers.

Should any captaincy be vacant, or the

incumbent be absent, a sergeant of the precinct is selected by the Superintendent or by the Board of Police to possess and exercise all his powers. Sergeants in rotation daily inspect the beds, bedding, clothes, and habits of policemen in their respective districts, and give to prisoners or lodgers memoranda of articles taken from them. One of the number goes on patrol with his section or platoon, vigilantly attends to duty throughout the tour, and returns with his men at its close. All of the 152 sergeants are required to have something of the military martinet in their composition, but not more than good taste and discipline justify. As such they report all derelictions from duty and all violations of order.

Sergeant T. V. Holbrow is keeper of the House of Detention, at 203 Mulberry Street, and returns daily to the Chief Clerk the number and names of committed and discharged witnesses who are unable to furnish security for appearance in criminal proceedings, and the number of those who remain in custody. He also reports weekly on the sanitary and dietary condition of his unique mansion. All letters addressed to the inmates must be open, submitted to his inspection, and also to delivery or retention as he may judge best. All conversations with the imprisoned are held in his presence, noted by him, and reported to the district Inspector. He himself is inhibited from converse with them, except in so far as their safe-keeping, comfort, or convenience is concerned.

Personal examination (April, 1886) of this dubious residence discovers that it consists of two buildings on the same lot, of which the one fronting on the street is allotted to women, who may go up and down its five stories at pleasure, but cannot leave it by front or rear. The back building is occupied by males, whose lavatory and bath-room are on the ground-floor; six bedrooms, with five beds in each, on the second, third, and fourth stories, and room for exercise in the fifth. The dining-room on the front lower floor displays the plain, wholesome food provided at so much per meal by the lady purveyor at the cost of the city. Six hundred volumes of light literature, history, biography, and travel beguile the tedium of captivity. Three women and fourteen men are held in durance questionable. One of the latter is deftly braiding horse-hair chains; the rest are vegetating in uncanny seclusion. All have been brought

PATROL WAGON.

hither since the 12th of the month. Unfortunates have occasionally been detained as long as four months, or even longer. Foreign residence, lack of fixed abode, probable purchasability, unwillingness to testify — as in the case of complainant strangers despoiled in houses of ill fame —and inability to give bail are held by many to warrant this forcible detention of witnesses to homicide or felonious assault. Here their board is free, remuneration by District Attorney or Judge probable, safety from bribery or intimidation assured, and presence, when needed to satisfy justice, secured. The Society for the Prevention of Cruelty to Children sometimes causes commitments to this establishment.

Opinions about the House of Detention are variant. It is a prison, and a gloomy one, although fare and lodging may be better than what the majority of miserable inmates ordinarily enjoy. Humanitarians, such as Mr. William Delamater, wish to see it abolished. The Police Report for 1885 regards it as "not only a blot upon the fair fame of this community, but a standing rebuke to the proper administration of justice in this great city." It is true that the wealthy criminal is often liberated on bail, while the poor friendless witness of his guilt is confined in jail. Here justice and liberty are at manifest odds. In 1885 the number of committals was 307; of discharges, 314; the average number of days' confinement to each prisoner, about 17; and the average price of meals for each person detained, $12 56. Add to the cost of food and maintenance the salaries of officers in charge, and the expenses of an institution "not demanded by justice or humanity" are seen to be considerable.

The duties of the 177 roundsmen—two to each platoon—include constant patrol, wise action in exigent cases, and exemplary conduct. Clerical offices and telegraphic operation when in-doors, behind the desk, are exacted of them.

The bulk of the police force, corresponding to the privates or enlisted men of the regular army, consisted on the 1st of January, 1886, of the 2396 patrolmen. On the 15th of June, according to the return of Deputy Chief Clerk Delamater, the native nationality of the 2936 men of all ranks and grades then constituting the police force was as follows: United States, 1745; Ireland, 974; Germany, 136; Austria, 4; Italy, 5; Switzerland, 1; Canada, 13; England, 30; Finland, 1; Scotland, 14; France, 6; Bavaria, 1; Nova Scotia, 2; Denmark, 1; Sweden, 2; West Indies, 1. Thus the United States have contributed 59.46, Ireland 33.17, and all other countries 7.37 per cent. of the whole. The Hibernian element, including those born in this country, is decidedly predominant. Naturally enough, those in whose constitution habits of subordination to authority have been ingrained by generations of servitude are most watchful and resolute when the enforcement of law is intrusted to their hands. Whatever their ancestral antecedents, the New York police have invariably illustrated the virtues of implicit obedience, self-control, manly courage, and intelligent fidelity. The club is at times quite freely used. The ideal policeman is only an ideal. The actual is but an approximation to the imaginary archetype, because he is only a man under all the limitations of the commonplace American citizen. Still, we are fain to believe he is a decided improvement upon the first uniformed policeman (July 8, 1693), who was invested by order of the Mayor with "a coat of ye citty livery, with a badge of ye citty arms, shoes, and stockings," charged to "ye account of the citty." He certainly is a vastly emended edition of the star-labelled functionary of 1850, whose favorite roosting-place was the barrels of a corner grocery, and who was commonly conspicuous for absence when his presence was most grievously needed. Out of the 700 or 800 more or less applicants for appointment every year, it is matter of congratulation that so few unfit men are successful.

Every candidate is duly examined as to his fitness for the service. This fitness must be of perfect physical health and superior muscular and physical development. Stature should not be under 5 feet $7\frac{1}{2}$ inches on the bare feet, avoirdupois, without clothing, of 138 pounds, and naked chest measurement of $33\frac{1}{2}$ inches. Any disease bars acceptance, and is ground of dismissal. He must also be neat and cleanly in person, and free from the use of private medicine at the epoch of appointment. Intellectual qualification must be equal to the due discharge of police duty. Besides the ability to read and write the English language understandingly, he must be sufficiently ac-

THE NEW YORK POLICEMAN OF 1693.

quainted with municipal, State, and national law to comprehend the nature and extent of his functions. This, together with expert professional knowledge, is acquired in the School of Instruction under the officer in charge and his assistants.

The School of Instruction has two departments, one for drill in the school of the soldier and of the company, and the other for instruction at Police Head-quarters. In the latter, Sergeant Henry O. Corbett instructs neophytes in about two hundred rules of patrol duty.

The undergraduates are further instructed as to the authority of policemen under the Code of Criminal Procedure. Police powers under the Sanitary Code are also made clear. No curriculum of instruction in pastoral theology, clinical surgery, or legal procedure is more exhaustive. Not one is so thorough. A surgeon sent by the Society on First Aid to the Injured adds the finishing touches by a course of five lectures. Examination follows, and if the examined pass the ordeal, each receives a certificate from the society. Familiarity with rules and duties is to be subsequently kept alive by comprehensive study of the Police Manual.

The moral character of every applicant must have the voucher of five petitioners for his appointment—all of whom certify from personal knowledge to his sobriety, industry, and good conduct—and also the corroborative testimony of independent official investigation. He must also endure the test of civil service examination by Inspector Byrnes, Hugh Bonner, the chief of the Fire Department, and the secretary of the Board. This puts his memory, knowledge of localities, and aptitude for business to the proof. Vacancies are filled by those who have passed highest in open competitive examinations, and have borne the athletic trials of Wood's Gymnasium and of preliminary drill. Promotions are regulated by the same standard. Preference in appointment is given to such as have been honorably discharged from the military or naval service of the United States in the civil war. One month of satisfactory probation is followed by certified appointment, but does not exempt from triennial inquiry into general fitness for continuance in service. Neither political nor religious opinion or affiliation can legally affect appointment or promotion. Both are professedly based upon positive merit. The Board of Police is equally divided between the two great political parties; a majority of the captains is said to belong to one, and a majority of the sergeants to the other; the inferior officers and men are equally divided between both. Religion and politics—the two things about which ordinary men care most—are supposedly ignored in presence of known and sworn duty. The persistence with which both intrude themselves into all human arrangements may, notwithstanding, lend some color of justification to the boastful assertion of power to "get a man on the police."

Investiture with all the rights and responsibilities of the baton is, according to the Police Manual, to be justified by the subsequent course of the appointee. He is required to be truthful and respectful, not meddlesome, prompt to quell disturbance, not to maltreat or use unnecessary violence toward citizen or criminal, to fill the measure of police regulations, not to drink nor to accept rewards, free passes, or tickets. He is expected to illustrate the golden virtue of silence, and to abstain from indulgence in some games, while permitted to play in others. The use of slang is forbidden to him; nevertheless, what he doesn't know of this peculiar form of language is not worth acquaintance. He is not allowed to borrow money of fellow-officers. On election days he must exercise due vigilance

in removing all ballot booths from within 150 feet of the polling-places. Fire-telegraph keys are to be faithfully kept, complaints and violations of city ordinances reported.

The privileges of police-officers are of such obvious value as to invest their position with the attribute of desirability. Unlike their brethren in the United Kingdom of Great Britain and Ireland, they may vote for all elective officers, but may not be active or offensive partisans. They may, with consent of the Board of Police, receive rewards for extraordinary and meritorious services. While actually on duty they are not liable to military or jury duty, nor to arrest on civil process, nor to service of subpoenas from civil courts. Each class of officers has a distinctive uniform; all are under impartial rules of transfer and promotion, and are paid monthly. Salaries range as follows: Doorman, $1000; Patrolman, $1000 for the first year, $1100 the second, and $1200 subsequently; Roundsman, $1200; Sergeant, $1600; Police Surgeon, $2200, Captain, $2750; and Inspector, $3500. After twenty years of service each member is entitled to retirement from active duty, and to an annual pension of $600. He may be in the full health and vigor of manhood, but the authorities have no power to refuse his legal rights. Steps that ought to be successful have been taken to remedy this defect in the pension laws.

Limitation is commensurate with privilege. The knights of the club are debarred from membership in fire or military organizations, from soliciting contributions for political purposes, asking any citizen to interfere in their relations to the force, conferring presents or testimonials upon other members, and from circulating subscriptions for charities without permission of the Board. All the time of every policeman must be bestowed on duty; his post is to be perpetually perambulated, his residence established in the city and known to his superior, his bed and bedding in the station-house, his presence at the roll-call, and his energies at command until his resignation—if he should resign—is accepted by the Board of Police.

Reprimand, delay or forfeiture of pay, or dismissal from further employment, follows upon intoxication, disrespect or insubordination to superiors, neglect of duty, disobedience to orders, incapacity, immoral or injurious behavior. The Corporation

PRISONERS BROUGHT INTO ESSEX MARKET COURT.

Counsel is employed to defend them when charged as members of the force, if there be apparent grounds of defense. Dismissals are announced to the entire corps. Court squads, organized for the service of criminal processes and the execution of Police Court orders in criminal cases, are subject to the same disciplinary provisions. Appeal to the civil courts is allowed. Whether the proceedings in the trial before the Police Commissioners have been in harmony with the forms of law is then the subject of inquiry. If not, the dismissed officer is reinstated. Chancellor Howard Crosby, in the first number of *The Forum*, strongly objects to this, and says: "As it is at present, the Police Commissioners of New York know the abominable character of some men on the force, but cannot dismiss them, because the civil courts with their abounding technicalities will at once reinstate them. The thing has been tried, and with this result. Thus the police captain may defy the Board of Commissioners, for they dare not remove him. The Legislature should make the Board's power final." Men of large and long experience differ from the energetic reformer in respect of this matter, and

maintain that the review of police trials by the civil courts is necessary to justice; that it preserves officers from the pique of politicians, imparts independence to police action, and strengthens fidelity by probability of redress from the higher constituted authorities. The Police Department prefers primary trial of an officer accused of felony or misdemeanor by a criminal court. If conviction follow, vacation of office is simultaneous, and clerical action alone is necessary. Superintendent Murray speaks of a policeman who on his "day off" left the station-house at 6.20 A.M., was convicted of drunkenness and disorderly conduct at 11, reported to the Superintendent and thence to the Police Board, and by 1 P.M. had ceased to be a member of the force. This course of action was certainly "short, sharp, decisive." In the Bureau of Records and Complaints, at the Central Office, the records of all complaints, civic or official, are preserved; papers are made out, subpœnas issued, and notes of procedure in all cases kept.

Doormen—77 in all—are the uniformed officers who exercise the functions of general house-keepers, maids-of-all-work, jailers, etc., at the several station-houses.

Changes in *personnel* of the police force in 1885 were such as indicate faithfulness, aspiration, efficiency, and healthy movement: 44 of the members died, and 77 were retired; only 2½ per cent. of all the days of service were those of sickness, and most of the sickness was clearly traceable to the unhealthiness, discomfort, and defective plumbing of barrack accommodation.

Clerks and employés belong to the Police Department, but not to the police force, although subject to many of the same regulations.

Each of the higher officers is held to the faithful performance of duty by a bond executed by himself and by two resident freeholders as sureties. That of the Property Clerk is for $25,000; of the Superintendent, for $20,000; of the Inspectors, for $15,000; and of the Captains, for $10,000.

How and to what extent the objects of the police system are accomplished by the metropolitan organization is of vital interest to the public. The *prevention of crime* is the most important object in view. To this end the patrolman devotes himself, or ought to devote himself. He acquires a sight acquaintance with residents, scrutinizes strangers, and suppresses criminal energies. The security of dwellings and other buildings, the surveillance of suspects and disorderly houses, the arrest of criminals, and the irregularities of servants, are within the scope of his action. In 1885 no less than 1190 buildings were found open, and were secured by the police. Among them were banks, churches, factories, 61 shops, and 765 stores. Suspicion of complicity with thieves is suggested by these figures. The patrolman is expected to search suspicious characters and parcels abroad at unseasonable hours, and thus to prevent the crime of housebreaking. Under section 1, chapter 747, Laws of 1872, he arrests sellers or possessors of obscene books, pictures, model casts, articles of indecent or immoral use, and thus prevents the corruption of society and the ruin of numerous lives. Repression, not cure, is the work of the police.

Gambling implements, lottery tickets, or lottery policies—all occasions of theft and embezzlement—the police aim to seize and destroy. In 1885, 122 persons were arrested for gambling, and 30 for keeping gambling-houses. Publicity of this vice has ceased, but those who wish to indulge

in it will always find opportunity. Perverted ingenuity tasks its powers to create the means. Magisterial and judicial dignity is sometimes fascinated by "poker," and declares it to be a social and defensible amusement. Nevertheless the police have secured the conviction of some poker-players. "Pool-selling," "book-making," or the registration of bets on sporting events, is an annoying and pernicious form of gambling to many citizens, but not to all police-magistrates. Some of them have held that the gambler should see the event on which he stakes his money before he can be held for infraction of the law. Fortunately the opinion of the Counsel to the Corporation overruled that of these unwise Solons, and offenders were driven from the city to follow their nefarious trade in other localities. The number of arrests for all forms of gambling was 303; of these 152 were discharged, 115 convicted, and 36 left in suspense. The lottery and policy business is so nearly broken up that only 33 arrests were made, and these mainly of peripatetic venders who travel from one customer to another to book their ventures.

The sale and use of intoxicating liquors are well known to be the most prolific source of pauperism, intemperance, and crime. Public sentiment is not sufficiently educated to insist upon total prohibition. It consents to license, and the closure of saloons and bars on Sundays, prohibits sale to minors and drunkards, and endorses the Civil Damages Act. But it fails to speak with legislative precision. Legists and jurists, who may or may not love alcoholic stimulants, hamper and restrain the police by conflicting opinions as to their powers and duties. Failure to enforce the Sunday law is more frequently the fault of the police judiciary—whose trustworthiest supporters are liquor-sellers, —than of police-officers. The latter indignantly speak of notorious cases where the plainest evidence has been ignored by judicial Dogberries, and the flagrant offenders dismissed to prosecute their injurious business unpunished. Whatever of improvement is visible on Sundays is mainly due to the police, who in 1885 made 2144 arrests for violation of the Excise Law, of which 1715 were for transgressions of the Sunday clauses: 255 convictions, 735 discharges, and 1154 cases undecided do not afford too much encouragement to zealous fidelity in the future,

ONE OF THE BROADWAY SQUAD.

whatever their influence upon the official status of the eleven police justices—of whom three at a time are assigned to preside in the Court of Special Sessions—may be. Publicity should be given to the disposition of every case brought into court. If this were done through one or more reputable newspapers, it is not at all probable that so many as six thousand bailable cases would at any time in the future, as at one epoch in the past (Chancellor Crosby being the authority), be found pigeonholed in the District Attorney's office in New York. It is assuredly not the fault of the Police Department that judicial courts are taxed beyond their powers of administration, and that district attorneys are, as alleged, so occupied with the management of unbailable cases as to find no time for the prosecution of bailable ones. Many thousand cases of felony and misdemeanor are now pending in the criminal courts. Some of these have been waiting for trial for several years. The Grand Jury of the city has recommended the establishment of an additional criminal court for the special trial of excise cases.

On election days the office of the police is to protect the ballot-boxes. Much of the elective machinery is under the control of the Bureau of Elections, which consists of Chief J. J. O'Brien—who holds office for three years at an annual salary of $5000—aided by three patrolmen, who act as clerks. This Bureau endeavors to obtain unobstructed expression of the popular will by sending out in the months of July and August the requisite blanks on which applicants inscribe their own names for appointment as inspectors of election and poll-clerks. Captains of precincts inquire into the fitness of the candidates. Republicans are usually appointed first, then the Tammany, County, and Irving Hall Democrats, in proportions determined by the Board of Police, and are sworn into office by the Chief. Neglect of duty by those thus sworn in is a State-prison offence. Lists of voters in each house, maps of election districts, and posters are sent to inspectors on registration days. A copy of each register is filed with the Bureau of Elections within forty-eight hours of the close of registry, and the possible insertion of fictitious names hindered, if not prevented. The registry in possession of the Bureau becomes the final authority on voting qualification. On election days the in-spectors again receive an ample supply of stationery, including statements of canvass, poll lists, and tallies. One statement of the canvass is sent to the Bureau of Elections, one to the County Clerk, and another to the Board of Supervisors; one of the tallies is forwarded to the Bureau and one to the Mayor within twenty-four hours of the close of the canvass, to prevent tampering with the returns. This has been attempted. In 1879 two men were sentenced to the State-prison for two and a half years in punishment of this offence, which was betrayed by the scratching on the bank-paper return. On the evening of election days statements certified by inspectors of votes cast for candidates are carried by police-officers to the station-houses as soon as the contents of each box have been counted. Thence they are sent by special messengers to the Bureau of Elections, where all returns are collated and filed away for reference. Election nights cause busy scenes in the bureaucratic office. All the police clerks lend a helping hand. The returns of Assembly districts, footed up by sergeants behind their desks, are reported in the room of the Police Board.

This Bureau also preserves record of the death of all males over twenty-one years of age, and of all convicted of felony, or sentenced to penitentiary or State-prison, in order to the correctness of the registry lists. Maps of Judicial, Assembly, Senate, and Congressional districts as arranged—really by the Bureau, but responsibly by the Board of Police—are drawn up in this office. Two large rooms, bursting with huge volumes and assorted documents, illustrate the painstaking care with which the elective franchise is guarded.

Situated as New York is, upon an island whose encircling waters are crowded by the shipping of all maritime peoples, it needs the energies of a special body of police to quell mutinies, arrest quarrelsome or insubordinate sailors, preserve order among the vessels, prevent smuggling, and check depredations upon marine property. This body it has in the Harbor Police, under the command of Captain E. O. Smith. Its duties are chiefly performed upon the water, and are invaluable to shipping interests. The steamboat *Patrol* is the dread of predaceous watermen, and is manned by a thoroughly efficient crew.

Special patrolmen are appointed to par-

FOOTING UP ELECTION RETURNS.

ticular duties on the application of firms and corporations, and are paid by them. A system of raps with the club on the sidewalk calls up wanted policemen, brings the assistance of more than one officer at fires, riots, or other emergencies, and indicates the route of a policeman in pursuit of any person in the night-time.

Arrested persons are conducted to the station-house, and thence, after longer or shorter detention, to a District Police Court. Of these there are six, in different parts of the city. There the prisoners are charged with specified offences, and committed, bailed, or discharged by the sitting magistrate, according to the evidence adduced. The "Record of Arrests," kept by the Chief Clerk in the Central

Office, is alphabetically arranged, and contains the name, age, color, sex, nationality, occupation, state in life—whether married or single—of each person arrested; also the complaint, name of complainant, name of officer making the arrest, date of arrest, and disposal of the case. The number of apprehensions in 1885 was 74,315—an increase of 4061 over that of 1884; 54,898 were males, 19,417 females; 29.33 per cent. of the whole were arrested in the Fourth, Sixth, Tenth, and Fourteenth precincts, which adjoin each other, and contain as miscellaneous a population as can be found on any spot of equal size on the globe. Assault and battery, disorderly conduct, intoxication, larceny, vagrancy, violation of Corporation, Health, and Excise laws, constitute the majority of offences. 34,374 whites and 1897 blacks were natives of the United States, 20,115 of Ireland, 8288 of Germany, 2458 of England, 3151 of Italy, 791 of Poland, 88 of China, and the rest of many different countries. More than half were of foreign birth, and of the native-born very many were of foreign extraction; 8041 were under twenty years of age, 26,673 from twenty to thirty years, 18,483 from thirty to forty, 11,927 from forty to fifty, and 7191 over fifty years old; 24,172 were married, and 50,143 single. The percentage of single persons arrested was 67.47, against 61.60 in 1872 —an increase accounted for by general disinclination to marry. 71,120 were able to read and write; 3195 had not any literary education; 7 were, or professed to be, clergymen, 3 authors, 25 teachers, 16 students, 66 editors and reporters, 1457 bar-tenders, 2391 clerks, 3087 drivers, 1272 house-keepers, 3393 house-workers, 13,466 laborers, 1517 prostitutes, 1707 peddlers, 1065 printers, 1182 rag-pickers, and 20,108 of no occupation.

Conspicuous among the several divisions of the police force is that of the Nineteenth Sub-Precinct, with quarters under the Grand Central Depot. In addition to limited patrol duty, the members maintain creditable order among the pushing hackmen who crowd the entrances to that vast edifice. They also protect the incoming and outgoing passengers who, to the number of over five millions annually, patronize the New York Central, Harlem, and New Haven railroads, which terminate here. So effective is their activity and skill that no confidence man, sharper, or pickpocket cares to come within their reach. Runaway boys are frequently apprehended on telegraphic notice from parents or guardians, and sent back to their friends. Telegraphic orders from police authorities and sheriffs in every part of the country to arrest fugitive criminals receive prompt attention. One of those gentry who had escaped from Adrian, Michigan, with $20,000 worth of sealskins, was caught at the window of the ticket office while demanding the rebate due on his ticket. The whole of the missing property was recovered.

The Broadway Squad, composed of 44 officers and men, is as famous in the police world as the gigantic grenadiers of Frederick the Great in the military. All are over six feet in height, and are far more commanding in presence and symmetrical in person than the unfortunate Prussians. From Thirty-fourth Street to the Battery they render highly appreciated assistance to pedestrians compelled to cross Broadway, and also regulate the endless procession of vehicles passing up and down that magnificent thoroughfare.

The Mounted Squad consists of 106 men, attached to five distinct precincts between One-hundred-and-tenth Street and the northern limit of police jurisdiction. The distances to be covered necessitate equestrian locomotion. On the several drives, such as St. Nicholas and other avenues north of the Central Park, nine policemen are specially assigned for duty during the day. Bestriding spirited steeds, trained to stop runaways by galloping alongside, the sturdy riders often incur great risks, but seldom fail to accomplish their object, or to save the lives and limbs of affrighted carriage occupants.

The *detection of crime* is a secondary function of the police force, but is one of such romantic and morbidly fascinating character that it possesses absorbing interest for the great majority of readers. The Detective Bureau, with apartments and records at Police Head-quarters, includes forty detective sergeants, under the orders of Inspector Thomas Byrnes. This officer, whose celebrity vies with that of Fouché and Vidocq, has been in command since 1880.

On May 25, 1882, the Detective Bureau as now constituted was created, at the urgent solicitation of Inspector Byrnes, by the State Legislature, and the salary of each detective sergeant raised to $1600.

ARRESTING A THIEF AT THE GRAND CENTRAL DEPOT.

Ward detectives serving under the captains of their respective precincts are not included in this particular branch of the force. Inspector Byrnes is a native of Ireland, but is of American training. Entering the force in 1863, he rose through its several grades to his present office. Weeding out all the worthless and inefficient, and supplying their places with young, active, and intelligent men, he instructed and organized the latter on his own plans. The Detective Bureau soon attained to national importance. Special attention was paid to Wall Street. Skilled thieves, the "best men" of their nefarious occupation, prized it as the richest of their hunting grounds. Fat purses were abstracted, tin boxes containing money, bonds, and valuable papers fell into their hands, and knavery was jubi-

lant. Now that district is to them as paradise to the lost spirit in Moslem legend. They may view afar, but may not enter. Any thief found below a line drawn across the city through Fulton Street is seized at once and compelled to account for himself. If the explanation be not satisfactory, the grip of the law tightens around the culprit, and the familiar jail again becomes his home. Ten or twelve detectives are always on duty at a room in the Stock-Exchange. On call, one or more can be sent to any place in the lower section of the city within two or three minutes. "From the 12th of March, 1880, until to-day, they have not lost a ten-cent stamp in Wall Street by a professional thief—not a penny, not a cent," is not an empty boast. It is sober truth. Somebody did steal President Simmons's over-

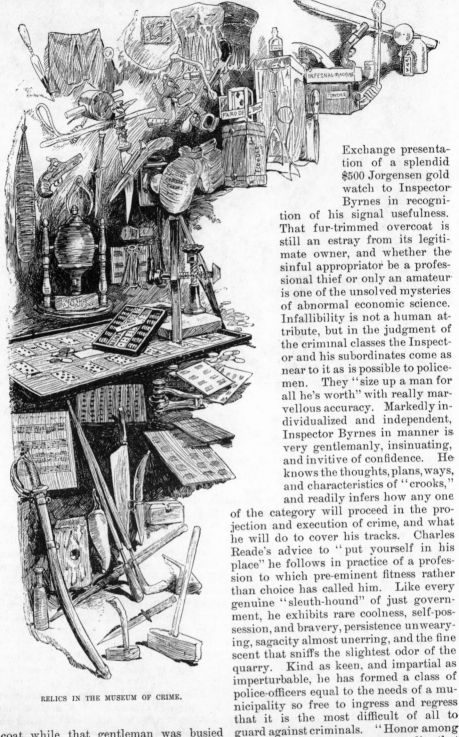

RELICS IN THE MUSEUM OF CRIME.

Exchange presentation of a splendid $500 Jorgensen gold watch to Inspector Byrnes in recognition of his signal usefulness. That fur-trimmed overcoat is still an estray from its legitimate owner, and whether the sinful appropriator be a professional thief or only an amateur is one of the unsolved mysteries of abnormal economic science. Infallibility is not a human attribute, but in the judgment of the criminal classes the Inspector and his subordinates come as near to it as is possible to policemen. They "size up a man for all he's worth" with really marvellous accuracy. Markedly individualized and independent, Inspector Byrnes in manner is very gentlemanly, insinuating, and invitive of confidence. He knows the thoughts, plans, ways, and characteristics of "crooks," and readily infers how any one of the category will proceed in the projection and execution of crime, and what he will do to cover his tracks. Charles Reade's advice to "put yourself in his place" he follows in practice of a profession to which pre-eminent fitness rather than choice has called him. Like every genuine "sleuth-hound" of just government, he exhibits rare coolness, self-possession, and bravery, persistence unwearying, sagacity almost unerring, and the fine scent that sniffs the slightest odor of the quarry. Kind as keen, and impartial as imperturbable, he has formed a class of police-officers equal to the needs of a municipality so free to ingress and regress that it is the most difficult of all to guard against criminals. "Honor among thieves" is one of the time-worn lies that

coat while that gentleman was busied with matters connected with the Stock-   guard against criminals. "Honor among thieves" is one of the time-worn lies that

THE MUSEUM OF CRIME.

he denounces with emphatic scorn. He says: "I never met a thief in my life, provided he could benefit by peaching on his confederates, from whom I could not find out anything I was desirous to know. There is no such thing as honor among thieves."

Interviews with the Inspector are had by special request. His private office is adorned by photographs and crayon drawings, whose subjects are associated with police affairs. Some of the men reporting to him are said to be college-bred, and can pass muster in the best society. All are chosen in view of individual aptitude for certain kinds of work. The stamp of officialism is about the last of which there is any trace. Keeping *incognito* as much as possible, the chances of prompt detection are multiplied. "Crooks" are now afraid of their shadows; great robberies have ceased, and minor crime been reduced over eighty per cent. Detectives more or less closely imitate the example of their chief, who says: "Every evening I make it a point to meet some of these men in their resorts, and learn from them the whereabouts of their friends, and what they are doing. One crook of consequence generally knows what other good men are doing. In this way I keep posted, and

know in what part of the country all the sharp men are. As experts are liberated from the State-prison I follow their tracks in this way." For the secret police of European countries, and for the private detectives in this, Inspector Byrnes entertains undisguised contempt. Crime, in his opinion, is a fine art, and criminal detection a science. "Set a thief to catch a thief" is a hoary mendacity. "In the long-run the honest officer is a match for the smartest thief." Detective opinion of the morality of American life, private or official, is not of roseate hue. The bribe-taking Aldermen of 1884 have not improved its complexion. Of Henry W. Jaehne, their former Vice-President, but now in Sing Sing through the Inspector's remarkable power of making rogues talk, he is represented as saying: "Jaehne thought I had more proof against him in regard to Mrs. Hamilton's stolen silver than I really did have, and I was careful not to undeceive him. As it was, I knew that he was a rascal, without having proof of the fact, until I had gained his confidence to such an extent that he admitted his guilt as to the bribery."

In the Photograph and Record Department, in charge of Sergeant Thomas H. Adams, are preserved about 60,000 portraits of between 6000 and 7000 criminals. Many of them have been received from other cities, and are not included in the Rogues' Gallery, which contains the busts of the "best people" arrested in New York. When a professional is photographed, fifty copies of the negative are taken, and the "pedigree" of the person printed on the back of each copy. One copy is then despatched to each precinct, where the pedigree is entered on the record-book, and the picture placed in the Rogues' Gallery, as at Head-quarters. The remainder are retained for the use of officers, and for exchange with the police authorities of other cities. Gallery and record-book are the patented inventions of Sergeant Adams. Portraits of deceased criminals are removed from their infamous companionship, as are those of the four per cent., more or less, of living ones who turn from their evil ways when young, and by years of well-doing entitle themselves to this favor, which is granted at their own request, seconded by that of reputable business men. Should they relapse, their portraits are returned to the case. The record of each of the 1700 originals in the Rogues' Gallery comprises full physical description and biography. One of them is, or pretends to be, a graduate of Corpus Christi College, in Cambridge, England. "Hungry Joe," ex-Governor Franklin J. Moses, of South Carolina, Bertha Heymann, "queen of the confidence women," "Whiskey" Short, who distilled whiskey from swill in Sing Sing State-prison, Annie Riley, who speaks five or six languages, "Ike" Vail, "king of the confidence men," bank burglars, forgers, and counterfeiters of strikingly intellectual countenance, are conspicuous among them. Basing his estimate on the reliable data at command, Sergeant Adams concludes that one-third of the "best people" are liberally educated, one-third fairly educated, and

the remaining third, with the exception of a very small number, so far educated as to be able to read and write. The youngest and most inexperienced are also the most reckless of criminals. These run all risks. Laziness is the cause of half the criminality in the land; temptation by successful thieves and by immoral reading, of the other half. Want has but little to do with it, except as it makes small thieves. These, by contact with hardened men in prisons, which are often schools of crime, develop into professionals.

The Museum of Crime, opposite the private office of Inspector Byrnes, is a shuddering horror; not so much from what is seen as from what is suggested. Speaking likenesses of shop-lifters, pickpockets, burglars, and eminent "crooks" glare from the walls upon visitors. Sledge-hammers whose heads are filled with lead, drags, drills, sectional jimmies, masks, powder-flasks, etc., that were used in the Manhattan Bank robbery of October 27, 1878, challenge inspection in their glass cases. The rascals made away with $2,749,400 in bonds and securities, and about $15,000 in money, on that occasion; but, thanks to our unequalled detective system, did not retain all their booty. Here are samples of the mechanical skill of Gustave Kindt, alias "French Gus," a professional burglar and maker of burglars' tools, which he let out to impecunious thieves on definite percentages of their robberies. The assortment of burglarious kits, tools, keys, wax impressions, etc., is complete. The genius of Kindt and Klein, so wofully perverted, ought to have made their fortunes in legitimate fields of operation. Nat White's bogus gold brick; Mike Shanahan's eighteen-chambered pistol; counterfeit Reading Railroad scrip; the lithographic stone on which ten or twenty thousand spurious tickets of the elevated railroad were printed; stones for printing fractional currency; bogus railroad bonds used by confidence operators; the black caps and ropes of murderers; the pistols wherewith various persons were slain; the lock curiosities of Langdon W. Moore, who knew how to open combination locks through studying their emitted sounds; the box in which the same thief, known as "Charley Adams," put $216,000 in government bonds, stolen from the Concord Bank, Massachusetts, in February, 1866, and which he first buried four feet below the surface of the Delaware River,

THE SANITARY SQUAD.

and then dug up and surrendered when under arrest; the pipes, pea-nut oil, lamps, liquid raw opium, and pills used for smoking in opium joints—are all here.

Instinct and experience unite to awaken profound dread of the Detective Bureau in the breasts of the criminal classes who understand police statistics. In 1885, Inspector Byrnes reported that 1080 males and females, including 7 detained as witnesses, were arrested for felonies and misdemeanors by his branch of the police force: 1 was hung, 98 were sent to State-prison, 88 to the Penitentiary, 12 to the City Prison, 23 to the Elmira Reformatory, 2 to the Workhouse, 4 to the House of Refuge, and 1 to the State Insane Asylum; judgment was suspended in 10 cases, 31 were fined (and $1612 collected), 103 delivered to other authorities, 318 discharged, 228 disposed of in other ways, and 161 left pending. The sentences involved 620 years' imprisonment, and the property recovered amounted to $121,202.

In the *prevention of calamities* the police force is not less efficient. To see that the street lamps are duly lighted and burning, that leakages or breaks of water pipes are quickly repaired, that rabid animals are killed, that diseases, noxious or inflammable substances, or explosives perilous to the public are reported, and that steam-boilers are legally inspected, is part of police duty. The presence of about six thousand steam-boilers—stationary, used for rock-drilling, pile-driving, barges, scows, elevators, etc.—in the city would be a constant element of danger were it not neutralized by the Steam-boiler Inspection Squad of 21 men under the Bureau of Steam-boiler Inspection and Engineers.

The *prevention of endemic diseases* is another important function of the Police Department. Disease frequently originates in and is propagated by the uncleanliness and filthy habits of ignorant and reckless people. Ashes, garbage, rubbish, dirt, and vile fluids, accumulating about the premises or in the streets, have bred the pestilences before which prayer has been powerless, and which have swept out the citizens with the besom of destruction. The Sanitary Code forbids all such practices, and police activity is employed to squelch them. Instruction is provided for the uninformed, and certain punishment for the wilful offender. Whatever malignant, infectious, contagious, or epidemic sickness may break out is reported forthwith. Pawn shops—so often the "fences" for concealing stolen goods— liquor and beer saloons, cheap lodging-houses or dormitories that are frequently mere fetid, crowded, human sties, abound most in the precincts infamous for poverty and crime, and cause plentiful toil for the Tenement-house Squad of the Sanitary Company. This includes thirty officers detailed by the Police Commissioners to assist the Board of Health, under whose orders they act, while reporting to and being paid by Sergeant Washington Mullen. They furnish protection, but not labor, when assisting the Sanitary Superintendent to vacate premises by order of the Board of Health. Sewerage, drainage, ventilation, and whatever pertains to the safety of life or health, is thus brought into relation to the Police Department. The 32,597 violations, including all grades of nastiness or negligence, of the Sanitary Code, reported by them in 1885, disclose the need of such a force, 125,045 inspections attest its activity, and 16,705 complaints its fidelity.

Charity and equity are elements of police duty, for the due observance of which the members of the force are held responsible. Lost children are necessarily numerous in tenement-house districts. Many of the small waifs know little of English, but all find favor in the eyes of the big, burly, warm-hearted protectors, who think of the cribs in their own homes. "I'd rather tackle a man twice my size than that chap," said a perspiring policeman as he deposited a dirty, tearful, kicking juvenile on the floor of Matron Webb's room at Police Head-quarters. The telegraph alarm sends description of person and clothing to all stations. Most of the estrays are soon reclaimed. Children rescued from inhuman parents or guardians by the Society for the Prevention of Cruelty to Children are also placed in care of Matron Webb until disposed of by the courts. 4308 lost children were cared for in 1885, 4087 restored to friends in New York, 7 to friends in other cities, and 214 unclaimed or rescued ones committed to the care of the Commissioners of Charities and Correction, or to that of corporate or denominational institutions. The 112 foundlings received during the year met with care that should have been bestowed by despairing or unnatural parents, in homes, asylums, and private families. Many were adopted. All particulars that might lead to the discovery of parents are preserved. Truant children come under the supervision of the police; but the laws in connection with compulsory attendance at school are not rigidly enforced.

The Bureau of General Information, established in June, 1885, on the recommendation of Superintendent Murray, has charge of the records of all missing persons, lost children, foundlings, persons found dead in the streets, etc., etc. Letters, averaging about one hundred monthly, from all parts of the country and of the world, requesting information about relatives or friends not heard of for a long time, arrive at the Central Office. The utmost pains is taken to acquire the desired information, and due answer is returned to the anxious inquirers. One young man, inquired about by friends in Algiers, North Africa, was found at the Hotel Brunswick, and the questioning letter put into his hands. Of the 203 males and 59 females inquired about as missing in 1885, 196 males and 55 females were found and placed in communication with their friends; 11 only were unaccounted for. Very mysterious circumstances surround some of these cases. Of 154 runaways from home, 143 were returned; of 87 persons found dead, 43 were subsequently identified at the Morgue, and the 44 unidentified—homeless, friendless, alone—laid to rest in obscure graves.

Stranded strangers applying for help are assisted. Immigrants lost on arrival are sought and restored to acquaintances. Utter indigence is relieved by nocturnal lodging in clean cells at the station-houses, and that without too strict regard to the morals of the lodgers: 72,832 males and 61,513 females thus found shelter in 1885. Petty thieves, beggars, tramps, drones, and a small remnant of worthy folk eagerly seek these temporary refuges. 6803 persons who were sick and destitute, insane, or injured in various ways, were conveyed to station-houses and hospitals by ambulances, and 141 sent to their homes. Dead bodies of unknown persons, found in the waters and public places of the city, are conveyed to the Morgue, at the foot of Twenty-sixth Street, East River: 143 persons, committing suicide in one way or other, as well as the bodies of those who met with accidental death, afforded this repulsive employment to the police in 1885. Stray swine or cattle are delivered to the keeper of the public pound; beggars apprehended and sent to institutions or dealt with as vagrants; children dancing in the streets for gain arrested; and lost or stolen property restored to claimant owners. This last is ordinarily done through the Property Clerk, whose office at Police Head-quarters embraces the most miscellaneous variety of pistols, watches, jewelry, silver-ware, forged bonds, male and female clothing, horse-blankets, cigars, sides of beef, chests of tea, sacks of coffee, boots and shoes, etc., to be found on the continent. His store comprises everything except a piano—and Mr. John Harriott has had a piano lid—from a coffin to a diamond pin. Diamonds and jewelry valued at $200,000 have been in custody at one time. These articles are all held for evidence against prisoners, and are not handed over to claimants without regular orders from judicial courts. The unclaim-

ed and unawarded are sold every six months, and the proceeds paid into the Police Pension Fund. During the year 1885, 1711 different lots, valued at $755,356 73, came into the hands of the Property Clerk, and 650 lots, valued at $44,126 32, were delivered by him.

The *protection of interior communications* is an important part of police duty in the populous city of New York. The force is called upon to disperse crowds, to regulate processions and parades, to prevent racing in the streets, to supervise the driving of private and public vehicles, and to remove all obstacles to free locomotion to the Corporation Yard.

The Ordinance Squad, in command of Sergeant Joseph Stewart, investigates the facts and circumstances of applications for licenses issued under direction of the Mayor. Nearly 30,000 investigations were thus made by its 63 members in 1885.

The protection of interior marine communications is intrusted to the Steam-boat Squad and to the Harbor Police. The first, also called the Third Precinct, under Captain Gastlin, includes 109 men, among whom are six detectives. These guard the docks from Jackson Street, East River, to Fourteenth Street, North River.

The *supervision of public amusements*, under the provisions of State law, and the apprehension of all offenders, enter into society's requisitions upon its police pro-

PATROL BOAT.

RIVER AND HARBOR POLICE.

tectors. Masked balls, with their special opportunities of indecency, immorality, and crime, entail the obligation of alert vigilance. The $4465 for 263 masked ball permits, and the $1940 for 776 pistol permits, received in 1885, were paid over, as the law directs, to the Police Pension Fund. Prize-fights or slugging matches, under the hypocritical pretence of scientific play for "points," they are now instructed to prohibit.

In *the communication of recent intelligence and information* the metropolis lags behind some of her more enterprising Western sisters. Telegraphic boxes that responsible citizens might use ought to be judiciously scattered over the whole area of police jurisdiction.

The Police Telegraph system, under Superintendent James Crowley, is, so far as it goes, an admirably effective one. Notice of arrests, fires, lost children, riots, and multitudinous matters is promptly diffused. Inquiries or searches ordered through it are posted in the sitting-room of each station-house. Its record of transactions is perfect, and throbs with excitement. In 1885 the number of messages sent over the wires of this bureau was 82,383. Of these, 57,334 related to coroners, sick cases, accidents, elections, etc.; 20,129 to dead animals; 1656 to general orders, arrests, and missing persons; 993 to property lost, stolen, or found; 648 to lost children; and 1713 to fire locations. At the Central Office the police lines are divided into five sections. By means of switching, two sections are connected, and general alarms sent to all stations. The office itself is connected, directly or indirectly, with the head-quarters of the Fire and other departments, with the police head-quarters of other cities, with railroad stations, prisons, banks, hospitals, asylums, factories, public schools, etc. The blotter, kept by three clerks, is a perfect diary of police experience since 1856.

The entire cost of the Police Department in 1885, as indicated by the report of the treasurer, was $3,679,421 78. The Police Pension Fund has an invested capital of $94,000; disbursed for pensions, etc., in 1885, the sum of $267,935 93; and received from various sources, $309,181 27. 662 men, women, and orphans are its beneficiaries.

Life on Broadway
(1878)

LIFE ON BROADWAY.

"I look down into all that wasp-nest or bee-hive, and witness their wax-laying and honey-making and poison-brewing and choking by sulphur. I see it all. Couriers arrive bestrapped and bebooted, bearing Joy and Sorrow bagged up in pouches of leather; there, top-laden and with four swift horses, rolls in the country baron and his household; here, on timber-leg, the lame soldier hops patiently along, begging alms: a thousand carriages and wains and cars come tumbling in with food, with young Rusticity, and other raw produce, inanimate or animate, and go tumbling out again with produce manufactured. That living flood, of all ages and qualities, knowest thou whence it is coming, whither it is going? From Eternity, onward to Eternity."—*Sartor Resartus.*

LIFE on Broadway is pretty nearly every thing. It is the broadest farce, the heaviest tragedy, and the most delicate comedy; it is tender, severe, sad, and joyous— an available text for the satirist, the moralist, the humorist, the preacher, and the man of the world. No ambition, passion, or creed the inside of an orange is by cutting it through the middle; and if, in a sort of geographical vivisection, a scalpel should be drawn down the middle of New York, it would fall into the channel formed by Broadway. The effluence is at the southern extremity of the city, and the affluence is on

SCENE ON UPPER BROADWAY.

may not be studied in its magnificent parade, which puts together things that by nature are widely apart, and effects a grand *ensemble* of vividly dramatic contrasts.

Topographically, as well as by the selection of traffic, the street is the main artery of the city. The best way of finding out the borders of Central Park, the street coursing almost due north and south for a little less than four miles.

On account of its centrality and directness, it is touched by nearly every moving inhabitant of the city in his daily walks: if he is going from north to south, he prefers it to the other avenues, because it is straight and its pavement is good; and if he is going from any quarter east to any quarter west, he must intersect it at some point in gaining his destination. The country visitor coming from the Jersey and Long Island ferries feels secure when he reaches Broadway, and while he keeps to it he can not go very far astray, no matter what his destination is. It is not only a channel of commercial traffic, but a favorite promenade of the idler and pleasure-seeker, and though the acquaintances of a man may be few, a walk up or down Broadway is sure to confront him with somebody that he knows.

The crowd is not distinctively fashionable, though well-dressed people preponderate; workmen in fustian and poverty-stricken work-girls appear in the stream, besides threadbare adventurers and the abject devotees of the gutter. It is a crowd greater in numbers and steadier in its flow than any thing London can show in Fleet Street or the Strand, and it mixes up the most dissimilar elements of nationality and condition. The night is never so dark or so stormy that the footfall of pedestrians and the rumbling of vehicles are altogether hushed. The occupants of the front-rooms of the hotels, waking

LOWER BROADWAY.

at any hour, can still hear the reverberations of the traffic, which swell toward morning into a deafening roar, and continue without lull throughout the day. The procession is endless. When all the rest of the city is asleep, Broadway is awake, and looking through its vista between the two bead-like strings of lamps, we still see some pedestrians plodding along on various missions of crime, industry, pleasure, or charity.

Whence come they, whither go they? asks Carlyle's German professor from his look-out tower. It is apparently the same crowd from day to day and from year to year; the faces are the same, and so are the passions shadowed in those faces. Individuality is subverted.

ONE OF THE BROADWAY SQUAD.

If we stood under the portico of one of the hotels yesterday and watched the procession, we may stand there to-day and see it over again without detecting any great difference, its recurrence reminding us of the band on the wheel of a machine. But the individuality subverted in externals is strong enough in the minds of the crowd. When we apprehend that the least intellectual and the least important of the human beings who are passing before us has his own pet scheme of life, his own secrets, his own theories—that he is a veritable microcosm in himself—how profoundly significant the procession becomes!

Our point of view is not introspective, however, for it would be vain and aside from our purpose to attempt an unravelment of the psychological complexities underlying the faces of the throng. What we are after is the surface glow of the picture—the superficial episodes, the exhilarations of the traffic—the light and shade and the dramatic spirit of the thing. There is cheeriness, impetuosity, vehemence, and brilliancy in a Broadway crowd. We have said that London shows nothing to equal it, and Paris itself can hardly surpass it. It has a Champagne sparkle even in the parts where business is supreme; its tread is elastic, buoyant, and almost rhythmic, as it follows the rattle and roar of the vehicles; and that rattle and roar, made by the pressure of hundreds of wheels and hoofs on a resonant pavement, are like the *crescendo* movement of a heroic symphony. Nervous people and people from the country can not enjoy it; it is bewildering, painfully so, to them; but the active citizen whose nerves are in good condition finds stimulation in the friction and the noise. Visions of Broadway and its throng have appeared to the writer in the mountain pine forests of the West, when the retrospect has added brilliancy to the well-remembered scenes, and it invariably leaves an indelibly vivid impression on the stranger, no matter how short his stay may be.

Let us stand near Trinity Church at about eleven o'clock on a fine morning, or, as a beginning, let us ascend the steeple. The street is straight for nearly two miles, when it turns slightly to the northwest, the slender gray spire of Grace Church marking the turning-point. Its name is unjustified by fact: the breadth is inconsiderable, being farther reduced apparently by the great height of most of the buildings, and the sur-

when all the patriotic bunting is unfolded, the view is more brilliant and ragged than ever; but what engages us most is the crowd—that uneasy mass of black dots which resemble the pen-and-ink kisses of an amorous correspondent. Has the reader ever noticed a swarm of flies buzzing on the

INTERIOR OF A BROADWAY STAGE.

face is depressed as far as Canal Street, where a gentle ascent begins. The variety of architecture is extraordinary. Every material has been used in every style—brick, iron, glass, marble, granite, brown stone, yellow stone, wood, and stucco. Small, modest dwellings of a much earlier period, with old-fashioned dormer-windows projecting from the upper story, and modern plate-glass show windows inserted in the lower story, are threatened with suffocation by buildings twice or three times their height. The Sierras are not more serrated than the cornice lines of Broadway, and the effect is not at all satisfactory to an artistic eye. Sign-boards hang out and flag-staffs rise from nearly every building. On a gala day,

outside of a grocer's window? That is another resemblance which the crowd has. The black dots seem to eddy, to rise and fall in constant commotion. There are hundreds of them, and whatever their actual dress may be, they appear from a great altitude to be black, which, excepting Sunday-school festivals, is the case with all American and English crowds.

The steady progress made by each shows that the confusion is not quite hopeless, and if we fix our attention on a particular one, our interest is immediately enlisted, and we follow its course with the patient eagerness of an astronomer who devotes himself in constancy to one only of the alluring heavenly bodies. We can form no idea out of

A BENCH IN UNION SQUARE.

the varied possibilities as to what manner of man the speck upon which we have set our gaze is, nor as to the errand upon which he goes, nor as to the thoughts that occupy him. It may be an exquisite with a lordly, leisurely strut, or a shabby clerk with bent shoulders and a family of six to support on as many dollars a week, or an observant literary man with eyes wide open to suggestion, or a pickpocket with no less strong powers of observation in another direction, or a commercial drummer with samples in hand. It glides slowly along, in and out among the other specks, and after a while it is lost, and we seek for it again in vain.

Mankind will not bear looking at from an elevation. The thin partitions of social classifications melt in the distance; sumptuousness of dress and grandeur of person are of no account; the millionaire and the beggar are indistinguishable. A communist might gaze happily on the world from Trinity steeple; for while all others would be reduced to a common level of insignificance, he himself would be above them all, and that is communism of the practical sort.

As we come down to the street again, the chimes burst into the strong melody of a hymn, and ring out the promise of the Eternal Rock in tones that the uproar of the traffic can not drown. The grand old church there, amid the busiest turmoil of commerce, embodying centuries of suffering and victories in its Gothic architecture, is an appeal to veneration which few can resist; and as the music of the chimes breaks upon the din, the most abstracted of the passers-by glance up at the historic sanctuary. How utterly absorbed most of the faces that we see are! Money-making is a strong passion, and money-making in this neighborhood is a game of chance. A few doors from Broadway, on Wall Street, is the Stock Exchange, where scores of men are striving for wealth

with the fierceness of maniacs. Other men flit by us on the street whose eyes are fixed with feverish intensity as they ponder over their schemes. In times of panic the fever reveals itself in wilder faces and more hur-

A FLOWER GIRL.

ried steps, and the student who complains of the intellectual drain that is put upon him, might find consolation in the overwrought and exhausted condition of the men whose brains are occupied in the apparently easy problems of the markets.

Bank messengers with actual bags of gold and packages of paper convertible into gold; office-boys with saucy faces and no less saucy manners; shrewd detectives with quiet, unobtrusive ways, altogether unsuspicious; telegraph boys in neat uniforms, carrying yellow envelopes that contain words penned ten minutes previously in California; railway magnates more important than many kings; spruce clerks and laborious porters —are included in the throng which passes before us in an almost solid body.

All is not toil and trouble with the merchants, however. Across the way is the white marble façade of a celebrated restaurant, where, after a successful stroke of business, a lucky handling of wheat or Erie, the masters of the situation make merry over the costly vintages of Champagne and Burgundy, sometimes prolonging their revels to an hour when all the adjacent streets are dark and vacant, and Trinity spire points solemnly to the deep blue night sky.

Soon after six o'clock the high pressure of the traffic down town abates, the offices are closed, a single lamp being left burning in each to reveal the interiors to the policeman, and the tired-out workers seek their homes. By nine o'clock the street is quiet.

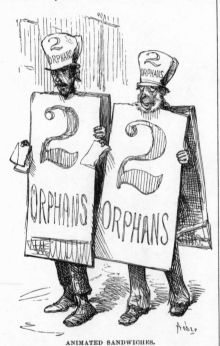

ANIMATED SANDWICHES.

A few pedestrians pass to and from the Brooklyn ferries at Whitehall. Between midnight and four o'clock the telegraph and newspaper offices send out their wearied operatives. The street is never quite empty, but the rapid change that takes place at night-fall, previous to which every stone and flag has seemed to have a voice, suggests a visitation of palsy.

A short distance north of Trinity, Park Row slants off from Broadway, being separated from the latter thoroughfare by the new Post-office and City Hall Park. Lights are burning over there all night. Men smirched with ink and pale with toil are coming and going constantly. Those high buildings are the offices of the great morning newspapers—the *Herald*, the *Times*, the *Tribune*, the *Sun*, and the *World*. The upper stories, in which the editorial and composing rooms are situated, blaze with light, and on the ground-floor a paler beam shows the advertising-rooms, where a few sleepy clerks await the last advertisements. The imagination can not encompass the nervous reach and power of the influence which those steadily burning lamps symbolize. Sitting under the trees of the Park, which is an agreeable break in the high-walled street, we are passed from time to time by reporters hurrying to their offices with rolls of "copy" bearing on every current topic—lectures on evolution, sermons, theatres, fires, murders, receptions, funerals, and weddings. An hour or so later the same slaves of the lamp pass us again as they go home; later the editorial writers are seen, and later still the proofreaders and compositors. The editor-inchief drives home in a *coupé*. The lawgivers and law-makers—people in themselves mighty, but not as mighty as he—have waited upon him in humility, and accepted a moment's audience as a boon. He is the incomparable planet of American civilization, although the lustre of the satellites sometimes outshines the planet itself, and as he composes himself in the corner of his modest carriage, his brain reflects in epitome the history of the world for a day. On a calm evening we can hear the roar of the presses on our bench in the Park, and in that roar we fancy that we can make out the articulation of the power which the myriad white sheets are to have in the morning.

While the lower part of Broadway is filled during the day with urgent business men and is deserted at night, the upper part is chosen for purchases and promenade by a much more brilliant throng, and is busy both night and day.

About two miles from the foot of the street the northward-bound traveller finds himself emerging from the close quarters of the street into one of those verdurous squares which lend a great charm to the city. In the mornings and afternoons the benches and the asphalt walks of this bit of country in town are crowded with whitecapped nurse-maids attending prettily dressed children; more or less disagreeable idlers, varying in distinction from the tramp to the slightly overcome tippler; and the pedestrians, who are glad enough to vary the monotony of the flag-stone sidewalk with a glimpse of the smooth grass-plats and the shelter of the trees. In the evenings lovers in pairs take the places of the *bonnes*, and the club man does not wholly despise the opportunity for meditation afforded by the common benches, which are inclosed by grass and foliage, and near the tranquilizing murmur of the fountain. The lamps hang among the foliage, and the square is bounded by high buildings; the bells of the fanys, the Arnolds and Constables, and the Lords and Taylors, are concentrated within these limits or in the immediate neighborhood, and woman in her most elegant attire appears in quest of new additions to her already voluminous apparel.

Woman out of the house is always magnificent, and she is never so elaborate in her toilet as when, with the plea of nakedness on

SCENE IN UNION SQUARE.

horse-cars and the rattle of other vehicles are half subdued, and the trees give one a sense of sequestration, although a few strides would bring us back to the street again.

Looking out from Union Square, as this oasis in the desert of buildings is called, we get an idea of how interminable a Broadway crowd is.

About a quarter of a mile farther north Madison Square relieves the confinement of the street with fountains, grass, shrubs, and trees, and between the two such a parade may be seen on fine afternoons, especially Saturdays, as no other city in America, and few other cities in the world, can show. The great retail houses of the Stewarts, the Tif-

her lips, she sallies out on a shopping expedition. On such occasions she surrounds herself with an atmosphere—or we had better say incense—through which she looms in proportions not altogether her own; a spirit of imperativeness and supremacy invests her, and the men among whom she mingles drop into a sort of nebulous inferiority. A masculine spectator is quite apt to overlook the presence of men; the men are there inevitably, but they wriggle helplessly and insignificantly in the feminine sea of furbelows.

So much in the way of generalization; and now to be more specific. It is the writer's unbiased opinion, well fortified by the comments of others, that more pretty faces and

MADISON SQUARE.

exquisite costumes are to be discovered between Twenty-third Street and Union Square on a fine afternoon than a month's investigation will reveal in any other city. This is not to be interpreted as praise of any particular type of American beauty. All types are aggregated in that fluttering stream of feathers and petticoats. The looker-on passes through a confliction of ecstasies in the contemplation of all the varieties. Constancy becomes an impossibility when all that is dark and sensuously melting in woman flits by in a compact brunette, to be succeeded by all that is fair and heavenly in a *spirituelle* blonde—when Perfection seduces us one moment in the *petite*, and the next moment embodies herself in a voluptuous amplitude of rosy flesh.

Though all the women we see are not pretty, an entrancing proportion are, and a still larger proportion are attired with a discriminating liberality of taste which employs vivid color without a suggestion of gaudiness. Another characteristic is the vivacity of manner, and the abundant use of flowers, both natural and artificial, as a decoration. In the time of violets and roses the air of this overheated city street is as fragrant as a garden. Nearly every woman wears a bouquet in her breast, and a perfect legion of sidewalk peddlers add to the sweetness with small bunches held out for sale in baskets and on trays.

Most of the commodities visible are those which women buy. The dry-goods stores preponderate, and after these are the glove stores, where plaster arms display the monstrous absurdity of twenty-two-button kids; the stationers', where the last fashions in note-papers and cards are revealed; the fancy stores, whose windows are filled with miracles of tortoise-shell and ivory carving and expensive ornaments for the house and the person; the photographers', where pictures are sold of the last idol of the hour; and the confectioners', whose sweetmeats are put up in the daintiest and most extravagant packages. Even the hawkers seem to understand the sex from which they are to expect patronage, and adapt their wares accordingly. An effectual appeal is made to woman's softness by the sleepy Spitz pups which are temptingly held out in the palms of a fancier's hands, where they resemble balls of wool; and a stronger appeal yet is made by the one-armed soldier, whose barrel-organ has a hard time in making itself heard above the noise of the vehicles. Other vendors offer pressed ferns, toys, plants, and photograph-holders. It may be imagined from the presence of the sidewalk merchant that the crowd is not *par excellence* fashionable, and it is not; but it is prosperous, gay, and animated.

When the business of her brief hour is partly over or finished, the outer woman having been provided for, the inner woman refreshes after her own fashion and in her own haunts. No man with a grain of proper feeling in him can be at ease in Purcell's during the women's shopping hours. It is singularly and unaccountably unpleasant to see a room full of women eating, no matter how dainty the food may be. At Maillard's a mild infusion of the male element makes the sight more endurable, and there we may learn what a stickler for the minor elegan-

SPITZ PUPS.

cies of life my lady is. The plate, the linen, the crystal-ware, are all flawless. The *menu* is on satin paper in gold and delicate tints, wrought into suggestions of cherubs and paradise.

A tenet exists in the unwritten constitution of the polite world which prescribes an early hour after which women shall not be seen unescorted on Broadway, but they remain beyond it and until the iron shutters of the dry-goods stores are drawn down, and the commercial men appear on their way home or to their clubs. Approaching darkness is most effectual in driving them home—they can not resist the terrors of that; and when night is come, another phase of "life" is uncovered by the glare of the many hotels, billiard halls, saloons, and supper-

rooms which are situated between Twenty-third Street and Thirty-fourth Street.

The lights are so numerous and bright that we have no difficulty in making out the faces and dresses of the nocturnal promenaders; the doors of all the public resorts are thrown wide open to us, and if we are not disposed to moralize too much, we can enjoy the excitement of the billiards, or the solace of coffee and cigars in a snug little alcove window, which is like the private box of a theatre, and from which the Vanity Fair outside is like a grand performance prepared for our own particular amusement.

Carriages go by in which we discover opera and ball dresses; the men on the sidewalk move along saunteringly, nearly every one with a cigar in his mouth, and the crimson tips of the weeds glow in the air like so many setting suns. The entrances to the hotels are filled with loungers and gossips. These are the men who, in their own estimation, make the world—the men who act in it, and talk about it, and take pleasure out of it.

The night-birds hover about the scene until the day-laborers begin to appear again, and the lights in some of the places of entertainment are not put out until sunrise.

What we have aimed at, and all that we have been able to obtain, in our superficial glance, has been a few of the more salient phases of the street. All the episodes of a walk on Broadway could not possibly be described in the space to which our article is limited.

There are the show windows, which make a complete international exposition of industries; and it would be difficult indeed to think of any thing that could not be bought on Broadway. If in some way the rest of the city should be demolished, Broadway could supply the survivors with every necessary and luxury of life, from dinners at Delmonico's to marmoset monkeys, from Cashmere shawls to household furniture à

THE TOY-WOMAN.

la Eastlake, from colossal bronzes to silk stockings, and from cigarettes to refined lard.

Taking the curious exhibits only, what a variety there are! Here is a little oyster saloon with two windows. One window is filled with moist dark green moss, upon which a stock of live frogs have flattened themselves underneath the sign of "fried frogs' legs," and just inside the shop a glowing range and frying-pan are ready to finish the business for the captives. In the other window several groups of lobsters have been made by a few touches of paint to resemble card and dinner parties with such verisimilitude that we wonder why so simple and available a disguise is not used oftener in this lying world. Around another window a crowd are watching a bulbous-headed child who is demonstrating the action of a patent swing called the "Baby Walker," which has a diabolical tendency to produce some brain

are the street vendors, who often offer interesting studies. The eloquence of the vagabond whose commodity is small tablets of grease-erasers, and of his twin brother in humbug, the man with the dentifrice, brings a laugh into the most serious face. Neighbor to these is an ambiguous foreigner in a Turkish cap, with odorous Tonka-beans for sale; and the next peddler is a philosopher, who is apparently quite oblivious of every thing except the patent threader with which he threads and rethreads a needle while he mumbles the advantages of his invention.

A few years ago a precocious youngster attracted large audiences by his drawings on the sidewalk. His materials were a few bits of chalk hoarded in a torn trouser pocket, and with these he rapidly drew political and legendary characters on the flag-stones. No policeman being near, he fell earnestly to his work on his knees, and a life-sized

SHOW WINDOW.

disease in any infant sacrificed to it. Next door an athletic salesman is exhibiting an adjustable chair, which is susceptible of so many complicated twists and turns that its possessor must be constantly in danger of involving his limbs in its machinery; and a little lower down the street the attraction is a hive of uncomfortable-looking bees, which are sailing in and out among the crowd, and making honey for a summer drink, dispensed by their owners at five cents a glass. Here a toy-shop window has been converted into a miniature lake, upon which tiny steamboats are puffing about, and there a pretty girl is fingering a pianolike machine which obviates the use of a pen in writing. The dramas which reproduce Broadway scenes are always successful, however destitute they may be of intrinsic merit, the exhilaration of the reality diffusing itself into the pasteboard mimicry.

But the crowd and the show windows are not the only diversions. Besides these there

figure soon appeared in plethoric blotches of red, blue, and yellow. An amused crowd gathered and silently watched the swift motions of the little vagabond's hand. Whose portrait would it be? In the earlier stages of its progress every body thought he could detect Captain Kidd, but an unforeseen touch quickly dissipated that notion; then it seemed to be bold Ben Butler, and then the late Mr. Eddy as Ingomar the Barbarian. Thus exciting the curiosity of his critics, and holding a dozen faces spell-bound, the artist completed his subject, working several more blotches of yellow into the legs, and mixing a little brown with white over the face. It was only "a Turk," indisputably crude; but was there no zeal and cunning in its execution? We fancied that we could see both, to say nothing of the brighter light in the none-too-clean face of the artist as he rubbed the colors on the flags. Besides, if this lad had no gift or love for his occupation, why did he choose it? His father was a cartman, and his mother sold apples at a corner; his brothers and sisters were shoe-blacks and news-vendors. Why did he not follow their example? We might ask a string of questions, but we do not like the interrogative way of putting things. It is simpler to postulate. The lad was allured to his occupation by his love for it, his love for it grew out of his sympathy with it, and his sympathy with it was inborn and co-existent with an ability to master it. That is our case related in the manner of the "House that Jack Built," modified.

Recently two new-comers appeared among the street exhibitors—an old man and a little girl, who illustrated and offered for sale a new system of lightning arithmetic. The man had a pale, intelligent, studious face, and wore a threadbare suit of black. The girl, who was about fifteen or sixteen, spoke in a modest but business-like manner, and was dressed in a tasteful suit of gray—an attractive, womanly little body, who won the hearts of all spectators. The father carried a small blackboard and an easel, and when the inexorable policeman was out of the way, a convenient street corner was selected for an exhibition.

The Broadway police belong to a special squad, and are noted for their intelligence, politeness, and military bearing. It is a picture to see one of these Apollos in buttons escorting a timid lady through a maze of vehicles, or carrying a school-child across the street in his arms, and sometimes the picture is heroic.

Many odd characters drift in the crowd; advertising handbills without number are thrust upon us; our ears are assailed by the deafening tramp of feet and the crash of the wheels; misery and merriment, pomp and poverty, in various shapes, file before us. What a matchless pageantry it is!

Then there are days when the whole aspect of the street is changed, as in a rain-storm,

LIGHTNING CALCULATOR.

when the pedestrians almost disappear, and the sidewalk and pavement shine with smooth moisture; and as in a snow-storm, when the fleecy white plays miracles with appearances. But to even glance at all the phases of Broadway within the limits of a magazine article is, indeed, impossible.

The Metropolitan Newspaper (1878)

THE METROPOLITAN NEWSPAPER.

"They were passing through the Strand as they talked, and by a newspaper office, which was all lighted up and bright. Reporters were coming out of the place, or rushing up to it in cabs; there were lamps burning in the editors' rooms, and above, where the compositors were at work; the windows of the building were in a blaze of gas. 'Look at that, Pen,' Warrington said. 'There she is—the great engine—she never sleeps. She has her ambassadors in every quarter of the world, her couriers upon every road. Her officers march along with armies, and her envoys walk into statesmen's cabinets. They are ubiquitous. Yonder journal has an agent at this minute giving bribes at Madrid, and another inspecting the price of potatoes in Covent Garden. Look! here comes the Foreign Express galloping in. They will be able to give the news to Downing Street to-morrow; funds will rise or fall, fortunes be made or lost. Lord B—— will get up, and holding the paper in his hand, and seeing the noble marquis in his place, will make a great speech; and—and Mr. Doolan will be called away from his supper at the Back Kitchen, for he is foreign sub-editor, and sees the mail on the newspaper sheet before he goes to his own.' And so talking, the friends turned into their chambers, as the dawn was beginning to peep."—*Pendennis.*

AFTER a midnight walk down Broadway, a few months ago, two gentlemen crossed the breezy interspace of City Hall Park as the yellow disk of the illuminated clock in er side several of the larger buildings were luminous in the upper stories, which seemed like rows of lamps hanging in the air.

These were the offices of the great morn-

UP-TOWN DELIVERY.

the tower marked one. A few outcasts were asleep on the benches; the foliage swayed, and broke the rays of the lamps into an irregular flicker; the high dark buildings on the Broadway side rose massively, like the embattlements of a fortress, but on the oth-

ing newspapers, which are concentrated within an eighth of a mile, and the animation glowing in them brought Warrington's apostrophe to the mind of one of the gentlemen, who repeated it to his companion.

Clustered among scores of other publish-

JAMES GORDON BENNETT: NEW YORK HERALD.

ing offices, loomed the buildings of the *Trib-une*, the *Herald*, the *Sun*, the *World*, and the *Times*, white wreaths of steam rolling up from their roofs and from the gratings over the press-rooms. The press-rooms extended beyond the buildings under the sidewalk, and the pavement vibrated with the beat of the machines, which were already tossing off parts of the papers, the insides or the outsides, leaving a reserve of space for the news that might arrive afterward. Where the heat had penetrated the hard flags, some newsboys had curled themselves in innocence and dirt. Others lay asleep on the steps, where the most important and most hurried of the larger contributors to journalism kindly forbore from disturbing them. Occasionally a telegraph messenger dived into the entrance of a building, then an errand-boy from the post-office with a pile of newspapers and letters, and then a reporter from some late meeting up town. As a matter of appearance more than any thing else—as the last "form" admitting advertisements had long since closed—a clerk sat in the advertising office, on the ground-floor, and drowsed, with the lights half down.

The two gentlemen entered one of the offices, and began to ascend that long stairway by which all editorial rooms are attained, custom and economy invariably putting editors in a garret, whence they may look down, physically and mentally, on the world they write about. More telegraph

boys, compositors, proof-readers, and reporters passed the visitors on the stairs, who, when they had explained their business to an inky office-boy, were admitted into the *sanctum sanctorum* of a celebrated morning paper.

A close, low-roofed, smoky room, lighted by innumerable Argand burners, and filled with little desks, at which sat, stooping, busy men, puffing cigars or pipes, and scribbling with pens or pencils at lightning speed—that was the next scene opened to them. On some of the desks there were piles upon piles of newspapers from points as far apart and as varied as the capitals of Europe and plaintive outposts on the far Western plains. A little tin box shot up and down a wooden shaft in the middle of the room, into which rolls of manuscript were put by an office-boy, who rushed from desk to desk and gathered the sheets as they came from the writers' hands. From time to time a nervous, sharp-voiced, imperative gentleman, in a very much soiled linen duster, called to one or the other of the workers, and gave orders which would have been quite unintelligible to a layman, who might have mistaken the establishment for a slaughter-house when he heard a pale-faced

HERALD BUILDING.

W. H. HURLBERT: NEW YORK WORLD.

to the ceiling, and the pens sped over the pages of manuscript paper. The writers bent to their work with tremendous earnestness and concentration; there was not one of them who had written less than a column of matter that night, and some were closing two and three column articles, which contained nearly as many words as five pages of *Harper's Magazine.* They were pale and care-worn. One of them was heading and sub-heading cable dispatches from the seat of war, another was writing editorial paragraphs on the important telegraphic news that came in, another was damning a new play in virulent prose, another was revising a thrilling account of a murder, another was transcribing his stenographic notes of a speech on the inflation of the currency, another was putting the finishing touches upon a well-considered article criticising a debate in the French Assembly, and another was absorbed in the description of a yacht race. The little tin box in the shaft bounced up and down more frequently, and the night editor became more nervous and imperative than ever, as the fingers of the big clock on the wall went beyond two. The pages of manuscript were sent up one by one, and long moist proof-sheets came down from the composing-room. Then the "cut-

little gentleman requested to "make a paragraph of the Pope," "cut down Anna Dickinson," "double-lead General Grant," "put a minion cap head on Peter Cooper," and "boil down the Evangelical Alliance." But making a paragraph of the Pope simply applied to the compression of some news concerning him into that space; "the minion cap head" intended for the venerable philanthropist meant the kind of type to be used in the title of a speech or lecture of his; and "boiling down" and "cutting down" were two technicalities expressing condensation. The gentleman in the linen duster was the night editor in charge, the despot of the hour, and the intermediary between the writers and printers, the latter being on the floor above, and the little tin box in the shaft communicating with them.

By three o'clock the last line of "copy" must be in the printers' hands, and from midnight until that time a newspaper office in the editorial department is in a state of nervous intensity and activity for which I can imagine no parallel.

The smoke from the cigars and pipes rolled up

THE WORLD AND THE EVENING MAIL.

ting down" began, and some of the writers saw articles that had cost them hours of research annihilated by the stroke of a pen, or reduced from columns to paragraphs —not on account of unimportance, but simply because there is always a superfluity of matter, contrary to the erroneous notion that the editor's great difficulty is to fill his space—and in some instances even the paragraphs were finally omitted to make room for unexpected news that arrived later. Telegrams were still

GEORGE JONES: NEW YORK TIMES.

coming in at half past two, but soon after that hour one dispatch brought the words "good-night," and that meant the closing. The night editor and his assistant now disappeared into the composing-rooms, where they remained to superintend the making-up of the forms, and the men at the desks prepared to leave, or threw themselves back in their chairs for a chat and some more smoke.

The composing-room at night is all a-glitter with lights strung under reflectors, which throw the strong beams down on the type-setters, who are actively fingering the little metallic letters. The paper columns of manuscript are transformed to leaden ones, and the leaden ones are framed into pages of six, seven, or eight columns each. Then the pages are stereotyped, by which process duplicate or triplicate impressions are taken of them, and they are finally put on the press, which finishes the business of making the paper.

In the neighborhood of the newspaper offices in Printing-house Square and on Park Row there are several queer basement restaurants, where coffee and cakes or other simple refreshments are sold for ten or fifteen cents. During the day their patronage comes from newsboys and shoe-blacks, but after dark they are popular with the journalists, who gather around one of the common little tables to eat a modest supper before going to their homes. Liveliness of conversation after such work as the slaves of the lamp have done would scarcely be expected, but the writer has heard many and many a brilliant story in these symposia, and has seen men with world-wide reputations sharing the hot buttered cakes and somewhat suspicious coffee. Later they go to their homes, and before they are in their beds their paper is issued. Thousands buy it and read it and grumble at it, and only a few of the more reasonable and reflective ever think what a prodigious embodiment of thought and action it is, and how dull and much worse the world would be without it.

To begin at the

THE TIMES BUILDING.

beginning in the description of a metropolitan newspaper is not an easy thing, for where the beginning is, after the issue of the first number, can not be said with certainty. Before one issue is complete, preparations are making for the next, and at the moment the night editor saw the last "form" put on the press that morning when the two visitors were in his office, special correspondents were already working in the interests of the paper at London, Paris, Berlin, and St. Petersburg; they were travelling on horseback and on camel-back, in steamers and railway cars, and by many conveyances much less common; they were attached to every exploring expedition, and were listening to debates in the great Parliament Houses; they were unearthing antiquities in ruined cities, and interviewing

J. M. BUNDY: NEW YORK EVENING MAIL.

able writer, with resources at his command that especially qualify him for his position, and his coadjutors are mostly young men of ambition, who have done wisely and well in beginning their career at the bottom of the ladder.

Some years ago, when the writer held the place of second assistant to a noted city editor, his superior was approached by a fashionably dressed and pleasant-faced youth, who prefaced a request for employment with the statement that he had recently graduated from Princeton, and presented several excellent letters of introduction. The editor politely said that he would be glad to have him try his hand among the reporters, at which the applicant shrugged his shoulders, and replied, with unconscious impudence, that he expected a chance as "special correspondent, editorial writer, or something of that sort." Poor boy! his ambition overleaped itself,

DAVID M. STONE: JOURNAL OF COMMERCE.

Prime Ministers; in brief, they were everywhere, and it can be said of them, as something similar was said of the British flag, that the sun never sets upon them, and that they never sleep.

But the local work of the day begins in the City Department, which includes the city editors and reporters, and which exemplifies the thoroughness of the system by which a metropolitan newspaper is made. In the number and ability of the staff, and in the completeness of organization, we believe that the journals of no other city compare with those of New York. In London, Manchester, and other English towns, local news is gathered in a hap-hazard fashion; but in New York every point to which news may possibly come is occupied with fidelity and diligence by experienced men.

The city editor is usually a well-paid and

JOURNAL OF COMMERCE.

WILLIAM CULLEN BRYANT: EVENING POST.

and fell upon the other side. The City Department was full at that time of clever graduates, who, besides having distinguished themselves at Harvard, Cornell, Yale, Williams, or Brown, had that natural aptitude for journalism which never so surely manifests itself as in the willingness to subordinate ambition to practicable opportunities. We had with us the poet of the (then) last year's class at Yale, who was doing all sorts of literary drudgery, and who had since advanced to an enviable position in his profession; and the staff included any number of other really able descriptive writers and news-gatherers, who never for a moment considered a reporter's place beneath them.

The old Bohemian element that once sullied metropolitan reporters has been almost entirely cast out. Some of the beery, illiterate, vulgar representatives remain, but the characteristic *attaché* of the city staff is a polite, shrewd, and intelligent gentleman. The outcry against the "interviewer" is occasionally justifiable, but the phase of journalism which he represents is a concession to public appetite and demand that is not always voluntary on the part of the journalist. The politician or financier who is followed from club to club or aroused in his house at midnight by a pertinacious reporter is not to be blamed for considering the reporter a nuisance; but, ten to one, the latter is more mortified by the indignity of his mission than the former is troubled by the intrusion. The desire of an influential newspaper to obtain one's opinion on any subject is a compliment to which few men are insensitive, and it often happens that the person interviewed is more disposed to talk

than the interviewer is to inquire. The poise of the man's head will be prouder as he reads the paper on the next day, and he will unblushingly complain before his family of the interviewer's impertinence!

The expense incurred by a prosperous newspaper in gathering local news is heavy. The city editor is paid from fifty to one hundred dollars a week, and his assistants are paid from thirty to forty dollars; the reporters receive from twenty-five to thirty-five dollars a week, and as many as thirty are employed on salary by one paper, in addition to a large number of others who are paid by space, that is, according to the quantity of work they do. The price paid to outsiders, or "specials," as the unsalaried men are called, is about eight dollars per column—a column containing between sixteen hundred and two thousand words—and a writer who combines ingenuity and good descriptive powers with experience and industrious habits can earn more by special work than the best salary.

The city editor arrives at the office about ten in the morning, and his staff is waiting for him, excepting those members who were assigned to duty on the night previous, and who are already at their posts. His own and all the other morning papers are on his desk, and from them he derives many suggestions for the day's work. A line in an obscure paragraph of one contemporary may give him the idea of a long article; an announcement in another may remind him of something that would have otherwise escaped his attention; and a "beat" in a third —*i. e.*, some news which his own paper does not contain—may remind him of the ardu-

WHITELAW REID: NEW YORK TRIBUNE.

ousness of his position. His knowledge of city affairs and people is almost limitless. Should any one ask him the way to the obscurest alley, he could tell it in an instant. He knows every man in office and out of office, his hours and his haunts. A letter of introduction from him would secure admittance to the murderer in his cell, the prominent divine, the railway magnate, or the popular lecturer. He knows not only the streets and numbers of the residences of men who may have facts to give on any topic, but has directions to their clubs, churches, billiard-rooms, saloons, and places of business at his tongue's end. He is a walking directory, with much information never before introduced.

After an hour's hard work with scissors, paste pot, and a scrap-book containing all

riety of assignments proves how wide a scope a reporter's experience may have, and how constantly he drifts from "grave to gay, from lively to severe"—standing by a death-bed at one hour, and the next sharing the festivities of a dinner at Delmonico's, or watching a horse or yacht race. In making the assignments the special abilities of the men are remembered. Jones, Merlin, and Taber are stenographers, and are sent to assemblies which require long reports. The proportion of stenographers in the staff is small, however, as *verbatim* work is not often required. Mr. Cleveland has had a large experience in financial circles; Mr. Allen is an irresistible "interviewer," and the "must" added to his assignment means that General Butler is to be interviewed whether he likes it or not; Aldrich, who is

DISTRIBUTING PAPERS—EARLY MORNING.

notices received at the office of events to occur on this day, he assigns his staff to duty, and many who were not relieved until 1 or 2 o'clock A.M. are again at work before 11 A.M., such being the hardness of a reporter's life. The assignment book is brought out, and entries are made in this manner, the names on the right representing those of the reporters:

Oyer and Terminer Court..............Jones.
Wall Street............................Cleveland.
Interview General Butler (*must*).......Allen.
Council of Political Reform..........Merlin.
Yacht Regatta. ....Chambers.
Special on Liquor Frauds.............Gillham.
Funeral at Christ Church.............Smith.
Special on Election (*see note*).........Sullivan.
Auction at Leavitt's...................O'Brien.
Autumn Weather (*a neat ¶*)..........Aldrich.
Dinner at Delmonico's (*half column*)...Taber.

When the book is fully made out, the va-

ordered to write a neat paragraph on autumn weather, excels in description; Sullivan is thoroughly posted in politics; and Chambers is famous as a yachtsman. Special articles are those in the preparation of which special sources of information are used, or those describing matters that are not of mere transient interest, such as markets, ferries, or street cars. The most trustworthy and capable men are employed in this service. "See note" means that a letter has been written containing full instructions, which will be found in the reporter's box; but with the ordinary assignments no other orders are given than the brief line in the book, and the man must decide the length and the treatment of the article for himself. One who fails to accurately gauge the value of his assignment, who overestimates or underestimates it, can not expect

HUGH HASTINGS: NEW YORK COMMERCIAL ADVERTISER.

advancement; in fact, the successful reporter must not only have a quick apprehension for what is news, but he must also be able to find subjects for treatment without any suggestions or assistance of any kind from the editors.

The perfection of discipline maintained in the City Department would greatly surprise the people who imagine that a great newspaper puts itself together, and that the editor's most onerous duty is the filling of space. The precision with which nearly every thing is done would be creditable to the cadets at West Point. Each man as he receives his assignment draws a line under his name to indicate the fact; failures to obtain news which other papers contain is punished by suspension from duty or dismissal; faulty English or delay in supplying "copy" elicits a savage reprimand from the city editor, and unless a man is heroically attentive to duty the various penalties will break him.

While the assistant city editor is required to keep track of all details, the city editor himself is wide-awake on all points. But his remarkable ability is best seen when occasion arises for a "spread." Thirty or forty men are then dispatched to various points, selected with an immediate perception of their value and strength. The affair is as momentous as a battle, and woe betide the man who is found wanting! An ocean passenger steamer is wrecked on the Jersey coast, and the earliest intelligence reaches the city at about noon—we imagine this for the sake of the example. The first thing to

be done is to get several men to the scene of the disaster, and if no regular line of travel is open, special conveyances are chartered regardless of cost. The passengers saved, the captain, the pilot, the men of the life-saving station from which the wreck was discovered, the agent of the steamer, the officers of other vessels in port, and every one who can throw some light on the disaster must be seen and interviewed. Most of these people are so fraught with their own troubles that they will not readily yield answers to the reporters' interrogations, and the latter only succeed in extorting statements from them by a degree of quiet persistence that would be deemed highly creditable in any other cause.

We have imagined that a brief telegram announces the wreck in the city about noon. Two hours later the scribes are on the spot, having reached it by a private steamer or a special train. The day is raw, misty, and miserable, and the great vessel looms through the ghostly atmosphere—a blot of darkness—with the surf beating over her and breaking on the low, sandy beach. There is plenty of activity and excitement; the life-saving station and the neighboring cottages of fishermen are filled with women passengers, who have been brought through the surf; the life-saving car is passing from the vessel to the shore with living freight, and the reporters elicit what information they can as they assist the surfmen and wreckers in the work of succor. Rain, mist, and spray are of no consequence to the newsgatherers; the day may be bitterly cold and wet, and they may have come from the city in light and insufficient clothing; their fingers may be almost frozen; but the notebook and pencil are in constant use, and the moisture drops over their writing in troublesome pools as they beseech and besiege the surfmen in dripping tarpaulins, who have landed from the wreck. Then

COMMERCIAL ADVERTISER.

the hour comes when, having drained every source of information, they must make for the nearest telegraph office, which is probably at Long Branch, and a race takes place among the representatives of different papers for precedence in the use of the wire. The competition involves strategy, but they all reach the office within a few minutes of each other, and settle down to the writing up of their accounts, handing the operator page by page as it is completed. An essential quality in all journalists, and especially in correspondents or reporters, is facility of perception, decision, and expression, and if they are without it in the beginning of their careers, the recurrence of the necessity for it develops it. A critic may find many grammatical lapses and inelegancies of language in the printed descriptions of those tired-out men who are scribbling, with empty stomachs, in all sorts of uncomfortable positions, to the nervous tick-ticking of the busy Morse instrument which is putting electricity into their words under the dark waters of the New York Bay. It is a very easy thing to find fault with them, and it may be very true that their style is artificial and their diction either impoverished or redundant; but it is outrageously unfair to take no account of the pressure under which they work out their fluent productions, to say nothing further of the unfavorableness of their condition to literary composition. Their note-books have been reduced to a pulp in the rain and spray, and the pencil marks are all blurred; the notes themselves are disconnected and meagre, having been gathered hurriedly from hurried people; but out of the chaos, without having time for revision, the Froissart of his day, as some one calls the reporter, weaves a continuous, lucid, graphic narrative of the wreck, and not of the wreck alone, but also of the voyage preceding it, incorporating a full abstract of the log, and conversations with the captain, pilot, officers, crew, and passengers, and furbishing the mosaic of detail with a strong picturesqueness of epithet that would not be unworthy of a much greater literary artist. Each man has written between two and three columns before midnight, and lest the intellectual reader fails to understand how great an achievement this is, we advise him to test the matter by putting himself under a cold shower-bath, and then trying to compose, in his wet clothes, an acceptable three-page article for this Magazine within four hours.

The telegraphic dispatches are supplemented by a mass of other facts which have been gathered in the city, such as a history and description of the steamer, the value of her cargo, the amount of the insurance; and when the paper appears in the morning the account of the disaster covers nearly a whole page, and is a marvel of completeness.

In reporting large meetings the number of stenographers on the staff is increased. Let us suppose, for example, that a political

EVENING POST BUILDING.

demonstration is to be made at the Cooper Union, and that the *Tribune* is arranging to report it. Many of the speeches are to be published in full, and altogether the proceedings will fill from twenty-five to thirty columns of the next day's paper. Four or five members of the permanent staff can report *verbatim*, and all the rest can make good synopses, which in most instances are sufficient. Some of the principal speakers have written their orations, and greatly help the city editors by lending their manuscripts in advance, which are put into type, but others have made no preparation, and the usual corps of short-hand men is augmented by recruits drafted for the occasion from the law-reporting firms of the city. In reality five or six meetings are to be held, one in the hall and the others outside, and the city editor-in-chief divides his staff into five or six squads, which are each assigned to a particular stand, under the direction of one of their own number. The men are next assigned to a "take," that is to say, each man takes notes for fifteen minutes, more or less, in turn, and then rushes to the office, where he writes his matter up. Thus the first "take" has been edited and put into type hours before the man assigned to the last "take" has left the hall.

This brings me to the night editors of the City Department, by whom all the matter

and a small vessel cruises about the harbor night and day in search of the in-coming ships and steamers which bring foreign papers and letters.

Should we follow the reporters from the time they leave the office in the morning until they are relieved at night, we would be led to stranger scenes than the Jersey coast, and among stranger people than the surfmen at the wreck. One man becomes a detective in the unravelment of some municipal fraud, and is closeted at one hour with a justice of the Supreme Court, the next hour with a notorious gambler in his saloon, the next with a prominent politician in the sumptuous parlor of a fashionable club, and the next with a poverty-stricken ex-office-holder in a garret. Every grade of society and every neighborhood are visited by him in his investigations. No rebuff discourages him, no accumulation of disappointments exhausts his patience, and nothing satisfies him except the information necessary to the complete-

REPORTER IN THE BAGGAGE-CAR.

ness of his article. Another would be found with a squad of health-officers and policemen inspecting the sub-cellar tenements of a poor neighborhood, or "raiding" the infamous resorts in Greene or Mercer Street; another passes the day at a religious conference, another at a horse-race, another in the ante-room of a sick millionaire's chamber, another amid the strife of Wall Street, and another at a meeting of coopers, or boiler-makers, or physicians, or actors, or seamen. The scenes change without intermissions. Now the music is slow, now it is lively; now mirrors and crystal pendants to the candelabra multiply the lights, and then the darkness is made darker by the pale and sickly flicker of a taper. All the woe and gayety, the penury and the splendor, the crying want and the spendthrift luxury, of the great metropolis are known to the reporter as no other man knows them. That facile pencil of his punctures every vein of life, and no place is too inconvenient for its use. In the street car as he rides down town to his office, in the dépôt while he waits for a train, or in the train amid the distracting noise of the locomotive, he plies it with superlative energy and industry.

of the reporters is read and revised. They are two in number, and their positions are of great responsibility. Beginning duty at five or six o'clock in the afternoon, they are occupied until two in the morning improving bad English, condensing diffuse articles, toning down broad or libelous statements, and preventing all waste of space.

The City Department includes several smaller departments, to which regular men are permanently assigned. The police department is one, and an able reporter is constantly stationed at head-quarters to gather the news that arrives there of crimes, fires, and other disasters. The mayor's office, the coroners' offices, the surrogate's office, the courts, the head-quarters of the Fire Department, and every point at which an item may be gleaned, are also occupied,

CHARLES A. DANA: NEW YORK SUN.

Some time ago an *attaché* of a morning paper was sent by an afternoon train to Norwalk, Connecticut, for the purpose of investigating a hunted Ring thief's transfer of property. He reached South Norwalk after four o'clock, and then rode to Norwalk in a slow street car. The only train by which he could return to the city was the Boston express, due shortly after nine, and in the four hours intervening he had to interview several people and make long abstracts from the county clerk's records. He had not begun to write out his material when the train started; but sitting on one trunk in the baggage-car, with another trunk for a desk, he wrote an article a column and a half long during the two hours' journey to the city—an article of the greatest importance, which needed no correction of the editor's, though the baggage-men had been playing an uproarious game of euchre, and the locomotive had been whistling furiously at every one of the numerous crossings, during its composition. Such activity as this is common among reporters, who develop above all other things, as I have said, the indispensable ability to work under pressure.

By one of those broad generalizations with which the world is apt to content itself, many people, in thinking of a great newspaper, place at its head a miscellaneous sort of person who does every thing in connection with it, writing every thing, reading every thing, and listening to every body. When they can fix upon his name, they address all communications to him personally, and the writer has seen envelopes at the *Tribune* office containing notices of births, marriages, deaths, and other such

trifles—trifles as matters of news—carefully and secretly inscribed to Mr. Greeley.

But the metropolitan newspaper is a machine with too many ramifications for the control of one man, and the vast mass of details involved in its production is classified and distributed among the several members of a large staff of sub-editors, the editor-in-chief holding his subordinates responsible.

The one who resembles the fanciful creation of the public mind most is the day editor in charge. He receives and opens the mail, distributing the various matters which it brings among the several departments, putting foreign correspondence in the hands of a foreign editor, news relating to art in the hands of the art editor, local news in the hands of the city editor, political news in the hands of the political editor, scientific news in the hands of a scientific editor, and agricultural news in the hands of an agricultural editor. Each of these editors has a special branch of the paper to look after; and in addition to them there is a dramatic editor, who attends exclusively to theatrical matters; a financial editor, who reviews the money market; an "exchange" editor, whose duty it is to read the hundreds of papers sent in from outside towns; and a literary editor, who is devoted to book reviewing and literary news. Master of all is the editor-in-chief, who directs the policy of the paper, writes occasional leading ar-

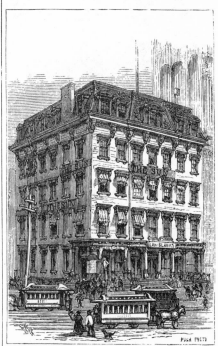

THE SUN BUILDING.

ticles on momentous questions, and supervises the whole intellectual establishment.

The office hours of the editor-in-chief are light, but his position is the hardest on the staff, for the responsibility of all the utterances of the paper falls upon him, and the care follows him from the office to his club, and from his club to his bedroom. He is never off duty. A private telegraph wire connects the office with his house, and questions and answers are flashing over it at all hours. If he seeks repose at his club, he has scarcely lighted his cigar and curled himself up in an easy-chair when a "print-

ernoon he again reaches the office, where a crowd of callers are anxiously waiting for an audience with him, among them being office-seeking politicians who want recommendations—which they will not get; philanthropists who want to enlist the influence of the paper in some scheme of Utopian form; authors who want puffs; unemployed journalists who want positions; and many others who want to make suggestions in regard to the policy of the paper, the general burden of all their business being in some "want." The editor closets himself immediately after running the gauntlet of these

WAITING FOR AN AUDIENCE WITH THE EDITOR.

er's devil" appears before him with proofs; if he goes to the opera, he is summoned from his box in the middle of the performance by a messenger with a note from the managing editor; he is called from the ball-room and the most fascinating of partners into an anteroom, where another "devil" is in waiting with more proofs; and when he draws the curtains around his bed and is falling asleep, the little telegraph instrument on his study table awakens him by its sharp tinklings, which impatiently demand advice from him in regard to the treatment of some momentous news which has come in since he left the office—it may be the resignation of a ministry, a declaration of war, a speech by President Hayes, the death of a king, or a Russian victory on the Danube.

Between two and three o'clock in the aft-

importunates, and opens his private mail, indorsing some letters, which are handed to his private secretary, and destroying many others. An usher then serves the cards of the callers upon him, some of whom are referred to the sub-editors, or to the managing editor, who stands in relation to the editor-in-chief as the captain of a flag-ship stands to an admiral, the executive officer being the day editor in charge; others are dismissed; and a few—a very few—are admitted. It is almost as easy to slide up hill as to obtain an audience with the chief editor of a metropolitan newspaper, whose *sanctum* is hedged in by a divinity which is not apparent in the proportions or the furniture of the modest apartment.

In personal interviews or in letters dictated to his secretary he communicates with all his principal assistants, giving them topics for articles, and hints as to the tone which the articles are to have, or correcting errors in their work of the previous day. His correspondence is voluminous, and occupies him, with the secretary, who writes in short-hand, until six or seven o'clock, when he disappears, to re-appear later in the evening. He is courted every where. Cabinet officers, leaders in the world of art, literature, and science, judges, and millionaires —all are desirous of standing well with him, and do not stint their efforts to win his favor.

When the time comes for going to press, the night editor has sixty or seventy columns of matter in type, and the capacity of the paper is about forty-eight columns. All the news and the articles are desirable, but something must be omitted, and the chief at his house is called upon by his telegraphic instrument to decide. Then, perhaps, some accident happens to one of the "forms" as it is being stereotyped, or a second edition becomes necessary, to admit some news that arrives after three o'clock, and he is again aroused. It is sunrise before the little instrument is quiet, and the paper is issued before its chief is thoroughly asleep.

Large as the salaried staff of editorial writers is, contributions are often purchased from outsiders for the editorial page and the news columns, and the authors, whose names do not often appear, are frequently eminent specialists in literature, science, and art. A contrast thrusts itself upon us here between the editorial pages, so called, of the New York and London papers. Those of the latter are absorbed in most instances by political subjects or abstruse matters of social science; but the reader of our metropolitan journals finds on the editorial pages, in addition to the political "leaders," agreeable essays on nearly every variety of topic.

Besides having its own staff of reporters and correspondents, the metropolitan newspaper also shares the facilities of the Associated Press, which, both in its history and its methods, is exceedingly interesting. I write of it *ex cathedrâ*, as my facts were supplied by the general superintendent, Mr. J. W. Simonton.

Exactly what the association is, very few understand. Some suppose that it is a newspaper, and it receives requests from country journals to "exchange;" others mistake it for an advertising agency; and even among some newspaper men many curious misconceptions of its objects prevail. It was started, long before the telegraph was a practical success, by four New York papers, and its sole aim was co-operation in the collection of marine news;

but with the development of the telegraph it expanded, and it was reorganized in its present form twenty-six years ago by the proprietors of the *Journal of Commerce*, the *Courier and Enquirer*, the *Express*, the *Tribune*, the *Sun*, and the *Herald*. The *Courier and Enquirer* being merged into the *World*, the latter paper secured the franchise of the former, and the *Times* was admitted to the partnership in 1851. The association is composed of the several papers, not of the individuals who own or control them, and so the proprietorship or policy of a paper may change without affecting the position of that paper in the partnership.

It collects news primarily for its own seven members, taking for the use of all a common dispatch, narrating Congressional proceedings or any event of general interest, and reducing the cost to each by dividing between all the expenses of reporting and telegraphing. But its scope was enlarged soon after its organization, and it now sells news at stipulated rates to over five hundred other papers published in every part of the

THE TRIBUNE BUILDING.

continent. Its agents are scattered over the whole world. Its London offices are never closed, and the news arriving there is forwarded under nearly three thousand miles of ocean at all hours as rapidly as it is received. Confining itself to no arbitrary limit, its daily cable tolls are seldom less than three hundred dollars, and sometimes they are four times that amount. North and Central America are covered by its own agents; and by arrangements with the great news agencies abroad, including Reuter's, it receives the news collections of the latter from every part of Europe, Asia, Africa, and South America. In well-populated regions of the United States sub-associations are formed, which give the local papers fuller details of local affairs than more distant papers would require; and in sparsely settled districts, where news items are not frequent enough to warrant the appointment of regular agents, the telegraph operators are authorized to employ men of ability in the interest of the association whenever any calamity, disturbance, or excitement occurs.

As the dispatches reach the general agency they are handed to the manager of the manifolding-room, under whose direction copies are multiplied for distribution, the manifolding process enabling one writer to make from twelve to twenty-six copies at a time, by means of a very tough oiled tissue-paper alternated with carbonized paper, and an agate or carnelian point substituted for a pen or pencil.

OSWALD OTTENDORFER: STAATS-ZEITUNG.

When a page of manifold is written, the office assistants separate and envelop the copies, which are sent to the city newspapers by messengers. Other copies are handed to agents representing sections of the papers in the North, South, East, and West, who edit them, each agent eliminating whatever will not interest his particular constituency, and adding any thing of value that he can obtain from other sources.

The distribution is effected by telegraphic delivery at many different points along a continuous line of wire at the same instant of time. The system involves combination reports, which are forwarded to all who share them at or within certain fixed hours, arranged by contract with the telegraph company. Though the reports to Boston are sent direct at all hours, the same report is repeated to all other places in New England on a combined circuit; that is to say, New York is put into telegraphic connection by a single wire si-

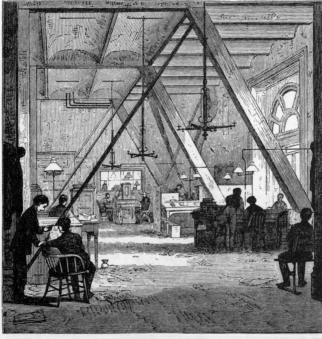

ASSOCIATED PRESS ROOMS.

multaneously with New Haven, Hartford, Springfield, Worcester, and other points East where there are papers entitled to the news. In each town or village an operator takes position at his instrument when report hour is called, and is ready to write the report in manifold as it comes over the wire. Another operator writes the message by the transmitting instrument in New York, and that one writing sends it to all points on the circuit. The receivers are

purpose. Washington receives a full *résumé* of the general news of the world, forwarded from New York, and also dispatches from New Orleans, Mobile, Charleston, Richmond, and other points. Each of these Southern cities is interested in the news of the others, and to supply them with it a summary of all that has been received at Washington is included in the combination report, which, being delivered at all points, gives back to each city some of its own news. This drawback

GETTING NEWS FROM STEAMER IN NEW YORK BAY.

highly skilled in the business, and read by sound without the aid of the recorded Morse characters.

The telegrams to the Western press are sent in the same manner, being delivered simultaneously at Pittsburgh, Wheeling, Cleveland, Cincinnati, Chicago, St. Louis, and other principal points. At Cincinnati, Detroit, Chicago, St. Louis, Milwaukee, and Memphis condensed abstracts, known as "pony" reports, are made and forwarded to smaller towns, whose papers can not afford the cost of the longer dispatch. Philadelphia, Washington, and Baltimore are also served in combination, and reports to all points south of the Potomac are made up by an agent placed at Washington for that

is inseparable from a combination system, and though it involves some waste of telegraphed words, the saving to the papers is very large.

The Canadians take the Associated Press news from Buffalo to Toronto, whence it is distributed throughout the Dominion. The Pacific coast is served partly from Chicago and partly from New York, the agent of the California press in Chicago being furnished with "drop copies" of what is sent from New York, so that he may avoid duplication. Other "drop copies" of the reports going to California are also taken off the wire at Salt Lake City, Denver, and Cheyenne for the use of local papers.

The charges to outside papers are adjust-

IN THE PRESS-ROOM.

ed on a liberal basis. Thus, while a poor country paper may receive the same combination report that a strong and influential paper in a great city receives, it is not charged more than ten per cent. of the amount assessed upon the latter—assessed not arbitrarily, but with the consent of all. The aim of the association is, first, to get news, and second, to get in return the highest amount the paper using it can afford to pay; but equal use of the news by papers competing with each other in one place involves equal charges to all of the competitors. Some of the poorer papers in the South receive the combination report of the whole world's news—all charges paid—for fifteen dollars a week, while the charges for the same matter to a metropolitan paper often amount to over five hundred dollars a week, and occasionally fifteen hundred dollars a week. The Western, New England, and New York State associations pay the parent institution fixed sums per month for the use of news delivered to their reporters at desks in the New York office, and make their own contracts with the telegraph companies. All others have direct accounts with the New York office or its local agents.

THE EXPRESS BULLETIN.

At the end of each week the cashier makes a statement of all disbursements and receipts of that week. The deduction of the receipts from the expenditures invariably shows a large deficit, which, divided by seven, gives the amount or share to be paid by each of the seven New York papers forming the association.

The American Press Association is an organization similar to the Associated Press, and supplies news to a large number of papers, including the New York *Evening Mail;* but it is not as extensive in its resources or its business as the older concern, the success of which is owing principally to the remarkable executive ability of its superintendent, Mr. Simonton.

We know from experience what drudgery and exhausting labor befall the man who is bound down to the desk of a metropolitan newspaper—the exacting discipline, the unremitted application, and the unsatisfactory results, which break the hearts and rack the brains of many promising writers. But beyond the compensation, which exists for all who are ambitious, in sharing the anonymous power of the press—a power which all people appreciate, consciously or unconsciously, despite their disavowment—is the exhilaration of the profession, the sharp competition, the swift action, and the inner view of men and manners which the journalist obtains. It is this exhilaration that keeps and sustains many who would otherwise endeavor to escape a business which is both arduous and underpaid.

To-morrow morning the reader will find his paper on the breakfast table—price two, three, or four cents—and, unless our article has impressed him, he will read it and cast it aside without thinking of its suggestiveness as an epitome of civilization, or of the enormous mental and mechanical labor it has cost. But cavil as he may, that moist sheet, fresh from the marvelous machines of Hoe, Walter, or Bullock—served at the door by the same urchins that the two visitors saw asleep over the warm gratings of the press-rooms—is the very essence of our times, embodying the highest results of discovery in all times.

NEWSBOYS WAITING FOR THE PAPER.

Games of the City Street
(1904)

Marbles—And He Takes the Alley.

GAMES OF THE CITY STREET

By ROBERT DUNN

The wind blows East,
The wind blows West,
The wind blows over the Cuckoo's Nest;
    Shall he go East?
    Shall he go West?
Shall he go under the Cuckoo's Nest?
    Hon-pon-kuck-a-da-hook!
    Hon-pon-kuck-a-da-hook!!

AS long as spring in New York is still the old spring of warm days and many long twilights, you cannot pass such a place as Tompkins Square, at Avenue A and Tenth Street, without hearing that song and that refrain some afternoon when school's just out. Or, skip over a great distance and many nations and pass Hudson Park, the queer polygon where Eighth Avenue begins, or Bayard Park on the lower East Side, or any of the green oases, uptown and downtown, in the tenements deserts of the city.

In hon-pon, two boys are "it": master and cuckoo. The cuckoo is picked by a round of "Eeny Meeny," or of fist-knocking for the pebble; and he, in turn,

Cold Enough for a Fire.

chooses his master, who stands erect against a park fence or house wall. The cuckoo, facing him, bends forward at right angles, and rests his head against the master's stomach. He is blindfold, and the master lays his fists on the cuckoo's back. And now the littlest boys, a-tiptoe, shrill and lithe, and the big boys, long-trousered and loungy, scheming how to "put up a game" on some mamma's pet—the thin, freckled, spectacled lad who lives in awe of a window opening down the block and a shriek coming from home —all are shouting "*Hon-pon-kuck-a-da-hook! Hon-pon-kuck-a-da-hook!*" with mixed vigor and falsettos.

The master, choosing a certain boy in the crowd, patent to all but the cuckoo, repeats the rhyme

> Shall he go East?
> Shall he go West? etc.

and pauses for the cuckoo to name the direction. Then the master leans over and whispers to the boy chosen to run

to some point east or west within the bounds of three or four blocks agreed on for the game, and wait; around the corner, or in a far tenement hall or a doorway. If the cuckoo's order is to go under the nest, the master has nothing to say, and the boy must double himself up and crawl beneath the cuckoo. It's best to be sent there, as will be seen, and wonderful how many small bodies can squeeze under him.

So all the boys are disposed of one by one, jointly by master and cuckoo, neither (save in going under the nest) fixing by himself any boy's fate. The rhyme is repeated to each by the master, the refrain by the crowd; and by this time every boy is supposed to have one good hard knot in his handkerchief, or a rag of some sort; but double knots, or knots with stones in them or knotted straps and ropes, are not allowed.

When all are out, the master cries, "All out"; the cuckoo stands erect, tears off his bandage, and the real play begins. The master shouts, "*Hon-pon-kuck-a-da-hook!*

Hon-pon-kuck-a-da-hook!! Hon-pon-kuck-a-da-hook!!!" The third repetition is a signal for every one in hiding to foot it, fast as legs can carry him, back to master and cuckoo at goal. Fun and confusion begin. The last man back is the proper mark for a good beating with every knotted handkerchief; but as every man is the last man in, until the one next him in hiding distance from goal shows up, every player as he arrives gets a good beating. The first get fewer knots on their polls, and the later ones more and more; for, as soon as one boy has run the gauntlet, he turns in to chastise his successors. The actual last man gets a long basting from the whole gang; but as for the men under the nest, they come in for no trouncing at all, and have nothing to do but to wield their knots, while the actual last fellow is rewarded by being made the next cuckoo, with choice of a master.

No test of strength or skill enters a game like this, and that is why it is typical of city boys. Look close, and you will see that hon-pon offers countless chances, as the boys say, "for a whole lot of skin." Chums and enemies, personal likes and dislikes, divide every street gang. So the city boy uses his games to rub in or to avenge prejudice and preference; and for the humor therein—now, don't call it bullying. In hon-pon, for instance, the master will send a boy he has a grudge against, or the sweet child for whose benefit the game may have been proposed —who'd have been called cry-baby if he'd refused to play—to the most faraway corner in bounds to make sure he'll be the last victim of the knotted handkerchief. And the blindfold cuckoo, after a friendly whisper, gets a nudge on his knee from a chum to signal *he* must be sent under the nest.

Games like this are more popular in the heart of the city than the local variations to be mentioned on prisoner's base, hi-spy, and cops and robbers (these the most eclectic terms, I hope). For this, city conditions are responsible; not so much

An Exciting Moment in the Game.

that narrow and crowded streets, cranky old men who live alone and rush out at you, fuming in spectacles and carpet slippers, at the least noise on their door - steps, or the mountain- ous hydra - clubbed blue- coats, ponder- ous of motion and with no sense of humor — with whom every gang has its vendetta — are dampers on manlier games. The rings and horses and horizontal bars that ornament the sward of Mr. Riis's parks and school yards are field enough for competition in muscle building.   But they are no outlet for the big per cent. of devil in every boy. Horseshoe-the-mare gratifies the deuce in a boy even better than hon-pon; and grown-ups, not too grown, who know the carpet-slippered old fossils of a neighbor-

Top-spinning in the Park.

hood, have been known to laugh as they passed and saw the prank in swing.   And unless it were for teachers' favorites, boys weak-eyed from overstudy and too much home   supervision, horseshoe-the-mare would be impossible.   It is played thus:

The gang is in a restless mood. "Let's go get Georgie," says one of the crowd; "he's never been shoed." George is the teacher's favor- ite, the inoffen- sive innocent. He is waylaid on the way home from school and coaxed to come play. It is proved to him the crowd can't possibly live unless he's with them, and may- be flattery like that isn't irre- sistible, coming from boys George has al- ways feared and looked up to, imagining they have de- spised and

One Pair of Roller Skates can be Made to do for Four.

looked down on him. So Georgie agrees to play. Some one suggests horseshoe-the-mare as a good game, and after one or two boys have pooh-poohed it—for a blind—it's agreed to be all right for a dull afternoon. Instantly a clamor rises; every boy wants to be the mare, until a big one in the gang, with the big boy's lazy halo of authority grounded in rumors that once in a while he smokes a cigarette, settles the matter by patronizing George, saying it's only polite and nice to let little Georgie be the mare.

"You be gentleman"—"I'm blacksmith," a couple shout, and gentleman and blacksmith scuttle off to return with a long piece of some mother's clothesline. The gentleman harnesses Georgie, knotting the rope so hard about his chest that he never can undo it alone; and while he puts his mare through her paces, making her stand, rear, trot, and gallop up and down the block, the blacksmith is off for his shop. Now the game must be played in a dwelling-house district; for, of course, the blacksmith's shop is the front stoop of the carpet-slippered fossil.

The gentleman reins in his prancing mare before the blacksmith in his shop, and shouts that her off hind foot needs a new iron. He shouts loud in case Mr. Carpet-slipper is asleep. "Who-a! who-a!" he calls, backing the mare into the bottom step, *backing her*, remember, "who-a! who-a!" as the blacksmith rubs the mare's mane and fetlocks cautiously, lifts up a foot and hammers away at the boot-sole with a chunk of coal. Whereupon the gentleman sneaks up the steps and ties the reins to the fossil's door-knob.

"It's a fine mare you have," says the blacksmith behind her back as the gentleman descends.

"Sure, that it is," replies the gentleman, "and how much do I owe you?" he asks.

"Oh, five dollars I guess," says the blacksmith, and a beer-keg stamp is handed over.

"Get-arp, get-arp!" both shout, hitting the mare over his shins, and little Georgie makes a plunge forward—stumbles—yanks the bell knob. . . .

The old duffer from behind the bell is doing for Georgie, invoking God, the police, parents, the devil, and untying the harness knot all at once. Wild cries of "Horseshoe-the-mare! Horseshoe-the-mare!" make hideous every corner.

Franker games, many like those we've all played, have been grouped into three classes, and the names simple variations of each will pass under in separate sections of the greater cities is curious.

The hi-spy class includes, among many others, ringalevio (Brooklyn name), kick-the-wicket, sixty-o, throw (or fling) the stick, I-spy-the-wolf (East Side), Yankee-dar-oo, (or nar-oo) (Harlem and Bronx) and Yoller. The rules of each merge and conflict with the rules of all. No one differs very much from plain hide-and-seek, but hide-and-seek is a girl's game, where you have to "lie low" until you're found, I believe.

The "it," for instance, in ringalevio stands up against the goal or base, blindfold or "not peeking," and counts while the crowd hides. (If he counts sixty, the game may be sixty-o.) When he starts to hunt, he shouts "ringalevio" for warning. Generally the common rules of hi-spy are followed, except in yankee-dar-oo, which is in some ways more like hare and hounds. The hiders in yankee-dar-oo are given two blocks' start, and whenever one turns a corner he must shout "yankee-dar-oo" to give the "it" or "hound" the scent; and each one caught has to be tagged three times, not simply seen, and the goal raced for. In throw-the-stick, the boy who touches base before the "it," grabs a stick there, and hurls it as far as he can, freeing those already caught, and giving each time to hide again while the "it" is "shacking" it back to base. In yankee-dar-oo, as the hiders, or hares, are caught they have to pitch in and help the hounds; and yoller is a version of yankee-dar-oo for after-dark use, in which the hound need only see the hare to have caught him.

In some cities, prisoner's base is despised as a girl's game, but though New York boys feel they do not compromise themselves by playing it, its versions, under names like ring-rover or come-over, grand-daddy, corey, and pump-pump-pull-away, are more popular. Two opposing goal lines, often street curbs chalked off for ten yards or so, with a danger area between in which the "it" tries to catch the players as they run from goal to goal, is the principle under

An Alert Type of Street Urchin.

all. In ring-rover, whenever the "it" yells,

> "Ring-rover, ring-rover,
> Come over, come over,"

every player must make a dash for the other side, past the "it," who tries to catch and tag him three times. In versions that allow you to cross at your own sweet will, the "it" only has to tag to catch; and in nearly all versions the boys caught stay between the goal to help him. Other rules vary minutely according to the name and locality of the game, though nearly everywhere the custom is for the first man caught

An East Side Newsboy.

to be "it" the next round, and for the catchers to rush in and grab whom they can when all the players are on one side; this provided, he shouts the title of the game, "Pump-pump-pull-away!" or "Corey!"

Hop-a-da-goose (Brooklyn version) is more distinctive and has a lyric as well.

A rectangle, about six by ten feet, is marked on the sidewalk with chalk, or coal, or arc carbon. This is the den in which the "it" can walk on both feet, but may leave only by taking a hop-skip-and-jump. If he wants to go farther than that he must hop on one leg.

The players to be caught crowd around him, shouting,

Hop-a-da-goose, hop-a-da-goose,
Come out of your den,
Whoever you catch
Is one of your men.

"It" doesn't take his hop-skip until the players, getting braver and braver, crowd closer and closer upon the den. Then he makes a dive for them with the hop-skip, chasing beyond by hopping on one leg within bounds. But if he lets the other foot touch ground, he can catch no one until he has run back to his den, before which every player may pile in and beat him with a knotted handkerchief. As he catches each man he must shout

Hop-a-da-goose, hop-a-da-goose,
I'm out of my den,
For I have just caught
One of your men.

Versions of hare and hounds, like cops and robbers, and chalk-corners, in which the 'scent is given by arrows marked on walls or pavements, need no description. Where rocks are scarce, duck-on-the-rock has become a game played with a baseball —roly-boly. The crowd's hats are lined up on one curb, and a boy with the baseball from the other tries to toss it into some one's hat. Whoever gets it so, runs to get the ball while the crowd scoots the other way. As he picks it up, he shouts, "Stand!" at which all must stop in their tracks, while the ball is hurled to "sting" any one in sight; and the boy hit "rolls" for the next round. A baseball is used, too, in "over," which is played only on the city's skirts, where you live in low frame houses, gabled and with yards. The gang divides into two sides, the one given the ball throwing it over the house-top to the crowd on the other side. If the ball isn't caught the first time, it is thrown back; if not the second time, it passes to the other side. When it is caught, the crowd having it stampedes around the house, and whoever is caught and tagged by the boy holding the ball under his coat —the point is, the other side never knows who holds it—goes over to the invading party. The game is won by the side which takes all the players.

But as Fourth-o'-July is peer of all holidays, so the doings of Launchin' Day excel games of any sort whatsoever.

Launchin' Day (in pronouncing *don't* Boston the "au") is the greatest East Side field day, Durbar, Derby Day—what you will—and it comes on August first; why, no one knows, except it has to come in summer.

The grounds are all East River docks, haunted by longshoremen and by dock rats, who will tumble overboard, all dressed, for anything from a peanut to a penny; especially the bulkheads around Fulton Market and the Dover Street dock, just up from the Brooklyn Bridge, which the crazy bridge jumpers intend—before-hand—to strike for. On August first, the longshoremen are out bright and early to egg on the carnival. The first victims are the very poor urchins sent out at dawn to spear drift-wood in the river by bending a horseshoe nail and fixing it to the end of a broomstick.

"Better get yer clodes off," advises a slouchy truck-handler, to the poor child tying up his bundle of rocket sticks drifted in from Coney on the early tide. But before the boy can cry out or run or peel off, the dock rats are on him with a whoop.

"Over wid ye," they shout, and "Over wid ye," echo the 'shoremen. The kid whimpers he can't swim. "Can't help," says a big rat; "dis is Launchin' Day."

The rats watch him shriek and splutter in the wash among the piles, until the psychological moment of the third sinking, when all hands dive over with another whoop, and make the gallantest, splash-iest sort of rescue. "D——n, why don't youse learn to swim?" is the leader's sym-pathy to the sobby, shivery kid on the pierhead, as he avenges himself with all his father's oaths, and as his head is full of proper resolutions about learning to swim. And ten to one, by next Launchin' Day he's a rat himself.

And by noon every boy who has poked his nose out of doors within three blocks of the river has had his ducking and made his resolutions to be a swimmer. The rats are bored, fearfully bored, and no reform school holds anything more vicious than a dock gang bored on Launchin' Day. In the afternoon you will notice rats snooping around lumber piles and hiding in saloon doorways across the street on the lookout for something. And gen-erally it is found. Past will walk a kid rather better dressed than any rat, maybe with a dash of Grand Street ribbon in his sailor hat, or a little velvety Fauntleroy effect to his trousers. But the rats know he can't swim. He is seized, and over he goes, ribbons and all. The rescue follows at the psychological moment. Then, dripping and weeping on the bulkhead, he gets no advice about learning to swim. He is left alone, and maybe he isn't lonely.

In a while a crowd of strange faces, pitying and sympathetic, gathers about him. They ask where he lives, and if he wants to go home. Boo hoo! Indeed he does. They lead him, with cusses for the rats and "de cruelties of Launchin' Day," to his mother's door. The bell is rung. Then,

"See here, Willie," they say, "we've a-rescued youse from drownin', ain't we? An' youse stick to telling your mother dat, and not peach on us. We've a-rescued you, see, and we'll kill youse if you tell her we ain't."

Mother appears at the door and grasps her lost child.

"Missus, your kid was shootin' craps on de Dover Street pier dis afternoon," says the leader, "an' he tumbles overboard, an' Mike an' us jumps in, an' saves his life. We don't know what he's worth to youse, an' mebbe his clothes is all spoiled, but our gettin' wet is worth about two dollars' doctor bills to our healt'."

Very often the gang—for of course it's a relay of the same crowd that chucked Willie over—gets the two dollars. But there are some wise mothers, even mothers of Fauntleroys—particularly if they have had other children treated so. One thing is certain, by next August Willie can swim, even if he has had to tease his mother to take him to Brighton Beach to learn.

So the day ends, as the rats locate the cop's favorite saloon and strip for a last swim, doing the "front air" and the "back air" (back and front double somersaults). Some one says, while all are playing porpoise, "Let's chaw 'em," and half the gang scrambles ashore and knots up all the clothes of the other half, and shouts, "Cheese it—the cop," to put him on that swimming without tights is going on; and the cop chases off all to hiding.

" Heads or Tails ? "

The Brooklyn Bridge (1873)

JOHN A. ROEBLING.

THE BROOKLYN BRIDGE.

PEOPLE who seventeen years ago divided an amphibious existence between New York and Brooklyn will long remember their arctic voyages in the East River during the severe winter of 1866-7. There were days in that season when passengers from New York to Albany arrived earlier than those who set out the same morning from their breakfast tables in Brooklyn for their desks in New York. The newspapers were filled for weeks with reports of the ice gorges, and with vehement demand for and discussion of the bridge, which all agreed must be built at once from New York to Brooklyn.

Public feeling was soon highly gratified by the announcement that leading citizens of Brooklyn were moving in the matter, and that a bill for chartering the New York

Bridge Company had been introduced into the Legislature then in session at Albany. The popular excitement gave but a timely lift to a movement already ripe, and to a charter already placed before members of the Legislature and government of the State, months in advance of the session, while the waters of the East River were sparkling in the warm sunshine as if ice gorges were never to be known. As early as 1865 Mr. William C. Kingsley, of Brooklyn, of whom the public has since heard much in connection with this enterprise, had employed an eminent engineer to draw a plan and make estimates for a suspension-bridge very nearly in the location ultimately fixed for the present work.

The charter originally and provisionally fixed the capital at $5,000,000 (with power of increase), and gave the cities of New York and Brooklyn authority to subscribe to the capital stock of the company such amount as their Common Councils respectively should determine. This latter was in effect a sort of "caution money," or a guarantee of the sound interest which those who were to govern the work ought to take in it, for it was wisely judged that neither private capital nor municipal management could be relied on to carry such a work successfully to completion. Public credit must be joined with private enter-

WASHINGTON A. ROEBLING.

prise, in the hands of men who had too much at stake in the work to permit it to be perverted to political purposes.

But by the time the foundations of the towers—the chief difficulty to be overcome—had been successfully completed, popular jealousy of a company enjoying the control of so much public expenditure began to make itself felt in various ways, and to serve as the instrument of various personal and political rivalries and enmities. At the same time, the work was so well advanced, and its plans and methods so firmly fixed by what had already been done, that its friends now felt prepared to resign the great enterprise entirely to the two cities (acting through a commission or board of trustees, appointed half by the

Mayor and Comptroller of each city, and including those officials), and prepared a bill to that effect, which was approved by the Legislature and accepted by the city governments. Under the charter thus amended the bridge is public property, 66⅔ per cent. to be paid for and owned by the city of Brooklyn and 33⅓ per cent. by the city of New York, the actual payments by the private stockholders having been reimbursed and their title extinguished. The engineers, etc., as well as the principal working members of the directory, retained their places as from the first, so that the work is, after all, a unit from beginning to end.

On the organization of the company, in May, 1867, one month after the passage of the incorporating act, John A. Roebling was appointed engineer (May 23, 1867), and he made his report of surveys, plans, and estimates on the 1st of the following September. In March, 1869, a board of consulting engineers was convened at the request of Mr. Roebling to examine his plans, and also to report upon the feasibility of the work. In the following May a commission of three United States engineers was appointed by the War Department to report upon the general feasibility of the project, and particularly as to whether or not the bridge would be an obstruction to navigation. The plans of Mr. Roebling were fully indorsed by both boards of engineers, the government commission recommending, however, an increase of five feet in height. The work of preparing the site of the foundation of the Brooklyn tower was commenced January 3, 1870, but Mr. Roebling did not live to see the first stone laid in the magnificent structure that was to crown his illustrious career. In the summer of 1869, while engaged in fixing the location of the Brooklyn tower, a ferry-boat entering the slip thrust the timbers on which he stood in such a manner as to catch and crush his foot. The injury resulted in lock-jaw, from which he died sixteen days after.

A fit successor was found in his son, Washington A. Roebling, who had not only been the accomplished associate of his father in some of his principal works, but had aided him most efficiently in the preparation of the designs and plans of the bridge. We say a fit successor was found, for at this time, when the grandest monument of engineering skill the world has ever seen is practically completed, certainly no other testimony is needed as to the great engineering ability and pre-eminent fitness of the younger Roebling to direct such a great undertaking. During the fire in the Brooklyn caisson in December, 1871, Mr. Roebling became himself a victim to the "caisson disease," but even from his sick-room his oversight of the work has not flagged.

Before the actual work of construction had commenced, however, it became apparent that in order to more perfectly adapt the structure to its intended uses, and to make ample provision for the rapidly increasing volume of inter-urban commerce consequent upon the development and growth of the cities, considerable modification must be made in the original design. The changes were, of course, in the direction of not only a larger and more capacious structure, but also of increased solidity and strength throughout. Such changes involved a very considerable addition to the cost. Mr. John A. Roebling originally estimated the cost of the bridge at $7,000,000, exclusive of the land required, which has cost about $3,800,000, and the time of building at about five years. The actual cost of the bridge, when completed, will be about $15,500,000, which, as compared with the original estimate of $10,800,000, shows an increase in cost of nearly $5,000,000. The items of additional cost are as follows: First, the United States government required an increase of five feet in height, making the clearance under the centre of the bridge 135 feet. At the same time it was decided to widen the bridge from 80 to 85 feet. These changes involved an increase of 8 per cent. in the cost of the entire bridge, including superstructure, towers, foundations, and anchorages. Second, the amount set apart for building the foundations of the towers in the original estimate was found to be entirely inadequate. For the New York tower a pile foundation was originally intended, whereas it was found necessary to go down 78 feet to the bed-rock, and the cost of labor in compressed air at such unprecedented depths proved to be four and a half times as much as was anticipated, as was also that of excavating the hard

conglomerate under the Brooklyn tower. Third, steel was substituted for iron as the material to be used in the construction of both the cables and the suspended superstructure, thereby vastly increasing the strength of all the parts. The items thus far enumerated foot up nearly two millions, which covers the excess in cost on the bridge proper. In his original plan and estimate, Mr. John A. Roebling contemplated approaches constructed of light iron girders, or trestle-work, supported by pillars of brick or stone, but it was concluded to build entirely of granite and brick—a change that has resulted in one of the finest masonry viaducts in the world. This involved an increased expenditure of about one and a half millions. The archways have been constructed with a view to their utilization as warehouses, and $400,000 has been set apart by the trustees for the placing of fronts and floors in them. As Mr. Roebling in his original report says, the cost of these improvements should not be charged in that of the bridge, and it was accordingly omitted by him. Then there are the station buildings and the elevated railway structures that are now building on the approaches, making a connection of the system of rapid transit of New York with that of Brooklyn when it shall have been built. Of course this was not originally contemplated, and it has swelled the cost of bridge by nearly half a million. Finally, there is a comprehensive item which could not have been anticipated, but which would be underestimated at half a million, namely, the preliminary expenditures, general superintendence, interest and discount on city bonds, and expenses legal, medical, funereal, and prandial. These additions to the cost, however, would never have swelled to so large an amount if it had not been for the needless and costly delays caused by the failure of the city of New York to promptly provide its proportion of the necessary funds. That this has caused an enormous increase in the cost of the bridge is well known, but it would be difficult to name an amount. The land expenses will be largely redeemed by the rentals the cities will receive from the warehouses under the approaches.

The principal ferry to Brooklyn takes a diagonal course up stream to a point determined by the abrupt falling off of the heights near Fulton Street. The bridge takes its Brooklyn departure in obedience

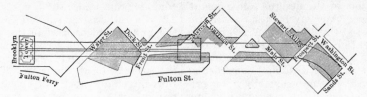

SITUATION PLAN OF BROOKLYN APPROACH.

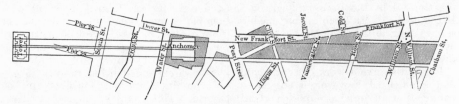

SITUATION PLAN OF NEW YORK APPROACH.

to the same topographical consideration. Its course is a straight line drawn from near the junction of Fulton and Main streets, Brooklyn, to the terminus fixed upon in New York, on Chatham Street, opposite the City Hall. This line and terminus were fixed upon as the result of Mr. Roebling's exhaustive examination and discussion of the question in his first report, of September 1, 1867, and no reason has been found to modify or to question the wisdom of his conclusions.

This line strikes the river at its eastern or Brooklyn shore close alongside of the north slip of Fulton Ferry. Its course across the river is not exactly at right angles to the shore, but makes a little down stream, striking the New York side at the foot of Roosevelt Street—four blocks further up stream, however, than the still more oblique ferry route. Here, then, are four points defined in a straight line: the two ends, and the two points at the water line, 1595½ feet apart, to be connected by the bridge proper with a single span. Three points in the air line of the bridge are also determined: the central altitude of 135 feet above mean high water required by the United States government, and the two terminal elevations, in New York and Brooklyn respectively, of 38.27 and 61.32 feet above high-water mark. The rise from these two to the central altitude gives the line of the bridge a gentle upward curve from either end to the centre, where it will be fifteen feet higher than at the towers, and forty-six feet higher than at the anchorages.

The adoption of a suspended span of 1595½ feet, at a height of 135 feet, also determined (in combination with other mathematical and mechanical considerations) the height of the towers (276⅔ feet) from which the span must be suspended, and two other points in the air line of the bridge, at which the ends of the suspension cables are secured—in other words, the anchorages—for the cables are not to pull on the tops of the tall towers, but to rest on them with nearly a simple vertical pressure, being not even fastened; and thus, so far from tending to pull the towers over, the suspended weight tends only to hold them in position. The cables are

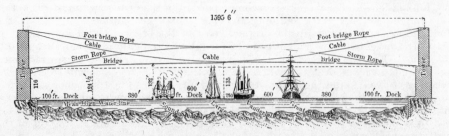

ELEVATION OF BRIDGE, SHOWING TEMPORARY ROPES USED IN CABLE-MAKING.

VIEW OF THE BRIDGE FROM NEW YORK.—After a photograph by Theodore Gubelman.

Tower | Cable Cable | Tower
Cable Cable

-------------- Horizontal wind braces beneath bridge

HORIZONTAL PROJECTION OF CABLE SYSTEM.

therefore anchored inland, at a distance of 930 feet back from the towers on each side.

The anchorages are solid cubical structures of stone masonry, measuring 119 by 132 feet at the base, and rising some 90 feet above high-water mark. Their weight is about 60,000 tons each, which is utilized to resist the pull of the cables. The mode of anchoring the cables will be described in its proper place. Suffice it for the present to conceive them thus anchored by their extremities on each side the river 930 feet back from the towers, and at the water-line on each side lifted up with a long, lofty, and graceful sweep over the top of a tower 276 feet high, and drooping between the two towers in a majestic curve which one can liken to nothing else for grandeur but the inverted arch of the rainbow.

Rising from the towers at an elevation of 118 feet above high-water mark in gentle but graceful curve to the centre of the river span, where it meets the cables at an elevation of 135 feet above high-water mark, is the bridge floor, an immense steel frame-work bewildering in its complexity. The frame-work consists essentially of two systems of girders at right angles to each other. The principal cross-beams or girders supporting the floor proper are light trusses thirty-three inches deep, placed seven feet six inches apart, and to these are attached the four steel rope suspenders from the cables. Half-way between these principal floor beams are lighter ones, to give additional support to the planking. To unite these cross-beams together, and to give the proper amount of stiffness and strength to the floor, there are six parallel trusses extending along the entire length of the bridge. The floor beams are further united together by small longitudinal trusses extending from one to the other, which, together with a complete system of diagonal braces or stays, form a longitudinal truss of eighty-six feet in breadth. It will be seen, thus, that this combination has immense strength, weight, and stiffness, laterally, vertically, and in every direction. To relieve the cables in a great measure of this enormous burden, and at the same time effectually prevent any vertical oscillations in the bridge floor, there is a multitude of suspensory stays of steel wire ropes diverging from the tops of the towers to points about fifteen feet apart along the bottom of four of the vertical trusses. These stays extend out for a distance of 400 feet from the towers, and are of themselves capable of sustaining unaided that portion of the great frame and its load in position. At the towers the frame-work is firmly anchored down, and again confined against the lifting or pushing force of the wind by a system of under-stays lying in the plane of the floor, so that no conceivable cause can ever disturb its rigid fixity of position and form. At and near the centre of the span, however, where these stays do not act so efficiently against any tendency to distortion, and to still further unite and stiffen the whole system, the two outside cables are drawn inward toward each other at the bottom of their curves. By this means each of them presents its weight in the form of an arch against an oblique pressure from below and the opposite side, and resists more or less in

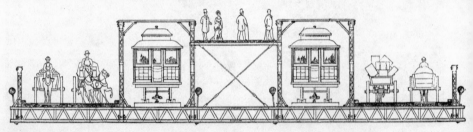

SECTION OF BRIDGE, SHOWING FOOT, RAIL, AND CARRIAGE WAYS.

the same way any force from the like directions. The two inner cables at the
same time are drawn apart at the bottom
of their curves, thus approaching each its
outside neighbor, and pairing with it, so
as to combine their opposing arches against
lateral forces from either direction. The
weight of the whole suspended structure
(central span), cables and all, is 6740 tons,
and the maximum weight with which the
bridge can be crowded by freely moving
passengers, vehicles, and cars is estimated
at 1380 tons, making a total weight borne

the river. The vertical trussing forms outside parapets eight feet high above the
common bridge floor, for the security of
vehicles, etc., while the inner lines of the
same will form inner parapets to the cars
and footways, supplemented by wire net-
ting which will break the force of the wind.
The intermediate avenues, one on each
side of the footway, will be occupied by
cars, constantly and rapidly moving back
and forth from terminus to terminus by
means of a stationary engine and endless
wire rope.

THE BROOKLYN ANCHORAGE.

by the cables and stays of 8120 tons, in the
proportion of 6920 tons by the cables and
1190 tons by the stays. The stress (or
lengthwise pull) in the cables due to the
load becomes about 11,700 tons, and their
ultimate strength is 49,200 tons.

The great frame, as above described, presents on its upper side five parallel avenues
of an average breadth of sixteen feet, separated by the six vertical lines of trussing, which project upward like so many
steel fences. The outside avenues, devoted
to vehicles, are each nearly nineteen feet
wide. The central avenue has a width of
fifteen and a half feet, and is elevated
twelve feet above all the others, for a footway, thus giving to the pedestrians crossing the bridge an unobstructed view of

The great steel cables, fifteen and three-
quarter inches in diameter, are not, however, limited to supporting the main span, but
are prolonged over the tops of the towers,
and descend thence to the anchorages on the
shores, at distances, as before stated, of 930
feet. The portions of the cables suspended from the towers to the anchorages support the shore spans of the bridge, which
are constructed precisely like the central
span already described. The anchorages
are therefore the next feature of the work
to be noticed. They are structures at once
exceedingly simple and satisfactory to the
mind. There is little more to imagine
than a great four-square mass of masonry, with a pair of broad arched passages
through it, partly to exclude superfluous

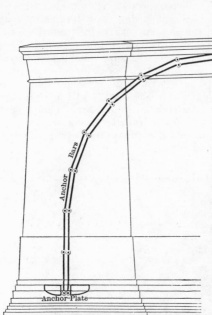

SECTION OF TOP AND BACK OF ANCHORAGE—SIDE VIEW.

passes a round iron bolt or key, which is drawn up against the plate, fitting in a semi-cylindrical groove, and thus the first link in the anchor chain is constructed and made fast. The link bars average twelve and a half feet long; and in the first three links, where the pull from the cables is least felt, they are seven inches wide and three inches thick, being swelled at the ends sufficiently to preserve their full strength with eye-holes five to six inches in diameter. The bars of the fourth, fifth, and sixth links are increased in size to eight by three inches, and after these the size is nine by three, with the exception of the last link, in which the number of bars is doubled, and the thickness halved. The pins or bolts connecting link to link are turned shafts of wrought iron five feet long and five to seven inches in diameter.

The four great anchor plates being set in position at the bottom of the masonry, each with the first double ninefold link of its anchor chain made fast through its centre, and standing erect above it, the masonry is next built over the anchor plates, and close around the chain bars, to the height of the latter, and extended over the whole area of the structure to the same height. Then the second link or set of chain bars is set, the eyes of the new nine fitting between those of the former nine, and the heavy bolt passing through all the eighteen eyes at once, and uniting each of the two ninefold links with a joint like that of a hinge. Each new link after the first two is now made to incline forward to the bridge a little more than its predecessor, forming a regular curve, so adjusted as to bring the chain out near the opposite (upper) corner of the structure to that from which it started. Here the cables enter the face of the anchor wall for about twenty-five feet, and meet the ends of the chains. The bars of the last link number thirty-eight, arranged in four tiers. There are nineteen strands in each cable, and the end of each strand is here separately bent and fastened in a loop around an eye-piece of cast iron,

cost, and partly to afford convenient avenues for locomotion. The dimensions of this mass are 90 by 119 by 132 feet, and its weight, which is its chief importance, the inconceivable amount of 120 million pounds. At the bottom of the structure, and near its rear side from the bridge, are imbedded four massive anchor plates of cast iron, one for each of the cables. These plates measure $16\frac{1}{2}$ by $17\frac{1}{2}$ feet on the face, and are $2\frac{1}{2}$ feet thick at the centre. The weight of each plate is over 46,000 pounds. And yet it is far from being a solid mass, which would waste perhaps half its material in perfectly ineffective positions. On the contrary, it is formed like a star, with many rays stretching from a massive centre, and tapering to their extremities, where greatly reduced strength and narrowed bearings are quite sufficient for the simple purpose of uniting the resistance of the superincumbent masonry upon the point of pull at the centre. This point is made by two rows of nine parallel oblong apertures through the two and a half feet of solid iron, and through these apertures pass eighteen forged bars of iron, with an eye at each end. Through each of the nine eyes, matched in position as one, below the under side of the anchor plate, called a "shoe," having a groove in its periphery to fit the strand. The ends of the strands are thus "eyed" like the link bars, and fraternize with the last set of the latter, fitting between them eye to eye, and keyed together with them by the eye-bolt. The ends of the great cables are now anchored fast with what seems to the imagination an enormous superfluity of weight and strength. It seems as if the cables would be torn apart ten times over by a force that was sufficient to pluck out their monstrous spread

To make assurance fourfold sure, the metal for this, as for every part of the work, has been tested by means of specimen pieces under the enormous power of the hydraulic press to its breaking point, a wide margin being always required above

TESTING STEEL.

of iron roots from the foundations of that solid cemented mass of rock. Undoubtedly this is true; but the intention of the engineer is not merely to equal the strength of the cables with that of their anchorage, but also to give the anchorage a solidity to be absolutely unaffected in the slightest degree by the incessant pull of loads and tug of storms for a hundred years, so that no loosening or vibration can ever be initiated.

the highest possible strain that it is estimated can ever come upon it.

All this is plain work. The anchorages are far within-land. But the great suspension towers to be connected by the central span of the bridge must be pushed out to the extreme wharf line in deep water, for even then the breadth of water to

RELICS FROM THE FOUNDATION.

be bridged at one spring is such as no engineer ever attempted before—nearly 1600 feet—and not only the difficulty but the cost of the work is increased in an enormous ratio by every foot of added length in a single span. We have therefore before us here one of the most interesting problems and one of the most brilliant triumphs of engineering: to build great works of masonry up from beneath the bed and through the rushing tides of a deep arm of the ocean, with all the precision and cemented solidity of the dry-land anchorages we have just been viewing. This part of the work, therefore, was first in order: this achieved left nothing problematical, whether as to availability or cost, in the remainder of the work.

Probably to the end of time thoughtful spectators unversed in the mysteries of engineering will pause, as they now do, before these gigantic towers, more wonderful than the Pyramids, with the everlasting sea beating their mighty bases, and will perplex themselves in vain to imagine by what means the granite masonry could have been laid so solid and true beneath not forty feet depth of rushing tides alone, but eighty feet below their surface, on the rock which those tides had not touched for untold ages.

To explain this mystery in one word, the submarine portion of the tower was really built above-water, in the open air, and thence sunk toward its bed as soon as built. But this is to put a new mystery in place of the first, for how could such a mass of masonry be set firmly to a hair's-breadth in its bed against the mighty current, or how could its bed be excavated to this enormous depth to receive it?

The principle of the diving-bell, supplemented by the air force-pump, or compressor, is the solution of the difficulty. Only the diving-bell must be a peculiar one, made to carry on its back the giant tower as it dives to the bottom, as it delves into the bowels of the earth, and as it reposes at length and forever on the rock. It is technically called a *caisson* (having been first used in France), from its resemblance to an inverted chest. Imagine your diving-bell, or caisson, made of an oblong form, corresponding to the shape and size of its burden, with a margin of eleven feet excess on all sides. You must, of course, also have it built with sufficient durability of material and strength of mass both to carry down the masonry entire, without flinching, and to rest under it forever without yielding or decay. It will be best to have the sides of our oblong diving-bell flare a little, and on the inner side to taper them to a sort of edge (well shod with heavy iron), so as to make room for the laborers within to excavate conveniently to the very extremity of the dimensions of their diving-bell. To obtain sufficient strength and rigidity in the

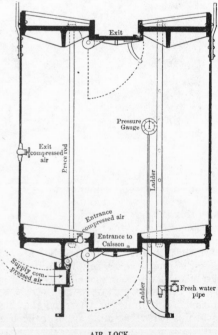

AIR LOCK.

THE CAISSON.

structure for its tremendous back-load, let its entire top, 102 feet by 172, be built to a thickness of 22 feet of dense Southern pitch-pine in timbers twelve inches square, laid in solid courses crossing each other, fastened with powerful through-bolts, and all the joints and seams filled with pitch. (The bolts and angle-irons of this caisson at New York aggregated 250 tons.) Let the sides be eight feet thick at their junction with the top, built in the same manner, but tapered on the inside, as already suggested, down to an iron-shod edge only eight inches thick, and let the iron bolts and angle-irons, of course, be so strong and numerous that nothing can loosen timber from timber save by tearing each stick into splinters. Further, let the back or platform that is to carry down the great tower in its descent to the bed-rock be supported at intervals by six cross partitions of solid timber four feet thick, with a door in each for communication between the compartments thus formed. These partitions, like the four sides, will ultimately rest on the bed-rock, and bear their part of the monstrous and everlasting load. Finally, let the whole cavernous interior be lined with boiler iron, seamed air-tight, for its perfection as a diving-bell, and for protection against the danger of fire, which experience in building the first or Brooklyn tower of this bridge has shown to be im-minent at all times while working by gas-light and with blasting explosives in compressed air.

Of course there must be means of ingress and egress for men and materials. There must be a well-hole through the top, and an iron well leading to it from the open air above-water for the men to go in and out. It must be lined with iron, continuous and air-tight with the lining of the interior, and must have an air-tight iron door, or rather two successive doors with an air-tight chamber between them large enough for a gang of men to enter, that the outer door may be closed on them while the inner door is opened to admit them to the artificial submarine cavern. This chamber is called an air lock, and its principle is like that of a canal lock, or still more exactly that of a pump. In going out, the men enter the air lock while its outer door is closed tight, and after the inner door through which they entered is closed behind them the outer door may be opened for their egress. Thus the loss of compressed air by the entrance and exit of a gang of men is simply what the air lock will contain and no more.

This would be too tedious a process, however, for the removal of the excavated earth. For this purpose water locks are used. The iron wells for the removal of material descend through the caisson into open pits in the ground below the level at which the water is held down by the compressed air. The water of course rises in the pits and wells to that level, and thus the compressed air is "locked" out of them, while the earth and stones dumped into the pits by the miners in the caisson tumble to the bottom of the wells, where they can be got at by simply reaching under water. In each of these wells operates a Morris and Cummings dredging-machine (either of the grapnel or "clam-shell" pattern, as each was required), like those constantly seen at work at one point or another in this and most other harbors where slips and channels have to be made or deepened, or cleared of deposits, the difference being that these are of the second class in size and power, adapted to the capacity of the caisson and workmen for supplying them with materials. While the harbor machines of forty horse-power remove 2000 cubic yards of mud per day, the caisson machines of twenty-five horse-power can raise 1500 yards; and without working their full capacity, clear the pits of earth as fast as it is practicable to mine it in the caisson. The iron "clam-shell" scoop of the machine descends by its chain to the bottom of the well with its jaws open, plunging into the mud, where the jaws are drawn together by the action of the machinery through another chain. This action operates like the pull of a ship's cable on the anchor, dragging its fluke downward into the bottom. In like manner the flukes of the dredging scoop are forced down into the mud as they are drawn together, and grasp a giant handful, exactly imitating, to use Mr. Roebling's expression, the action of the human hand in picking up handfuls. The force of this grasp is illustrated by the fact that large rocks are picked up as well as earth and small stones, even when only a corner of the rock is seized between the valves of the scoop. All the rock blasted out in Hell Gate by the vast submarine excavations was picked up from the bottom and raised in this way.

While the caisson with its entrances and appurtenances approaches completion in the ship-yard, arrangements must next be made for placing it in position on the bottom of the stream. First a slip or dock must be built to fix it in the exact position of the intended tower. The "water lot" marked for occupation is levelled as well as possible by dredging, and a row of piles is driven as deep as possible along the landward line, a length of 172 feet. At right angles with this a row of piles is driven out 102 feet into the river from each end, making three sides of an oblong inclosure or stockade. Into this inclosure the caisson is towed. The exact lines of the pier foundation are mathematically fixed by the engineers, and the caisson is placed in the proper position to a hair by blocking and wedging on all three sides. It now rises and falls with the tide, however, and is therefore not yet capable of being exactly and finally placed. The next business, accordingly, is to commence the foundations of the pier on the massive platform or raft of solid timber 22 feet thick and 102 by 172 feet square, which we have figuratively called the back of the submarine monster which is to carry the whole burden down to its final bed. The huge squared blocks of granite are now laid at leisure in hydraulic cement in uniform courses, and soon their weight overcomes the buoyancy of the caisson, and settles it to the bottom, with its top still visible above-water. The compressed air is now let into the diving-bell interior, forcing the water out beneath the iron-shod edges of the sides where they rest on the bottom. This done, the workmen can go down into the very wet cellar, and complete the levelling of the earth under the supporting edges of the structure. Now, while the caisson barely touches bottom by its weight, but does not rest too heavily, the engineers can, with their mathematical instruments and wedges, finally adjust the mass in exact position, and by easing away the bottom under it wherever required, with much patience, they at length get it level, and uniformly supported by blocking placed under its cross partitions. A few more blocks of granite laid on will make it immovable. All is now ready for the dredges to begin lifting out the mud and stones which the men of pick, shovel, and wheelbarrow pour into the water locks or wells beneath the dredging shafts.

Many formidable difficulties have thus been surmounted, and the curious observer now sees how everything so far can be done by the puny hand of man when guided by his mighty mind. But with our thoughts fixed on the mountain-like mass of rock descending full built, we are staggered still by the difficulty of letting it down eighty feet into the submarine earth, with its position as plumb and level and unchangeable at every moment of descent as that of the cornerstone at rest in its bed under any great building on land. If it should sway from its position ever so little, the mathematical accuracy and beauty of the whole after-work would be marred, and what power on earth could move it back a hair's-breadth toward its place? If a side or a corner should be hindered or hastened in its descent a little more than the rest, the mass would be wrenched and disjointed by its own irresistible weight, and the disintegrating force thus initiated within the structure could never be eradicated or counteracted. But the mode of achieving this miracle of descent — not only moving mountains, but moving them to a hair, through the earth, as the piston descends in the cylinder of a steam-engine — is so commonplace and simple that it seems almost childish. No machinery of vast and imperceptibly slow leverage or screw-power, and of admirably scientific adjustment, is here called to our aid. Nothing but pine blocking under the six cross partitions of timber on which, as on so many legs or feet, the monstrous burden-carrier stands. As fast as the earth is dug away to make room for the descending tower, the blocking is knocked away to let it down. Impossible? Let us see. Suppose a blocking at every two or four feet beneath the supporting partitions, can not we knock out alternate blockings all round? True; but how shall we knock out the rest, and what would become of the structure deprived of support now at this point and now at that, and pitching downward this way and that with rock-rending force? Not so fast. By knocking out the alternate blockings we have just doubled the weight and compression on their fellows. By such increased com-

WRAPPING THE CABLES.

pression of its supports the tower has settled in some measure, of course, and in the most uniform measure possible. Now we just drive in again the blockings we have removed, as tightly as possible, after levelling away the earth under them. But it is evident that we can not drive them as tight as they were before under the actual weight of the tower. Besides, the new ground they now rest on is susceptible of fresh compression. Therefore, if we next knock out the blockings before undisturbed, the tower will settle down on the replaced blockings as far as its weight can compress them and the new ground under them. The fact proves to be that one complete process of this kind lets the tower down about one inch by the compression alternately of the two sets of blockings and the subjacent earth.

But what if our blockings should be driven tighter or prove harder, themselves or their foundations, at some points than at others: will not this produce an unequal settling, and strain the integrity of the masonry? No; for both the weight and strength of the mass are so predominant as to make nothing of such minor resistances, and the only result is that the presumptuous block is crushed. This mode of equalizing the pressure by its own irresistible weight was frequently observed. Again, if it be asked how we are to restrain so uncontrollable a mass from veering in one direction or another from its true position as it descends, the answer to this difficulty also is given by that same uncontrollable weight. Since it can not be influenced in position a hair's-breadth by all the power that man could bring to bear upon it, it will be equally insensible to all the fortuitous forces that would bias the direction of a more limited mass in descending, such as bowlders temporarily encountered by the under edges of the caisson at particular points, or the pressure of the tides. The mass and its movement are too majestic to suffer any influence whatever from such casual obstructions. Only if an obstruction were permanently left in the way at one point, while the caisson was lowered at other points, could such causes act against the plumb descent of the structure.

The last operation, after laying bare the bed-rock, and testing its soundness and solidity at all points, is to fill up the caisson with a solid hydraulic concrete, which will harden into rock and unite itself immovably with the rock on which it rests, becoming to the caisson what a tenon is in a mortise. This concrete is rammed as tightly as possible under the roof of the caisson; but if it be impossible to drive it as tight as if the weight of the tower actually rested on it, this is not amiss. For the continued and increasing weight on the wooden supports will certainly compress them further in time, and will eventually, in all probability, bring the weight of the tower firmly, if not altogether, upon the incompressible concrete with which the caisson is filled.

With regard to the danger of decay in wood, which presents itself to most minds in this connection, experience has long since shown that, when buried beyond reach of air and changes of temperature, wood is perfectly incorruptible, and will endure, so far as we can judge, as long as stone. Oxygen, chemically free as it is in air, is the agent of decomposition, and in its absence all substances are alike incorruptible. The sea-worms make no trouble at the depth below the bottom where we have left our timber platform. It may safely be trusted to support the bridge between New York and Brooklyn as long as there shall be need of it.

The caisson for the Brooklyn tower was towed into its berth on the 2d of May, 1870. Ten of the fifteen feet thickness of timber in its roof were built on after this, *in situ*. On the 15th of June the first granite blocks were laid on the timber. They are of from four to seven tons weight. The masonry, faced throughout with granite, is partly built of the less expensive blue limestone from Kingston, New York. The compressed air was let in, the water driven out, and excavation commenced on the 10th of July. The bed being a tenacious conglomerate of clay, sand, and bowlders, extending to a great depth, it was not necessary on this side to sink the pier to the bed-rock, and at forty-five and a half feet beneath the bottom of the river the caisson was filled up with concrete and left in its final position. The latter operation was completed on the 11th of March, 1871. Two months had been lost by the accident of a fire in the caisson, requiring the interior to be flooded with water to extinguish it. This accident cost $15,000, and its recurrence in the New York caisson was guarded against by a lining of boiler iron throughout, at an expense of $20,000.

The New York foundation was a work of much greater magnitude and difficulty. From the sandy nature of the ground it became necessary to sink the pier to the bed-rock, seventy-eight feet below high-water mark. The process was not different in method, but was much more trying to the workmen, from the greater pressure of air required in the caisson to keep out the water. The caisson was placed in its berth in October, 1871, and rested on the rock in May, 1872, after less than one year's work in sinking it to its bed.

The construction of the towers above the water line was, of course, a simple though enormous piece of mason-work. The Brooklyn tower was completed in May, 1875, and the New York tower in July, 1876. Everything was now ready for the work of cable-making, into which, having already anticipated the construction of the great floor or bridge proper, we must enter somewhat minutely, to give the reader a clear idea of its curious and interesting processes.

THE DRUMS—SPLICING THE WIRES.

Let us first imagine the cable as constructed—simply a bunch of wires, not twisted, but laid parallel, and bound together by a continuous wrapping of wire. The wires are of size No. 7, or a little over one-eighth inch in thickness; they number over 5000 in each cable, and make a bundle 15¾ inches thick. To lay and bind this prodigious bunch of wires straight and parallel would be impossible except by subdividing the mass into skeins or strands, which are first laid and bound separately, and afterward united. Each cable contains nineteen strands of 278 wires each. They are formed precisely like skeins of yarn or thread. Each skein is a continuous wire almost exactly one million feet, or nearly 200 miles, in length, passing from anchorage to anchorage, back and forth, 278 times. The turns of the wire at each extremity of the skein pass around a solid block of iron shaped externally like a horseshoe, with a groove in its periphery, in which the bend or bight of the skein lies as a skein of yarn is held on one's thumbs for winding. Each shoe or eye-piece is fixed (after the strand is finished) between the ends of two anchor bars, a seven-inch iron bolt passing through the three, and so connecting the strand with the great anchor chain at either end. After a skein is fully laid in position (passing, of course, over the tops of the towers) it is compressed to a cylindrical form at every point by large clamp tongs, and tightly bound with wire at intervals of about fifteen inches throughout its length. The men who do this work go out for the purpose on the strand in a "buggy," so called, which is a board seat slung by ropes from the axis of a grooved wheel fitting and travelling on the strand as bound together. When the

FARRINGTON CROSSING THE SPAN.

strands are thus completed and duly regulated, the final work of wrapping the cable is accomplished in a similar manner, as hereafter described.

But to follow the process of construction, we return to the day when the towers and anchorages stood complete, but disconnected, with the intermediate spaces occupied only by the trackless air, and the question was how to initiate a connection between them all. To this end a three-quarter-inch wire rope, long enough to reach from anchorage to anchorage over the tops of the towers, was coiled on board a scow by the Brooklyn shore. First, its end was hoisted up the water face of the Brooklyn tower, and passed over the top, let down the land face, and then carried back to the top of the anchorage, and made fast. Next—waiting until an opportunity when the river was clear of vessels at that point, and stationing boats to warn coming vessels to halt—the scow was towed across to the New York tower,

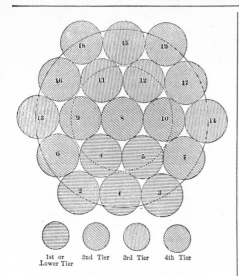

1st or   2nd Tier   3rd Tier   4th Tier
Lower Tier

SECTION OF CABLE, SHOWING STRANDS.

paying out the wire rope into the water as it went. The end remaining on board was then hoisted up the water face of the New York tower, passed over, and lowered again on the landward side. Then it was made fast to a drum connected with a powerful steam-engine, which wound up the rope from the bed of the river and over the tower, until it swung clear from side to side in mid-air, and the first connection between the shores was made. It remained only to carry the New York end back to the anchorage, hoist it up, and secure it in position there.

A second span of three-quarter-inch rope was carried over in substantially the same manner, and the ends of the two were then joined at the anchorages around grooved driving-wheels or pulleys, making an endless belt or "traveller" revolving by steam-power throughout the whole distance from anchorage to anchorage.

To accomplish the succeeding operations would require men to work hanging on this slender cord all the way from tower to tower. Mr. E. F. Farrington, the master-mechanic who superintended this part of the work on the bridge, and who had previously been engaged on the suspension-bridges at Cincinnati and Niagara Falls, now took the resolution to make the first passage of the line, and to give his men as good an example of courage and confidence as they would ever have occasion to copy.

On Friday afternoon, August 25, 1876,

the running gear for the endless traveller rope was in readiness. A boatswain's chair, consisting of a bit of board for a seat, slung by the four corners, with as many short ropes uniting in a ring overhead, was secured to the traveller rope at the Brooklyn anchorage, and Mr. Farrington took his seat on the slung bit of board for a private trip over the line of the future bridge in sight of his men. Having made his preparations so quietly, and being so quiet a man, his surprise was great, on looking down from his high starting-point, to see the house-tops beneath him black with spectators, the streets far below paved, as it were, with upturned faces, the ferry-boats conveying like stacks of humanity, and the New York shore crowded in a similar manner. As he gave the signal to start the wheels and swung out, with the rushing rope hissing and undulating like a flying serpent through the air, the boom of cannon far below announced to the modest and unsuspecting aeronaut that his intended private trip for the encouragement of his men was a public triumph. Away went the whirring rope, invisible or like a spider's thread to the eyes below, bending and swaying with the human weight that rode its cantering waves, to all appearance self-impelled, like some strange creature of serpentine flight, sweeping first downward toward the house-tops till the deepest curve his weight could give the slender rope was passed, and thence soaring sharply upward to the top of the first tower in his course. Here he gave a signal to slow the rope nearly to a stop, while the men on the tower, with excited cheering, lifted the rope and its slung rider over the parapet, supported both across to the other side, and launched them off the dizzy height again. Again the cannon roared, and the myriads of spectators swung their hats and cheered with wild excitement, while all the steam-whistles on land and water shrieked their uttermost discordance. The trip occupied twenty-two minutes, and at the end the explorer was glad to hide from the pursuing crowds that would fain have caught him as a trophy and carried him through the streets in triumph.

It was after this an easy matter to carry across the other carrier ropes; the ropes from which the "cradles," or hanging platforms, for regulating the wires, were suspended; those which supported the foot-bridge for the workmen, over which sight-seers were sometimes allowed to pass ; and the "storm cables," which, stretching upward from the towers below the roadway, steadied the temporary structure against the wind.

Meanwhile all was ready in the large sheds that covered the Brooklyn anchorage for the regular and long-to-be-protracted machine-work of cable-making. Thirty-two drums, eight feet in diameter, were rigged in the position of carriage-wheels just clear of the floor, eight drums behind the destined position of each of the four cables. Hundreds of coils of wire, already delivered in the yard below, had been dipped in linseed-oil and dried again and again. A screw thread had been cut on every end of wire by a convenient machine constantly at work for this purpose (opposite ends being cut with right and left screws respectively), and the little steel coupling tubes, with inside screw-threads to match, had united fifty-two coils, or nearly ten continuous miles of wire, upon each of the thirty-two drums.

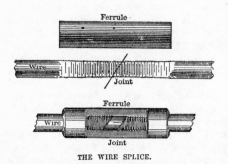

THE WIRE SPLICE.

Now the shoe, or eye-piece, around which the skein of wire to form a strand of the cable is to be turned at each extremity, is secured in a temporary position on the anchorage, and the work of winding the skein is begun. A wire is fastened to the shoe, and passed around a sheave or grooved pulley fixed and suspended to the traveller rope by iron arms reaching up from its axle. The traveller rope is set in motion, and bears forth the sheave, carrying the bight or turn of wire before it, thus taking across two spans, or a complete circuit, of the wire at once. On reaching the New York side (which takes about eight minutes) the bight of wire is passed around the shoe, completing once the circuit of the skein. The sheave, released, returns empty to the Brooklyn side.

Next the circuit of wire that has been carried across must be "regulated," that is, adjusted to the exact length and height required by its place in the strand. On the top of the Brooklyn tower, first, a clamp is fastened on the first span of wire —i. e., that directly reaching from the end fastened at the Brooklyn anchorage—a small tackle-block is hooked on, and two men haul up the slack between the tower and anchorage until the regulator men in the cradle signal that the position is accurately adjusted at their respective points. A similar regulation is made on the New York tower to adjust the curve of the wire between the towers, and the same process is likewise repeated on the New York anchorage, until the fall of the wire off that point is also accurately located. The return span is then adjusted in the same manner, in reverse order, beginning at the New York tower. On the Brooklyn side, when the last span of this circuit of wire is adjusted in position, it is passed around the shoe, held fast, and the bight is again placed on a sheave, and the traveller starts again to carry over a second circuit of the skein. Thus the skein is wound round and round its eye-pieces at either anchorage with unbroken continuity, with uniform tension, and with exact parallelism between all its threads, until the full number of 139 circuits has been made, and 278 wires are ready to be bound together in a round and solid cord three inches thick. On either side the eye-piece, of course, the cord is parted, and for a few inches is bound in two separate strands of 139 wires each, but it is shortly brought into one, leaving a loop at each end of the strand, inclosing the eye-piece or shoe, which, as before stated, is pinned between and together with two of the eighteen anchor bars in which the great anchor chains unite with each cable. Strands for each of the four great cables are made and placed simultaneously. A circuit of wire is laid and regulated in about thirty minutes, including ordinary delays. Two travellers are running, so that four circuits, or eight full lengths, of wire might be laid per hour. If weather never interfered, the 21,000 wires of which the four cables are composed could have been laid in less than a year. In point of fact, however, as it was useless to make the strands faster than the engineers could locate and adjust them in the cables—which is the grand difficulty of the work—it was doing well to lay forty wires on an average each working day.

On the commencement of impracticable weather in winter, such as incrusts the wires with snow and ice, it becomes impossible to regulate the wires properly. Then the work is necessarily suspended for the time being.

But the chief delay, as before remarked, arose from the difficulty of regulating the strands from two causes—sun and wind. Obviously the unity and strength of the cable depend on getting each strand into its exact and peculiar place. As the locations of the individual strands vary in height, the strands must vary in length. Each must hang in its own peculiar length and curve to a mathematical nicety; for if left but half an inch too long or too short for its true position, it will be too slack or too taut for its fellows, and it will be impossible to bind them solidly in one mass, and make them pull equally together. In the abstract this is a matter of exact mathematical science. But in practical engineering the actualization of the calculations is interfered with by variable forces which can not be resisted, evaded, or calculated. The chief of these in cable-making is temperature, which fluctuates so irregularly and unceasingly that the length of the strand is rarely the same for an hour together; and what is far more baffling to the engineer, the different spans are unequally acted on by the sun. One curve is in shadow while another is in full sunshine; one is exposed vertically to the sun, while another is struck by its rays at an extremely dull angle. In short, when the sun shines the several curves of each strand are all "at sixes and sevens," too unstable in position to be adjusted. The same is true of them in another sense when they are kept swaying and undulating by the wind. Hence the engineers can do nothing with them except at hours when two conditions concur—freedom from the influences of wind and direct sunshine. The hours from daylight to sunrise (when calm), and occasionally a few hours of calm and cloudy weather, are the only times available to the engineer for adjusting the length of his strands. This is done by changing the position of the "shoe." The figures of the engineer show that the deflection of the cables from the tops of the towers is 127.64 feet at 50° F., while at 90° it is 128.64 feet—a variation of nearly one-third of an inch for every degree of temperature, so that the engineer is likely to find his cables varying as much as half a foot in height in the course of a day. In short, the ponderous thing, though neither small nor agile, has a trick in common with the minute and lively insect which, when you put your finger on him, isn't there.

The running and regulating of the cable wires commenced June 11, 1877, and the last wire was run over October 15, 1878. The nineteen strands for each of the four cables having been thus made and located, the final operation is to unite and wrap them with wire. This is done by a little machine. An iron clamp is provided, the interior of which is of the size and cylindrical shape of the cable before wrapping. The temporary fastenings of wire around each strand are removed as fast as this work proceeds, and the clamp, screwed tightly, compresses the nineteen strands together, symmetrically arranged in a true cylinder, with the odd strand in the centre, and the other eighteen filling two circles around it. The wrapping machine follows up the clamp, and binds the cable with a close spiral wrapping of wire. This machine or implement consists of an iron cylinder cast in halves, to be bolted together about the cable, compressing it firmly. A reel or drum of wire encircles the cylinder. The wire winds off the drum through a hole in a steel disk on the rear end of the cylinder, whence it passes with a single turn around a small roller attached to the disk, and thence to the cable. The disk is turned by hand by a lever attached to it, and thus the wire, being held in severe tension by its turn around the roller, is tightly wound on the cable, and as it advances in its spiral or screw travel pushes forward the cylinder from which it is reeled.

The cables, thus completed, were ready for their load, the floor or bridge proper, already described. The suspender bands were next put on the cables; to these are attached the wire rope suspenders, and these in turn hold the steel floor beams of the roadway. The suspender bands are made of wrought iron five inches wide and five-eighths of an inch thick. The bands are cut at one point, and the two ends turned outward, so that they may be opened (by heating), and placed over the cables. The two ends, or ears, which hang vertically down when the bands are in

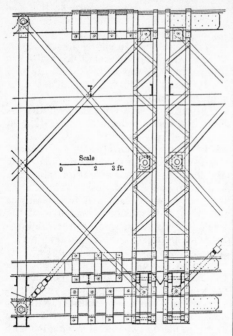

Scale
0 1 2 3 ft.

EXPANSION JOINT IN CENTRE TRUSS.

place, have holes through them for a screw-bolt one and three-quarter inches in diameter, which serves as the support of the suspenders, and also for tightening the bands and the cable. By the aid of these suspenders at short intervals all the way, it was easy to place, first, the cross-beams of the bridge floor, beginning with those nearest each anchorage and each face of the towers. The nearest suspenders hanging ready to receive the first iron beam had only to be drawn in and attached thereto by their clamps or stirrups, and the beam was swung out in position, ready to support planks for the workmen to stand on and launch the second beam, and so on. The cross beams being laid and braced together, forming the horizontal truss, the vertical truss-work is also put in, with the diagonal bracing below the floor, and the stays from the towers both above and below, and the bridge is at last ready for the planking.

The suspenders are for the most part at equal distances from each other. But it will be noticed that at the centre two suspenders from each of the four cables hang close together, sometimes but a few inches, sometimes more than a foot, apart. These give the clew to that problem of en-gineering and puzzle to the public as to how the expansion and contraction, by heat and cold, of the floor or bridge proper, are to be provided for. The great span may be said to be in two pieces or half-lengths, connected at the centre by an "expansion joint." Each half of a truss is attached to one of the two suspenders mentioned, and the two halves are connected by plates attached to one, and sliding in channels or ways in the other. No weight comes upon these guide-plates, as the two suspenders support the halves of the truss independently of each other. The planking is so arranged as to be always continuous, and the iron rails for the cars are at this point split in half lengthwise, so that one half plays upon the other, guide-rails on either side protecting the cars.

At 118 feet above high-water mark each of the towers of the bridge is divided into three masses by the two broad openings, $31\frac{1}{2}$ feet wide, which here commence. The six lines of the great steel trusses or framework forming the bridge pass, unbroken in their continuity, through these openings of the piers, resting on the masonry underneath, and firmly anchored down to it by huge bolts and ties of wire rope. An idea of the strength of these trusses may be obtained when it is considered that for over one hundred feet out from each side of the tower they are of themselves, without any support whatever from the cables or stays, sufficiently strong to carry all the load that may ever come upon them. The openings continue to the height of $120\frac{1}{2}$ feet, where they are closed by pointed arches. Above these arches the reunited tower rises thirty feet higher, where it receives a set of iron bed-plates, on which rest the "saddles" in which the great suspension cables ride. These are iron castings in the form of a segment of a circle, with a groove to receive the cable on the upper and convex side. The under and plane side lies on a layer of small iron rollers held in place by flanges on the surface of the bed-plate. The object of these is to give sufficient play to the bearings on which the cables rest to prevent the cables themselves slipping and chafing in the saddles if affected by the force of storms or variations of load, or when lengthening and contracting under changes of temperature. From the saddles each way the cables sweep downward in a graceful curve, the landward ends entering the an-

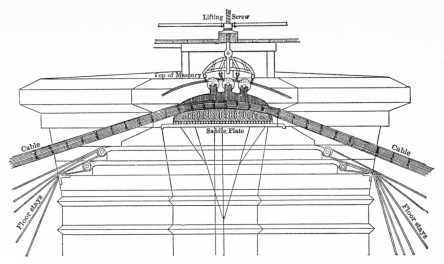

SECTION OF TOWER, SHOWING SADDLE-PLATE AND LOWERING OF STRAND INTO POSITION.

chor walls, as already described, and supporting the shore ends of the bridge, while the main bow, or inverted arch, hanging between the towers, holds up the central truss of nearly 1600 feet span.

A great work of engineering is a battle with nature, in which, as in other wars, Death must take his toll. There have been employed upon the works at one time as many as six hundred men, a small army in themselves, and in the fourteen years since the master-mind, John A. Roebling himself, became the first sacrifice, more than twenty men have been fatally hurt. Several more have been victims to the "caisson disease,"* resulting from working in compressed air; but, despite the dizzy height, no one has fallen from the main span into the water below. Besides the fire in the Brooklyn caisson, which cost no lives, and the fall of the derricks on the Brooklyn tower, which had more serious results, there has been

one great accident only; but the imagination can scarcely picture anything more dreadful. On June 19, 1878, one of the great strands broke loose from the New York anchorage, carrying with it the "shoe" and its ponderous attachments. As the end swept from the anchorage it dashed off several of the men at work, and then, with a frightful leap, grazing the houses and peopled streets below, it landed for the instant in the bridge yard close under the New York tower. The great weight mid-stream whizzed it over the tower with frightful and increasing rapidity, and the whole span plunged madly into the river, narrowly missing the ferry-boats that ply, crowded with human freight, below the line of the bridge. In these years the enterprise has lost also its president, Henry C. Murphy, and its first treasurer, J. H. Prentice, as well as its chief engineer. But, in strange and happy contrast, there has not been a single break in the engineering staff, Engineers Martin, Paine, Collingwood, McNulty, Probasco, and Hildenbrand having served continuously, most of them from the very first. And now all the extraordinary engineering difficulties are overcome, and with them the vexatious delays from unfriendly opposition, political feuds, the stoppage of financial supplies, and the adoption of a new structural material. In a few years these will have been forgotten, and the forty million passengers who are

---

* The "caisson disease" is the result of living under atmospheric pressure greatly above that to which the human system is normally adapted. The blood is driven in from the exterior and soft parts of the body to the central organs, especially the brain and spinal cord. On emerging into the open air, violent neuralgic pains and sometimes paralysis follow. Advanced consumption is, on the other hand, stayed, and sometimes remedied, by compressed air. Dr. Andrew H. Smith, surgeon to the Bridge Company, reported one hundred and ten cases of the "caisson disease," of which three were presently, and probably more finally, fatal.

expected to cross the bridge yearly will think only of the great boon that emancipates them from the delays of fog and ice, the possible collisions, and the old-time delays in waiting for the ferry-boats. Yet the ferries will still have plenty to do.

The summer of 1883 will be memorable for the opening of the great bridge, uniting New York and Brooklyn into a metropolis of nearly two million people—a population that will soon outgrow Paris, and have only London left to vie with. The bridge is practically a new street, belonging jointly to the two cities, and making with Third Avenue, the Bowery, and Chatham Street, New York, and Fulton Street continuing into Fulton Avenue on the Brooklyn side, a great thoroughfare fourteen miles long, already continuously built up, from the Harlem River to East New York. This is longer than the great street which stretches east to west across London, under its various names, from Bow to Uxbridge Road, spanning the valley where was once the Fleet brook by that other fine work of engineering, the Holborn Viaduct. The bridge roadway from its New York terminus opposite the City Hall to Sands Street, Brooklyn, is a little over a mile long (5989 feet), and it will take the pace of a smart walker to make the aerial journey, with its arched ascent, in twenty minutes. The cities will probably decide, confining the tolls to vehicular traffic, not to charge him the one cent first proposed for the privilege of taking this trip on "foot's horse." But for five cents he can jump at either end into fine cars, built on the pattern of the newest Manhattan elevated cars, which move apparently of their own volition, until one finds the secret in the endless wire rope underneath that is worked by stationary engines on the shore and makes continual circuit, across under one roadway and back under the other. These will take him across in a little less than five minutes, and it is not improbable that through trains will ultimately convey passengers from the northernmost end of New York over the Brooklyn Elevated that is to be, bringing them nearer to the health-giving beaches of Long Island by nearly half an hour's time.

But the wise man will not cross the bridge in five minutes, nor in twenty. He will linger to get the good of the splendid sweep of view about him, which his æsthetic self will admit pays wonderful interest on his investment of nothing. The bridge itself will be a remarkable sight, as he looks from his central path of vantage down upon the broad outer roadways, each with its tide of weighted wagons and carriages of his wealthier but not wiser brethren, and nearer the centre the two iron paths upon which the trains move silently and swiftly. Under him is the busy river, the two great cities now made one, and beyond, completing the circuit, villa-dotted Staten Island; the marshes, rivers, and cities of New Jersey stretching to Orange Mountain and the further heights; the Palisades walling the mighty Hudson; the fair Westchester country; the thoroughfare of the Sound opening out from Hell Gate; Long Island, "fish-shaped Paumanok," with its beaches; the Narrows, with their frowning forts; the Bay, where the colossal Liberty will rise; at last the ocean, with its bridging ships. And when he takes his walks about New York he can scarcely lose sight of what is now the great landmark which characterizes and dominates the city as St. Peter's from across the Campagna dominates Rome, and the Arc de Triomphe the approach to Paris, and the Capitol on its height our own Washington—the double-towered bridge, whose massive masonry finds no parallel since the Pyramids. Those huger masses were the work of brutal force, piling stone upon stone. The wonder and the triumph of this work of our own day is in the weaving of the aerial span that carries such burden of usefulness, by human thought and skill, from the delicate threads of wire that a child could almost sever.

The New York
Working Girl
(1896)

THE NEW YORK WORKING-GIRL

By Mary Gay Humphreys

"I AM an original working-girl."

The women from Murray Hill who had come down to Cooper Union to confer with the women from Cherry Hill about the feather-workers' trouble looked up incredulously at the shirt-maker's exultant boast. The statement of fact was plain enough, but not the meaning of the tone. That there could be anything but necessity in getting up early and working late six days in the week, for a sum of money ridiculously unimportant in their eyes, seemed incredible.

An original working-girl, as the shirt-maker expressed it, is, in fact, a new type. She is a girl to whom work is a necessity, but a burden she takes up lightly and gladly. It means independence, freedom, power. It means association, companionship, organization. It leaves her free to do with her life what she chooses. The regularity that her work exacts she knows is good for both body and mind. She has a pride, which she feels is not wicked, in being one of the cleverest of workwomen. If there is extra work to be done, she is booked to do it. This gives her satisfaction. Certainly she does not earn money enough to suit her. But if she cannot make more she doesn't mean to take less, and is ready to try conclusions with a light heart.

In all probability she has not been to school since she was thirteen years old. Since then her education has been conducted by experience and the newspaper. Neither is an inefficient teacher. On the contrary, so ably has this been done that her mind is a storehouse of facts that make her valuable frequently for purposes of reference to people who have been through college. Her experience directs her mind toward matters of public importance, and these include how public men have stood with regard to them. Not infrequently she has had the career of some legislator assigned by her organization to her watchful eye. Whatever has at any time engrossed the public mind she is informed about.

When she turns at a strike meeting and asks your opinion about the restriction of immigration, it is not a question of Shakespeare and the musical glasses, nor has she loaded up with information in order to unload it upon somebody else. You have no opinion, and it is worth while to frankly admit it, in order to arrive at her opinion and how she got it. She was a shirt-maker. The girls had the trade in their own hands, and made good wages. First one black man got in, and he brought his brother and his son. Pretty soon the room was half-filled with men in shiny clothes and big black beards, who brought their relations. The girls first objected because they made the factory towel so black with their dirty hands. After that the girls brought their own towels, but the black men seemed to choke up the room and swallow all the air. Then work began to give out; the black-bearded men were taking it home to do nights when their wives and daughters could help them. The old people and the little children, who could do nothing else, pulled out the bastings. The boss found he could get his work done cheaper and save in rent and fuel. At last prices were cut until the girls might as well strike or starve. They struck.

It is irrelevant but instructive to know that they made a gallant fight and lost. The black-bearded men came in greater force and took all the work home; the factory was given up, the girls thrown out of work. Thus was the question of immigration pressed upon them. It was discussed privately in their union, and publicly at Cooper Union. To talk about it was like talking about any other question pertinent and personal. The arguments were those familiar; but one may be mentioned. Every working-girl born in this country is an American—Irish-American, German-American are not terms she uses; she may go without a meal, but her birthright forbids her to content herself with black bread and coffee like the black - bearded men. During a great strike in a neighboring, thread-mill the complaint was bitter against the imported Scotch girls, who wore shawls on the head and took their places. American girls eat meat and wear bonnets. This is neither vanity nor gormandizing, but a sense of that decorous, orderly mode of life that becomes the free people of a free country. Of this the immigration laws tend to deprive her, and her patriotic instincts rebel.

In other matters she is instructed in like manner. No university education is more costly. Eight years ago she began to entertain views on convict labor, after a now historic strike, disastrous both to employers and employed. This strike shows so many of the chivalrous, picturesque, economic, and insidious features of a labor contest that it is worth relating it somewhat in detail. A newly imported superintendent, desiring to show his zeal by increasing the firm's profits, cut down the wages of the cutters. The cutters, men, and well organized, struck. The operators were hundreds of girls, unorganized. To render the strike effective it was necessary that they, too, should go out. Behind them were the ironers, eighty strong - armed women with a good union. One of the offices of a union is to know the state of the market. The situation did not warrant the reduction, and the ironers attempted to rally the girls to the defence of the men. The superintendent posted a notice of petty restrictions to the ironers at this juncture. It was scarcely posted when one, now the historic leader of the revolt, laid down her iron, sat down on her ironing - table with folded arms and swinging feet. In an instant eighty women were sitting on tables with folded arms and swinging feet. The superintendent came up and removed the offending paper, but it was too late ; the spirit of revolt had spread ; the girls went out, and the ironers were locked out. The proprietor was kind, everybody had been glad to work for him. But he was more remote than the president. The strike lasted for months, the firm never recovered its custom, its name is now effaced from

the business of the country ; the prisons and the houses of mercy came forward with cheap bids for the ironing, and the laundry work of the town was practically transferred to institutions.

Nothing has tended more directly to weaken allegiance to the church than that religious houses were permitted to use their unfortunates to interfere with the wage-earning power of honest workmen. In the case of the State what the ironers experienced, so also have the shoefitters and the overall - makers. But also in the case of the State the working-girl has seen the ingenuous little ballot put an end to convict labor in the prisons, and the lesson, as it pertains to her welfare, has not been unheeded. The typical working-girl is a good deal of a politician. If she was not the backbone she was the spinalcord of the Anti-Poverty Society, and Mr. Henry George has a fine following in her ranks. She is up in ward politics, and calls Jim, Mike, and Barney by their first names. But her interest is farther-reaching. She goes to hear speeches at Cooper Union, and has views on tariff reform. Sometimes she works out economic problems in her own way.

A group of boxmakers were talking about the flattering messages sent by the uptown ladies to two girls of a working-girls' club who were doing the janitor's work so that her wages could be saved for the club. Finally, one girl said she wasn't so sure about it being a good thing. Girls who worked hard all day, she thought, ought not to be taking on more work after hours. Besides, there was Mrs. Flanagan, who needed the money. Sometimes it seemed almost wrong to save money.

This made a great outcry. If there was one lesson that was eloquently dwelt on at the club it was that of economy, the virtue of saving. The girls were learning dressmaking so that they could make their own dresses, and millinery, that they might trim their own bonnets. This they pointed out. But the other girl said it seemed to her it would be almost better to be doing overwork, for then she could give her clothes to some other girl to make and she could be earning too. It seemed to her that the best thing in the world would be to have everybody earning more. That would be better than to have a few saving money.

"But everybody knows that the way to get rich is to save money. There was Peter Cooper, Mr. Stewart, and Mr. Astor. That was the way they did."

"That is what everybody tells us," persisted the other girl; "but I don't believe they got rich by sticking to saving. I get along better than I used to. There was a time when I never had more than one dress a year, and I would contrive until I would get a blue ribbon for my waist, and another for my neck, and one for my hair. Although you may say I couldn't afford them, I'll never forget the pleasure the ribbons gave me."

The girls didn't agree to this at all. They loved ribbons, of course, but everybody agreed that ribbons were not only an extravagance, but a foolish extravagance. The other girl said she was not so sure of that, for in a far-off way she was helping to keep the girls who made the ribbons. She liked to think that.

"But you can't be right, Maggie," said, in painful hesitation, a girl who especially loved to decorate herself. "Nobody talks that way. Everybody says we must save. If you put money in banks and let it lie, when you have enough you can live on the interest of the money."

The girl called Maggie said that might be well enough for some people, but most folks had to hustle if they wanted money, and a good sight hadn't anything to hustle about.

"I was up to Cooper Union to a political meeting this fall," she continued, "and a man there said that the trouble was, everybody was doing too much. The factories were so full that there was not enough people to buy what they made; so the stock stood and rotted, and the men who owned it failed."

"That's true," said another girl, "for after the season closed my boss had his lofts stacked with cloaks fairly rotted, and we were laid off for months."

"But it wasn't because there wasn't enough people to buy the cloaks, but because they couldn't buy them. Now,

if I could earn more I would have been one of his customers myself. I needed a cloak."

"But what would you have us do, Maggie, if we're not to be savin' money?"

"I'm not saying that exactly. I'm only sayin' that I believe in doin', not savin'. I'm not setting the world right. Only if I had my way none of us would have to work so long and so hard, and then there would be more work for everybody; and then everybody could earn and everybody spend; and everybody would have to keep on working, earning, spending, and round and round we would all go working, earning, spending. Of course, some people would not get so very rich, but we would all be better off; and as we all kept going around, working, earning, spending, I believe we would get lifted higher up, as if we were all riding along on the thread of a screw."

This actual but incidental conversation illustrates how the circumstances of the New York working-girl's life lead her to the consideration of subjects that are not usually forced upon the magical period of youth. Occasionally they go deeper than the conclusions of experience. One class in political economy, held at Cooper Union, is recalled. There may have been others. The girl thrown out of work because her factory has been closed by a trust, has her attention drawn to this new engine of dismay; and there are plenty of orators at Golden Rule Hall, if more pretentious places are wanting, to stimulate, if not satisfy, inquiry. The educational value of a union is not usually dwelt upon. Some organizations are avowedly educational.

One scene is recalled. It took place during the feather strike, when a well-known woman in the educational world was to address the girls. She began brusquely: "You talk about your rights. You have no rights." Such toying with abstract propositions was not above the comprehension of the girls. But the lady soon left the well-worn paths of easy generalization for the more dangerous ground of the specific. The chief concern of the working-girl should be not wages but to do good work. It

In Front of a Box Factory in Hester Street at Six O'clock.

was impossible to get any sort of work properly done. This difficulty she illustrated by the unceremonious ripping of some shop-made article of her own. From thence she proceeded to comment on their feminine tendency to dress, and to lay down plain directions for spending their money.

The audience stirred uneasily. Before she was seated half a dozen girls were on their feet. A shirtmaker, with flashing eyes and incisive speech, gained the floor. "You say we have no rights. What rights have you that we haven't got? You are better dressed, have more learning and more money than we have. But these things give you no more right to come down here and tell us what we shall wear, and how we shall spend our money, than we have to go uptown and tell you how you shall spend your money and what you shall put on. You complain about the ripping of your gown. Do you know anything about the life of the girl that sewed that seam? I wonder what sort of work you would do on bread and tea, or a chocolate éclair to stifle your hunger? You know all about books. I don't; but I know that you can't do good work on an empty stomach. Let

us have fair wages, so that we can feed ourselves properly, and we will give you good work."

No attempt is made here to render the rude eloquence with which these things were said; but when the girl ceased, flushed and breathless, uptown and downtown broke into cheers. The first speaker was a large-minded woman, and hastened to take the girl's hand and assure her that her heart was right if her words had been misplaced. Such girls are not among the legions of the Working-Girls' Clubs. The well-meaning women who are prepared to tell the working-girl everything—what books she shall read, and to see that she is "washed be'ind the ears," fail to understand how little such advice is needed. After a lecture of this sort before the Working-Women's Society from a woman earnestly desiring to be of benefit to a number of working-girls whom she was invited to meet, a feather-worker said:

"How astonished would that lady be if she heard the girls that curl feathers at our table. We have such a good time. We talk about books that we read—good books that she seems to think we know nothing about. We talk

Laundresses Support the Cutters' Strike.

about the theatres, and newspapers, and the things that go on about town. We may use bad grammar, and our speech is rough, but it is never vulgar, as she seems to think, or she would never say the things that she has just said to us."

The typical working-girl belongs to a union, or a local assembly of the Knights of Labor. A union is the most absolute of democracies. Even in "mixed unions," as the organization of both men and women are called, the woman has the same right of speech and office as the man. She has, per-haps, been presiding officer, wielded the gavel and served out parliamentary rulings to the men. All this is favorable to her self-respect; the girl takes pride in her station, and to her condescension finds no reasonable basis. When the up-town ladies take off their good clothes and address her as "sister," she accepts it good-humoredly as a sort of pose; but she would rather see some gracious

Knows a lot about local politics.

feminine adornments, that she might get a hint for a new gown she has in her own eye. Nor has she any craving for sweetness and light as it is diffused through the medium of calisthenics, palms in blue-and-white pots, and China silk curtains.

A committee looking up statistics of wages in the trades visited one of these centres for the dissemination of refining influences. Some young girls were going through a musical drill. The fair-haired college girl who was in charge came forward. The questions were addressed with propriety to her, as in many of the clubs, at that time, it was found that conversation about trade matters was not allowed.

"I'm sure I don't know," the young woman said.

"What trades do your girls work at? May we ask them?"

"Certainly," was the amiable reply. "We never ask the girls anything about outside mat-

The Enemies of the Working-girl.

ters," she added, as if a principle were involved. The girls were asked, and answered freely, but their fair-haired patron was plainly anxious to get back to her woven paces. One of the committee, a boxmaker, looked on curiously.

"Why do they do that?" She was told it was a species of feminine dancing.

"And she takes the trouble to teach them that, and doesn't know whether those girls have homes, or anything about their real lives. That's what I call sugar-coating poverty."

The same views were commonly expressed, and sometimes more bitterly, as if there was a conspiracy abroad to make working-people contented with their lot. In every case it is just to the working-girl to say that these views were prompted by the apparent indifference to such vital matters as wages and conditions of work. "Let us have fair wages, and all these things shall be added unto us," they said, impatiently. The time was inauspicious. To the cigarette-girls' strike, to the shirtmakers' strike, had succeeded the feather-workers' trouble. So frivolous an article as ostrich feathers had been the source of one of the largest and

best-paying industries in town. For several years each season had seen a cut, until a day's work scarcely furnished a living. The energetic girls pieced out their wages by night-work, but several girls had ruined their eyes working on black feathers, and the experience of the shops was that night-work demoralized the trade, the strong and selfish prospering at the expense of the weak. The season opened with another cut. The state of the trade demanded it, so they were told. This to the girls, who knew that feather boas had "come in," did not seem reasonable; moreover they attached importance to the fast time the boss's horses were making that they read of in the daily papers. They liked the boss, and were glad when he gave the dust to everybody on the road. But, plainly, the horses were costing too much; they could not support the expense.

Two girls wrote to the Working-Women's Society a despairing cry for help. It was offered. Two members volunteered to distribute the hastily printed "call" to a conference of feather-workers. Those who have never stood picket, nor handed out circulars in the shadow of a disaffected factory, with the chance of being invited by the police to "move on," have failed to experience moments of gleeful terror that stirs the blood like a tonic. The girls came out, took the white missives slipped into their hands, and read them after they had turned the corner. Their indifference was discouraging; but by six o'clock the rooms were jammed. The firm was interceded with by women not connected with the trades, but without avail. Here occurred a curious entanglement, which illustrates what a complex creature is woman and how constant a factor is sex. It was well known by the girls that the situation would be taken advantage of by rival houses to "down" the boss, who had always laid down the law in his union—that of the employers. They liked his bluff, burly ways, his friendly address, and, as was said, took an interest in his fast horses as an indulgent mother does in the long-tailed hobby of a spoiled child. They did not mean the trade should leave him any more than that they would suffer their own grievance. It was necessary to get all the girls out. How could they be reached? It was

Scab!

only common prudence not to talk to them on the street.

The feather-curlers are the aristocrats of the trade. What the feather-curlers would do all the feather-workers would do. Now the feather-curlers have to have sharp knives. This is done at various little shops in the neighborhood. The girls leave them at night, and get them in the morning. A descent was made on these little shops in the early morning, and each girl's knife wrapped in one of those blood-stirring appeals that are part of the literature of strikes. The ruse was successful. House after house came out; the feather-working industry was paralyzed. The girls formed a strong union. Women from uptown offered their services; meetings were held; money was subscribed; a benefit was given. The pinches of poverty were scarcely felt in the excitement, in the hand-to-hand fight with the bosses before the Committee of Arbitration, and in the accounts of the beauty, eloquence, and prominence of the feather-workers so generously parcelled out by the chivalrous young reporters.

Such are among the mitigating influences of a strike; there are proud functions that possess less advantages in some respects. That in the struggle of wage-winning some personal satisfaction may be snatched is only incidental to a struggle altogether serious. The employers made overtures and the conclusion of the feather-workers' strike was, from every point of view, a picturesque and significant accomplishment. For days two high contracting parties met in the rooms of the Working-Women's Society, the one a committee from the Feather-Girls' Union, the other a committee from the Association of Feather Manufacturers, arranging the scale of prices under which the girls would go back to work. This went into every branch of a complicate trade in which the variation of a fraction of a cent meant thousands of dollars to the employer. There were debates and arguments; point after point was stoutly contested; yet so thorough and accurate was the girls' knowledge of the trade that the schedule established by them was practically accepted.

Pickets.

Night-work was abolished, the agreement ratified by both parties, and the strike called off. In almost every trade the management of these details would fall to men. But the feather trade is a woman's industry, and that a handful of girls, a few weeks before working each for herself, could so quickly and intelligently enter into deliberations of such moment, shows something of the mental discipline and unconscious education that take the place of schools in the working-girl's life.

When the amendment to the Factory Law was passed providing for women inspectors, one of the first appointments was a boxmaker. She had left school at thirteen, and, excepting a few months at night-school, had no other education than that given by her trade and the newspaper to which she gave flattering attention. The distance between a boxmaker earning eight dollars a week and a State official makes a dizzy leap. Her new duties brought her into personal relations with great corporations, the clerical landlords, the manufacturing magnates, as well as familiar with the humble dens of the sweaters; they involved not only the enforcement of the law, and sometimes legal proceedings, but discretion, knowledge of human nature, and large measures of that sense miscalled common. Such an article as this would indeed be lacking if it failed to discover the uprightness and thoroughness with which this working-girl has performed the duties of her new estate, and the high esteem and respect in which she is held by her chief and those with whom she has had to do.

The sense of power that has accompanied these changes, among its varied influences, gives the factory-girl a dignity of character that the unorganized saleswoman cannot match among her more attractive surroundings. A man prominent in labor matters says that in time of trouble there is no loyalty that compares with that of the working-girl; she stands firmest; stays out longest; is less amenable to those insidious influences that are the most fatal with which the working-people have to contend. A gentleman, whose opinions a number of centuries have thought worthy respectful consideration, has said that under the same circumstances men and women will act pretty much in the same manner. It is suspected that the ethics of women are influenced somewhat by their physique. The human impulses are the same ; and working-girls standing picket in a strike have been known to use arguments of force as the men sometimes do. An outsider can scarcely comprehend the complexity of emotions, casuistry, personal reasons, abstract propositions, and sense of the picturesque that have combined to bring forth the word "scab." When in a turbulent meeting a peacemaker rises to say, "I don't think it very polite for one lady to call another lady a scab," the speech has no humor except to one in some remote mental perspective. Others bend their heads to escape the fast flying words, praying that they may be averted.

The daughters of the black-bearded men who carried dismay among the American girls in the eighties take to organization like ducks to water, as indeed do now their fathers. The Russian, Pole, Bohemian, who can speak no other English word, can say "union." The union of the Hebrew girls, allied to the United Brotherhood of Tailors, is the largest and most prominent in town. They are for the most part undersized, and it is worth a journey to some ill-smelling hall on the East Side to see some mite of a creature in a trim matronly gown and a Psyche knot address a mass of wild-looking, excited men.

One of the perplexities of the web in which both working-men and working-women are together ensnared, is that they who should be natural allies are industrial enemies. The organization of women into their unions on the part of men, these alliances offensive and defensive, are not prompted by chivalry, the natural impulse of the strong toward the weak, but by self-preservation. The argument is brief and conclusive. Women at cheaper wages are used to cheapen the labor of men. Organize women, insist on equal wages for them, and brawn will tell. Machinery is on the side of the women. The type-setting machines, responsive as the piano to her nimble fingers, at this moment illustrate the situation. The incidental fact that when she goes out to lunch

A Meeting at Cooper Union.

she returns, and on Monday morning she is in her place, is in her favor. The working-girls themselves, forced into this unnatural antagonism, are on the side of the men. The lessons of experience have been too searching. There was a strike, or perhaps a lock-out. A father goes out with the men; the girls take their places at lower wages; a daughter is one of the girls; perhaps, too, the wife. The women are now the breadwinners. The man can get

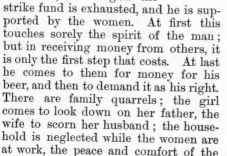

A Type of the Born and Bred American Working-Girl.

no work; at length the strike fund is exhausted, and he is supported by the women. At first this touches sorely the spirit of the man; but in receiving money from others, it is only the first step that costs. At last he comes to them for money for his beer, and then to demand it as his right. There are family quarrels; the girl comes to look down on her father, the wife to scorn her husband; the household is neglected while the women are at work, the peace and comfort of the family is destroyed. This is not an imaginary situation, it is the tragedy of countless homes.

Pythagoras Hall, just off the Bowery, was dedicated to Labor and the Muses. Nor was the goddess of Deportment forgotten. "Gents will please take off their hats when they are dancing with the ladies," used to be one of her reminders on a black and white placard, that he who danced might read. Here, in packed meetings, to which no man

Margaret Finn, Factory Inspector.

was allowed, working-women from every part of town, when the days were very black for them, met and talked over the matters that pressed them so nearly. However other women from whatever point of view come to regard marriage, the rank of the working-women are solid for husbands and homes. The ideal state is one in which the man earns the money and the woman cares

for the children and the house. At these meetings the labor question, from whatever point of view it was considered, returned by one road or another to this. If it is a question of child labor, it is bad for the child, but it tends to drag down men's wages. For married women to work in the trades is almost immoral; they should attend to their homes and their children. The severe labor, the long hours, the nervous strain on the growing girls exhausts their vitality and unfits them to be wives and mothers. And oh, the pathos and despair of a situation that continues to crowd women into the ranks of the workers and to lower the wage-earning power of the men until marriage becomes more and more an impossibility to both.

From time to time the uptown women came to these meetings to urge the working-girls to leave the factories and go into domestic service. There were many reasons why they were disinclined to this. Girls used to regular hours and prescribed duties objected to the irregular hours and desultory duties of the household. Better scanty food, a hard bed, and personal freedom, than material comforts and only every other Sunday out. It may be dearly bought to be one's own mistress and to go and come at will, but these are possessions not to be rashly sold. But hearken to the final, the conclusive answer.

"The men whom we may hope to marry will not visit us in other people's kitchens."

There is no impression more difficult to efface from the minds of the well-intentioned women than that the entrance of girls into industrial pursuits lowers their moral standard. This is not always formulated thus plainly, but it is implied in their efforts to mitigate the conditions of women working for their weekly wages. If they establish a comfortable boarding-house or lodging-house, they set up moral safeguards frequently so rigorous that self-respecting girls refuse to enter them. If they organize classes for recreation or improvement, it is considered quite within their province to address these classes with words of warning and personal advice that it would be considered impertinence to address to girls in other walks of life. If they desire to get legislation in behalf of working-girls at Albany, it is the moral aspect that is urged out of all proportion of the legitimate reasons in its support. The alliance between poverty and crime is by no means exclusive.

The fact that a girl spends nine hours a day in a factory working for her daily bread is an argument in her favor as against Satan and all his works.

This is not an unsupported assertion. From the investigations made by the United States Commissioner of Labor, both in this country and Europe, it appears, according to the official reports of the prison authorities, that in Manchester out of fifty women only eight came from factories, while twenty-nine came from domestic service. From the investigations of M.

Minnie Rosen, Walking Delegate of the Garment Makers' Union.

Lottie Persky, Chairman.

Esther Friedman, of the Executive Board.

Reybaud, in France, he reports a decreasing criminal list in a constantly increasing factory population. From the police records of Fall City, one of the largest manufacturing centres in this country, the operatives, who are 38 per cent. of the population, supply only 33 per cent. of the arrests. In Lynn, the shoe factories, which furnish 28 per cent. of the population, supply but 22 per cent. of the arrests. The factory population of Lowell, which is 30 per cent. of the whole, furnishes but 22 per cent. of the arrests. These facts are representative. Regular employment is conducive to regular living, and as a rule does not harmonize with intemperance and crime. These investigations, carried more particularly into the lives of working-women, only resulted in the same conclusions borne out by the police of twenty-two cities in which inquiry was made. In this city it is proper to add that by far the largest proportion of women seeking the hospitalities of such institutions as the Nursery and Child's Hospital are not from factories but from domestic service. The averages of women working in factories and shops barely, in the best of times, reach $5 a week. "It is easy enough to be virtuous on five thousand a year," Mrs.

Rawdon Crawley once remarked, but that the working-girl must dress and maintain herself on $5 a week, discloses an integrity of character for which she has not had credit.

The vice of the working-girl is suspicion. Distrust is fostered in the trades. A new superintendent puts her on piece-work. Nothing could be better; she is a clever work-woman. But the work gives out. She is laid off a half-day, a day, two days. She discovers that the work is sent out of town to women in their homes who can afford to work for less prices. She can have the work if she will work at their rates. Or she discovers she is working on high-grade work for low-grade prices; the numbers by which the grades are known have been changed. A shrewd manager is fertile in ruses for lowering wages in return for his own advance in salary, dependent, perhaps, on his success. A large number of the disturbances in factories, so perplexing to the public, are from such causes. When the enthusiastic economist, with illustrated diagrams, demonstrates to her the superior nourishment in beans, and how to grow plump on twelve cents a day, she is persuaded that this is only another argument to keep down what she calls a living wage. Faith in human nature is one of the dearest possessions of youth. The working-girl is indeed defrauded when she learns so early to distrust.

Her most admirable virtue is self-sacrifice. The girls in the unions, as with the men, are always the cleverest, the most skilful in their trades. They are the workers who have the least need of a union. For a working-girl to pledge each week a certain sum from her scanty wages in the interest of those who are less able to stand alone, is an act of self-denial, which by no means gets the recognition to which it is entitled. Hunger and cold strip the human heart bare. The countless acts of self-sacrifice that attend a long strike almost persuade that the poor only know how to be generous.

The femininity of the working-girl has withstood all the shock of modern agitation. When the cares that infest the day have fled, bright is the night and many the pleasures it brings. The Bowery is a gay promenade, and there women may walk in its splendor of noonday in the safety that Fifth Avenue does not afford. The theatres are open; there are lectures at Cooper Union, perhaps a "Lady Gotham" Ball given by the Shirt-ironers' Union, and one of the great functions of the winter. But most dearly the working-girl loves a moonlight picnic. A union picnic is not the *al fresco* entertainment its name suggests. It is as formal in its routine as an uptown cotillion. The union encourages a certain orderliness of mind and observances of titles and forms that find expression in the working-girl's amusements. The lady floor-managers are intent on their duties; the grand promenade that opens the festivities is a gravely decorous and imposing rite.

No girl is expected to dance with a man who does not belong to a union unless he promises to join, for a picnic is also a proselyting occasion. The men are laid under the same embargo. This is also part of the fun and make-talk of the affair. There is no girl who has not a trim gown for the dance, for the window displays of Grand and Fourteenth Streets keep her informed as to fashions and cut, and her skilful fingers do the rest. The commingling of nationalities gives vivacity and variety to the scene; interesting are the many types of feminine comeliness.

Here is a girl, tall, slender, with well modelled features. Yesterday she was making shirts. Last night she was speaking at the Social Reform Club. This afternoon she was at a conference of the uptown women in a luxurious drawing-room. To-night she dances, coquettes with her admirers, plays at the old, old game of man and maid. She is no longer a type, she is just Girl.

The World's Greatest Aqueduct (1909)

THE WORLD'S GREATEST AQUEDUCT

WATER FROM THE CATSKILL MOUNTAINS TO THE CITY OF NEW YORK

BY ALFRED DOUGLAS FLINN

Engineer, Headquarters Department, of the Board of Water Supply of the City of New York

THE Catskill Mountain water system being constructed for New York City is one of the most notable engineering enterprises ever undertaken. Ranking with the inter-oceanic canals at Suez and Panama, the Assuan irrigation works in Egypt, and the projects which are converting western America's arid wastes into fruitful fields, the Catskill aqueduct, with its tributary reservoirs, probably surpasses any one of them in the variety of problems to be solved. Although undertaken by a municipality, these works in magnitude and cost compare with national enterprises.

Imperial Rome's longest aqueduct was fifty-seven miles in length; the Catskill aqueduct will be ninety-two miles long. Rome, with hordes of laborers from conquered domains, carried its aqueducts at the hydraulic gradient across valleys on imposing masonry arches. Modern explosives and rock-drills enable New York to tunnel in solid rock beneath valleys and rivers, avoiding masonry, which is now expensive, and which is likely to suffer in New York's severer climate.—THE EDITOR.

CATSKILL MOUNTAIN water, gathered from brooks that have been fed by melting snows and copious rains, and have tumbled over rocky slopes into the streams of the mountain valleys, will in a few years be served to the inhabitants of New York City. The project ranks as the greatest municipal water-supply enterprise ever undertaken, and as an engineering work is probably second only to the Panama Canal. The need of the water is much greater than is realized by a majority of the citizens or by the guardians of their interests.

Nothing can so quickly and completely disorganize the complex activities of a modern community as a shortage of suitable water; no single agency can so rapidly spread disease and death as a polluted water-supply. For several years New York has been using more water than its sources of supply can safely be depended upon to furnish in a series of dry years, such as have occurred within the memory of men who have scarcely reached middle age. Continuing years of abundant rainfall have masked the danger to which engineers have repeatedly called attention.

In 1905, as the result of a movement promoted by civic bodies in the days of Mayor Van Wyck and Mayor Low, a bill was introduced into the legislature, on the initiative of Mayor McClellan, which, becoming a law, enabled the city to start new systems of water-supply that, with the already existing permanent works, should ultimately give New·York the best and largest water-supply ever known.

As thousands of water-wise Americans know, New York City ("old New York") has used Croton River water for more than two generations. Similarly from the Ridgewood system of wells, streams, and reservoirs, Brooklyn has drawn its supply, often scanty. Approximately five hundred million gallons of

117

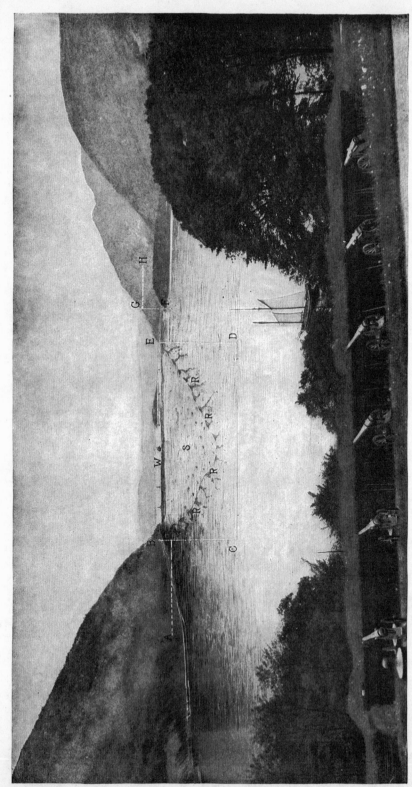

VIEW, LOOKING NORTH FROM THE WEST POINT WATER BATTERY, OF THE HUDSON BETWEEN STORM KING (ON THE LEFT) AND BREAKNECK, WITH VERTICAL SECTION OF THE AQUEDUCT TUNNEL UNDER THE RIVER

The rock-bed of the Hudson is indicated by R, R; S is the body of sediment between the river current and the rock-bed; W, the black line indicating varying depth of river water; A, B, aqueduct tunnel emerging from Storm King; B, C, tunnel shaft now being sunk from the shore of Storm King; C, D, aqueduct tunnel about half a mile long to be bored in solid rock twelve hundred feet below the surface of the river; D, E, tunnel shaft now being sunk from the shore of Breakneck; E, F, G, H, continuation of the aqueduct tunnel into Breakneck, with a rise to flow-level, whence the aqueduct will proceed to the enlarged Kensico reservoir.

water are consumed by the metropolis every day, a stream which would flow hip-deep between the buildings in Fifth Avenue's fashionable shopping district at a comfortable walking pace. For every man, woman, and child this allows a daily average of 125 gallons. Or, to put it still another way, for all domestic, manufacturing, and public purposes New York uses every day water which weighs about eight times as much as its population.

Compared with the 130, 140, 200, 220, and 320 gallons used every day for every person in several large American cities, New York's allowance is moderate, especially when one recalls the character of business and the methods of living which prevail in the metropolis. Liberal, even lavish, domestic use of water is not waste. The very necessities of life demand that there should be a maximum supply, in order to provide for the average demand for the individual. The word "waste" should be properly interpreted. Its use in writing about water-supply has been unfortunate, for it has been employed both technically and popularly to characterize quite different conditions in the economy of water. To let a dozen glassfuls flow from a faucet in order to get one cool draft is not waste so long as this is the least expensive way to get cool water. In a broad sense, to permit water to flow from the faucets through cold winter nights is not waste so long as this is the least expensive way to protect one's plumbing fixtures. To allow even large volumes of water to spill over the lowest dam of a watershed is in no sense waste when the city has already taken from the stream all that it can use, or when the saving of occasional discharges of this sort would cost more than to get the same quantity of water, of equal or better quality, from another stream. Doubtless some water is carelessly or wantonly wasted in New York City, but not nearly so much as some persons assume. Waste should be discouraged and curtailed, but waste of water can no more be wholly prevented than the waste of energy and time. But if all the waste which it would be reasonably practicable to stop ceased, New York would still require more water-works to provide beyond peradventure for present needs and future growth.

Croton River drains into New York's reservoirs the water of 360 square miles of forest and farm, and can safely furnish about 336,000,000 gallons daily. Two aqueducts, one thirty-four miles long, built in 1842, and having a daily capacity of 80,000,000 gallons, and the other thirty-two miles long, built in 1891, and having a capacity of 300,000,000 gallons, bring this water to the city. To procure 500,000,000 gallons of Catskill Mountain water daily, over 600 square miles of mountain and meadow will be brought under tribute, several large reservoirs created, and an aqueduct ninety-two miles long built, with many miles of conduits within the city limits.

The extent of these existing and proposed works is not readily to be comprehended even when reduced to the common money measure. For the portion of the Catskill works needed to bring into the city every day unfailingly 500 million gallons an expenditure of $162,000,000 is estimated. But these disbursements will be spread over many years, and the burden will not fall heavily, except for possible temporary difficulties in raising ready money for construction payments. Indeed, the cost of water for every person will be on the average less than one cent per day. Furthermore, these water-works, well managed, will not only pay interest on the investment and cost of operation, but in a relatively few years will pay the capital cost. It is reasonable to believe that the works will be as permanent as those of Rome.

Because of its antiquity and impressive ruins, the water-supply of ancient Rome is doubtless the most famous in the world. In 97 A. D. the imperial city had no fewer than nine aqueducts, with an aggregate length of 263 miles; but if the water that all those aqueducts could carry (estimated at 84,000,000 gallons per day) were put into New York's Catskill aqueduct, it would rise only to the height of about three feet and three inches.

In the angle of the State west of the Hudson and south of the Mohawk are hundreds of square miles of territory partly forested, but in the main little cultivated and sparsely populated. From time to time the large timber has been cut; the farms have depreciated. From the hills tens of thousands of square feet of blue-stone have been quarried for sidewalks,

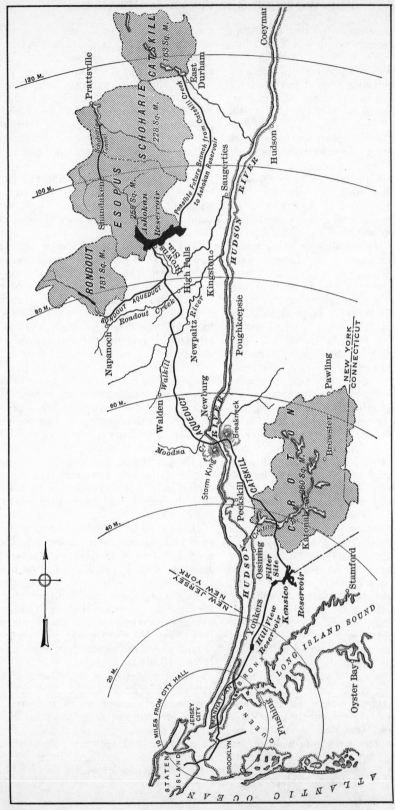

MAP OF THE CATSKILL AQUEDUCT SYSTEM

The shaded sections west of the Hudson indicate the watersheds which will fill the Ashokan and other reservoirs. At Storm King a tunnel aqueduct will pass under the river to Breakneck; thence the aqueduct will cross the southwest corner of the Croton watershed to the enlarged Kensico reservoir, south of which is shown the site for the filters, and farther on the great equalizing Hill View reservoir.

but within twenty years even this industry has been almost supplanted by the use of Portland cement concrete. There remain the bracing air, the attractive scenery, and the abundant rainfall; and thousands of holiday-seekers flock thither. Their entertainment now constitutes the most profitable business of the region, and will not be interfered with by the project. The city, therefore, is not destroying large commercial or agricultural industries, but is simply making the highest use of one of the principal resources of the region, its water.

After repeated investigations, the most thorough of which were those of the Burr-Hering-Freeman commission, eminent engineers appointed by Mayor Low in 1902, several large streams in the Catskills were selected for successive development as needed. Esopus Creek, above the best dam site, has a drainage area of 257 square miles; Rondout Creek has a useful watershed of 131 square miles; above the selected point of diversion, Schoharie Creek drains 228 square miles; and 142 square miles of the basin of Catskill Creek can be utilized. Thus, with the addition of several minor streams, a total water-gathering area of 885 square miles has been found, which, it is conservatively estimated, will yield even in a series of dry years about 770 million gallons daily. These waters are all of exceptionally high quality, and, barring Catskill Creek, are remarkably soft. In this respect even the latter suffers only by comparison with the unusual softness of the others.

Although turbulent torrents of great volume rush through the gorges of these mountain creeks in flood-time, in late summer the streams could all be run through a four-foot pipe, one of the street mains of a large city. But a great community does not use water in any such irregular fashion, and nature must be regulated to meet the necessities of man. The flow must be controlled, so that flood excesses may supplement drought deficiencies. Great impounding, or gathering, reservoirs are the means which engineers employ to this end. In the Catskill scheme eight large impounding reservoirs are contemplated, of which the first to be constructed, and by far the greatest, is the Ashokan reservoir on the Esopus. In the southeastern corner of this mountain region geologic forces

have provided a great basin in which can be stored not only the waters of the Esopus, but also part of the water of the other streams. Through one of the ridges a tunnel aqueduct ten miles long will bring in the Schoharie contribution, while the Catskill Creek water will flow through an arched masonry conduit, to be built mostly in trench along the eastern slopes of the mountains for thirty-two miles. From the Ashokan reservoir the main aqueduct, called the Catskill aqueduct, will convey the water to the northern boundary of New York City. Into this aqueduct, about six miles below its starting-point, a branch aqueduct will bring the water from Rondout Creek.

But what is an aqueduct? How large is this one? If the curious inquirer will visit Peekskill, New Paltz, or High Falls, where construction is in progress, he will come upon a great trench, in some places thirty feet wide at the bottom, with steam shovels, rock-crushers, concrete-mixers, and hundreds of men and horses at work. Here and there stretches of concave concrete paving have been laid in the bottom of the trench. Elsewhere this paving is being covered by a large concrete arch, thus forming a great tube, or conduit, shaped something like a horseshoe, seventeen feet high and seventeen and a half feet wide inside.

Over this concrete conduit, wherever it is not wholly buried by the depth of the trench, an embankment of earth will be built, except where the trench is mostly through rock, where the bank will be made partly of the rock fragments. Through this aqueduct a railroad coach could easily pass, with a man sitting on top, and there would be room on each side for a man on horseback. In this aqueduct water will flow at the maximum speed of four feet per second, or two and three quarter miles an hour, a comfortable promenading pace, or at the average daily quantity rate of 500 million gallons. This quantity of water, flowing at the velocity mentioned, would make a stream about four feet deep in the ordinary cross-town street of the Borough of Manhattan.

This is the cut-and-cover, or open-cut, type of aqueduct, and is built along the hill slopes or across the flat lands wherever the topography permits a trench to be dug at the proper elevation. In this kind of aqueduct the water flows freely, as in a brook, and not under pressure, as in a pipe under the street. Of the cut-and-cover aqueduct there will be approximately fifty-four miles.

But the topography and geology of the Hudson valley do not permit the Catskill

very thoroughly combined in special machines. When first made, such concrete is plastic or fluid, according to the proportion of water, and can be formed or cast into any desired shape; but in a few hours it sets, or hardens, and rapidly becomes like stone, continuing to increase in

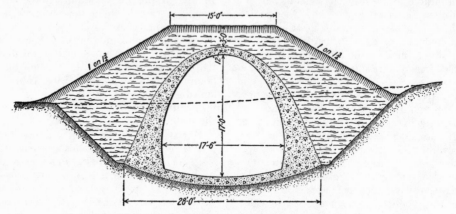

SECTION OF "CUT-AND-COVER" AQUEDUCT, BUILT OF
CONCRETE, WITH COVERING OF EARTH

aqueduct to follow a smooth grade. To avoid long and expensive detours around hills, and to pass ranges of mountains and hills which it would be impracticable to go around, tunnels are being driven through them at the same elevations that the cut-and-cover aqueduct would occupy if the topography were more favorable. Since, however, tunneling is more costly than open-trench work, the size of the aqueduct in these tunnels is less, the dimensions inside being thirteen feet, four inches wide, and seventeen feet high. In order to get the same quantity of water through them, a more rapid flow is necessary, and therefore the slope is a little steeper. Of such tunnels, known as grade tunnels, there will be twenty-three in all, aggregating thirteen and a half miles in length, or approximately as long as Manhattan Island. Virtually the whole length will be in solid rock, and, whether in rock or earth, will be lined with concrete, so as to provide a smooth, clean surface for the water and to prevent the falling of rock or earth from the roof or sides.

In passing, it may be well to explain that the concrete which will enter largely into the construction of the aqueducts and dams is a mixture of Portland cement, sand, crushed stone or gravel, and water,

strength for months, and more slowly for years. Portland cement, a heavy, gray powder, is manufactured in many parts of the country, but that used in the Catskill works will doubtless come mostly from the Lehigh Valley district of Pennsylvania and from the vicinity of Catskill village, New York. The suitability and availability of concrete greatly facilitate and cheapen the construction of dams and aqueducts, displacing more costly brick and stone masonry. Forms of construction which would be impracticable with the latter are entirely feasible with concrete. In building the aqueduct, the soft, fresh concrete is placed against steel plate forms, or molds, erected in the trench or tunnel, thus securing a smooth, clean surface for the water.

The pathway of the Catskill Mountain water from the great Ashokan reservoir to New York City will have many an up and down, and some of the "downs" will be deep. West of the Hudson, several tributaries with broad valleys trend generally northeasterly, so that the aqueduct has to cross these valleys. The great river itself has to be passed, and east of it lies the important valley of the Croton, and at the southerly end of the aqueduct for about two miles even the high land is so low and the real estate so expensive that a tunnel under light pressure is the most economical type of conduit.

These valleys are so far below the natural level at which the water will flow that it will have to be carried across them under great pressure; for the valleys are

Of course it has not been wholly feasible to avoid all these difficulties, but by going to great depths, satisfactory conditions have been found.

Two of the most important and beautiful valleys are those of the Rondout Creek and the Wallkill River. The Wallkill

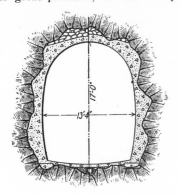

GRADE TUNNEL IN ROCK, LINED
WITH CONCRETE

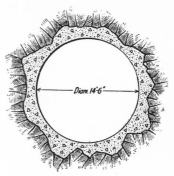

PRESSURE TUNNEL IN ROCK,
LINED WITH CONCRETE

much too wide for the stone arch construction which the very mention of the Roman aqueducts at once suggests, or for any other kind of bridge of the great height necessary. The most permanent and economical form of construction, therefore, is a tunnel through the solid rock, passing not only beneath the visible streams, but also under the pre-glacial gorges, now filled with earth and hidden from view. It is of the utmost importance that these tunnels should be driven through strong, sound rock, so that there will be not only no leakage of water, but sufficient weight and strength to resist the pressure which the water will exert due to its distance below the hydraulic gradient, or natural flowing level, for cut-and-cover aqueduct.

Before these pressure tunnels could be designed, a great deal of information had to be obtained about the geology of the valleys. Hundreds of drill-holes, with individual depths often of several hundred feet, and aggregating many miles, had to be sunk through the earth into the rock in order to determine its character at different points, as well as its depth, so that the tunnels might be located safely, avoiding as far as practicable the rocks which were too weak or difficult for tunneling.

valley was found to be very simple geologically, Nature being satisfied with one kind of rock, through which tunneling will probably proceed with no more than the ordinary difficulties. Rondout valley, on the other hand, is somewhat of a geological museum, containing at least twelve different kinds of rock, varying from the hard quartzite conglomerate, locally known as Shawangunk grit, to soft, water-bearing, and treacherous sandstones and limestones. Sound, strong granite is found beneath the Hudson River and on both sides at the selected place for crossing between Storm King and Breakneck mountains, the picturesque northern gate of the Highlands of the Hudson, about four miles above West Point.

Several years of hard work will be required for driving and lining these tunnels. For the Rondout siphon,[1] besides the shafts at each end, six intermediate shafts, making eight in all, have been provided to aid in construction, so that the digging of the tunnel may proceed at fourteen points. To aid in constructing the Wallkill tunnel, four intermediate shafts will be used. Each of these tunnels is about four and a half miles long. For the siphon beneath the valley of Moodna Creek, stretching south to the Hudson

[1] By way of explanation, aqueducts, or conduits, beneath valleys are frequently called inverted siphons, or simply siphons, because of their similarity to true siphons turned upside down. Of course there is no siphonic action.

River, five miles long, there will be seven shafts. A shaft about 1200 feet deep is thought to be necessary on each bank of the Hudson. To cross beneath the Croton reservoir, a tunnel with two shafts 510 and 560 feet deep will be required. These pressure tunnels, aggregating seventeen miles in length, will also be lined with the most substantial concrete masonry. Inside this lining, the waterway will be circular, with diameters ranging from fourteen feet to sixteen and a half.

If to the new tower of the Metropolitan Life Insurance Company, at Madison

tunnels, being a more expensive type, have smaller waterways than the grade tunnels, and the water will flow through them at higher velocities.

Besides the great valleys to be crossed by pressure tunnels, there are many others too narrow or of too unfavorable geology to be crossed economically by tunnels. Steel pipes, incased in concrete and lined with cement mortar, will be used for passing these depressions. Three pipes will be laid across each valley, but only one will be laid at first, the others being deferred until the increase in the demand

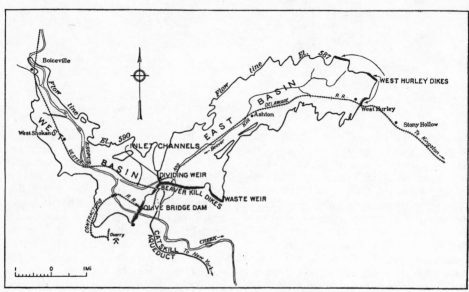

MAP OF THE ASHOKAN RESERVOIR

Square, New York, there were added the height of a Fifth Avenue mansion, it would approximately equal the depth (708 feet) of the shaft at the southerly end of the Rondout siphon. Even in the shallower Wallkill siphon the cages carrying men and materials up and down from the tunnel level will travel a distance (in the deepest shaft, 480 feet, in the shallowest, 350 feet) greater than that from the sidewalk to the top of the towers of the Park Row Building, for a number of years New York's tallest building. From the bottom of each of the working shafts tunneling will be extended for an average distance of nearly half a mile before the headings from adjacent shafts will meet. When finished, each tunnel will be large enough for a subway train to pass through. Pressure

for water makes the expenditure necessary. In general the diameters of the pipes inside the lining will be approximately nine and a half feet north of Kensico reservoir, and eleven feet south of that reservoir. At each end of every siphon, and at every reservoir, there are to be buildings containing appliances for controlling the flow of the water, known as siphon-chambers and gate-houses. A total of seventy buildings for this and other purposes along the aqueduct will be required.

The Ashokan reservoir (Ashokan is an Indian name meaning "place of fish") will be situated about fourteen miles west of the Hudson at Kingston, eighty-six miles in air line from New York, and will center about the hamlet of Brown's

Station on the Ulster & Delaware Railroad. It will be formed by a chain of masonry and earth dams having a combined length of over five miles. Another dam about half a .mile long will divide the reservoir into two basins. It will be chain of dams. Nearly a mile long on top, it has a maximum height above its foundation of 240 feet. Its central portion is being built of solid masonry, with a top length of 1000 feet, minimum top width of twenty-three feet, and a maximum

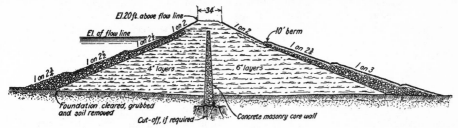

TYPICAL SECTION OF DIKE OF THE OLIVE BRIDGE DAM AND BEAVERKILL DIKES

twelve and a half miles long, and the average width will be a mile. When the reservoir is full, its water surface will be 590 feet above tide; it will contain 128,-000 million gallons, sufficient to cover Manhattan Island to an average depth of twenty-eight feet; 190 feet will be the maximum depth of water behind the dams, and fifty feet the average throughout the reservoir. With a shore-line of forty miles, it will have a water area of 12.8 square miles, and a nearly equal additional area of land has been taken to protect the margins. Approximately forty miles of new highway and thirteen miles of new railroad will have to be built. A concrete arch bridge at the dividing dam will afford connection between the northern and southern sides of the reservoir. Seven villages and many scattered dwellings and other buildings now dotting the valley will have to be razed. From forty small cemeteries all the bodies in 2500 graves must be removed. All trees and brush will be cut and taken away or burned. The landscape will be changed, but, guarded by the somber mountains, Ashokan Lake will add to the attractiveness of the scenery.

Olive Bridge dam is the greatest of the

width at the bottom of 190 feet. This portion of the dam closes the main gorge of the Esopus. Concrete core walls are being built in the earth dams. These earth dams, or dikes, are thirty-four feet wide on top, and have flat slopes, so that their thickness at the bottom is great, reaching a maximum of 800 feet in the earth portion of Olive Bridge dam. If all the earth, rock, and masonry to be handled in constructing Ashokan reservoir were to be put in one heap, they would form a pyramid having a base a quarter mile square and of an equal altitude. The great pyramid of Cheops, in Egypt, was originally 756 feet square at its base and 481 feet high. Its volume, therefore, is only one eighth that of the material to be moved in building this one reservoir of the Catskill water-works.

Construction of the main dams of the Ashokan reservoir was begun in the fall of 1907, the contract, amounting to more than twelve and a half million dollars, having been awarded to MacArthur Bros. Company and Winston & Company. To provide for the thousands of laborers, many of whom have families, a great camp or temporary town has been built close to the scene of operations. This town has hundreds of houses, schools, a bank, a church, a hospital, a water-supply system, a sewerage system with a disposal plant, a great

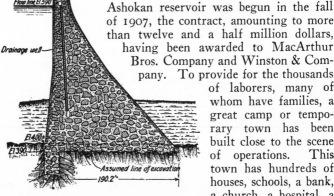

MAXIMUM MASONRY SECTION OF
THE OLIVE BRIDGE DAM
From the lowest foundation to the parapet
this dam is 240 feet high.

general store, a large bakery, a mess-hall, an office building, blacksmith and machine shops, streets, park, band-stand, bath-houses, ice-house, fire department, police, electric lights, and telephones. Great quarries and sand-pits are being developed to furnish materials for the dams, and ten miles of standard-gage railway, not to mention several miles of narrow-gage, have been laid, connecting with the Ulster & Delaware main line. For seven busy years Camp City will flourish, and then it will be obliterated as completely as possible.

Near historic White Plains, thirty miles north of the New York City Hall, the valleys of the Bronx River and Rye ponds afford opportunity, by constructing one large dam, to form a reservoir of great capacity, approximately 40,000 million gallons, with its water surface 355 feet above tide. Its watershed is insignificant, but in it can be kept, relatively near the place of consumption, a water reserve sufficient to insure against the distressing results of accident to the aqueduct northward. Indeed, if necessary, that part of the aqueduct could be out of service for several weeks for inspection or repairs. Hence it also virtually safeguards the continuity of the flow from the Ashokan reservoir almost as well as if a duplicate aqueduct for these seventy miles had been built at much greater expense. To be sure, a second aqueduct will be needed in the distant future, but the reservoir will continue to perform this function of insurance toward the two. From Kensico reservoir, also, in the future, additional aqueducts and pipes can be led in various directions, to distribute water to different parts of the vast district which, in all probability, will ultimately be dependent upon it.

Kensico dam will be of massive masonry, 1830 feet long, rising 150 feet above the ground and nearly 300 feet above its deepest foundation in the ledge rock underlying the valley. Conspicuously in view from the four-track suburban line of the Harlem Division of the New York Central Railroad, it will be the greatest monument to the city's enterprise of all the Catskill water-works structures. Ten years or more will be required for its building.

Just north of the city line, in Yonkers, on a large, flat-topped hill, will be built Hill View reservoir,[1] an equalizing reservoir of approximately 900 million gallons capacity, to regulate automatically the differences between the steady flow in the aqueduct from Kensico reservoir and the fluctuating consumption in the city. This reservoir will be made by digging to an average depth of about twenty-five feet (maximum forty-four feet) over a large part of the hilltop, and using the earth thus obtained to build the sides of the reservoir higher. Its water surface will be 295 feet above tide, about 3000 feet long, and 1500 feet wide, and the water will be thirty-six and one half feet deep. A great concrete wall will divide the reservoir into two basins, and in this wall will be formed a by-pass aqueduct, so that water can flow to the city without entering the reservoir, whenever it may be necessary to clean or repair the reservoir. The reservoir will be lined with concrete and stone paving. There will also be a by-pass around Kensico reservoir. From the paths on top of the embankment of Hill View reservoir magnificent views will be had of New York, the adjoining towns, the Hudson with its Palisades, and the blue waters of Long Island Sound.

From Hill View reservoir an extension of the Catskill aqueduct will deliver the water into the distribution pipe systems in the streets of the five boroughs of Greater New York. The busy, congested streets, already underlaid with subways, water and gas pipes, sewers, electric conduits, and other structures, and bordered by tall buildings having one or more stories underground, cannot well accommodate the great number of large pipes that would be necessary to bring Catskill Mountain water from Hill View to the consumers. Furthermore, the annoyances and dangers incident to digging so many big trenches and laying the pipes in the streets would be quite intolerable. If this pipe-laying could be done quickly, the bother might be endured; but it would unavoid-

[1] London dedicated in the spring of 1909 Honor Oak reservoir, a covered masonry reservoir 824 by 587 feet, occupying, with its embankments, fourteen and a quarter acres. Hill View reservoir will be 3000 feet long and 1500 feet wide, and will occupy, with its embankments, 163 acres.

Ultimately Hill View reservoir will have a concrete, groined-arch roof, supported by pillars of concrete.

COMPLETING THE ARCH OF A SECTION OF CUT-AND-COVER
AQUEDUCT BY DEPOSITING CONCRETE ON MOLDS

Earth will be piled above the concrete and sodded.

ably spread over several years. Indeed, it might be said to be perennial, when repairs and replacements are taken into the reckoning, and a main distribution system of great pipes would be costly. Hence it is deemed wise to avoid as far as practicable the use of steel or iron pipes for the extension of the Catskill aqueduct for delivering water into the city.

Beneath the borough of the Bronx, Manhattan Island, and the edge of Long Island there is solid rock. Therefore a way of escape from many of the pipe troubles appears. Starting from Hill View reservoir, a great tunnel, like those under Ron-

SECTION OF CUT-AND-COVER AQUEDUCT
NEAR PEEKSKILL

This section was built in accordance with the
drawing shown on page 712.

dout and Wallkill valleys, is to be driven deep into the rock, hundreds of feet below the street surface, and lined with concrete. Thus, disturbance of the streets will be avoided, and a permanent conduit will be secured. Shafts through which tunneling operations are to be conducted will be spaced from 3000 to 5000 feet apart at points where little inconvenience will be caused. After construction, these shafts will be the connections between the tunnel and the main pipes of the street distribution system. This tunnel will pass beneath the Harlem and East rivers, but the crossing of the Narrows

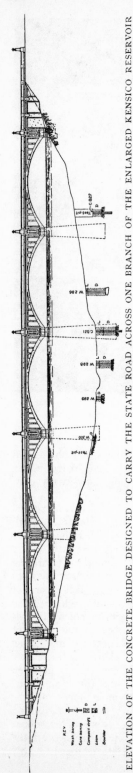

ELEVATION OF THE CONCRETE BRIDGE DESIGNED TO CARRY THE STATE ROAD ACROSS ONE BRANCH OF THE ENLARGED KENSICO RESERVOIR

to Staten Island will be made by heavy pipes, because the rock there is at too great a depth, and the quantity of water too small, to make a tunnel worth while. As a matter of precaution, two parallel pipes will be laid beneath the water some distance apart, and a reservoir to contain a reserve store of water will be built on high land on the island.

The fountains of Versailles are famous, and thousands make pilgrimages to see them in their beautiful settings when the water is turned on. Two fountains of far greater volume —scores of times as great—will be incidental features of the Catskill water-works. At times water in reservoirs, as in natural ponds, becomes impregnated with unpleasant tastes and odors, due mostly to very small organisms which, in a favorable combination of conditions, develop in unusual numbers. Although not deleterious, or not seriously so, the products of these organisms are disagreeable. Aëration has been proved by experience and experiment to be an efficacious and inexpensive means for removing these tastes and odors, and the most convenient form of aëration for the present purpose has been found to be nozles of a simple design arranged as fountain-jets. Of these great aëration fountains, one will be built where the water is drawn from Ashokan reservoir and the other at Kensico reservoir. In each fountain there will be upward of 2000 jets in symmetrical groups within a basin 500 feet long by 250 feet wide. By using different combinations of these nozle groups, various quantities of water, up to the full capacity of the aqueduct, can be aërated. With appropriate landscape settings, these gigantic fountains will be also a lasting source of enjoyment.

In order further to safeguard and improve the quality of the water, filtration is to be provided, and northwest of White Plains a site has been selected for a great sand-filter plant which will be of about twice the capacity of the largest plant now in existence.

When all the works are completed, the Catskill water-supply will be one of the safest in the world. Its gathering-grounds are topographically and geologically of unusual excellence and are sparsely populated. Wide marginal strips of forest and meadow will protect each impounding reservoir. These great artificial lakes will afford long storage for the gathered waters, giving opportunity for the beneficial action of sun, wind, and sedimentation. By these various means pollution will largely be prevented, and objectionable bacteria, tastes, and odors will be almost wholly removed or destroyed.

Goethe once wrote, "Dem Menschen ist ein Mensch noch immer lieber als ein Engel."[1] And so perchance the reader may be possessed of sufficient human interest to inquire by what marshaling of men's brains and brawn these great works are to be wrought. By appointment of Mayor George B. McClellan, under special legislation, John A. Bensel, a civil engineer, Charles N. Chadwick, a business man, and Charles A. Shaw, formerly president of the Hanover Fire Insurance Company, constitute the Board of Water Supply of the City of New York. They were chosen from lists of three names presented respectively by the Chamber of Commerce, the

[1] To mankind men are always dearer than angels.

VIEW OF THE SPILLWAY AND DAM OF THE PRESENT KENSICO RESERVOIR

In shadowy outline the proposed new dam has been drawn on the photograph. It will be on the average 400 feet north of the old dam and its parapet will stand as here shown 125 feet above the water-level seen in the photograph, a greater height of dam (about 175 feet) extending beneath this water-level. Steps will ascend both hillsides to the west. The present State road is shown in the foreground.

Manufacturers' Association of New York, and the Board of Fire Underwriters. Mr. Bensel is president of the board, and succeeded Mr. J. Edward Simmons, who resigned in January, 1908, and is now president of the Chamber of Commerce.

Two bureaus comprise the board's forces. In the Administration Bureau are the secretary, auditor, chief clerk, and purchasing agent, adjuster of claims, and chief of aqueduct patrolmen, each having a necessary corps of assistants, totaling for the bureau about 125 persons. Consulting Engineer John R. Freeman is the engineer adviser of the commissioners. At the head of the Engineering Bureau is Chief Engineer J. Waldo Smith. On his staff of consultants are Professor William H. Burr, Mr. Frederic P. Stearns, Allen Hazen, George W. Fuller, and a few other engineers and scientists of national and international reputation. Mr. Charles L. Harrison is Deputy Chief Engineer. Because of the geographical extent and the magnitude of

the works, the Engineering Bureau has been organized in four departments: the Headquarters Department, with Alfred D. Flinn, Department Engineer, has charge of preparing designs and specifications for the dams, aqueducts, and other structures; executive and civil-service matters, inspection of manufactured materials for construction, and preparation of real-estate maps and documents for all the departments, and in addition surveys and construction within the city limits. The Reservoir Department, with Carleton E. Davis at its head, is charged with all surveys and construction on the watersheds. Its chief work at present is the Ashokan reservoir, with its great dams and the headworks of the Catskill aqueduct. From the headworks to the divide of the Croton watershed sixty miles of Catskill aqueduct is under the care of the Northern Aqueduct Department, Robert Ridgway, Department Engineer, to whom falls the Hudson River crossing and the great siphons under the Rondout, Wallkill, and Moodna valleys. The remainder of Catskill aqueduct, with Kensico and Hill View reservoirs and the filters, falls to the Southern Aqueduct Department, with Merritt H. Smith as Department Engineer. The departments are divided into three or more divisions, which in turn are subdivided into several sections. Including engineers, inspectors, stenographers, clerks, laborers, and other assistants, the Engineering Bureau contains nearly 1000 persons.

For purposes of construction, the work of building the reservoirs and aqueducts has been divided into many contracts, ranging in expenditure involved from a few tens of thousands of dollars to several millions. In the busiest summer, when the majority of these contracts will be simultaneously in progress, the contractors' employees will probably reach a total of 15,000, and the expenditure will approximate $2,000,000 per month. This autumn of 1909 will doubtless see 10,000 men at work, for by October the major contracts for the aqueduct will have been let, excepting part of the line between Kensico and Hill View reservoirs. Hill View reservoir will probably also be under contract; the main dams of the Ashokan reservoir are already in progress. A re-estimate of the cost of the Catskill project made since many of the large contracts were awarded shows that the original estimate of 1905 was sufficient, an unusual and gratifying fact in engineering projects of great magnitude.

Readers distant from New York may ask: "Why go so far for water? Why not take water from the Hudson, a relatively short distance above the city, just as many inland communities do from rivers on which they are situated?" Simply because the Hudson is a tidal estuary as far as Troy, and if sufficient water to supply even half the needs of New York were withdrawn in extremely dry seasons, the river water would be too brackish for domestic consumption as far north as ten or fifteen miles above Poughkeepsie, or eighty miles in air line from the City Hall, New York. It is only six miles farther to the head of the Catskill aqueduct. To be certain of maintaining an adequate fresh-water flow, large compensating reservoirs would have to be built on the headwaters of the river in the Adirondack Mountains to store the surplus waters of

wet seasons for discharge into the upper tributaries of the river at a suitable rate in dry seasons. Furthermore, much unpurified sewage enters the river above any point at which the city's works could be located. Since the water would be taken at tide-level, it would have to be raised several hundred feet by powerful pumps in order to deliver it in the city under suitable pressure. Hence, to obtain Hudson water, purify it, and convey it to the city, extensive and very costly works would be necessary; and when all was done, the supply would be inferior in quality. It has been said that the nineteenth century discovered dirt—that is to say, the true nature of filth and its relation to human health. In the light of that discovery, communities are learning to prefer clean water, if such is available. Consequently the Board of Water Supply, with the concurrence of other city authorities and the approval of the State Water Supply Commission, very sensibly concluded that it was more economical and prudent to take some of the Hudson water from some of the lower tributaries in the Catskill Mountains before it became contaminated, and at an elevation from which it could flow by gravity to the city and be delivered at a level 165 feet above that at which the Croton water is delivered.

An abundance of clear, soft, pure, and wholesome water is the most fundamentally essential commodity for any great community. New York City has expended to date for the construction of existing water-works, exclusive of interest and maintenance, about $137,000,000, not taking into account the investments of private water companies, several of which still purvey to portions of some boroughs. Recent projects for additional supplies from the Catskill Mountains and Suffolk County will involve during the next half-century the expenditure of about $225,000,000, and will increase the safely available daily supply to two and a half times that now available, and provide bountifully for the city's needs as far in the future as can be reasonably foreseen. And the Croton, Ridgewood, Catskill, and Suffolk County systems will be permanent, even if long continuance of the city's remarkable growth should in the distant future lead to a demand for water in excess of the combined capacities of these sources.

New York's present population is 4,500,000, and her daily consumption of water for all purposes from works owned by the city is, as I have said, 125 gallons per person. At this rate, a year's supply would be a lake twenty miles long, three miles wide, and having an average depth of twenty-five feet. The ordinary summer flow of the Niagara River over the American Falls is now about 8000 million gallons daily, which is only fifteen times the stream consumed in New York. It must be remembered that Yonkers, Mount Vernon, New Rochelle, and even more distant suburbs may be added to the metropolis, or at least to the metropolitan water district, in the not far distant future, making yet greater demands upon the water-works systems built by the city, and many local sources of supply will have to be abandoned because of insufficiency and pollution. With all these vast figures representing demand and expenditure, it is comforting to find by computation that the average cost of all water for domestic, public, and manufacturing uses each day to each person will be less than one cent, including maintenance, interest on capital investment, and sinking fund.

Of the great works for collecting and conveying the Catskill Mountain water, many of the most difficult and interesting parts will be totally hidden from view after completion. Indeed, of the Catskill aqueduct scarcely anything will be visible except the long, neatly graded embankments over the cut-and-cover portions and the occasional buildings housing the gates and other devices for controlling and measuring the water. Most conspicuous will be the great reservoirs, with their huge dams of masonry and earth. Many of these visible structures will be comparatively inaccessible. It is fitting that these conspicuous structures should be made esthetically pleasing, not by elaborate and expensive ornamentation, but by simple and dignified treatment. Here the dominant civil engineer will be aided and guided by the architect and the landscape engineer.

Subterranean river! The mere name has always held a mysterious and romantic fascination. A reversed subterranean river is what the Board of Water Supply is creating. Instead of beginning with tiny streams in dark fissures of the rock or some surface rivulets which sink out of sight, this river will start at its large end from the Ashokan reservoir, an extensive artificial lake, and flow for scores of miles without change of volume, coming to the light only in the beautiful Kensico Lake and Hill View reservoir's huge bowl, whence it will ramify through the hundreds of miles of tunnels and pipes beneath the city streets, issuing finally through faucets and hydrants in thousands of jets to serve those who have bidden it flow thus in constraint. Several years of very active work must, however, elapse before Esopus water will reach the city.

The French Quarter of New York (1879)

SCRIBNER'S MONTHLY.

VOL. XIX.　　　NOVEMBER, 1879.　　　No. 1.

THE FRENCH QUARTER OF NEW YORK.

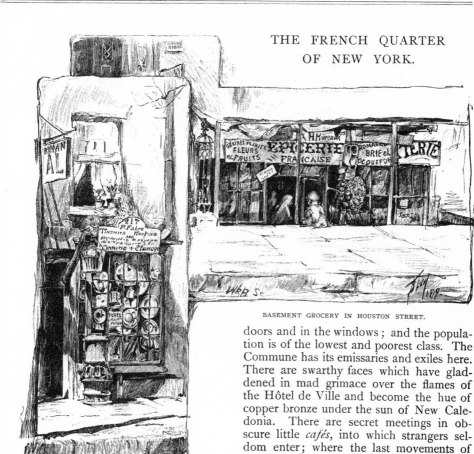

BASEMENT GROCERY IN HOUSTON STREET.

TIN-SHOP IN GREENE STREET.

I confess to finding no little pleasure in lazy explorations of the region that lies west of Broadway, south of Washington Square, and north of Grand street. This is the *Quartier Français* of New York. The commonplace, heterogeneous style of the buildings, and the unswerving rectangular course of the streets are American, but the people are nearly all French. French, too, is the language of the signs over the doors and in the windows; and the population is of the lowest and poorest class. The Commune has its emissaries and exiles here. There are swarthy faces which have gladdened in mad grimace over the flames of the Hôtel de Ville and become the hue of copper bronze under the sun of New Caledonia. There are secret meetings in obscure little *cafés*, into which strangers seldom enter; where the last movements of the Nihilists are discussed, and the would-be regicide is commended over draughts of absinthe and more innocent beer. Mademoiselle Berthe, with her little sisters, fabricates roses and violets out of muslin and wax in the high attics of the tenement houses. Madame Lange, with her arms and neck exposed, may be seen ironing snowy linen in front of an open window. Here is Triquet, *le charcutier ;* Roux, *le bottier ;* Malvaison, *le marchand de vin ;* Givac, *le charcutier Alsacien*, and innumerable basement restaurants, where dinner, *vin compris*, may be had for the veriest trifle.

135

The brazen faces of idle and vicious women stare out of the half-closed lattices at the passer-by, and there are shady alleys, unsafe to the stranger unattended; but the denizens of the quarter are mostly industrious, thrifty and honest. They earn little and spend less. They talk French, and retain many of the customs of the motherland. It is notable how insular and exclusive they are; for Broadway, with its assimilative influence, is the eastern limit of the district.

Turning down Grand street into Greene one day, with half a dozen steps my friend and I were transported in imagination to France. At No. 95 we descended into a basement, the specialties of which were indicated by the sign over the door: "Sabots et Galoches—Chaussons de Strasbourg," but the specialties were not immediately visible in an abundance of the varied merchandise of a general store. The small panes in the window were not made to admit an abundance of light, and that which would have come in was obstructed by the sample articles displayed along the sashes. The roof was low, the counter wide and the proportions

RESTAURANT DU GRAND VATEL IN BLEECKER STREET.

of the room were partly concealed by the long, loaded shelves. There was a perplexingly mixed quantity of small-wares, kindling wood, herrings, leather, groceries, and other preparations, the wrappers of which bore the marks of French exportation. Probably the neighbors had no alimentary want that could not have been satisfied out of the multiplicious stock. The delicate drab pots of *pâté de foie gras* were visible among much grosser articles of plebeian diet; but despite the array of wares and the sufficiency, no customer was there when we entered, and none came in while we remained. A bell attached to a spring over the door tinkled violently to announce us and subsided with a nervous quiver. All was so quiet and antique in the little store that we dreamily thought of Miss Hepzibah Pyncheon, and half expected to see her come out of the inner room, which was open to inspection through a windowed door. But instead of the tall, angular, forbidding shop-keeper of Salem, a courtly old lady issued forth in a white Normandy cap, and saluted us with a charmingly dignified courtesy: "*Bon jour, Messieurs.*" She was old and white-haired, but her manners and face had a lavender-like reminiscence of the queen of a long-ago *rosière*. That was a fancy of my friend's, who asked to see some *sabots*. "*Ah, oui !*" said Madame, and suspecting that customers so unusual as we were could only want them for private theatricals, or, perhaps, a fancy dress ball, she brought out of a recess a pair with red tops and a garniture of bright-headed nails. My friend shook his head; we wanted the real *sabots des paysans*, and she laughed at the idea as she showed us a pair of the coarse wooden shoes with stiff uppers that may be seen on the feet of the plodders in agricultural France. She told us that there was very little demand for them; that they cost a great deal to import, and that the lowest price at which she could sell them was seventy-five cents! They did not seem dear, and my friend, who is an artist, bought them in expectation of finding a future use for them in one of his pictures. "We make smaller ones to order," Madame told him. He replied he might require a pair, and when he inquired about the size and

he exhibited his hand, she laughed again, and perhaps thought of the *rosière* with whom he had associated her. "Ah, yes," she answered, "but ladies always wear them padded with cotton wool." We then asked her for one of her business cards. "It is quite unnecessary, *messieurs*," she remarked: "I am known all over the *quartier*." This was said with a delicious air of mock dignity and another profound courtesy. Through the glass-door separating it from the shop, we could see into the further room, where by the light of a strong lamp a man was putting together the parts of some delicate machinery; and this was Madame's husband, who adds to the profits of the store his earnings as a watch-maker. The humble scene was so essentially foreign that, having said "*Bon jour*" to Madame, we went into the street with more than three thousand miles of distance imagined between us and our actual situation. Just then, too, while the bell over the door was still audible in dying pulsations, a man brushed past us with a bristling crop of black hair, a coarse black mustache, small black eyes, and a sallow

LANDLADY OF THE "GRAND VATEL" AND HER PARROTS.

FRENCH BAKERY IN GREENE STREET.

complexion; he wore a blue blouse, and carried his hands in his pockets; this surely was Jacques, unalienated from the idle crowds around the wine-shops of Belleville.

While, as we have said, most of the people in the quarter are of the industrial or criminal classes, there is also a scattering of impecunious music-teachers and professors of languages, who maintain themselves with a frosty air of shabby-gentility on a very, very slender income. Literature and art have devotees in a peculiar condition of allied mental exaltation and bodily penury domiciled in the dismal-looking houses, over the doors of which a sign proclaims "Chambres Meublées et Pension,"—men whose lives have no fruition, and whose occupations do not embitter them by their futility, but are held in higher esteem than by much more successful votaries. After his unprofitable labor of the day, the poor professor repairs to a restaurant, where he sits down to a dinner of five or six courses; he bows profoundly to the landlady, who is cordial or severe in her recognition according to the items on the little slate which records her accounts; he waves his hand airily to some acquaintance, and leisurely begins his meal. He has *soupe aux croûtons, veau à la Marengo, pommes frites,* a small portion of *Gruyère* and a bottle of wine. He eats appreciatively after the manner of a *bon vivant;* he uses his napkin gently and frequently; he glances blandly at the surroundings; watching him, you would suppose the viands were the choicest of the season, exquisitely prepared, while in reality they are poor and unsubstantial stuff, the refuse, perhaps, of better restaurants. Having finished the edibles, he calls for a "gloria," that is, black coffee and cognac, and sipping this, he communes with his fancies which come and vanish in the blue waves of cigarette smoke. His aspect bespeaks perfect complacency—"Fate cannot harm me; I have dined to-day." It is the happy knack of his kind and country to extract the fullest enjoyment from the least considerable materials, and he returns to his attic, or seeks some *café* for the rest of the evening, in a mood of blissful contentment.

It is in the restaurants and *cafés* of the region that we learn the frugality of the denizens. Here in Bleecker street, at the corner of an intersecting thoroughfare, is the " Restaurant du Grand Vatel," named after the celebrated and heroic cook of Louis the Fourteenth, who, utterly chagrined at the failure of a certain fish to arrive in time for one of his dinners, ended his life by running a sword through his body. The sign of this restaurant indicates an exceedingly moderate tariff, thus: *Tous les plats*, eight cents; *plats extra variés; café supérieur*, three cents, and *café au lait*, five cents; but the *menu* is such a marvel that it is worth reproducing. A dish of soup and a plate of beef and bread are ten cents; *soupe aux croûtons*, that is, with toasted crusts, costs five cents; *bœuf, legumes*, ten cents; *veau à la Marengo*, twelve cents; *mouton à la Ravi-gotte*, ten cents; *ragout de moutons aux pommes*, eight cents; *bœuf braisé aux oignons*, ten cents; *macaroni au gratin*, six cents; *celeri salade*, six cents; *compote de pommes*, four cents; *fromage Neufchâtel*, three cents; *Limbourg*, four cents, and *Gruyère* three cents. Bread is one cent extra. Think how far fifty cents will go in so reasonable an establishment! The professor's dinner, wine included, costs him the extravagant sum of forty cents, and with five cents added for a roll and a cup of coffee in the morning, that sum covers his daily expenditure for food.

The floor is sanded, and the little tables are covered with oil-cloth, each having a pewter cruet in the center. A placard flutters from the wall, announcing a grand festival, banquet, ball and artistic tombola in celebration of the eighth anniversary of the bloody revolution of March 18th, 1871, under the auspices of the " Société des Réfugiés de la Commune,"—"Family tickets, twenty-five cents; hat-room checks, ten cents "—from which we gather that the " Restaurant du Grand Vatel " has some queer patrons. The landlady sits behind a little desk in a corner. She is a woman of enormous girth, with short petticoats which reveal her thick, white woolen socks; her complexion is dark, her eyes are black and deep, and large golden rings dangle from her ears. A little man with red hair, and loose, slovenly slippers, who shuffles untidily about, is Leroy, *le propriétaire*. Two revolutionary parrots are perched over Madame's head, and break the silence by their horrid cries. "*Tranquille !*" cries she, tapping them with a cane, and they remain quiet for a few minutes, to resume their shrieks until she again admonishes them. No customers are present, and the *cuisinier* is staring idly out of the window. His hands and arms are very dirty, but his head is crowned by a *toque* of unsurpassable whiteness. The *garçon* also is unoccupied, and stares wonderingly at my friend and me, who are trying a six-cent dish of *macaroni au gratin*, which proves to be not altogether unpalatable. By and by a faded little gentleman enters, whom we at once recognize as one of those incommunicable acquaint-

TAVERNE ALSACIENNE, INSIDE AND OUT.

ances that become familiar to us in the passing throngs of a great city—we see them day after day and year after year, until every peculiarity of their features is

fitting as exactly as an epidermis; a silk hat with an obsolete flat brim, and a pair of prunellos; conspicuously pinned to the lapel of his coat were the ribbon and silver

MAKING ARTIFICIAL LEAVES.

impressed upon our memory; we see them growing older and grayer, with the fluctuations of fortune manifest in the shabbiness or fashionableness of their attire; but we never *know* them, and always pass with a greeting that is mute. This little gentleman who enters the "Restaurant du Grand Vatel,"—how many years is it since we first saw him? Long as the time is, we do not detect the least change in him. What he was, strolling out of the *quartier* into the leafy quiet of Washington Square one morning in spring six years ago, he is still. There is a degree of imperishability about him. We were struck then by the elasticity of his diminutive but graceful figure, his military bearing, and the superlative neatness of his dress. He wore a suit of dark blue cloth, the double-breasted frock coat

cross of some foreign order; the cloth was thread-bare, the hat no longer glossy, and the boots were by no means water-proof; he walked erect and with a measured tread and his black mustache was fastidiously curled. In every particular he is unaltered to-day; his clothing shows precisely the same degree of wear; his step is as buoyant, his face as fresh, and his mustache as black as ever. If his life had been suspended immediately after our first meeting, and his garments packed in camphor, secure from moth and sunshine, neither animation nor garments being resumed until now, the restoration could not have shown completer immutability. The genteel poverty of his dress and the dignity of his manners are combined with a placid reserve and an automatic precision of movement. "He is probably an old soldier and adherent of the Empire," said my friend, " and above a soldier a beau : punctilious in points of honor and Quixotically exalted in ideas. Truly, this is a pitiable exile for him. I can see a yearning for Paris and his old-time haunts in his eyes, but mixed with the bitterness of his fate is a sweet resignation."

The door opened, and a half-intoxicated, blear-eyed fellow entered with a great noise. Leroy tried to put him out, but he became effusively affectionate. "A good fellow," said the proprietor to us, " but he received a fortune from France a month ago and has been drunk ever since." Extremes meet at the " Restaurant du Grand Vatel." The poor professor and the gentlemanly old soldier set their " glorias" on the same benches with sottish artisans to whom labor is a *dernier ressort.*

At the " Taverne Alsacienne " in Greene street, a lower and more vicious class is to be seen. We enter a gloomy basement with an impoverished bar at one side and a much-worn billiard table at the end. It matters not what the hour is, whether it be in the forenoon, afternoon, or past midnight. A circle of men is gathered around the tables absorbed in piquet, écarté or vingt-et-un. Most of them are without coats, and the shabbiness of their other garments is lit up by a brilliant red bandanna kerchief or a crimson overshirt. Keen glances are shot at us; for the tavern has a certain *clientèle* outside of which it has few customers, and suspicion is rife at our invasion. A stranger in the " Taverne Alsacienne " is very likely to be a spy or a detective, and the *habitués* are sensitive under inspection. They are drinking wine, vermouth, and greenish-opaline draughts of absinthe. Staggering in unnerved and stupefied from the previous night's debauch, they show few signs of vitality until four or five glasses of the absinthe have been drunk, and then they awaken; their eyes brighten and their tongues are loosened—the routine of play, smoke and alcohol is resumed.

Besides the ordinary trades—the butcher's, the baker's, the grocer's, and the carpenter's —which are supported by all communities, and which in the French quarter have national representatives, the industries of the colony are limited, with a few exceptions, to artificial flower-making, leaf-making and feather-dyeing. In the attics of the tenement houses entire families are found engaged in one of these occupations. The materials are supplied by the large manu-

facturing firms, and out of muslin and wire roses, lilies and daisies grow in cheap profusion for the unfashionable trade. Sometimes one woman hires a number of children, paying each fifty cents a week, and the little hands are employed on the simplest details. Again, Mademoiselle Julie and her sister, Marie, work all alone in their " sky-parlor," and manage to live comfortably and decently on very small earnings, indeed. Embroidery is also largely engaged in, giving employment to both men and women; and sweetmeats are manufactured which rival in appearance the most appetizing imported bon-bons. One little shop is kept by an ingenious person, who devotes himself to repairing damaged bric-à-brac and art treasures; he promises to renew pictures blistered by fire, to put together a broken statuette so that not a trace of the operation can be seen, or to restore a precious meerschaum suffering from an aggravated fracture. All the occupations of the quarter are " light," requiring taste and adroitness rather than physical strength. Among others in the colony are large numbers of skilled artisans, who are brought from France for a term of years by such firms as Tiffany's, and who are handsomely paid.

It is not easy to form an exact estimate of the whole number of French in the city. We had been informed that it was about twenty thousand, and we visited the shabby little consular office in Bowling Green to verify the statement. But the consular agents did not know; the archives of a consular office are usually indeterminate or unavailable. M. Munier, editor of the " Courier des États Unis," fixed upon twenty-four thousand as the probable number, curiously divided by him as follows: about eight thousand permanent residents of the city, who have made it their final home ; about eight thousand who, like the imported workmen of Tiffany's, have come here to stay a period of from five to ten years, and eight thousand who are here " prospecting," and do not usually remain more than two or three years. The names of eight thousand are in the city directory. At least one-half of the whole number do not speak English fluently, or at all among themselves, and about one-third are ignorant of the language. Neither the proprietor of the " Restaurant du Grand Vatel," nor he of the " Taverne Alsacienne," nor the polite old dame who sells *sabots*, can talk except in their native tongue. But a school for teaching English to French adults has been opened by the Board of Education, the female department in Marion street, and the male department in West Thirteenth street; these are well filled. There are four homes, and giving money to others or finding employment for them. Two daily newspapers are published in the French language, the largest of which is the "Courier," a

THE COOK OF THE GRAND VATEL.

French churches in the city,—one Roman Catholic and three Protestant,—and at least twenty French benevolent societies, one of which, the "Société Culinaire Philanthropique," is very wealthy. The "Société de Bienfaisance" fills a position of varied usefulness in helping the sick and penniless, sending the old and infirm to their former member of the Associated Press. Many years ago, the late James Gordon Bennett described its proprietors as "the three starving Frenchmen," but its circulation has so increased that it is now a very valuable property.

There are gaps in the quarter which are filled by Americans, Germans and Italians.

Even the berated Asiatic has opened his laundry next door to that of Madame Lange—he copper-colored, reticent, assiduous; she florid, voluble and coquettish. The lowest element in the quarter is American; and the invasion is continuous, taking away the national distinctiveness. By and by there will be no French Quarter, and we shall seek in vain for a blue blouse, the " Maison au Carreau Cassé," the " Rendezvous des Zouaves," or the " Restaurant 'du Grand Vatel."

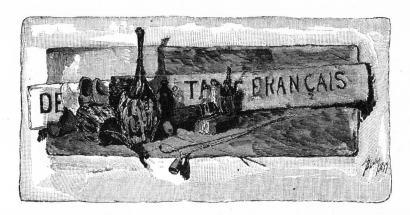

Pratt Institute
(1893)

THE PRATT INSTITUTE.

WITH PICTURES BY LOUIS LOEB.

WELVE students in its art department, five years ago, was the germ from which has sprung the Pratt Institute in Brooklyn, with its aggregate to-day of nearly four thousand students. Variety in its plan has come with development, but the conception of its founder underlies all its many lines of educational work, and binds them into unity. The Institute is not a heterogeneous grouping of departments. It is a collection of schools, each complete in itself, but all auxiliary the one to the other in the common task of helping man to help himself.

If the reader were being personally conducted through the Institute, he would not in all probability be taken first to the department of industrial and fine arts, though there are reasons why I should take him there at once; for there was the nucleus about which the other schools of the Institute have been gathered, and it is in a sense the central department of the Institute, being the one to which other departments look for the instruction of their pupils in graphic expression.

If, instead of taking the elevator, we had walked up the stairway, we should have found the art department already stretching out its hand to us. All the way from the basement to the top floor of the building are neatly framed photographs arranged in chronological order, and showing the historical development of architecture, painting, and sculpture. Besides material of this sort in the class-rooms and studios, the museum and library of the Institute contain much of interest to art students.

If our visit is made during the day, most of the students whom we see are those who have come for thorough and exhaustive training in art-teaching, or in some branch of industry or of fine art. Such students work five days of the week, both morning and afternoon. Then there are those employed in some trade or art during the day, who wish to gain such knowledge as will improve their prospects for advancement in their line of occupation. Such students work three evenings of the week. So popular are these evening classes that they fill eleven large studios. The students come year after year to perfect themselves in architectural drawing, in mechanical drawing, in drawing from the cast and from life, or in clay-modeling and wood-carving. A decidedly smaller number comprises those so situated that they cannot study during the whole day, but come for instruction in the afternoon three times a week.

When these students, with their varied aims, have filled the rooms, the scene is most attractive. Perhaps the chief attraction to the ordinary visitor is that all seem to be striving after and making some tangible attainment. The thoughtful onlooker sees rather, in the very atmosphere of such work, a silent culture which may only be dimly hinted at by the thing attained; and it is true that the endeavor in the art and other departments of the Institute is to make the work not only practical but educative. Nevertheless, as we look at this group drawing from casts of the antique, yonder one working from life, this from the costumed figure, and yet others painting still-life groups in oil and water-color,— students, in short, doing all phases of fine-art work,— the practical eye can see that most excellent results attest the value of the instruction, and the talent of many of the students. There seems to be something in the method here which stimulates originality in the student, and, while checking wrong tendencies, allows the individuality of the pupil to come out in his work. One thing in the policy of the school deserves mention. Any visitors acquainted with art instruction would notice the large number of teachers. Not only are there many instructors, but they are employed for a long enough time during the week to enable them to give the student personal criticism and aid.

Among the students of fine art, some of these whom one sees drawing from the cast or working in water-color may have as their aim industrial art. The principle kept constantly in view is *that efficient special training must rest upon sufficient general training in art.* In the industrial-art studios the good results of this intelligent policy are manifest in the specimens of finished work, and in much that is unfinished. Here are designs for wall-paper, carpets, book-covers, knife-handles, brass-work, fine work in silver and gold, all giving evidence of a training artistic, educative, and practical. Students are not allowed to work with the idea of selling everything they make, but the advanced class are permitted, after submitting designs to the instructors, to sell what they can find a market for. One thousand dollars' worth of designs was sold by the students last year.

Leaving the industrial-design studios, we come to a room where numerous specimens of work indicate very good results in wood-carving. In addition to instruction in the use and care of tools, and in technical methods in wood-carving, the student is required in the two-year course to practise free-hand drawing, design, clay-modeling, and to study the principles of construction. Across the hall from this room is the clay-modeling studio, where work is done both from the cast and from life. Here are gods and goddesses, and a group of earnest young women putting their best thought for the time being into clay. These are students of the normal art course. Most of them have had much experience as teachers in public and private schools, or have been engaged in various lines of art work. No other work of the art department is more vitally important than the training of competent teachers of art. The first graduate of the course went out in 1890, yet already sixty-one are employed in different parts of the country. Some are supervisors of drawing in large cities, others are teachers of drawing in normal schools and in high schools, and directly or indirectly are influencing the work of nearly 5000 teachers and of more than 245,000 students.

Next door to the clay-modeling studios are the architectural- and mechanical-drawing rooms. The aim of the instruction here is to turn out scientific, broadly trained draftsmen. The course of two years in each subject seems to be most carefully arranged with a view to much more intelligent and thorough instruction than the ordinary draftsman gets. These young men now working at the drawing-tables at some problem in construction or in design and composition, we may see later in the shops of the department of science and technology. Here we have one of many instances of the essential oneness of the Institute, the helpful reciprocity active between the different departments. It is considered that a broadly trained architectural draftsman should become familiarly acquainted with building methods. In the shops he is given practice in joinery, framing, and details of house-building, and studies the processes and materials employed in masonry, plastering, plumbing, and house-painting. In the mechanical-drawing course the student goes to the shop to learn joinery, turning, molding, forging, and machine-shop work. Both architectural- and mechanical-drawing students are given a course of experiment in the testing laboratories. Besides work in instrumental drawing, they are also required to practise free-hand and instrumental perspective, pen and pencil sketching, design, color,

and clay-modeling. That so much work in fine art should be made an organic part of the curriculum in the architectural-drawing course is certainly a favorable omen. It would seem natural enough that those who have so much to do with the antipodes of the esthetic as mechanical draftsmen, should need such training; but this fact has not been so generally recognized as to mar one's pleasure at seeing what is being done here in fine art in the mechanical-drawing course.

The art hall of the department, a large studio on the sixth floor, has top and side lights, and contains a conveniently arranged and most carefully selected collection of photographs illustrative of all phases of art. Beneath it are the art-needlework rooms, where the student is taught not only all kinds of embroidery, but is instructed in the making of designs. Lady visitors should not go to this room first, for the exquisite examples of ecclesiastical embroidery, tapestry, and banners, besides a thousand and one articles of household use in delicate and artistic designs and harmonies of coloring, will tempt them to stay too long.

Art-needlework suggests a natural transition to the department of domestic art, which gives morning, afternoon, and evening instruction in sewing, dressmaking, millinery, and physical culture to over twelve hundred students. Without any precedent in this country,—it might almost be said in the world,—the courses of instruction have been systematically graded, so as not only to insure a thorough knowledge of the subject, but to impress upon the pupil the value of order, accuracy, and economy. Besides instruction in methods and manipulation, the courses are designed to cultivate the pupil's taste. She is constantly led to consider the style of the making and coloring of hats and dresses from an artistic and hygienic standpoint. The instruction is broadened also by talks given in the class-room on the history and manufacture of materials and textiles used, and upon colors and form. Perhaps we shall hear the director of the department giving one of these talks as we walk through the pleasant, well-lighted rooms. If so, we shall listen to the doctrine that the desired end of the training given here is true economy of time, labor, and money in the attainment of beauty; and that this end may be more easily gained by studying the laws of art and nature, and trying to apply them to each article of dress or of household decoration. This is to be accomplished by putting much thought and some money into one really durable and beautiful thing in harmony with its use and surroundings, even though wilful fashion fly off at a tangent. This strikes a man as good orthodox reasoning; whether it is too far beyond the age to be more than a dream remains to be seen. It is also argued by those who have shaped these courses that physical culture is essential in teaching the principles of artistic dress, since a well-proportioned body is necessary to symmetry of effect in dress. There is, therefore, a course in callisthenics, which students are encouraged to take. A course in drawing is given under the direction of the department of industrial and fine arts, beginning with pencil practice, and including study of drapery, drawing of waists and gowns, practice in use of color, problems of design, and study of the human form.

All of this suggests the danger of making these courses too esthetic to help the very classes most in need of help. But there is a great elasticity about the general plan of the department. There are one-year courses for training professional dressmakers and milliners; there are evening courses for those already engaged in work who wish a broader theoretical knowledge; and there are classes to which those may come who desire to learn millinery and dressmaking for household purposes. It seems to me that nothing could be more democratic than the ideal of the Pratt Institute. Here are girls who have known the pinch of want taking up the work for a trade. Near by is a girl who comes from a household where are many children, and she is acquiring the knowledge for use in helping to clothe younger brothers and sisters. Side by side with these may be found the society girl, who is going into the thing for fun, but soon finds it no joke; the wealthy girl, who is managing a mission sewing-room; and in a room near by are the sweetest imaginable little seamstresses from six to twelve years of age. It is every one according to her desire here. There is an opportunity for broad and exhaustive training, or for more special instruction.

From the rooms of the domestic-art division a short trip in the elevator brings one to the kitchens of the domestic-science division. Here is a most unique exemplification of the adage, "Cleanliness is next to godliness." Pure air and plenty of it, limpid sunlight, spotless floors, tables, and cooking-apparatus — all this is most interesting and invigorating to one who is haunted with the ghosts of unforgotten boarding-house dinners. These cases of food products, and of the chemical constituents of food; the charts showing what the food must supply to the human body; the models of different cuts of meat — all these facilities for instruction are only a hint of what is attempted in the kitchens, lecture-rooms, and laboratories. Even a carefully prepared exhibit can but inadequately suggest an educational curriculum. In a word, it is the train-

ing of women in the sciences underlying the right administration of the house, and in the arts based upon those sciences.

Here is the normal class in domestic science taking a lesson in practical cooking; but with these students the knack of the culinary art is a subordinate accomplishment. As they are to be teachers, their time is chiefly employed in studying the science at the basis of the theory, and the theory underlying the practice. It is a liberal course which they are pursuing, including German, the physical sciences, biology, psychology, household economics, and applied chemistry. All instruction is by lectures, quiz, and laboratory practice. Besides these as theory, they are given practice in cookery, and in laundry work. It seems at first a far call from German to laundry work. But there is close logical sequence throughout the curriculum. The same students now studying the proportion of ingredients, effect of heat upon food, or engaged in the creation of some toothsome dish, may in an hour be at the Hoagland laboratory studying bacteriology.

Besides the classes in cooking open to normal students, there are a Saturday-morning class for school-girls, a housekeepers' class, and a course for physicians and nurses. In the above the instruction emphasizes theory. There are other morning classes, and also classes in the evening where cooking is studied with particular reference to practice.

Here is an interesting class in hygiene and home nursing. It is not intended to compete with the hospitals in the training of nurses, but to give the mothers and sisters of our households instruction that will fit them to meet emergencies coolly and effectively, and will make them more efficient in the care of the sick. The boy on the floor has just been drowned (hypothetically), and the physician is giving the class an object-lesson in the treatment of such cases. Robust as the patient looks, he is a youth of many maladies. Ever since the year began the class have been putting his broken arms and legs into splints, bandaging his contused head, poulticing him, and, in brief, doing all in their power to make him comfortable.

The laundry course rather astonishes one with its revelation of the variety of processes, and the range from coarseness to exceeding delicacy of material dealt with. We who have seen our hard-earned belongings go to the tub — to return, alas! in how altered a condition — breathe a prayer that many such courses may send out their influence through the kitchens and laundries of the land.

If one is a privileged guest at the Institute, he can speak from the fullness of appetite

ENGRAVED BY A. E. ANDERSON.

A CORNER IN THE LAUNDRY — DEPARTMENT OF DOMESTIC SCIENCE.

awakened and satisfied by the delightful cooking turned out by its classes. So popular are they that the number in each is limited. The latest class organized is a camping-class of ladies and gentlemen, the pioneers, it is to be hoped, of a general movement toward reformation in the camp kitchen.

Both of these departments — that of domestic art and that of domestic science — are really divisions of one great department giving instruction to nearly two thousand pupils. While we are yet in the hallway of this department, making our way toward other scenes, we come suddenly upon the myriad click of type-writers. We are all so familiar with the sound and sight that it is hard to realize that the invention is as modern as it is. In this room, an outpost of the department of commerce, a multitude of young girls are learning type-writing as a means of livelihood, or are acquiring the art as a part of their training as amanuenses. The department gives thorough training, morning,

"THE DAILY NEWS CO."

afternoon, and evening, in type-writing, phonography, bookkeeping, penmanship, English, Spanish, and arithmetic. Hundreds of young men and women are making a living by type-writing and phonography — arts which, added to a good education, make the amanuensis. Yet it was not earlier than 1872 that Mr. Cooper was persuaded to allow a class in phonography to be organized, and thus to open the field of stenography to the thousands young men and women who are now occupying it.

The public has become accustomed to thinking of business colleges as not worthy of serious thought. It is reassuring to find that the policy here is conservative, and that students are not admitted to any of the classes without such examination as will prove sufficient intelligence and education.

The development of the school is to be along the broad lines laid down by Sir Philip Magnus, who, after showing the advantage Germany has reaped from her superior schools for commercial training, says: "The study of

BALLOTING.

modern languages and of commercial geography, including the technology of merchandise, and the elements of science underlying it, constitute the groundwork of commercial education." Next year will see the beginning of a two-year commercial course, which will offer a broader training in commerce than has heretofore been attainable in any business college. The *raison d'être* of this course is suggested in the following quotation: "Boys are, as a rule, so anxious to leave school and obtain employment that they think they cannot afford the time necessary to acquire a high-school education, and devote a year or two in addition to commercial studies. The remedy for this is the establishment of schools to take the grammar-school graduate and give him a two- or three-year course in combined high-school and commercial work." The curriculum of the regular course will include history; commercial, physical, and industrial

geography; commercial law; mechanical drawing, and civics; English, political economy, and bookkeeping, or phonography and type-writing.

Crossing an iron-covered bridge from the department of commerce, we are in the high-school building. Perhaps we shall have a more vivid and lasting impression of the system of instruction in the high school, and of the nature of its curriculum, if we imagine ourselves to be spending a school-day with the classes. First, we shall meet with the whole school at chapel. Here, after the devotional exercises, the daily newspaper of the school is read. It is called the "Pratt Institute Daily News," and has a managing editor (one of the teachers) and twelve assistant editors, who also hold every other office on a newspaper from artist to printer's devil. Blackboards stretching around three sides of the assembly-room are filled each morning with important news,

LOUIS·LOEB·93·

STILL-LIFE CLASS — THE AQUARELLISTES.

ENGRAVED BY F. H. WELLINGTON.

each editor being answerable for the news he places upon his blackboard. Maps and pictures are drawn to illustrate important events. Biographies are accompanied by portraits. The exercise lasts only twenty minutes, and doubtless has its value not only in keeping teachers and students up to date, but in its educative discipline. Other exercises of the school, in-

ART DEPARTMENT—COSTUME CLASS, ART HALL.

tended to be supplementary to the study of civics and a training in practical politics, are campaign speaking, caucus, joint session of House and Senate, balloting, and registration.

The classes now disperse to their class-rooms, and we find ourselves in a cheerful class-room attending a recitation in English. The hour is passed in very practical composition work. Criticism on the part of students and teachers is to the point, and the conduct

·LOUIS·LOEB·93·

ENGRAVED BY PETER AITKEN.

DEPARTMENT OF SCIENCE AND TECHNOLOGY—FRESCO CLASS: DESIGNING AND EXECUTING.

of the recitation suggests not only intelligent preparation, but good class-room method. Written exercises are handed in, perhaps in the second stage of evolution, bearing the teacher's annotation and the students' corrections. If some magic rug could transport us to the literature-class up-stairs, we should find drawing hand in hand with literature study. At the blackboard are students making rapid sketches of costumes, of persons, and of buildings illustrative of the text. This is interesting as an experiment, and the students seem attentive. One of the greatest problems in school work is to give literature study its weight as an element of the first importance in the curriculum. Any method or methods which cultivate in the student not only interest but taste in literature are legitimate. Such is the aim in the use of the devices I have mentioned, and in a variety of others. The school is evidently not in the well-worn ruts. Now the class goes to a botanical class-room, where there are good microscopes in number sufficient for individual use. Here we come at once upon one tendency in all the work of the school. In literature, language, and science the laboratory method is employed. Another flight, and we find ourselves in the history class, where the blackboard illustration is in the form of graphic charts invented by the students, and showing the chronology and philosophy of the subjects as they understand these. Map-drawing is a daily class-room exercise.

In mathematics and in the sciences, as well

155

DEPARTMENT OF DOMESTIC SCIENCE — CHEMISTRY.

as in the studies mentioned above, the student is, by a variety of methods and by judicious questioning, thrown upon his own resources. His training is intended to be for increase in power, whether that comes through acquisition or through reasoning, or through both. It is not that so much ground shall be traversed, that such and such examinations shall be passed, but that the student shall grasp principles first, facts second, and learn to generalize and correlate. Such is, I am informed, the ideal striven after by the school. A long step in the right direction is a college preparatory class, supplementary to the regular course. This obviates the necessity of unduly pushing pupils in the regular course. From the botany-room the class is, after an hour, dismissed to the drawing-room, where we find them drawing from the cast. After this exercise and a recess for lunch, the boys go to the shops of the department of science and technology, where for an hour and a half they are engaged in pattern-making. The girls spend the same length of time in sewing in the department of domestic art and science. If we had cast in our fortunes with the second-year class, we should have gone with them to the physical lecture-room and laboratory for their science. But in each year of the course drawing and manual work are an organic part

of the curriculum. It is this feature which chiefly challenges public attention. Unfortunately, it is a feature which has given rise to much misapprehension, even among intelligent persons. As we go down to the shops with these boys, and watch them for the time being transformed into Vulcans at the forge, or learning by practice the secrets of founding and tin-smithing, or intent upon the making of a close joint in the carpentry shops, the question naturally comes, What part does all this play in general training? The theory is that while literature cultivates esthetically and ethically, while science stimulates observation, while mathematics trains the reasoning powers, manual training disciplines and strengthens the will.

In the third story of the high-school building is a room which reminds me that a kindergarten department has lately been organized. The free kindergarten, in which the students of the kindergarten training-class have living contact with the work which is to be their profession, is in another building. Perhaps we can imagine them there learning the secret of helpful fellowship with child life. The pupils of the regular kindergarten training course of two years are brought much under the influence of the art department, that they may drink in as

FORGE SHOP — FINISHING THE GATE.

ENGRAVED BY C. W. CHADWICK.

much of the artistic atmosphere as possible. It helps them to appreciate the beautiful through the pencil, and to gain in power of expression. The whole course is carefully arranged so as to be an efficient training for kindergarten work, founded upon a sound educational basis and a true spiritual insight. The psychology taught is that of Froebel, as found in his " Mutter und Koselieder." Besides the training-class, classes of young mothers have been formed to study the same book. Here they can learn what the proper care of children means, can gain insight into child nature, and can see how the faculties of every child may be quickened and directed.

Directions are given for introducing into the nursery the kindergarten materials in the logical order of Froebel.

We now leave the high school, going through the great central office of the building. Here are the secretary's rooms, and the offices of the Thrift, a savings-bank and building-loan association for the encouragement of habits of thrift. Amounts as low as five cents are taken on deposit. Here also is the editorial sanctum of the " Pratt Institute Monthly."

On the opposite side of the outer hall is an assembly-room used for public lectures, given as supplementary to the work of the various departments. Here also meets the choral society of the music department of Pratt Institute. If a stranger to the tonic sol-fa system should happen in when the choral society is practising, he would see much to astonish him in the feats of the singers in sight and sound reading, and in the rendering of the most difficult and classic music. Besides the advantages of the choral society for the practice and rendering of the best compositions, the music department has thoroughly organized courses. There is a

157

course for the training of teachers and supervisors of music, which has already graduated one class of successful teachers. A lecture course in music is open to all pupils. There is a class in kindergarten color-music, and a juvenile course held after school hours. Tonic sol-fa is the system in vogue, and the inspiring motive of the school's work is to bring all that good music means of esthetic and ethical influence within reach of classes now too much excluded from such advantages.

I have reserved one of the most interesting sights of the Institute until now. We are in the technical museum, which contains so many interesting things that the visitor is usually undecided what to look at first. In fact, the collection, though it contains much to interest the casual visitor, is intended mainly for the students. It illustrates the changes through which the native product passes in the process of manufacture. Here we see the lump of clay at one extreme, the graceful and most exquisitely artistic vase at the other. With this idea kept prominently in mind, much may be learned in a few hours here that many·hours in a library could not so clearly reveal. The varied usefulness of such a museum in any educational institution and community at once suggests itself.

Stepping into the elevator, we drop like a plummet to the first floor, and, turning to the right, are in the reading-room of the library, in a realm of silence, "far from the madding crowd." The large reference library back of the main reading-room has gained a reputation more than local. As we talk with the well·educated attendants, who are here on duty all day long, and at night when the library is open, we can guess the reason for the growing reputation of this part of the library. In these days time is as precious to the library investigator as to the business man, and any institution which meets him half-way to help him in his work earns his sincerest gratitude.

Retracing our way from the reading-room, whose two hundred periodicals are arranged very conveniently for use, we come into the free circulating library. Here are all the usual facilities to be found in circulating libraries, such as well-arranged and accessible catalogues, and, last but not least, intelligent and most obliging attendants. Even the poor woman who cannot remember the name of the book she wants, but knows it had red covers and was oblong, is sent away happy, if possible. Upon the walls are bulletined the resources of the library as those bear upon topics of present interest. Discussions growing out of the New Orleans incident, a festival such as Arbor or Memorial Day, the death of celebrated men, such as Spurgeon or ex-President Hayes—all such events

and occasions find there bulletin-boards covered with library references. Just at present we should find a great deal cognate to the World's Fair. The general public has free use of the books in the library, and teachers and students have special privileges. A course of talks on the use of reference-books is given chiefly for their benefit. The library has grown from 1000 volumes in 1888 to 40,000 at present, and is growing at the rate of five to six thousand volumes a year. Last year it had a circulation of 170,000 volumes. In some respects this library is unique. It differs from most circulating libraries in being connected with an educational institution, and from most school and college libraries in having the free and public circulating features. A branch library in Williamsburgh has a stock of 2000 volumes, and a yearly circulation of 28,000. Some of those whom we see busy now at the library shelves are members of the class in cataloguing and library methods, which attempts to train librarians for the smaller libraries. The course includes English and American literature and English composition. The attendance is good, and graduates are doing satisfactory work in desirable positions.

Descending one flight of stairs from the library to the basement, and walking through the large Institute restaurant, we come out upon a spacious quadrangular court. Crossing this diagonally, we enter the department of science and technology. This department shares with the department of domestic art and science the direction of the high-school students in manual work, and in addition furnishes their instruction in mathematics and science. Its other field is the instruction in scientific and technical subjects, and in the principal mechanical trades, of classes quite distinct from the high school.

We find the physical and chemical laboratories of the department on the fourth floor of its building. At night these are full of students, whose earnestness is in their faces, and is patent in the fact that after a hard day's work they are here at all. Such classes are peculiarly inspiring to the teacher, and I sometimes think that because of the receptiveness of the pupil and its reflex influence on the teacher more is accomplished in the same time than in ordinary day-classes. In both physics and chemistry these students are afforded all the facilities of laboratories which have been developed to an exceptional degree of efficiency. Individual experimentation is specially provided for and insisted on. The courses of study have been arranged with extraordinary care to secure the best results in acquisition and in training within the time allowed for each course. In physics the subjects emphasized are mechanics and heat, because of their practical bearing. The laboratory work follows the lecture, and gives the student opportunity to verify by actual experiment what he has learned in the lecture. The course in chemistry extends through three years, and includes a large amount of laboratory work. The elements and inorganic compounds, and their characteristic reactions, are studied in the first year. A thorough course in qualitative analysis runs through the second year, followed in the third year by practice in quantitative analysis and assaying. Every effort is made to give the student an insight into the conditions of actual practice. Many of the students in these classes are already engaged in manufacturing establishments where a knowledge of chemistry is necessary. The other scientific subjects taught in the evening are algebra and geometry. Care is taken to present the subjects simply, and as a direct preparation for the course in technology.

Under technology, the instruction is on the subjects of electrical construction, steam-engine, strength of materials, and machine-design. These classes reach young men already engaged in some technical pursuit, but in need of broader scientific knowledge. The marvelous extension of the application of electricity has made an imperative demand for such courses in electrical construction as this department offers. In all the technical subjects the instruction is by lectures, reinforced by laboratory practice. Even a visitor void of all mechanical trend finds something attractive in the sight of these young men computing the efficiency of an engine in the steam laboratory, or, in the testing laboratories, testing the strength of metal wires, or of material used in construction. And whatever impression one gets is deepened by the reflection that this is not play, but work which is both educative and of direct practical moment to the student.

The trade-classes are significant of that change which has come into the modern world from the introduction of the principle of division of labor. They are an attempted substitute for the old apprentice system, and are intended to give the greatest result at the least expenditure of time. This means that the learners shall be given a course of carefully selected exercises, each one of which illustrates a new principle. In the carpentry shops we find a model house almost finished. It was built by students, and in building it they have seen and practised all the processes of house-building. The same principle holds good in the teaching of plumbing and fresco-painting. An encouraging sign in these trade-classes is the coöperation of the trade associations.

The classes in fresco-painting deserve special mention, so praiseworthy is the attempt to elevate the standard in an art which is with us so much in our households. Here are the learners, working in little three-walled rooms, plastered on wall and ceiling. The instructor tells us that the purpose is not only to supply instruction in the technical practice, but to provide for thorough study of fresco-design. In the first year of a three years' course practice in technical operations is given. In the second year this technical side is left behind, and considerable time is spent on drawing from the flat and from the cast. The last year is devoted to composition of ornament, and to production of finished designs for friezes, panels, and ceilings.

The Pratt Institute is visited every week of its yearly session by hundreds of visitors. It is likely that only a small percentage of these grasp the scope or significance of the mission which the Institute is trying to fulfil. At the World's Fair may be found an exhibit so arranged as to show the detail and methods of the training, first by departments, then by courses, then by grades. Each department has its alcove, each case in each alcove containing work, charts, or other media suggestive of the progressive training afforded in the courses of that department. The methods and curricula in courses where the results of training do not become apparent to the eye in concrete material form are of course difficult to suggest. But even in the purely intellectual curricula much ingenuity has been shown in the indicating of method.

In addition to the general Institute exhibit above referred to, there is an alcove showing the work of the women pupils and graduates. The former is a presentation rather of the educational phase of the work; the latter aims to show how, while thoroughly educative, the Institute courses are valuable as a training in the arts and industries by the practice of which women may become self-supporting. The significance of such an exhibit cannot be even suggested in a few words. It is easy to talk sounding words about woman's emancipation. On the floor and walls and in the show-cases of this little room there is the blazon of a great victory. It is here evident that woman has not been crushed out of the battle for bread by the indiscriminating competition of the times. If invention introduced complexity into the industrial system, it also opened the way for woman's taste, skill, and deftness of touch. Almost every piece of work here is in some way connected with the idea of home. Woman's true emancipation, it would seem, does not take her from her mission as the maker and glorifier of home. The exhibit includes work done by women pursuing sixteen different self-supporting occupations learned at the Pratt Institute. The drawings, articles manufactured from students' designs, wood-carvings, dresses, bonnets, etc., cannot here be described. The whole exhibit is highly creditable and very interesting. Of the great host of 2,700,000 women who are making a living in professional or in industrial occupations, 1320 are known to have received their training at the Pratt Institute. From the normal art course have gone out 61 supervisors and teachers of drawing whose annual salaries average $768.06. Graduates from the courses in design, art-needlework, and wood-carving are holding positions as teachers, or are serving as designers in well-known establishments, or are practising their professions independently. Three alumnæ of the architectural course hold good positions in an architect's office. Ninety-six of those trained in cookery and laundry work are earning a livelihood, and doubtless exerting an influence for good; for what is more redolent of ethics than a well-cooked steak, or where will you find more character than in a well-laundered shirt-bosom? From the courses in sewing, dress-making, and millinery, 3888 women have graduated. Of this number 44 are teaching, and 589 are practical workwomen in their own specialty. Sixteen of the 44 teachers are earning an aggregate of $12,950, or an average of $893.75 each. The classes in phonography, type-writing, and bookkeeping have trained 704 women as stenographers and bookkeepers. Of this number 486 have taken positions at an average salary of $12 a week. The school in library training opened two years ago; and of its 34 alumnæ, 21 have positions as assistants in libraries.[1]

In reflecting upon the work of a great educational institution, especially one yet in its infancy as far as age is concerned, a natural inquiry is, What of the future? There are rocks ahead to be avoided, there are headlands to be weathered, and havens of opportunity to be gained. The building which the trustees have planned, and which it is hoped will be ready for occupancy in September, 1894, suggests something regarding the spirit and intention of the founder of the Institute. Though they are impressive because of massiveness and height, the present buildings of the Institute are, to say the least, not classic in exterior architecture; the reason for which was not a desire to limit in expenditure, nor a lack of appreciation of the beautiful, but a fear on the part of the founder that the idea lying in his mind might prove impossible of realization. Hence the

[1] The information in the above paragraph is taken from a pamphlet published for distribution at the World's Fair.

main building was put up so that if the school should not be a success, the structure might serve as a factory. The new building is to be not only admirably suited for its intended uses, but a thing of beauty within and without. Greatly increased accommodations for the library will be particularly valuable in its reference department. I know of no school having a better-managed reference library than that possessed by the Pratt Institute. In its new quarters it will have much greater space for growth, and will be enabled to offer largely increased facilities. If the ideal of the director of libraries is even approximated, the usefulness of the library to the various departments of the Institute must be incalculable. Another significant feature is an auditorium with a capacity for six hundred. Here are to be given courses of lectures bearing upon the work of the various departments. It is to be hoped that, not unmindful of the importance of their high school, the academic department of the Institute, lectures in history and literature may be heard in this exquisitely decorated auditorium. In the large art museum, which will occupy nearly all of the second floor, will be found casts illustrating the development of sculpture, ceramics, wood-carving, wrought iron, textiles, etc. Here the students may find material for object-lessons in the fine and the applied arts. On this same floor is a gallery for the exhibition of pictures. Not only will the honor productions of Institute students be displayed here, but occasional loan exhibitions will also be held. The art department will occupy the third and fourth floors, and the arrangement of studios, and the lighting of each, leave little to be desired. Broad balconies run about the central court of the building, and all rooms of the third and fourth floors open upon them. The walls of these balconies are to be hung with hundreds of Braun carbon prints illustrating the historic schools of sculpture, painting, and architecture, in such a manner as to form a large museum collection of these prints, which can be used by the public or by students.

Very imperfectly, and only in its general features, appears in the foregoing sketch an educational institution which is the living memorial not only of the beneficence, but of the character of its founder. I suggested at the beginning of this article that the germ of the institute was the twelve students who first sought its instruction. In a deeper sense, the impulse, or rather the steady conviction and faith, in the heart of one man was its creative cause, and is yet its vitalizing principle.

James R. Campbell.

The New York Stock Exchange (1885)

J. EDWARD SIMMONS, PRESIDENT OF THE NEW YORK STOCK EXCHANGE.

From a drawing by F. Dielman.

THE NEW YORK STOCK EXCHANGE.

THE New York Stock Exchange is a building, an association, an exchange of securities for currency or its representatives. Ordinarily speaking, it signifies the body of men by whom the change of securities for valuable considerations is effected in an edifice devoted to that purpose. This edifice occupies a portion of the space between Broad and New streets, has a frontage of 65 feet on the first and of 158 on the second thoroughfare, and has also an entrance on Wall Street. It

163

THE NEW YORK STOCK EXCHANGE.

is a solid and unpretentious but imposing structure, designed by James Renwick, the architect of Grace Church and the Roman Catholic Cathedral. Improved arrangements that will give an additional six-sevenths to the floor of the Exchange—now 53 by 140 in size—have been projected by the Governing Committee, and will doubtless be effected. The legal title to all the real estate owned and occupied by the association known as the New York Stock Exchange is vested in the New York Stock Exchange Building Company, of which Donald Mackay is president. The cost of the whole is over $1,800,000, and the amount annually expended by the Committee of Arrangements for its preservation and for the salaries of the different individuals employed therein ranges from $150,000 to $200,000.

Strangers are not admitted to the ground-floor except by courtesy. Entering from Wall Street, the Board Room, with its Babel of voices, is on the right, or New Street side. On the left, or Broad Street side, is the Long Room, devoted to telegraphic apparatus and subscribers who pay $100 per annum for the privilege of using it. A door through the partition affords direct ingress to the parlor sacred to brokers, who therein indulge

THE BOND ROOM.

in some reading, more smoking, and incessant draught and chess playing. Stock-brokerage and the latter abound in shrewd combinations. Between the Board and Long rooms are telephonic and telegraphic instruments of communication with near and distant offices. The famous Callahan "ticker," whose patent was purchased of the Gold and Stock Telegraph Company by the Western Union Telegraph Company, and which prints its electric messages on endless strips of paper, is perpetually at work during the hours of business. Its owners yearly pay $18,000 to the Stock Exchange for the privilege of giving information about transactions in the market. The Commercial Telegram Company also enjoy the same privileges on the same terms.

Inspection of the Board Room, littered with torn memoranda of executed orders, after the day's proceedings are over, discovers that the several stocks have their respective locations upon the floor. Here is St. Paul; a board informs us what the price of the last sale was and how many shares were sold on the day previous. Next comes Northwest. At the south end is Reading, also the New York Central. A row of sign pillars runs along the middle of the room from end to end. On the first we find, to the south, Lake Shore, Wabash Preferred, and Common. This stock is not in active demand; the figures show what was bid and what was asked, without any sales. On the second pillar is New Jersey Central and Denver and Rio Grande. In like manner prices and sales of the previous day are recorded of the Oregon Transcontinental and Texas Pacific on the third pillar, of the Missouri, Kansas, and Texas and the Louisville and Nashville on the fourth, of the Central Pacific and Manhattan Consolidated (Elevated) Railway on the fifth. Omaha Preferred, Western Union Telegraph, and Union Pacific also have their places on the right of the chairman's rostrum. Mining stocks are sold at the north end of the room. On the New Street side are the Canadian Pacific, Minnesota and St. Louis, Alton and

D. C. HAYS, TREASURER OF THE NEW YORK STOCK EXCHANGE.

Terre Haute, Rome and Watertown, Erie Second Consols, Mobile and Ohio, Chesapeake and Ohio, Rock Island, Pacific Mail, Ohio and Mississippi, Missouri Pacific, Ohio Central, sundry Southern roads, the Delaware, Lackawanna, and Western, and the Michigan Central. The names and figures of all these stocks indicate the vital relation of the Stock Exchange to the commerce and development of the country.

A bulletin-board apprises the brokers that certain of their number have been allowed extended time in which to settle with their creditors, and who are proposed for re-admission or election to the board. Two annunciators also attract notice. These instruments are covered with numbered knobs, one of them running from 1 to 340. A member is wanted outside; but no voice is strong enough to outscreech that Indian hubbub of bids and offers. The messenger whistles through a tube to the boy behind the annunciator; he replies, "Well?" and receives the order, "Put up 24"—the number of the broker wanted; 24 is put up; by pulling the knob bearing that number it instantly appears under the raised section of a tes-

sellated arrangement in front of a gallery —of which there are two—allotted to spectators. The eye of the broker catches the silent announcement, which is discontinued when it has served its purpose.

On the New Street side is a corridor, railed off from the Board Room, accessible to subscribers at $100 per annum, clerks and messengers, and permitting direct contact of client with agent. Three chandeliers, filled with 198 electric lamps, diffuse clear, soft, and abundant light when needed. The arrangements for heating and cooling the room are no less admirable. The ventilating apparatus is as effective as it is necessary, and cost $30,000. Not only does it supply pure air, but perfumes it at the same time. "What bouquet have you this morning, doctor?" is not an uncommon inquiry of the superintendent. Washington and also New York time is kept at the Stock Exchange. Punctually at 10 A.M. the gong strikes for the opening of business, at 2.15 P.M. for deliveries, and at 3 P.M. for the cessation of traffic.

In the second story is the office of the Committee on the Stock List, the Bond Room, where railroad bonds and bank stocks are bought and sold, the office of the President and that of the Secretary, and last, not least in attractiveness to strangers, the galleries, from which may be witnessed scenes compared with which street fights are nothing in point of earnestness and interest. In the third story are the rooms of the several committees, the assistant secretary, the stenographer, and the Glee Club. Mammon has some music in him. The sixteen (more or less) members of the club voice it in excellent style. Their annual concerts in Chickering Hall are fashionably and largely attended, and are sometimes repeated. Truth compels the statement that they engage the best vocal and instrumental assistance. Still, on organ and piano they are amateur experts.

The vaults under the building are among the strongest in the world, and contain 1032 safes for securities. Citizens not connected with the Stock Exchange hire about 400 of them. There are also rooms for messengers and members, with lavatories, closets, and other conveniences on the same floor.

Such are the present quarters of the New York Stock Exchange. They are in startling contrast with those of the

ON NEW STREET.

twenty-four brokers who met under a buttonwood-tree in front of what is now No. 60 Wall Street in 1792, and there created what has grown into the present organization. Their association was as crude as the resources of the country. Business was chiefly done at the Tontine Coffeehouse, a favorite resort for merchants, at the corner of Wall and Water streets. The commercial revival following the war

GEORGE W. ELY, SECRETARY OF THE NEW YORK STOCK EXCHANGE.

of 1812–15 made better organization an urgent need. The character and importance of current transactions called for a precise and binding system. In 1817 the New York Stock and Exchange Board was constituted after the model of that in Philadelphia, and its meetings were held, after 1820, in the office of Samuel J. Beebe, 47 Wall Street, next in a room in the rear of Leonard Bleecker's, and subsequently in the domicile of the old *Courier and Enquirer*. In May, 1817, it removed to an upper room in the Merchants' Exchange, on Wall and William streets. Thence it was ousted by the great fire of 1835, and for some years afterward held its sessions in a hall in Jauncey Court. In 1842 it returned to a hall in the new Merchants' Exchange, now the Customhouse. The board was then a close corporation, but an eminently honorable one, and decidedly averse to any publication

of its doings. The Open Board of Brokers, gotten up in the rotunda, in or about 1837, tried to force themselves into the association, and, failing in that, cut away the beams and dug out the bricks of the regular Board Room, in order to insert their heads and learn what was being done. In 1853 the board removed to rooms on the top floor of the Corn Exchange Bank, at the corner of Beaver Street, and from thence into Dan Lord's building, on Beaver, above William, near Exchange Place, where it was located in the panic of 1857, and also at the outbreak of the great rebellion.

In 1863, a second Open Board of Brokers, the first being defunct, was established in a dismal William Street basement, denominated the "Coal Hole." This soon had several hundred members, and did an immense business. Thence it passed into a fine hall on Broad Street—within one door of the Stock Exchange, which had fixed its quarters in the edifice now occupied, and which was built for its use in December, 1865—and by 1869 had acquired fully one-half the speculative business done on "the street." Warfare between the old and the new was annoying to both. Negotiation followed, and ended in consolidation. The government department of the old board was absorbed at the same time. Since then all have enjoyed equal rights and privileges in the same structure.

The members of the New York Stock Exchange are *sui generis*. In number they are eleven hundred. This limit was reached in November, 1879. They constitute an association, not a legalized corporation. In 1871 a perfect charter was drawn up by business men for the incorporation of the Stock Exchange. Tweed was then in the zenith of his legislative power. Thinking that the application presented an opportunity for making money, he caused false names to be inserted in place of the true, had it passed by the New York Legislature, and signed by the Governor. A hundred thousand dollars, or thereabouts, was asked for this superserviceable meddling, but both demand and charter were rejected by the indignant members.

The twenty-four brokers who signed an agreement not to buy or sell stocks for less than one-fourth of one per cent. commission, and to prefer each other in negotiations, increased in number slowly. Only

JACOB LITTLE.

twenty-five adopted the constitution of 1817. Among the thirty-nine who had signed it in revised form in 1821 were Nathaniel Prime, Leonard Bleecker, and other experienced bankers of the highest reputation. Exquisitely sensitive in matters of honor, scrupulous in regard for right, dignified and urbane in manners, they were worthy of the utmost confidence and regard. J. L. Joseph, whose firm was the agent of the Rothschilds, joined them in 1824, and the celebrated Jacob Little in 1825. Large accessions were received during the civil war, at the consolidation of the boards in 1869, and again in 1879, when the present maximum was attained.

The form of government under which the Stock Exchange acted for many years was that of pure democracy. Consolidation with the "government department"

CHAIRMAN JAMES MITCHELL.
From a drawing by F. Dielman.

erning Committee. Administrative and judicial powers are intrusted to the latter, whose decision in all cases is final.

The President of the New York Stock Exchange, elected in May, 1884, and unanimously re-elected in 1885, is J. Edward Simmons, a gentleman of the highest respectability, of established reputation, solid attainments, and enviable popularity. James Mitchell, the Chairman since the consolidation in 1869; Alexander Henriques, the Vice-Chairman since 1880; D. C. Hays, the Treasurer since 1866; Commodore James D. Smith, the Vice-President; and George W. Ely, Assistant Secretary from 1874, and Secretary since 1883—all possess the same characteristics. The services of the President are gratuitous, although their importance is such as to require his constant care and attention.

The President sees to the enforcement of the rules and regulations, cares for the general interests of the Exchange, presides over it when he chooses, and is a member and the presiding officer of the Governing Committee. In his absence the Vice-President assumes the same power and functions. The Chairman presides over the board when assembled for business, calls the stocks and bonds as they are printed on the list, maintains order, and enforces the rules. In his absence the Vice-Chairman discharges these duties. Neither, while presiding, can operate in stocks. The Secretary has charge of the books, papers, and correspondence of the Exchange, keeps record of the opening and closing of the different transfer books for dividends, elections, etc., of the various corporations in which it is interested, and posts the amount and date of such dividends upon the bulletin-board. The Roll-Keeper preserves a list of the members, and of the fines imposed upon them. He

on May 1, 1869, and with the "Open Board of Stock-Brokers" on the 8th of the same month, brought with it the adoption of a republican constitution, by which the government is vested in a committee of forty—divided into four classes, of which one goes out of power every year—and in its President and Treasurer. These constitute the Governing Committee, and, with the Vice-President and Secretary, are the officers of the Exchange. The President, Secretary, Treasurer, Chairman, and Vice-Chairman are annually elected by ballot of all the members present and voting, on the second Monday in May. The Governing Committee chooses the Vice-President, and also appoints the Roll-Keeper. Vacancies are filled by election, either of the whole body or of the Gov-

INTERIOR OF NEW YORK STOCK EXCHANGE.

W. E. CONNOR.

also collects the latter, and reports semi-annually to the Exchange.

Applications for membership are publicly announced, together with the name of the member nominating, and the name of the member seconding the applicant. The nominators are asked in committee if they recommend the applicant—whom they must have known for twelve months —in all respects, and if they would accept his uncertified check for $20,000. The latter query is crucial. The nominee is requested to state his age, whether he be a citizen of the United States, what his business has been, whether he ever failed in business; if so, the cause of his failure, amount of indebtedness, and nature of settlement. He must also produce the release from his creditors. He is asked, if indebted, what judgments have been given against him; if not in debt, whether he pays for the membership and the accompanying initiation fee with his own means ; whether his health be and has been uniformly good; whether his life be insured, and if not, for what reason; what kind of business he purposes to do; alone or in partnership. A copy of his statement is forwarded to him, and is read and certified by him as correct. Any willful misstatement upon a material point subjects him to lasting ineligibility for admission, or to deprivation of membership, as the case may be. Not less than eight

hundred admitted men have been thus questioned by A. M. Cahoone, Chairman of the Committee on Admissions. "The best policy is honesty," is the cardinal maxim of the Stock Exchange. Financial morality satisfies its requirements. Further than that is beyond its chosen province.

An elected member must sign the constitution and by-laws, pledge himself to abide by the same, pay an initiation fee of $20,000, or, if admitted by transfer, of $1000 in addition to the price of his membership. All new members are now admitted through transfer. In 1792 no initiation fee was demanded; in 1823, only $25; in 1827, $100; in 1833, $150; in 1842, $350; in 1862, $3000, and for clerks, $1500. Thence it rose in 1866 to $10,000, at which figure it stood until 1879, when it was raised to $20,000. There is little hazard in predicting a future rise to $100,000. Even at that figure it would be little if any higher than such a privilege has cost at the Paris Bourse. It ought to imply corresponding guarantee of the capital and character of the broker. The semi-annual dues amount to $25. Ten dollars for the Gratuity Fund are charged to the account of each on the death of one of the members. Fines also are charged in the half-yearly bills, and are levied on the exuberant and indiscreet at the rate of from twenty-five cents to ten dollars, at the discretion of the presiding officer, for such offenses as knocking off hats, throwing paper wads, standing on chairs, smoking in the halls (five dollars), indecorous language, interrupting the presiding officer while calling stocks, or calling up a stock not on the regular list. The revenue from fines is quite large. Some New York stock-brokers compensate themselves for strict legality in one direction by breaking minor rules in others.

A single membership in the Stock Exchange has sold as high as $32,500. At an average of $30,000 the whole number of memberships is worth $33,000,000. Some of the brokers are very rich; others comparatively poor. Estimating the average capital at $100,000, and multiplying this by 1100, we have $110,000,000, which, added to the value of the memberships, gives $143,000,000 as the capital invested by the members.

Generally speaking, brokers are of three classes. The first does a regular commission business; never speculates, except on occasions, and succeeds best. The second are the scalpers, who buy and sell in the hope of making one-eighth or one-quarter of one per cent. profit. These are the physiognomists of the institution. Reading the faces of associates who have large orders, they buy with the intention of selling to them at a rise. The scalpers are busiest when there are more brokers than business. Too smart to live, they usually die of pecuniary atrophy. The guerrillas are a sub-class of the scalpers, few in number, and by making specialty of dealing in inactive stocks have formerly fixed the unsavory appellations of "Hell's Kitchen" and "Robbers' Roost" upon certain localities of the floor. The third class is composed of traders in particular stocks, by whose rise and fall they strive to enrich themselves, in some instances closing contracts every day. One trader in Northwest for sixteen years is said to have accumulated a handsome fortune. The ideal broker is cool, imperturbable, unreadable, knowing or accurately guessing the movements of the great operators, able to buy the most stock with the least fluctuation, covering his tracks in the execution of a large order by purchasing in small quantities, and by shrewd selling at the same time. Washington E. Connor, partner and broker of Jay Gould, does presumably the largest brokerage business in the Exchange.

W. H. VANDERBILT.

The compensation paid to commission brokers ought to be satisfactory. It is one-eighth of one per cent. upon the purchase and upon the sale of all securities other than government bonds, estimated at par value, when made for a party who is not a member of the Exchange. No business can be done for less than this rate to non-members. The minimum rate charged to members is one-thirty-second of one per cent., except where one member merely buys or sells for another (giving up his principal on the day of the transaction), and does not receive or deliver the stock, in which case the rate must not be less than one-fiftieth of one per cent. The commission on mining stocks selling in the market at $5 per share or less is $3 12½ per 100 shares; if at more than $5 and not over $10 per share, $6 25; if more than $10 per share, $12 50. To members of the Exchange the minimum commission charged is $2 per 100 shares. Contracts for a longer period than three days carry six per

C. J. OSBORNE.

cent. interest. Any violation, direct or indirect, of these laws—even the *offering* to do business at less than these rates—is punishable by expulsion from the Exchange, and sale forthwith by the Committee on Admissions of the membership of the offender. The commission broker who carries stock for his customer and furnish-

es most of the money occasionally charges one-fourth of one per cent., or $25 per 100 shares. Ten bonds, at par of $1000 each, are reckoned equivalent to 100 shares, and are subject to the same commissions.

What compensation will these rates afford to brokers? For the year ending December 31, 1881, the transactions of the Stock Exchange are computed to have amounted to $12,816,246,600. Checks for this enormous amount were drawn and paid. The commissions thereon at one-fourth of one per cent. would be $32,040,616; which, divided equally among 1100 brokers, would give to each the snug little sum of $29,127. This, as related to the cost of his seat, is almost or quite equal to the Israelite's "shent per shent." Not all the brokers receive this remuneration; some receive five or six times as much. Profit is proportioned to size of sales and purchases. It is impossible, without possession of an abstract of each broker's business, to accurately estimate the amount of fictitious sales, or sales on "margins," as compared with sales to *bona fide* investors. It can not, we judge, be less, and is probably much more, than one-half of the whole.

Brokers may be either principals or agents, or both. Not all the great operators, such as A. W. Morse, Jacob Little, John Tobin, L. and A. G. Jerome, Daniel Drew, W. S. Woodward, Cornelius Vanderbilt, James Fisk, Jun., W. Belden, H. M. Smith, D. P. Morgan, D. O. Mills, C. F. Woerishoffer, William H. Vanderbilt, Jay Gould, Cyrus W. Field, James Keene, and Russell Sage, have been members of the Exchange. The last-named, as also C. F. Woerishoffer and others, are distinguished illustrations of the trading and commission broker combined in one. Examples are not uncommon of operators, even of brokers, selling "short" the stocks in which they are interested as directors. The Vanderbilts are reputedly as free from this vice as any of the money magnates in the street. One of the most popular brokers and large operators—bull or bear as an excellent judgment may dictate—is C. J. Osborne.

Stock-brokers have a dialect of their own that is caviare to the crowd. Like the trade-marks and "shop" terms of merchants, it must be explained to be intelligible to the multitude. It is pithy, pungent, scintillating, and sometimes rank. It precisely characterizes every variation and aspect of the market. A broker or operator is "long of stocks" when "carrying" or holding them for a rise; "loads" himself by buying heavily, perhaps in "blocks" composed of any number of shares—say 5000 or 10,000—bought in a the price from declining; "milks the street" when he holds certain stocks so skillfully that he raises or depresses prices at pleasure, and thus absorbs some of the accessible cash in the street; buys when the

CYRUS W. FIELD.

lump, and is therefore a "bull," whose natural action is to lower his horns and give things a hoist. He "forces quotations" when he wishes to keep up the price of a stock; "balloons" it to a height above its intrinsic value by imaginative stories, fictitious sales, and kindred methods; takes "a flier," or small side venture, that does not employ his entire capital; "flies kites" when he expands his credit beyond judicious bounds; "holds the market" when he buys sufficient stock to prevent "market is sick" from over-speculation; keenly examines "points"—theories or facts—on which to base speculation; "unloads" when he sells what has been carried for some time; has a "swimming market" when all is buoyant; "spills stock" when he throws great quantities upon the market, either from necessity or to "break," i. e., lower, the price. He "saddles the market" by foisting a certain stock upon it, and is "out of" any stock when he has sold what he held of it.

Brokers and operators are "bears" when they have sold stock, and particularly stock that they did not own, contracting to deliver it at some future time.

ADDISON CAMMACK.

They are then "short of the market." The disposition of the bear is to pull things down. The Wall Street bear is often found "gunning a stock" by putting forth all his strength and craft to break down the price, and especially when aware that a certain house is heavily loaded and can not resist his attack. He "buys in" by purchasing stock to meet a "short" contract, or to return borrowed stock; "covers," or "covers his shorts," by buying stock to fulfill his contract on the day of delivery. This is a self-protective measure, and is called "covering short sales." A "drop" in the price of a stock is to a bear the next best thing to a "break." He rejoices in an "off" market when prices fall. He "sells out" a man by forcing down the price of a stock that the person is carrying so low that he is obliged to let it go, and perhaps to fail. He groans lustily when the bulls get a "twist on the shorts" by artificially raising prices, and "squeezing," or compelling the bears to settle at ruinous rates. Neither "bull" nor "bear" is an altogether safe "critter." The latter, however, is reputed to be about four times as mischievous as the former, inasmuch as he rudely sells another man's property, whereas the bull contents himself with carrying his own.

The bear occasionally finds himself in a "corner," where it is impossible to buy the stock of which he is "short," and which he must deliver at a specified time. He growls and begs, but must pay what the holders of his contracts are willing to accept. Some relief is afforded by a "let up," or the withdrawal from the market of the "clique," or "pool," or combination of operators that cornered him. A "squeal in the pool" is the revelation of its secrets by one of its members, and a "leak in the pool" is when one of the parties sells out his interest without the knowledge of the others. Either form of defection yields some mitigation to the bear's sufferings. Very popular among the members of this special zoological class is the most extensive operator of their number—one whose strength of character defies opposition—A. Cammack.

Brokers demand "ten up," or a deposit of ten per cent. on the selling value of the stock, in order to insure the fulfillment of contracts. A "wash"—one hand washing the other—is an arrangement between brokers whereby one fictitiously buys what the other fictitiously sells of a certain stock, to keep up or advance the price, and thus to lay a foundation for real sales. "To wipe out an operator" is to confuse and overreach him so that he utterly fails. Sometimes the broker or operator is caught by "traps," or worthless securities. In that event he runs the risk of classification as a "gosling," or a "lame duck," who can not meet his engagements, or a "dead duck," who is absolutely bankrupt. He may even degenerate into a "gutter snipe," or "curbstone" broker, who belongs to no regular organization, has no office where comparisons may be made and notices served (as all members of the Stock Exchange must have), does business mainly upon the sidewalk, and is supremely happy in the light and warmth of the Subscribers' Room or corridor when he can raise shekels sufficient to pay for them. Quoting the vernacular of the Board Room: "The gutter snipe carries his office in his hat. Where one buys of another in New Street, and the market goes up, the buyer is on hand immediately after breakfast, but the seller and his office are absent, and *wikey wersa*." These last words are our old friends *vice versa* in guise of Romaic pronunciation.

Brokers are nothing if not classical—extremely so.

The technology of the Stock Exchange is too large for full quotation. "Conversions" are the exchanges of bonds for equivalent shares of stock, such bonds being called "convertibles." "Collaterals" are securities of any kind pledged for borrowed money. Pledging them is termed

to the Governors. "Differences" are money balances paid where stock is not transferred—which seldom happens. To lend "flat" means without interest. To "water" stock is to increase its quantity and impair its quality. To "pass a dividend" is not to pay it. There are other slang phrases used in connection with the business of stock privileges, which is **not**

RUSSELL SAGE.

"hypothecation." A "good delivery" is of certificates of stock or bonds legally issued, bearing satisfactory power of attorney on the back or appended, and transferred agreeably to the laws of the Exchange. A "bad delivery" is the opposite, and involves the right of appeal to the Committee on Securities, and thence

"recognized" by or done publicly at the Exchange. Privileges to receive or to deliver securities are bought and sold outside the institution. Russell Sage is the king operator in these peculiar transactions. Stock privileges are "puts" and "calls," or combinations of both. A "put" is the privilege of putting or selling to the one who sells it a certain quantity of a speci-fied stock at a designated price within a fixed time. A "call" is the privilege of calling for or buying a certain stock at a specified price within a given time. The seller of the put must be ready to buy, and of the call to sell, whenever called upon. A "straddle" is the option of ei-ther buying or selling; it combines the put and call in one, and differs from the "spread" in that the market price at the time of purchase is filled into the latter, while in the "straddle" the price may vary from that of the market, by agree-ment or otherwise. The cost of stock privi-leges varies with the length of time they have to run, the difference between the prices named in them from those current on the day the privileges are sold, the ac-tivity of the market, and other conditions, and is from one per cent. to three per cent. of the amount involved. Experts affirm that they have a duplex character—that of policies of insurance and that of tickets in a lottery. In exceptional cases only are they means of profit to any but those who issue them. Even the latter—with the exception of the shrewd operator now so conspicuous in the business, and possi-bly not even of him—are likely to come to grief, as the large majority of their prede-cessors have done. The gain of the holder is dependent, first, on favorable turns in the market, and next, on his ability and promptness in utilizing them. Keen in-tellect, prevision, nerve, watchfulness, and tigerish spring at opportunity must unite to prevent the loss of what is invest-ed in them. "Don't," is the best advice to those who seek advice about fooling with them.

The activities of stock-brokerage in-volve exhaustive drain of vital energy. The nervous force necessarily expended in rapid reasoning and quick decision is often directed into other channels to re-lieve the overtasked brain. The younger section of the broker tribe indulges in an annual regatta of its rowing association, in base-ball contests with the callow ath-letes of popular colleges, or in friendly struggles among themselves, in which the "Good Boys" are pitted against the "Bad Boys," in go-as-you-please pedestrian matches in the Central Park, in Bacchic dances to the entrancing music of Italian organ-grinders, in tremendous attempts at Græco-Roman wrestling, and in exaspera-ting "tug-of-war" contests at either end of

a stout rope. It also revels, in company with the elder, in the concerts of the Glee Club, and never fails to make the annual song festival at Chickering Hall, or the less frequent one in the Brooklyn Acade-my of Music, a grand success in respect of enthusiasm, flowers, and numbers. At the Christmas season it luxuriates in the blowing of tin horns and bugles, smash-ing of broker hats, pelting with blown bladders, wet towels, and surreptitious snow-balls, and in the sly insertion of the cooling crystals between the collars and necks of unsuspecting brethren. Hot pennies are sometimes substituted. If the victim whose spinal column glows with unwonted heat be of dynamite tem-perament, a fierce explosion is the inevi-table result. This same juvenile section is addicted to horse-play with unconscious intruders into the Board Room, and with subjects of practical jokes. The clothes of both grow rapidly worse for wear, and are badly marked with uncertain quota-tions of stocks in still more uncertain fig-ures in chalk. This is all the more incon-gruous in view of the faultless and al-most dudish attire of many of the mem-bers. Fashionable tailors can not crave better advertisement, nor florists more striking coign of vantage, from which to display their choicest wares.

This class of gentlemen reveals remark-ably affectionate interest in the advent of a new-comer to the broker household, cir-culates tidings of the joyful event, con-gratulates the blushing *père*, and takes up a collection for the purchase of some ap-propriate or inappropriate present to the infantine monarch. They are also some-what prone to the hazing of new members, and are not always discreet in the choice of methods. If the welcome be peculiarly hearty, the novice may receive a free ride around the Board Room, the transfer of quotations from the blackboard to the back of his coat, and see the necessity of new orders to his hatter and tailor. In vain does the Chairman use his gavel on such occasions. The spirit of fun is riotous, and does not hesitate to run off with that symbol of authority. At other times it may leave him alone in his glory to call the list in awesome silence to empty benches. These irrepressibles welcome some visitors with profound respect. Prince Hohenlohe is regarded in silence; "God Save the Queen" is sung with en-thusiasm in presence of Sergeant Ballan-

tine; and loud applause greets a brief speech from "Tom Brown." Oscar Wilde does not fare as well. The cheers are derisive, the jostling severe, and the sunflower knight finds it difficult to keep his æsthetic legs. A Manitoba insurance agent, looking like a Russian bear in his fur cap and hairy coat, enters the gallery. He is a blizzard to the brokers. They rub their hands, swing their arms, and outdo the pantomime of a half-frozen stagedriver. Eloquence affects them strangely when it springs from their own officers. Cat-calls, cheers, howls, and whistles testify to their high appreciation. The less there is of it, the better they like it. "I am sorry," is an exordium that evokes conflicting counsels, such as "Hire a hall," etc., etc. "Thank you," was the staple speech of one of the best secretaries the Exchange ever had, and never failed to bring down the house. The hilarity and practical jocosity at rare intervals overleap due bounds, and provoke fistic encounters, in which case the impromptu Sullivans and Morrisseys are parted, and then punished by temporary suspension from all privileges of the Exchange.

Repartee is piquant, always pointed, sometimes Falstaffian. In dull times the lovers of fun amuse themselves with parodies of election tickets, railroad regulations, and corporation circulars. Of the latter, that of the Great Bric-à-brac Company is a specimen. It proposed the manufacture of antique china, bric-à-brac, and bronzes out of old fruit cans, broken crockery, old iron, tin-foil tobacco wrappers, and other refuse. Domestic discussions were possibly reflected in it.

As a rule, the stock-brokers are a self-indulgent, genial, expensive, and generous class of fellow-citizens. They dine well, dress well, bubble over with animal spirits, bear bravely the reverses of fortune, and enjoy robust health. Many of them are graduates of colleges; few are rough and uneducated. Composed of the best blood of the people, they are not, as a whole, distinguished for literary achievements. Stephen H. Thayer is a contributor to the departments of poetry and criticism in the *Christian Union*, Brayton Ives is represented by newspaper editorials and by contributions to the *North American Review*, Strong Wadsworth is one of the ablest writers in *Johnson's Cyclopædia*, and Edmund C. Stedman, the American Rogers, is accomplished and brilliant in poetry and prose.

Failures in business are not so common with brokers as with their clients. One of the more prominent is credited with the assertion that "if there were no fools, most of the members of the Stock Exchange would have to retire from business." Not two per cent. of the latter become insolvent, but as folly is a constant quantity in human nature, the percentage of its exponents is much higher.

The employés of the New York Stock Exchange merit passing notice. Of these and of paid officials there are about 178. The employés, numbering over 160, receive salaries varying from $200 upward, and include about fifty pages, called "graybacks," from the color of their uniforms. These run errands from the floor of the Exchange to the telegraph department, whence some seventy-five blue-clad messengers convey messages and packages to and from the offices of the members. The pay-roll of the financial year ending in 1884 exhibits an expenditure of $119,082 for salaries.

One sergeant of police and ten privates are constantly on duty at the Stock Exchange, except on Sundays and holidays. On the 23d of May, 1884, thirty-five police officers were on hand; and in seasons of great excitement all the force available is sent down to protect the interests of this dominant financial institution.

The securities bought and sold at the New York Stock Exchange are certificates of stock, and bonds issued under national, State, or municipal authority, or by corporations doing business as common carriers, or in banking, mining, manufacturing, or other industrial pursuits. Securities evidencing debt and contracting to pay specified sums of money on a future day are denominated bonds. Certificates of shares (stocks) in the capital stock of corporations represent the cash contributed to each particular enterprise at the risk of the investors. In Great Britain railroad bonds are termed debentures, and are rarely secured by mortgage. "Stock" means public funds or government securities representing money loaned to the nation; and also the capital stock of railroad or other companies not distributed into shares. Petroleum stocks are excluded from the Stock Exchange.

Before any issue of bonds or stock is admitted to the privileges of the Exchange, it must pass the scrutiny of the Committee on the Stock List, and receive the approval of the Governing Committee.

Certificates of stock must be indorsed with an irrevocable power of attorney, containing a full bill of sale and a power of substitution, to constitute them a good delivery. Stocks and bonds—such as those of the Illinois Central, Cleveland and Pittsburgh, Harlem, and New York and New

BRAYTON IVES.

Haven railroads—that pass into the hands of permanent investors are infrequent subjects of traffic in the Exchange. Speculative or active stocks are commonly those of corporations ruled by directors in their own interest. History shows that such directors have, in some instances, by indirect methods, awarded building contracts to themselves, built railroads by means of "rings," turned them over, in more or less finished condition, at a profit of sixty or one hundred per cent. to themselves, to the company, and then have raised or depressed the price of stock at pleasure.

Government, State, and railroad bonds, bank stocks, and other securities are called twice a day in the Bond Room—at 11 A.M. and 1.45 P.M. Chairman Mitchell, whose memory is longer than his list of over six hundred securities, usually presides in the morning, and the vice-chairman in the afternoon. Stocks are not called in the Board Room. Formerly all bonds and shares were called in regular sequence, transactions effected in each as it was reached, and daily business closed with the exhaustion of the list. The secretary recorded all sales, and the members approved his minutes, which were final evidence of the terms of the contracts.

The cash value of the annual transactions of New York stock-brokers defies ordinary comprehension. On the 25th of February, 1881, 721,303 shares of stocks on the regular list were sold on the floor of the Exchange, 848,940 shares on November 22, 1882, and 3,022,407 in the week ending March 26, 1881. The largest single sale recorded is that of W. H. Vanderbilt to a syndicate of American and foreign bankers and railroad operators. Public sentiment being decidedly averse to the control of the New York Central Railroad by a single family, he, in deference to it, sold less than half his interest in it. But what he did sell amounted to the enormous sum of thirty million dollars. One hundred and fifty thousand shares, at 120, were sold outright, and the option of a hundred thousand more at the same price was subsequently taken up by the same purchasers. The securities daily bought and loaned are paid for by checks on city banks. The yearly business of the New York Clearing-house exceeds fifty billion dollars, and the principal part of this is from the transactions of the New York Stock Exchange. The London system of settlements twice a month by the payment of differences has failed of adoption in our chief money mart, and is certainly neither so safe nor so judicious as that of cash payments.

The methods of business in this national monetary institution are precise, positive, and suited to its nature. At 9.50 A.M. the members may enter the Board Room; at 10 the gavel of the presiding officer announces that it is open for business; at 3 P.M., precisely, it is closed. A fine of fifty dollars is imposed for each offense in public trading before or after these hours, and any contract thus made will not be recognized or enforced by the Governing Committee.

Collected in groups, like spring chickens in a rural boarding-house keeper's hen-yard, New York Central, Northwestern, Milwaukee and St. Paul, being special points of attraction, no sooner does the gavel fall than a dozen blending thunder-storms break loose. The air is rent by explosive cries, shrieks, yells, hoots, irregularly rising and falling in gusts ungovernable, broken only by the deep bellowings of broad-chested sons of Boanerges. And thus for five long hours the tempest rages, with accompaniment of flitting forms, fierce gestures, uplifted hands, tossing heads, and other inexplicable confusions that shroud the innocent spectator in appalling mystery. Here and there are individuals cool and collected as if in church, but they only throw the anarchic uproar into more striking relief. "Mad, sirs!—mad as March hares!" But there is wondrous method in this madness. Each offers the stock he has to sell—cries it loudly, number of shares, price. Buyers name the prices and conditions they bid for desired stocks. Hundreds are vociferating at the same moment; every ear is attent to what the owner wishes to catch. The brokers take it all in, sometimes buy and sell without looking at each other, so familiar are they with each other's voices; cry out while scribbling memoranda, "Take 'em," "Sold," "I bought 500 of you at 97," and afterward report to principals who the active traffickers were, thus supplying them with data for guessing at the trend of the market. In the Bond Room comparative order reigns. All are seated. Occasionally manners are free, laughter loud, and jokes practical. The bids and offers to sell are intelligible. Between bond calls the brokers who deal in these securities transact business in one corner of the Board Room, to which they descend by an elevator, with the stockbrokers from whom they receive orders. There the voices of the traffickers are torn into tattered shreds of sound, which convey no more meaning to the uneducated ear than the gutturals of so many Choctaws. At times the noise is terrible, especially in panics.

Heard by participants in the crushing throng, the sounds are distinct enough. "Five hundred [New York Central] at 85—at 4⅞." "Take 'em," shouts a buyer. "One hundred [Chicago and Northwestern] at 84, cash." "Eighty-three and three-quarters for 100," with shake of uplifted hand from buyer. "Sold," rejoins the seller. "Five thousand [Northern Pacific Preferred] at 42, buyer 30." "I'll give 41 for the lot." "Sold." "Hundred [Lake Shore] at ½, buyer 3." "Three-eighths, seller 3, for 100." (Delaware, Lackawanna, and Western) "—any part of 1000 at ½, cash." "One hundred at ⅜."

"I will give 117 for 500" (Chicago, Burlington, and Quincy). "Sold the lot." "I'll give ¾ [41¾] for 300" (New Jersey Central). "I'll loan 200." "I'll take 100, flat." "Fifty [Rock Island] at '10½." "Hundred at ⅝." "I'll sell 500 more." "Take 'em." "Give it for 500 more." "Sold." "What's the price?" (Lake Shore). "Three-eighths—½." "What ⅜?" "Why, 65⅜." "I'll give ⅜ for 1000." "Sold the lot." Bids are monosyllabic as possible. Names of stocks are not vocalized in the localities where the stocks are sold. Brokers waste no breath in trading. All offers made and accepted are binding. The securities on the free list are not called unless asked for.

Sales are either for *cash*, in which case delivery is made on the same day at or before 2.15 P.M., or in the *regular way*, when delivery is made on the day following, or on *time*, usually three, ten, thirty, or sixty days. More frequently option sales are for three days: when stock is cliqued they may be for thirty or sixty days. In option sales the delivery of the stock within the specified time may be at the buyer's option or at the seller's option. It must be within sixty days at the longest. In all option contracts extending over three days twenty-four hours' notice must be given, not later than 2 P.M., before securities can be delivered or demanded.

The sixty days limitation of contracts originated in one of the famous speculative ventures of Jacob Little soon after the panic of 1857. He had sold large blocks of Erie, seller's option, at six and twelve months. The "happy family," composed of the most eminent members of the board, combined against him. The day of settlement came; Erie shares had been run up to a high figure. At 2 P.M. the brokers prophesied that the Napoleon of finance would meet his Waterloo. At 1 P.M. he stepped into the Erie office, presented a mass of convertible bonds that he had quietly purchased in England, and demanded the instantaneous exchange of share equivalents for them. The requisition was met. Little returned to his office, fulfilled his contracts, broke the corner, and was Wellington and Napoleon in one. The convertibles were his Blücher and night. To prevent the repetition of such victories the present option limit was adopted by the Exchange.

Strictly legitimate use of the Stock Exchange is when the investor who buys for permanent holding pays the full price of the stock transferred to him and takes it away. Speculators who desire to find a more direct and easy way to affluence than that of patient toil, and therefore wish to buy more stock than they can pay for, are accommodated by brokers, who provide the money by means of a loan on the hypothecation of the securities. Loans are easily obtained in ordinary times to an amount within twenty per cent. of the market value of these collaterals. The speculator advances the difference between the current price and the sum borrowed. This difference is the *margin*. The margin is a magnificent instrument of stock speculation. Twenty per cent. is ample. Some brokers require much less. Ten per cent. is the rule. Traders not in the Exchange offer to do business for customers on a margin as narrow as one per cent. Just as long as the loan can be continued or renewed the broker may carry the stock until his client wishes to realize. Decline in current price decreases the margin and increases the risk of carrying. Therefore the broker calls for more margin from his principal. If it is not forth-coming, he sells out the stock to save himself from loss. If a number of brokers, similarly circumstanced, unload at the same time, the market is correspondingly depressed.

The financial institutions loaning most largely to brokers are the Farmers' Loan, Union, and United States Trust Companies, the Bank of the State of New York, the Fourth National, Union, Merchants', Mechanics', Gallatin, Leather Manufacturers', Importers' and Traders' Banks, the Bank of America, and the Bank of North America. The brokers also lend stocks and money to each other. Call loans of money on stock collaterals are commonly made at the north end of the Board Room.

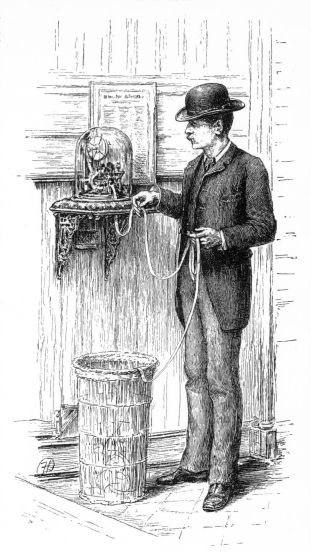

THE TICKER.

This used to be done on the sidewalk. The loan is usually about eighty or ninety per cent. of the market value of the collaterals, and bears interest at different rates, according to the condition of the money market. Statute law prohibits more than six per cent. per annum. Borrowers therefore pay commissions of one-eighth, one-quarter, one-half, of one per cent., or even one per cent., per diem—365 per cent. per annum—in panics to those who borrow for them. For weeks together the monetary stringency has been such as to command the higher rates. At other sea-

S. V. WHITE.

sons, when the market is easy, the rate of call loans scarcely averages three per cent. —at present it is about one and a half per cent. — per annum. Brokers also loan stocks, either "flat," *i. e.*, without interest, or with interest, to those of their number who have made "short sales;" or, in other words, have sold stocks they did not possess. The borrower pays the current price and delivers his stock; then waits for a drop in the price, buys as he can, returns an equal quantity of stock, and reclaims his money. If the lender does not call for his stock next day, the custom is to regard the loan as continued. If he does call for it, and the borrower fails to respond, then the Chairman of the Exchange may publicly purchase it under the rule, and charge the difference, if any, to the delinquent. Or the borrower may borrow the stock of another who has it to lend, and continue the process until the price falls and he can satisfactorily close his contract. The rates paid for the loan of scarce stock are sometimes extraordinary. Thus, in a recent scarcity of Northern Pacific Preferred, a Philadelphia owner hired a special train to New York, appeared at the Stock Exchange, loaned at two or three per cent. per diem, and soon returned worth several thousand dollars more than when he came. In the Lackawanna corner engineered by Deacon S. V. White, another Philadelphian loaned

a large quantity of the stock, cleared about $10,000 in a few hours, and complacently retraced his steps to the City of Brotherly Love.

All securities sold are actually delivered; all securities bought are paid for on delivery; all borrowed stock is returned; all borrowed money is refunded. There are but few exceptions to these rules. In cases of default the stocks involved are publicly bought or sold, under the rule, by the Chairman, the contracts closed, and the differences paid. "You must do as you agree," is the homely iron law of the Stock Exchange. Refusal subjects to inexorable suspension or expulsion.

Notes of sales as they occur are made by twenty-four quotation clerks, who are also telegraph operators, and send the news by "sounders" to the main offices of the Western Union and Commercial Union Telegraph Companies. Thence the news of sales is sent by "transmitter" from each office over the tickers, of which there are many hundreds in and out of the city, in the offices—private, in hotels, club rooms, etc.—of their patrons. There agents, speculators, and investors watch the fluctuations as they follow, and intelligently issue orders to their brokers. Boston, Philadelphia, and other cities are thus in instantaneous communication with the New York market. Publicity is also given to the history of each day's transactions by a printer who makes it his business, and who distributes copies of his printed list to subscribers.

Stock-brokers also establish private telegraph codes between themselves and clients, codes in which certain words stand for names, phrases, numbers, etc. Thus, "Boxwood of London wants capsicum," that is, 10,000 shares of a known stock. "Sell 1000 Bouncer," "Buy 500 Zulu," "Loan Hickory Toadstool," "Take all that Godly Goodbub has to sell," "Close out Sandringham sharp," are telegrams that recipients holding the key fully understand.

Four telegraph companies—the Western Union, Baltimore and Ohio, Bankers' and Merchants', and Mutual Union—receive and deliver messages at the Stock Exchange by public wires, and also by about one hundred private ones, owned by different persons. On one day, in the space of five hours, 5727 telegrams were received from or dispatched to various parts of the country; and 1904 messages sent by messengers to people in the neighborhood of the building. Such is the accuracy of the service that it is asserted mistakes have not occurred in the delivery of a million and a half of messages that would involve the loss of five hundred dollars. From one to two millions are annually paid by brokers for communications with European correspondents.

The ideal business of the New York Stock Exchange is unquestionably as legitimate as that of the Produce Exchange, or of any intermediary between the seller and the buyer. That there are grave evils incident to its operation is equally unquestionable. The war for the preservation of the national Union largely converted the American people into a nation of speculators. The rage for sudden wealth was further intensified by the discoveries of mineral oil and the precious metals. These created innumerable companies for the exploitation of mines, the construction of railroads, and other objects. Sudden and violent fluctuations in the price of stocks, and the daily report thereof in the newspapers, aggravate the speculative spirit. Considerations of morality and prudence are set at naught by those who will be rich, and who dream of opulence by other methods than the slow and steady measures of their fathers. Professional men, merchants, manufacturers, mechanics, farmers, widows, and spinsters, blinded by the glare of success, and hoping to strengthen their slender income, have adventured their savings upon the treacherous sea of Wall Street, and lost them all. To them the Exchange Building is a whited sepulchre in which fortunes lie entombed, a sea in which voracious sharks rend or swallow the little fish who dare to enter its troubled waters, a gambling saloon where deceit and desperation wait upon the players. It may have been such to them, simply because they made it such, not because they availed themselves of its real functions.

An immense amount of gambling is done in piratical relation to it, and in spite of the strenuous exertions of the stockbrokers to prevent it. The "bucket shops" situated in the large towns and cities of the country are the instruments by which it is carried on. The proprietors of these nefarious establishments surreptitiously obtain quotations from the Stock Exchange. Tickers are refused to them by the Western Union unless four members

of the board vouch for the worthiness of each applicant. The quotations desired are furnished by persons who have bound themselves to that telegraph company not to do so, and who have obtained injunctions from the courts restraining the corporation from removing their instruments. Former insolvent members of the Stock Exchange, now known as "exempt members," are among the users of the knowledge thus acquired. Because of this grievance the Chicago Board of Trade has compelled the Western Union to remove its tickers from their offices—a precedent that the New York Stock Exchange will probably follow unless this grievance be redressed.

In these bucket shops a blackboard, with list of stocks at prices quoted in New York inscribed thereon, is displayed. Speculative clerks and others are invited to bet upon these quotations, under the pretense of the put and call system. For example, one is induced to buy, on a margin of $1 per share, five shares of Missouri, Kansas, and Texas stock at $16\frac{1}{4}$. If it rises to $17\frac{1}{4}$, he gets back his margin and gains $5. If it drops to $15\frac{1}{4}$, he loses his margin or bet. The secret of ruin in thousands of instances is to be found in the gambling of bucket shops. Yet the wealthy patronize and are fleeced by them. Quirk of Knaveville keeps a bucket shop, and receives the quotations. He confidentially informs his trusting patrons that he has certain knowledge that an inactive stock is about to rise in price—say the Denver and Rio Grande, now selling at 9—and persuades them to venture $1 per share to the extent of 15,000 shares. This done, he telegraphs to a broker to "sell 3000, D. and R. G.—quick, quick," in blocks from $8\frac{3}{4}$ to 8. The selling broker, alone or with assistance, makes his offers, which are accepted by another broker to whom Quirk has telegraphed to buy the stocks offered at those prices. The last quotation, 8, fixes the price. The telegraph announces it at Knaveville. The $15,000 margin, minus the one-fourth of one per cent. brokerage on the fictitious sales, is swept into the swindler's pocket.

While the Stock Exchange has legitimate and invaluable uses, it is none the less true that it has been and is converted into a gambling arena by the great speculative operators, most of whom have sprung from the lower walks of rural life, who control the management of railroads whose stocks are active. The facts of good or bad harvests, freight or passenger traffic, rates of transportation, can not explain the fluctuations of their prices. The secret is to be found in the parlors of directors. There flaming reports of pros-

that are vain," the conspirators acquire colossal wealth. The New York *Times* of July 31, 1884, devotes the whole of its first page to the history of the Union Pacific Railroad, in which it affirms that Jay Gould, after the panic of 1873, purchased

JAY GOULD.

perity are prepared, and unearned dividends declared, to "bull" the stock. There accounts are "cooked" so as to exhibit decreased earnings, needless expenses for rolling stock and improvements of permanent way incurred, floating debts swelled, acceptances issued for discount, and that will purposely be allowed to go to protest when due, earned dividends passed, evil prophecies uttered, to "bear" the stock. By "ways that are dark and tricks

a controlling interest, buying, it is said, at 15 to 20, and eventually selling at 90 to par. Its securities then and for some time afterward were dividend-paying, by virtue of good management and high traffic charges. This fact he and his associates—for Jay Gould is often multitudinous—resolved to turn to their own account. He bought up the dishonored bonds of the Kansas Pacific for much less than par (40 and upward), and its almost worthless stock for next to nothing—1 to 4; and also purchased the securities of the Denver Pacific. Next he proposed the consolidation of the three roads under the title of the Union Pacific; effected the consolidation in 1880; loaded the old Union Pacific with $14,000,000 of Kansas Pacific bonds, $10,000,000 of Kansas Pacific stock, and $4,000,000 Denver Pacific stock, and received new certificates of the same quantity and face value as the old ones. Next this original genius and his fellow-directors, who knew his plans and possibly shared his profits, issued over ten millions of additional stock, and in 1879 and 1883 over seven millions of Union Pacific bonds. Such is the current report.

How was this series of feats accomplished? "Jay Gould pays for his knowledge," remarked a Wall Street veteran. He does retain the best legal talent in his service. He also employs the powers of the subtlest intellect in the market. "Matched orders" raise or depress prices without regard to intrinsic values. Brokers are intermediary agents. Orders to buy or sell stocks may come through half a dozen hands before reaching them. The fingers that pull the wires which set the puppets dancing are often enveloped in densest darkness. Cash advances from the principal owners of Kansas Pacific pay the coupons next due. Provision is made for the payment of those past due. Kansas Pacific credit rises. Its stock is dead—no demand for it at 4. Brokers receive orders to buy large blocks at 4, and those orders are "matched" by instructions to other brokers to sell equal quantities at 4. The stock is galvanized. Next come orders to buy at 5, 6, 10, 12, and orders to sell at the same figures. Again come purchases and sales at 20, 40, 60. Kansas Pacific is extremely active. It leaps up to 105—ten per cent. higher than Union Pacific—and is really worth no more than when at 5. Long before the top notch is reached other speculators buy this active stock at rising prices. The owners unload much of their burden, to the tune of shekels clinking into their coffers. Of course they are obliged to support the stock, and to buy what may be offered while prices are advancing. A consolidated mortgage for twenty-nine or thirty millions upon the Kansas Pacific is next issued, and new bonds, guaranteed by the Union Pacific, exchanged for the old ones. Money is advanced to pay the first six months' interest. This imparts to the road an appearance of strength. Better conditions of trade do really raise its value, but by no means to the extent fictitiously indicated. Blocks of bonds and shares are transferred to confiding investors during this interesting process, and what remain in possession of the manipulators are of greater worth than the original Kansas Pacific bonds and stock.

Corners of stocks are affairs in which few except gambling speculators are injured, and in which legitimate stockholders may profit from higher prices. They occur in stocks of which the amount issuable or issued is known, and which have been oversold. Too many operators have made contracts for future delivery, or borrowed stocks which they have sold and delivered. The bulls, in clique or pool, ascertaining or estimating the extent of the "shorts," quietly buy up all the stock in the market, and when the contracts of the bears mature, drive those animals into a corner.

Excessive stock speculation causes stringency in the money market, compels brokers who carry stocks with scanty supply of clients' funds to realize quickly, and thus forces prices below the normal standard. It aggravates panics by making it the interest and habit of the bears to circulate alarming rumors of trouble in banks, and of important firms about to suspend. Suspicion is intensified by remembrance of former failures. All stocks sympathize. The bears are then "wreckers."

On the principle that charity begins at home, the New York Stock Exchange has established a gratuity fund, amounting at present to $700,000. It also makes a voluntary gift of $10,000, free from all claims, to the heirs of a deceased member. One-half is paid to the widow and one-half to the children; if there be no widow, the whole is paid to the children; if there be neither widow nor children, the whole is paid to his legal representatives. His membership is sold, and the proceeds—less any dues or balances of unfulfilled contracts against his name—paid to his heirs. Of the income of the Stock Exchange from fees, dues, fines, and rentals, amounting to $300,000, one moiety, after defraying all expenses, is appropriated to the gratuity fund, and the other in rebate to the members. The natural increase of the gratuity fund will soon render further assessments unnecessary.

Life in New York
Tenement Houses
(1892)

The Home of a Thousand People.

LIFE IN NEW YORK TENEMENT-HOUSES

AS SEEN BY A CITY MISSIONARY.

By William T. Elsing.

FOR nearly nine years I have spent much of my time in the homes of the working people, on the East Side, in the lower part of New York City. I have been with the people in their days of joy and hours of sorrow. I have been present at their marriage, baptismal, and funeral services. I have visited the sick and dying in cold, dark cellars in midwinter, and sat by the bedside of sufferers in midsummer in the low attic room, where the heat was so intense and the perspiration flowed so abundantly that it reminded me of a Turkish bath. I have been a frequent guest in the homes of the humble. I have become

the confidant of many in days of trouble and anxiety.

I shall in this article tell simply what I have heard, seen, and know. I shall endeavor to avoid giving a one-sided statement. I have noticed that nearly all those who work among the poor of our great cities fall into the natural habit of drawing too dark a picture of the real state of things. The outside world has always been more inclined to listen to weird, startling, and thrilling statements than to the more ordinary and commonplace facts. If I were to crowd into the space of one magazine article all the remarkable things which

191

The Bright Side of Life in a Tenement-house.

I have heard and seen during the past nine years, I might give an absolutely truthful account and produce a sensation, and yet, after all, I should give a most misleading idea of the actual condition of the homes and the people with whom I have been so intimately associated. We must not crowd all the sad and gloomy experiences of a lifetime into a history which can be read in an hour.

What I have said applies especially to the homes of the people in the tenement-houses. An ordinary tenement-house contains five stories and a basement, four families usually occupying a floor. The halls in nearly all the houses are more or less dark, even during the brightest part of the day. In the winter, just before the gas is lighted, dungeon darkness reigns. When groping my way in the passages I usually

The Dark Side—under the Same Roof.

imitate the steam crafts in a thick fog and give a danger-signal when I hear someone else approaching; but even when all is silent I proceed with caution, for more than once I have stumbled against a baby who was quietly sitting in the dark hall or on the stairs. In the old-style halls there is no way of getting light and air, except from the skylight in the roof, or from the glass transoms in the doors of the apartments. In the newer houses a good supply of air comes directly from the air-shafts at the side of the hall. The new houses are not much better lighted than the old ones. The air-shafts are too narrow to convey much light to the lower floors. In the older houses the sink is frequently found in the hall, where the four tenants living on the same floor get their water. These sinks in the dark halls are a source of great inconvenience. A person is liable to stumble against them, and they are frequently filthy and a menace to health. In the new tenements the sink is never placed in the hall. In addition to the owner and agent, in connection with every large tenement-house, there is a housekeeper. The housekeepers are usually strong and thrifty housewives who take care of the halls and stairs, light the gas, sweep the sidewalks, and show the rooms to new applicants, and frequently receive the rent until the agent or landlord calls for it. Sometimes the housekeeper deals directly with the landlord, who comes once or twice a month to look at his property and collect the rent. The housekeeper is frequently a widow, who gets free rent in exchange for her work, and by

reduced rate in exchange for her services. There is never any difficulty in getting a good housekeeper. The landlord or agent sees to it that the housekeeper does her duty and the housekeeper watches the tenants. If they soil the stairs and halls, she reminds them of the fact in no uncertain way. If a careless tenant gives unnecessary labor to the housekeeper that tenant will soon be compelled to seek other quarters. The result is that the stairs and halls in all the large tenement-houses are remarkably clean. I have visited a great number of them, and can confidently say that I have never seen the halls of a large tenement-house in as neglected and dirty a condition as the corridors of the New York Post-Office. But the moment you enter the rooms of the occupants you often step from cleanliness into filth. The influence of the housekeeper and the sight of the clean halls and stairs is to some the first lesson in cleanliness, and is not without its beneficial effects. There is a slow but constant improvement in this direction, and every year strangers from many lands are getting gradually acquainted with the use, value, and virtue of clean water.

The housekeeper is frequently wanting in the older and smaller houses, which were formerly occupied by one family, but now serve as homes for three or four. Every tenant is here expected to perform a portion of the housekeeper's duty without remuneration. These houses are sometimes extremely dirty, and the death-rate is higher than in the larger and better kept tenements.

Pig Alley.

means of sewing or washing is able to provide food and clothing for her children. It pays the landlord to have one tenant rent free in order to have a clean house. If the house is small the housekeeper usually receives her rent at a

Let us leave the hall and enter some of the homes in the larger houses. To many persons living in a tenement-house is synonymous with living in the slums, yet nothing is further from the truth. It would be an easy matter for me to take a stranger into a dozen or more

A New Tenement of the Better Sort—One of Many Recently Erected by Private Enterprise.

homes so poor, dirty, and wretched that he would not forget the sight for days, and he would be thoroughly convinced that a home cannot exist in a tenement-house; but I could take that same person to an equal number of homes in the same section of the city, and sometimes in the same house, which would turn him into a joyful optimist, and forever satisfy him that the state of things is not by any means as bad as it might be. To the casual observer the tenement-houses in many portions of New York present a remarkable degree of uniformity. The great brick buildings with their network of iron fire-escapes in front, their numerous clothes-lines running from every window in the rear, the well-worn stairs, the dark halls, the numerous odors, pleasant and otherwise, coming from a score of different kitchens presided over by housewives of various nationalities — these are all similar; but the moment you enter the rooms, however, you will find every variety of homes, many of them poor, neglected, wretched, and dirty; others clean, thrifty, and attractive; indeed, as great a variety as exists in the interior of homes in an ordinary town. There

same time thousands of cheerful, happy homes in the tenement-houses. The floor is frequently as clean and white as soap, water, and German muscle is able to make it. The tablecloth and bedlinen, although of coarse material, are snowy white. The stove has the brightness of a mirror, the cheap lace-curtains are the perfection of cleanliness, and the simple furniture shines with a recent polishing. There is nothing offensive about the well-washed faces of the children. A few favorite flowers are growing on the window-sill. The room contains a book-shelf with a few popular volumes. A bird-cage hangs from the ceiling; the little

A Grandfather Cutting Carpet-rags.

are homes where the floor is bare and dirty, the furniture broken and scanty, the table greasy, the bedlinen yellow, the air foul and heavy, the children pale, frowsy, and sticky, so that you squirm when the baby wants to kiss you; but there is also another and brighter side. There are at the

songster seems to feel that his music is appreciated in this tenement-kitchen, and pours forth more rich and tender notes than are ever heard in the silent chambers of the wealthy. In such homes the oft-recurring motto, "God Bless Our Home," is not an idle mockery.

Poverty and Death.

A large number of tenement-houses in the lower portion of New York are only a little below the common up-town flat. It is often difficult to tell where the flat leaves off and the tenement begins. You get about as little air and sunshine in the one as in the other. The main difference lies in the number of rooms and the location. If some down-town tenement-houses stood up-town they would be called flats. The word *tenement* is becoming unpopular down-town, and many landlords have dubbed their great caravansaries by the more aristocratic name of "flat," and the term "rooms" has been changed to "apartments."

There are three distinct classes of homes in the tenement-houses; the cheapest and humblest of these is the attic home, which usually consists of one or two rooms, and is found only down-town. These are generally occupied by old persons. Occasionally three or four attic rooms are connected and rented to a family, but as small single rooms are sought after by lonely old people, the landlord often rents them separate-

ly. An old lady who has to earn her bread with the needle finds the attic at once the cheapest and best place for her needs. The rent of one or two unfurnished attic rooms ranges from $3 to $5 per month.

A large number of very poor people live in three rooms—a kitchen and two dark bedrooms. Where the family is large the kitchen lounge is opened and converted into a double bed at night. The rent for three rooms is generally from $8 to $12 per month.

The vast majority of respectable working people live in four rooms—a kitchen, two dark bedrooms, and a parlor. These parlors are generally provided with a bed-lounge, and are used as sleeping-rooms at night. The best room is always carpeted and often provided with upholstered chairs. The walls are generally decorated with family photographs and inexpensive pictures, and in some of them I have found a piano. These parlors compare very favorably with the best room in the house of the average farmer. The rent for four rooms is from $12 to $16 per month.

The rent is an ever-present and unceasing source of anxiety to a great many poor people. The family is sometimes obliged to go half clothed and live on the cheapest and coarsest food in order to provide the rent money. The monthly rent is a veritable sword of Damocles. To a poor woman who dreads the coming of the landlord, the most enticing and attractive description of heaven which I have been able to give is a place where they pay no rent. The landlords are of necessity compelled to be peremptory and sometimes arbitrary in their demands. If a landlord were even a little too lenient his tenement property would certainly prove a losing investment. The apparently unreasonable harshness of many landlords is often justifiable, and the only means of securing them against loss. Generally where a good tenant is unable to pay the rent on account of sickness or lack of work the landlord is willing to extend the time a few weeks. I frequently find families who are two or three months in arrears. In the majority of cases where dispossess papers are served, the landlord does not know his tenant sufficiently well to trust him, or the tenant is unworthy of trust. Very few of those who are evicted are compelled to take to the street. In most cases sufficient money is collected from friends, neighbors, and charitable people to procure another place of shelter. Occasionally, however, all the worldly possessions of an unfortunate tenant are placed on the street. It is a pathetic sight to see a small heap of poor household stuff standing on the sidewalk guarded by the children, while the distressed mother is frantically rushing from one charitable organization to another in search of help.

A poor German woman came to me last year and informed me that her furniture was standing on the sidewalk, and she knew not what would become of her. She had with her a beautiful little girl. The child cried continually, but the mother's distress was too great for tears. She begged me in God's name to help her. I gave her but little encouragement, and dismissed her with a few kind words. She left without heaping abuse on me or cursing the church for its neglect of the poor. A little later I went to the place where she informed me her furniture was and found all her earthly goods on the sidewalk. I inquired of some of her former neighbors about her character, and on being convinced that she was a worthy woman, rented two small rooms in a rear tenement. I found some young street-corner loafers, told them about the woman, and asked them to lend a hand in getting the furniture moved. There is no man so bad that he will not do a good turn for another if you approach him properly. These young roughs went to work with a will, and when the poor woman returned from her last fruitless attempt to collect enough for a new home she found everything arranged. She was thankful and happy. I did not see her until two months later. Then she appeared in as great distress as before, and showed me a new dispossess paper. She informed me that she had failed to find work, everything had been against her, but she hoped to get on her feet if I would once more help her. I told her it was impossible for me to do anything more for her; so she thanked me for my former kindness and departed. That afternoon I heard of a lady in Orange, N. J., who wanted a house-servant and a little girl as waitress. I immediately thought of the German woman and promised if possible to send her out to Orange as soon as arrangements could be made. I was soon in the little rooms of the widow and her daughter and expected to be the bearer of joyful tidings. When I finished she looked sadly at the few scanty pieces of furniture and said:

"If I go to the country what shall I do with the stuff?"

"My good woman," I said, "the stuff is not worth fifty cents; give it to the boys to make a bonfire, and do what I tell you."

"But I have not money enough to leave the city."

I provided the fare, the boys had a glorious time around their fire, and that night, instead of sleeping in her comfortless room, the poor woman was on Orange Mountain. It would have been a losing investment for any land-

DRAWN BY C. BROUGHTON.

ENGRAVED BY H. W. PECKWELL.

Evicted—on the Sidewalk.

lord to have given an extension of time to that woman, and yet she was a thoroughly worthy person, as the sequel

foreigner who took up his abode in a tenement-house fifteen or twenty years ago may be perfectly contented with his

A Hovel in the Italian Quarter.

proved; her old misery and trouble were at an end. She found a good home and gave perfect satisfaction.

Many other experiences like this, and my constant association with the conditions of tenement-house life, have, of course, led me to certain conclusions as to the best remedies, which I shall reserve for specific mention in the latter part of this article.

The population of the tenement-houses in lower New York is continually changing. There is a constant graduation of the better element. As soon as the circumstances of the people improve they want better homes. A

surroundings, but when his children grow up and earn good wages they are not satisfied with a tenement-house, and give the old people no peace until a new home is found. Sometimes a man who has led a bad life reforms and immediately seeks a better home for his wife and children. I know several men who were at one time low and degraded drunkards, who would have been satisfied with a pig-sty, who had torn the clothes from their children's backs, the blankets from their beds, and taken them to the pawn-shop to get money for drink; but through the good influences that were thrown around them, the wise counsel of friends, and the saving power of the gospel they became changed men. Their circumstances began to improve, the children were provided with clothes, one piece of furniture after another was brought into the empty rooms, until the place began to look like a home again. These men were charmed with the new life. Home became so dear a place that they are willing to travel an hour each morning and evening in order to make it still more attractive. They began to

This constant sifting of the best elements makes religious and philanthropic work in lower New York exceedingly difficult and apparently unfruitful, but none the less encouraging and necessary. The fact that the people leave the tenements in search of better homes is the best proof that a good work is being accomplished. A few months ago we celebrated the tenth anniversary of the dedication of one of our city mission churches. There were

The Monroe Model Tenement.

see the disadvantages of life in a tenement and found a new home on Long Island or in New Jersey.

six hundred present, and out of this number there were only twenty-four who were at the dedication ten years before. While the better class is being constantly sifted out of the tenements, a steady stream of new-comers flows in to take their places.

Successive waves of population follow each other in rapid succession. It is often impossible to tell what the character of the population will be in the next ten years. In 1830 the agents of the New York City Mission visited 34,542 families. Among this number there were only 264 who desired foreign tracts, showing that the population was then almost exclusively American or English-speaking. Now the English language is rarely heard in some of the lower parts of New York, except by the children. That section of the city between the Bowery and East River, Grand and Houston Streets, has been successively occupied by Americans, Irish, Germans, and is now fast coming into the possession of Russian and Polish Jews. The Jewish invasion has been remarkably rapid. Eight years ago I used to see occasionally a Jewish face on the streets or a Jewish sign over the stores. Now the streets swarm with them.

I recently made a careful canvass of a typical block and found 300 families composed of 1,424 individuals. The nationalities of the families were as follows: 244 German, 16 Irish, 11 American, 13 Hungarian, 6 Polish, 4 Russian, 2 Bohemian, 1 English, 1 Dutch, and 2 Chinese. Among the 244 German families there were 192 Jews, 38 Protestants, and 14 Roman Catholics. The German Jews are the most highly respected, and on this account many call themselves German who are in reality Russian or Polish Jews. These 300 heads of families are engaged in 72 different trades, occupations, and professions. There are 73 tailors, 17 cigarmakers, 17 storekeepers, 12 pedlars, 11 painters, 9 butchers, and 9 shoemakers in the block. The remaining 65 trades and professions are represented by 148 different persons. Thirty of the heads of families are Roman Catholics, 47 Protestants, and 221 Jews, and 2 have no religion. The Jews do not as a rule mingle to any great extent with the Christians. When they come in large numbers into a street,

the Christians gradually withdraw, and the neighborhood finally becomes a Jewish quarter. There are streets in New York where it is a rare thing to find a Christian family.

During the transition period, when a locality is neither Christian nor Jewish, an interesting state of things prevails—a Jewish family, a Roman Catholic family, a pious Protestant family, and a heathen family, as far as religion is concerned, frequently live on the same floor. Suffering appeals to our common humanity. In trouble and sickness these neighbors render each other assistance and often become warm friends. I have seen a Jewish woman watching anxiously by the bedside of a dying Christian. A Roman Catholic or Jewish woman will often stand as godmother at the baptism of a Protestant child. A pretty, black-eyed Jewess occasionally captures the heart of a young Roman Catholic or Protestant, and they have come to me to perform the marriage service. Persons of various nations and religious beliefs are sometimes present at a tenement-house funeral. Bigotry and national prejudice are gradually broken down and the much-abused tenement becomes a means of promoting the brotherhood of man and the union of Christendom. You may hear daily from the lips of devout Roman Catholics and Jews such words as these: "We belong to a different religion, but we have the same God and hope to go to the same heaven." Such confessions are not often heard in small towns and country districts, but they are frequent in the tenement-houses.

The Jews, who in all ages have been noted for their exclusiveness, are affected by this contact with Christians in the tenement-house. In DeWitt Memorial Church, with which I am connected, an audience of three or four hundred Jews assembles every week to hear Christian instruction. From the standpoint of social science such a gathering every week for the past eighteen months is significant. The Jew in every land has preserved his identity. Persecution has isolated him; when he has been most hated he has flourished, when he has been despised

An Invalid Supporting His Family by Making Lace.

he has prospered. Like the symbolic burning bush, the fires of persecution have not destroyed him. It remains to be seen whether he will preserve his identity in this country, where, as a citizen, he enjoys equal rights, and where the doors of the public school and the Christian church stand open to Jew and Gentile alike.

Whatever may be the nationality of the parents the children are always thorough Americans. The blond-haired, blue-eyed German children; the black-haired, dark-eyed Italians; the little Jews, both dark and blonde, from many lands, are all equally proud of being Americans. A patriotic Irishman gave a beautiful edition of "Pictu-resque Ireland" to one of the boys in my Sunday-school. The lad looked disappointed. His father asked him why he was not pleased with the present. He answered: "I want a history of the United States." We have a circulating library, patronized almost exclusively by foreigners. The librarian informs me that four boys out of every five call for United States histories.

The most powerful influence at work among the tenement-house population is the public school. Every public school is a great moral lighthouse, and stands for obedience, cleanliness, morality, and patriotism, as well as mental training. When the little children begin to attend the schools their hands and faces are inspected, and if they are not up to the standard, they are sent home for a washing. A boy who is especially dirty is sometimes sent down-stairs with the cleanest boy in school, and told to wash himself until he looks as well as his companion. Such lessons are not soon forgotten, and the result is the public-school children in lower New York present a very respectable appearance. The fresh-air excursions, with many other benefits, promote cleanliness. The heads of the children must be examined before they can enjoy a trip into the country. There is

or three weeks the pale-faced children return to the crowded city with renewed health and with larger and better views of life. I know boys who became so enraptured with green fields, running brooks, waving grain, and life on the farm that they have fully resolved to leave the city when they become men. One little fellow was so anxious to become a farmer that he ran away because his parents would not permit him to leave home.

The fresh-air work usually closes in October, but the young ladies connected with the "College Settlement" have added a new feature, which will

The Poor Helping the Poor—Distributing Thanksgiving Dinners.

no more beautiful and beneficent charity than this fresh-air work.* In two

commend itself to everyone who is acquainted with the condition of life around us. Every Saturday afternoon during the winter two of the ladies take a small party of children to their summer home. Saturday evening is spent in playing various games, or enjoying

You cannot do people very much good at long range. Hand-picked fruit is the best.

A Missionary Workshop—De Witt Memorial Church (non-sectarian).

a candy-pull, and having a general good time. On Sunday the children attend the country church, and Sunday evening, seated before a blazing open fire, a good book is read, or the ladies in charge give some practical talk to the children. On Monday the little party returns to the city and the house is locked until the following Saturday. Such a visit to the country will be indelibly impressed upon these children.

Last summer I took a party of boys from my mission church to Northfield, Mass., and attended Mr. Moody's students' conference. We pitched our tents in the forest, cooked our own food, and sang college songs around our campfire at night. In ten days I became thoroughly acquainted with the boys, and was able to help them in many ways. I believe if every minister, priest, rabbi, and Sunday-school superintend-

ent would select eight or ten young men and spend two weeks with them under canvas by the side of a mountain-lake or trout-stream, more good might be done in permanently influencing their lives than by many weeks of eloquent preaching.

To keep the boys off the streets, and to train them to habits of cleanliness, obedience, and manliness, military companies have been formed in several of our down-town Sunday-schools. It is astonishing how well a number of wild boys will go through military tactics after a few months' drilling. The hope of our great cities lies in the children of the poor. If we can influence them to become upright, honorable men and women, we shall not only save them, but produce the most powerful lever for lifting up those of the same class who are sinking. I know scores of children and young people who are far better than their parents. Some of the noblest young men I have ever known have worthless, drunken parents. Some of the most beautiful flowers grow in mud-ponds, and some of the truest and best young women in our city come from homes devoid of good influences ; but in all such cases uplifting outside help has moulded their characters.

While the people in tenement-houses are compelled to sleep in rooms where the sunlight never enters, and suffer many discomforts from overcrowding, especially in summer, there are certain compensations which must not be overlooked. The poor in large cities who have steady work are, as a rule, better fed and clothed than the same class in rural districts. Fresh vegetables, raised in hot-houses, or sent from Southern markets, are sold throughout the winter at reasonable prices, and in the early spring strawberries and various other fruits are for sale on the streets in the tenement district long before they reach the country towns and villages. In the poorest quarter of the city you find the so-called "delicatessen" shops, where the choicest groceries, preserves, and canned meats are sold. The clothing, too, worn by the young people is stylish and sometimes expensive ; anyone who walks through these

districts will be astonished at the number of well-dressed young people. A young woman who earns from $6 to $8 a week will often be dressed in silk or satin, made according to the fashion. The teeth, finger-nails, and shoes are often the only signs of her poverty. When visiting a stylish young woman's plain mother, I have sometimes seen all the finery in which the daughter appeared at church on Sunday hanging on the wall of a bare, comfortless bedroom not much larger than a good-sized closet.

The tenement-house people are not all thriftless, as the records of the down-town savings-banks clearly prove. Seven hundred out of every thousand depositors in one of the banks on the Bowery live in tenement-houses, and if it were not for tenement-house depositors several of our down-town savings-banks would be compelled to give up business. An abundance of cruel and bitter poverty, however, can always be found. The "submerged tenth" is ever present.

A widow, for instance, with three or four young children who is obliged to earn her bread by sewing, is in a most pitiable and terrible position. Hundreds of such weary mothers continue their work far into the night, with smarting eyes, aching backs, and breaking hearts. There is nothing which makes a man who has any feeling for the suffering of his fellows so dissatisfied with our present social system as the sight of such a poor woman sewing shirts and overalls for twenty-nine cents a dozen. There are good people in all our large cities who live just above the starving point. The average earnings of the unskilled laborers with whom I am acquainted is not over $10 per week. When a man is obliged to spend one-fourth of this for rent, and feed and clothe his family on the remainder, it is impossible to lay by anything for a rainy day. When the father is out of work for a considerable time, or when sickness or death enter the home, distress, hunger, and an urgent landlord stare him in the face.

It is easy for those who have never felt it to overlook the constant strain of poverty and the irritation which it causes in families which in circumstances of ordinary comfort would be contented. In such cases particularly can great good be accomplished by a visit from some clear-sighted and sympathetic person.

Recently I was invited to act as referee between a husband and wife. There were three little children and a grandmother in the family. The man worked in a cigar-box factory; business was slack and he was employed only half time. His average weekly earnings were $5. They had a debt of $11 at a grocery-store and another of $35 at an undertaker's shop. I know the family; both husband and wife are honest, sober, and industrious people. The wife wanted to break up housekeeping; the husband was opposed to this plan, and they had agreed to abide by my decision. I examined each one separately. I began with the husband and said:

"When a physician prescribes a remedy he must first know the disease. I want you, therefore, to tell me plainly why your wife wants to break up the home. There may be good reasons why her plan should be adopted. If you two cannot possibly agree, and are fighting like cats and dogs, then I may be in favor of breaking up. Tell me just how the matter stands."

He informed me that he and his wife had always lived in perfect peace. They never had any trouble except poverty. The wife had become completely discouraged, and the only way she saw out of the difficulty was to put the children into an orphan asylum and go out as a house-servant until she could earn enough to clear off the debt, after which she hoped to get her home together again. The wife and grandmother gave me the same account. The perpetual strain of poverty was the only reason for breaking up the home. For the sake of the three little children I decided that the home must not be broken up and promised to see that the debt at the grocery-store was wiped out and the family clothing was taken out of the pawn-shop. The grandmother was so pleased with the decision that she determined to become a servant and begged me to find a place for her.

In our large cities there is too much isolation between the rich and the poor. The charitable societies are often the only link between them. If the mother of every well-to-do home in our large cities would regularly visit, once a month, a needy family, a vast amount of good would be accomplished among the worthy poor, and distress would be unknown. Human nature is too selfish for such a happy state of things ever to be realized, but it is possible to bring the givers and receivers of charity closer together than they are. If some of the wealthier ladies who now give a few dollars each year to the charitable societies would seek through these societies to come into direct personal contact with the recipients of their charity, they would experience a deeper happiness and fully realize the blessedness of giving. Business men are too much occupied to make a monthly visit to the tenement-houses, but if their wives and daughters would undertake this work a new day would dawn for many a poor, heartbroken mother who is now hopeless and longing for death to end her misery. We are frequently asked, "Is it safe for a lady to visit these great tenement-houses?" We answer unhesitatingly, perfectly safe. The young ladies connected with the City Mission go unmolested into the darkest portions of New York. The first visit to a tenement-house might be made in the company of a city missionary, after which the most timid could go alone.

Nothing is easier than to make paupers out of the poor. Great discretion must be exercised, but the Charity Organization Society, the Society for Improving the Condition of the Poor, the City Mission, the Children's Aid Society, and other equally worthy institutions are ever ready to give direction to individuals who desire to do personal work. A few persons have through the City Mission come into personal contact with the poor, and the results are most gratifying.

While in a small town the distress of the poor is easily made known through friends and neighbors or the clergyman, in our large cities the most deserving are often overlooked and suffer most intensely; and it is these cases which are reached by personal visitation. The worthy poor are generally the silent poor. Their sufferings must be extreme before they make their wants known. There are many poor, upright, God-fearing old people who struggle against fearful odds to keep body and soul together, and yet they drift daily toward the almshouse on Blackwell's Island, the last and most dreaded halting place on the way to Potter's Field. I have nothing to say against the administration of the almshouse or the treatment of its inmates, but I do not wonder that old men and women who have led a good moral life would rather die than be stranded on the island and take up their abode among the broken wrecks of humanity which fill that institution.

It is very unwise to give aid without a thorough investigation. Not long ago a Polish Jew asked me the way to a certain street. I directed him, and he said : "Dear sir, I am in great distress ; my furniture is standing on the sidewalk in Essex Street, and my children are watching the stuff, while I am trying to collect a little money to get another place." He drew from his pocket a few coppers, and asked me to add my gift. I said : "I do not know you, and I am acquainted with a great many poor people whom I would like to help, but I have not the means ; how, then, can you expect any help from me?" Two streams burst from his eyes. The big tears rained down his beard and coat. "It is hard," he said, and bowed his head, buried his face in a red handkerchief, wiped off the tears, and passed on. I crossed the street. The tears of that sad man touched me. I turned, ran after him, and said : "Where is the stuff?" "In Essex Street." "What have you?" "A table, bureau, bed, and looking-glass," he replied. "Have you nothing small that I can take with me and loan you money on?" He pointed to his well-worn greasy coat, and said : "I have this." "Show me the stuff," I said. We walked together, and I endeavored to carry on a conversation with the stranger in German, for he was ignorant of English, but suddenly he seemed to have lost all knowledge of the German tongue in which

he had before addressed me, and was perfectly dumb. When we reached Ridge Street he finally spoke, and asked me to wait for him a moment while he went to see a friend. I said : "Look here, I want you to take me to the stuff immediately." He looked amazed and said : "What have I to do with you?" "A good deal," I replied ; "you either take me to the stuff or I take you to the police station." "Do you think I am a liar?" I said : "You must take me to the stuff or you are a liar." "Come," he said, "I will take you to the stuff." It was wonderful to see how that old man, who had moved so slowly before, walked through the crowded streets. I had all I could do to keep up with him. We soon reached Essex Street. It was Friday afternoon and Essex Street was in all its glory—old clothes, decayed meat, pungent fish, and stale fruit abounded. The Ghetto in Rome and the Jewish quarters in London and Amsterdam are nothing compared with Essex Street. At one place it was almost impossible to get through the crowd, and I left the sidewalk and took the street. In a moment my new acquaintance disappeared, and I have not seen him since. I have no doubt this man and many others like him are making a good deal of money by playing on the sympathies of poor people.

I have made it a rule never to give a homeless man money, but when his breath does not smell of whiskey I give him my card containing the name and address of a lodging-house. The card must be used the same day it is given. As some of those who ask for a lodging never use the cards, my bill is always less than the number of cards given out. One night a man told me he was tired of his bad life and he wanted to become a better man. I spoke a few encouraging words to him and was about to dismiss him, when he told me he was sick and needed just five cents to get a dose of salts. I took him at his word and immediately sent for the drug and made him take it on the spot. It is needless to say that he never troubled me again.

There remain many cases where charity is of no avail. Where poverty is caused by crime, no relief can come except by breaking up the home. Not long since I was called to take charge of the funeral of a little child. I groped my way up the creaking, filthy stairs of a small, old-fashioned rear tenement. I knocked, but heard no response; I pushed the door open, but found no one in the room, yet this was the place—"Rear, top floor, left door." I made no mistake. I entered the room and found a dead baby wrapped in an old towel lying on a table. I learned from the neighbors that the father and mother had been out collecting money to bury the child and had both become beastly drunk. I returned to the dead child, read the burial service, and thanked God that the little one was out of its misery. A little later a man came and took the body to Potter's Field. The parents had buried (it would be more accurate to say starved to death) six children before they were two years old. Very little can be done for such people. Cumulative sentences ought to be imposed upon them each time they are arrested for drunkenness, so that prison-bars may prevent them from bringing the little sufferers into the world.

A great deal is done by the various charitable societies for the relief of distress, but as far as my observation goes the most effective charitable work is done by the poor themselves. Thousands of dollars are given away in the tenement districts every year by the inhabitants of the tenements, of which no charitable society makes a record. I have never related a peculiarly distressing case of poverty to a poor person but there was a ready response, and out of their own poverty the poor have ministered to those who were in need of relief. The children of our City Mission school, who come from the tenement-houses, contributed last Thanksgiving-Day $80 for the poor in our immediate neighborhood. A club of fifty small boys and girls saved their pennies and bought thirty-five Thanksgiving dinners for the poor, consisting of chickens, potatoes, beans, turnips, and cabbages. The original plan was to have a head of cabbage go with each chicken, but the money gave out; this did not in any way disconcert the children, for they quickly solved the difficulty by cutting a cabbage into four parts, and putting a quarter into each bag. The children worked from 7.30 to 11 P.M. distributing the provisions. The members of this club visit the hospitals, sing to the patients, and furnish them with reading matter. During the past ten months they have distributed 27,901 booklets and illustrated papers. Last summer the children noticed that the flies troubled the sick people and there were no fans in some of the hospitals. They saved their pennies, which in most cases would have gone to the candy-store, and bought a lot of palm-leaf fans at a wholesale house. They bound the fans with variously colored ribbons and decorated them with scripture texts appropriate to the sick, and on Sunday afternoon presented them to the delighted patients. The poor give that which costs them something, and their joy is correspondingly greater. That the most spontaneous and beautiful charity flourishes in the tenement-houses will undoubtedly be a surprise to many, but it is a fact well known to all who have any large acquaintance with the poor in our great cities.

It is equally true that there is more virtue in tenement localities than is commonly supposed. Darkness and sin have much in common. The dark halls and crowded homes are not favorable to virtue, but nevertheless virtue is the rule and vice the exception. The people who live in tenement-houses are not fastidious about rules of etiquette and propriety. Young women sometimes allow young men to address them and caress them in a manner which would offend well-bred people, and yet these girls would indignantly resent any liberties which they consider dishonoring. Young people occasionally desire to be married secretly, and timidly ask if it is not possible for me to date back the wedding certificate three or four months; such cases, however, are not common. There are many hasty marriages where the consent of the parents has not been obtained; these sometimes end in a speedy separation. Young girls occasionally come to me accompanied by young men half drunk and ask me to perform the marriage ceremony. There are self-styled clergymen who put up conspicuous signs advertising the fact that they make a business of uniting young people in marriage. These hungry sharks are ever ready to give their services for one or two dollars, thus plunging thoughtless young people into misery. I have succeeded in breaking up matches which I knew would have brought certain ruin to the parties concerned. I always refuse to marry a young couple when I am not permitted to consult the parents before performing the ceremony. If a law were passed making it obligatory on young people to get a license from the civil courts before a clergyman could perform the marriage, some unfortunate marriages would be prevented. A few hours of sober reflection would bring both parties to their senses.

The young people in our cities are extravagant. Very few of them save anything. Many of them put all they earn on their backs, and sometimes have not enough to pay the wedding fee, and all the furniture for the new home has been bought on the instalment plan. When the young husband is sober and industrious the married life generally moves on smoothly. It frequently happens, however, that from the day of her marriage a girl begins to fade like a flower. In three or four years a bright young girl will degenerate into a careworn, ill-tempered, slovenly middle-aged woman, surrounded by two or three pale, ragged, ungoverned children. She spent her girlhood in a store or shop, and was never initiated into the art of housekeeping. Her husband finds the saloon a far more comfortable place than his home. When industrial training shall have been introduced into every public school and the girls get a thorough training in housekeeping we may look for improvement in the home life of the poor in our cities. The cooking classes in connection with the girls' clubs, the Young Women's Christian Association, and those opened in some of the City Mission churches are doing excellent service in training young women to assume the responsibilities of home-makers.

The influence of the church on the tenement population is not as great as it probably will be in the near future. The strongest churches have followed their constituents and moved up-town ; those which remained have languished, and in some cases have been compelled to close for want of active support. A new era has dawned. All religious denominations are interested in the churchless masses. New churches and chapels are being erected down-town, and there is a strong feeling in every quarter that the old stations must be maintained. The wisest men fully recognize the fact that if the churches among the tenement population are to do efficient work they must be well manned, richly endowed, and run at high pressure all through the year. Wherever church work has been pursued on these lines the results have been most gratifying. The workingmen, although not hostile, are generally extremely indifferent to religion. They are concerned about food, clothing, and a place of shelter for the present, and trouble themselves but little about the future. The fact that the church is beginning to take an active interest in the temporal welfare of the working people is already producing beneficial results.

The daily press exerts as great an influence over the parents as the public school does over the children. The workingmen in the tenement-houses constantly read the newspapers, and they read almost nothing else. What we need is not more learned lectureship foundations on the evidences of Christianity, but endowments to secure a large number of short, concise, popular prize essays on moral and religious subjects, especially adapted in language and style to the working people. If these prize essays were published in the Sunday papers they would be read by tens of thousands of workingmen, and be a most powerful means of doing good.

There are a great many things which might be done to improve the conditions of the poor, but most of the schemes proposed are altogether impracticable. If we could make the poor sober and industrious, and the rich unselfish and generous, poverty would soon disappear ; unfortunately we can do neither. We must take the world as we find it, and employ the best means to reach the desired end. I have seen a great deal of wretchedness and poverty in lower New York, and for some of these evils I can offer no remedy ; but if the following suggestions could be carried out I believe something would be done toward improving "darkest New York :"

First.—There is nothing the inhabitants of the tenement-houses need so much as more room, sunshine, and fresh air. At present the sun never shines in the bedrooms of three-quarters of the people of New York City. In some parts of our city the population is nearly twice as dense as in the most crowded part of London. Nowhere on the wide earth are human beings so crowded as in the tenement districts. The suffering in July and August is often intense. The bedrooms become unbearable, and the roofs, fire-escapes, and empty wagons are used as sleeping places. Thousands of little children do not see green grass during the entire summer ; they are virtually prisoners in their own homes. The only true remedy can come in a complete system of cheap rapid transit. If the happy day ever comes when a poor man can be carried to the green fields of Long Island, New Jersey, or Westchester County for five cents, then a wonderful change will take place. It is commonly supposed that the poor enjoy herding together like dumb brutes on a cattle train, but nothing is further from the truth. The only reason why so many people put up with the numerous inconveniences of a tenement-house is simply that stern necessity compels them to live in this way. At the present time, with all the inconveniencies of travel, many persons are leaving tenement-houses and seeking better homes in Brooklyn, Jersey City, and upper New York. If the North and East Rivers were spanned with railroad bridges, so that in twenty minutes a workingman might be ten miles distant from the factory or store, there would be a great exodus from the tenement-houses, and many places now used as homes would be turned into shops and warehouses.

Second.—A great blessing would be conferred on the crowded multitudes of the East Side if the long-promised and eagerly-desired small parks were opened. There are stone, coal, and lumber yards on the river-front on the East Side which would make attractive breathing spots for the children of the poor. If the Park Commissioners would bestir themselves, and with all possible haste provide the children of the poor with small parks and play-grounds they would confer an inestimable blessing upon the city.

Third.—Great improvements have been made in the construction and sanitary arrangements of tenement-houses, but still more must be done in the same direction. There are scores of horrible, pestilential rat-holes which are utterly unfit for human habitation. All such places ought to be condemned, and the Board of Health must be backed up by public sentiment in its endeavor to root out these plague-spots. Our city lots are not of the proper size to erect the large rectangular European tenements with a court in the centre, from which light and air can be conveyed into every room. A few such model tenements, however, have been built by associations of philanthropists and private individuals. More of these model tenements are needed. They will bring down the exorbitantly high rents which are now exacted from the poorest people. The model tenement will confer a great boon upon large families. It is often exceedingly difficult for a man who has seven or eight children to get rooms in the better class houses. The first question asked is, "How many children have you ?" I know families who have been compelled to pay a high rent for poor accommodations on account of the large number of children. A poor woman searched all day for rooms ; wherever she saw a place that suited her the old question, "How many children have you ?" was asked, and she was obliged to look elsewhere. One morning she sent all her children to Greenwood Cemetery, put on a black dress, and began the search of rooms. When she had found a suitable place the landlord asked, "How many children have you?" "Six," answered the woman, sadly; "but they are all in Greenwood." The landlord was satisfied that the children would do his place no harm. The woman paid a month's rent and took possession. There was a scene at night, but during the month the woman proved to be such a good tenant that she was allowed to remain permanently.

Fourth.—The saloon is the poor man's club, and flourishes most vigorously in the poorest sections of the city. Instead of denouncing the saloon on account of the numerous evils it afflicts on the poor, something better must be supplied to take its place. "Home is the sacred refuge of our life," but notwithstanding all that poets have sung and moralists have spoken, many workingmen are perfectly convinced that two dark bedrooms and a kitchen is not an attractive place in which to spend a pleasant evening with a friend. The saloon is the only substitute. When Orpheus passed by the cave of the siren he took his lyre and made such wondrous melody that sailors, enraptured by the music, spurned the seductive strains that were wafted from the dangerous cave. The fable has its application—give the workingmen something they will like as well as the saloon and you will strike at the root of the evil. There are excellent places, like Cooper Union and the Young Men's Institute; but these institutions cannot expect to draw those who live one or two miles away in another part of the city. If the workingmen were fully alive to the advantages afforded them they would undoubtedly be willing to walk a long distance, but the majority of them have no ambition to improve themselves. They spend their evenings in the saloons because they are always within easy reach and form agreeable meeting-places. It is absurd to denounce the saloon in unqualified terms. The multitudes who patronize them are not all absolute fools. Many simply seek to satisfy the craving after

fellowship which the Creator has implanted in their natures. The saloons are well-lighted, conveniently-located social clubs, provided in some cases with a pleasant reading-room, and always with obliging proprietors. Wise men are beginning to see that a substitute must be supplied to take the place of the saloon which shall retain all its good features and simply discard its evil elements. The churches of various denominations are taking a deep interest in providing attractive, well-lighted reading and club-rooms for the workingmen in our large cities. A great and beneficent work might be done by the Board of Educaton if free reading-rooms and libraries were opened in connection with every public school in the crowded portions of the city.

Fifth.—Good old John Wesley said, "Cleanliness is next to godliness;" but bathing in tenement-houses is exceedingly difficult and sometimes impossible. On pleasant days, when vast numbers of young men prefer the street-corner to the saloon, I have often stopped among a group of young fellows and said: "Boys, suppose a first-class swimming-bath were opened somewhere in this neighborhood, where you could for five or ten cents dive from a spring-board and plunge into a tank 50 feet wide and 100 feet long, full of warm, clean water, would you patronize such a place?" and the spontaneous and united answer always is: "You bet your life we would." I am fully convinced that if a first-class natatorium, with reading-rooms, library, and restaurant attached, was opened in some crowded district, the result would surpass all expectation. The baths have been remarkably successful in London. In one of these institutions over two hundred thousand baths were taken in a single year, and the receipts were more than $3,000 over the expenditures. Every humanitarian effort which is successful across the ocean does not succeed here, but from the sights which I witness every summer, when hundreds of young men plunge from the docks, lumber-yards, and shipping, at the risk of being arrested and having their clothes stolen, I am convinced that a swimming-bath would at once become immensely popular. The old Romans were wise in this respect. One of their great baths in our modern cities would be an effective means of aiding all forms of good work.

At the Christian conference held in Chickering Hall, in 1888, I endeavored to impress upon the audience the need of public baths. The good work begun at that time by the City Mission has been completed by the Society for Improving the Condition of the Poor. The first bath was opened last August, and the results are most satisfactory. Sixteen thousand baths have been taken in one hundred and fifteen days. One day in the latter part of August there were six hundred and sixty-nine bathers.

Sixth.—There is a great need of a universal loan association. The poor, as well as the rich, are frequently compelled to borrow money. Unfortunately the poor cannot get it at five or six per cent. There is no bank in the city which will loan a poor man money and take his old clothes, his wife's wedding-ring, or some little household treasure as security. Yet the poor man is forced to borrow. He has been out of work a few weeks. The landlord will come to-morrow. The children are hungry and call loudly for bread. In the dark bed-room lies a child with a burning fever. A physician has been to see the child. He is a kind-hearted man, he knows the hardships of the poor and does not expect his fee to-day; but of course the father cannot be expected to pay for the prescription he has just written. How shall the man get bread for those hungry children and medicine for this one who is sick? They have one last resort left—the household idols must be sacrificed. All the valuables are brought together. These little rings and lockets, and the silver cup which a proud uncle presented to the first baby boy; the father's overcoat and Sunday suit, with the mother's best dress, are all needed to make up the $10 for the landlord, and to get food and medicine for the children. The pawnbroker is ready to devour everything which has any value. The pawn-tickets are carefully put away, and the parents confidently hope that they will soon be able to redeem the things they have "put away." They redeem them at three per cent. a month, or else they finally lose them, not having received more than one-fifth of the actual value of the articles. I sent a boy to an East Side pawn-shop with a gold watch, the original cost of which was $150; its actual present value was certainly not less than $40. The boy received $5, and this was as much as he could get. I redeemed the watch the next day, much to the disgust of the pawnbroker. It would prove a great blessing to many people in distress if the Charity Organization Society, or the Association for Improving the Condition of the Poor, would open a general loan association. Two or three rooms in the United Charities Building, now in course of erection on Fourth Avenue and Twenty-second Street, would be well suited for this purpose. I fear, however, that no charitable society will undertake this work, from the mistaken idea many people have that such an institution would foster thriftless habits among the poor. Such persons forget that it is not a question of pawn-shops or no pawn-shops, but whether we shall have one large, reputable loan association, where the poor man's clothing and jewelry shall be as good as the rich man's real estate at a banking-house, or a vast number of little pawn-shops — those whirlpools in which the valuables of many poor families are swallowed. Thieves who want to get rid of stolen property, and thriftless drunkards who go to the pawnbroker to dispose permanently of their property at the highest prices, will continue to visit the pawn-shop; but persons who need a temporary loan to help them through a period of enforced idleness or sickness would be greatly benefited by a wisely managed loan association.

Seventh.—There is great need of trained nurses for the sick. Hundreds of mothers who are obliged to care for their homes during the day, are sitting at night by the bedside of sick children. If the sickness is of a temporary nature these periods of broken rest and double duty are passed without disaster. It frequently happens, however, that two or three children are sick at the same time. The mother is compelled to work night and day until nature gives way and she breaks down under the strain. Sickness brings increased expenses, therefore it is impossible for the husband to stay at home to take care of his family. If he does not work there will be no money next week for food, rent, and medicine. When the physician tells him that the end is near for wife or child, then he gives up his work. I have visited homes where I found the mother and all the children sick, and if it had not been for the occasional visit of a neighbor there would have been no one to give a cup of water to the sick or dying. Into such homes the trained nurse comes like a ministering angel. She lights a fire in the cold stove, bathes the sick, provides clean bedding, dresses the little children, puts in order the rooms, and when the place looks like home again, she takes from her basket some beef-tea, a little jelly, or some other tempting morsel for the sick. The mother, who has been lying hopeless in the dark bedroom, begins to revive, and watches with deep interest the ministering stranger, and with wet eyes says: "God bless you and reward you for what you have done this day." The nurse not only aids the sick, but is able by her counsel to help the mother when she has recovered. The friendly talks on housekeeping and the care of the children are often of the greatest value. The nurse also forms the connecting link between the hospitals and the invalids hidden away in the tenement-houses, many of whom would have been left to rot and finally to die on their filthy beds if the nurses had not found them and sent them to the hospital. The nurse does not stop to ask what the nationality or creed of the sufferers is. The only recommendation required to receive her services

is sickness and distress. The nurses of the City Mission are doing a noble work, but their number is too small and they must be constantly restrained lest they break down from overwork. Here is a work which can be done at once. Anyone who desires to relieve the suffering poor in the most direct and effective way can do it through a trained nurse. It would be a source of the purest happiness to many a man and woman, when they go to rest in their beautiful and luxurious homes, to know that $600, the saving, perhaps, of some needless luxury, is keeping a faithful nurse at work the entire year, moistening the fevered lips of the sick, or soothing the last hours of the dying. The Great Teacher of men consigned Dives to hell, not because of erroneous theological opinions, but because he neglected the beggar, who lay at his gate full of sores. Dives is among us to-day. He is clothed in the finest robes and fares sumptuously every day. Lazarus is also here. He lies in the cheerless bedroom of a tenement-house, hungry, sick, and full of sores. The two have been brought together for a purpose. The only salvation for our modern Dives lies in Lazarus.

Eighth.—There is need of greater coöperation among all good men. When we see anyone endeavoring to cast out social demons among us, let us not forbid him because he does not accept our creed or follow our party. Prejudice, narrow-mindedness, and bigotry have too long stood in the way of social reform. Wise men must recognize that whatever is good is of God. It makes no difference from what source it comes. When all good men shall work together on the broadest lines of social reform, great and beneficent changes will be brought about, and New York will continue to be a great, happy, and prosperous city.

Private Stables
of Manhattan
(1901)

PRIVATE STABLES OF MANHATTAN

By Robert Wickliffe Woolley

RICH men, and even those of moderate means, have few luxuries from which they derive more genuine pleasure than from their private stables. The townsman especially finds his horses and vehicles the source of much health and happiness, and the housing and care of them a deeply interesting occupation. America stands among the first of the countries of the world in the completeness and value of its private stables, yet here the industry—if I may so call it—is scarcely a quarter century old. The memory of man runs not to the contrary when the horse of high racing degree received any but distinguished consideration; but the exaltation, in cities, of the horse of pleasure, is of comparatively recent date. The equine aristocrat of the twentieth century, however, represents so very much gold; so much affection and thought is lavished on him, and he is treated with such consideration by his owner that his position may really, by comparison, be said to be regal. Practically little is generally known of the care and money expended on smart turnouts. One realizes they are costly, of course, and that they are just as one would have them were he or she the arbiter of fashion, but of the pains and thought expended upon the modern stable and its paraphernalia one's estimate is apt to be based on very imperfect data. Commodore Vanderbilt and his contemporaries, with all

MR. CORNELIUS VANDERBILT'S STABLE.

their wealth and excellent horses, never dreamed of expending sums on stables that even the average establishments of the kind in New York, Philadelphia or Chicago cost to-day.

Mr. Frank Work, one of the oldest and best known road drivers on this continent, inaugurated the new order of things, and to his example is due the credit for the many private horse palaces now in the larger cities of the country. When, in 1882, he ordered plans for a $50,000 stable from architect George Edward Harding, his friends and rich men generally accounted for his seeming prodigality by saying the horse was

With due respect to Mr. Harding, Mr. Work is responsible for most of the notably good features of the establishment. He has been all of his life a lover of the horse and a close student of all pertaining to it; he has paid liberally for speed and conformation, as well as for style and breeding, and is ever in the market for the latest and best things in harness, vehicles and stable appliances. It is small wonder that he should have, with the aid of an experienced architect, constructed a stable that really startled the horse world, and after twenty years has not been surpassed except in the matter of display and superfluous

MR. H. O. HAVEMEYER'S COACH HOUSE WITH STALLS BEYOND.

his greatest weakness. When the building, which is located in West Fifty-sixth street, was completed, however, it actually cost $140,000, and Mr. Work has frequently said he paid not a dollar too much. Though many stables since erected are more elaborate and ornate, this pioneer is second to none in convenience and comfort. In practical appointments—ventilation, drainage, heating, lighting, location and size of stalls, harness and carriage rooms, it is perfect.

appointments. This stable is famous also as the private club of its owner. Mr. Work provided quarters for himself as well as for his horses. On the second floor are bachelor apartments, including sitting-room, dining-room, bedroom, refrigerators, wine chests, etc. In the rear of these, and overlooking the stables and a small tan-bark arena, is a balcony where the noted road driver and his friends can sit on a winter's day and sip high balls and toddies, while discussing he fine points of a horse on parade. Hundreds of famous men have been entertained in these quarters, and every niche and corner is rich in memories.

Now let me turn from writing of the magnificence of the private stable of to-day and tell of one stable—and there are others somewhat like it—that I consider a marvel because of its completeness, the limited amount of space it occupies, its simplicity, and the smallness of its cost. This is Mr. Frederick C, Thomas's. in West Forty-

noted for more than twenty years for his smart turnouts, and is one of the most expert tandem drivers in the country. No man ever made such a showing at so little cost. His stable is his pride, and he declares his friends have voted him a horse crank. "Maybe I am," he said to me, "and I am rather proud of it. A crank generally knows something about his hobby."

Mr. Thomas has the most remarkable collection of harness in New York—probably in America—and the story of its gath-

MR. LOUIS STERN'S STABLE.

irst street. It is an ordinary three-story brick building, 25x60 feet, containing six stalls and a carriage room on the first floor, feed and harness rooms and offices on the second, and servants' quarters on the third. The woodwork is polished, the brick walls are clean and bare, the lighting and the ventilation perfect, and the whole cost a very small fraction of the amount that is usually expended on an unpretentious stable. Mr. Thomas has been

ering is well worth telling. He never had a large amount of money to spend at any one time on his horses or stable equipments, so from the start he was obliged to do everything on a modest scale. His knowledge of leather, of workmanship, of bits, etc., was equal to that of any expert. He knew where good harness was made, he knew how to direct the making of it in shops in which excessive prices were not charged, and he had taste. The oldest set in his collection

THE STABLES OF MR. H. O. HAVEMEYER AND COL. O. H. PAYNE.

is for a runabout, and it was purchased in 1884. A little later he bought a double set for a brougham, after that a tandem set, and so on. He didn't feel that he could afford to pay fancy prices: moreover, Mr. Thomas never bought harness just because a bargain figure was quoted on it, nor did he buy what he really wanted when he felt that by so doing he would tax his bank account. He simply made his collection as favorable occasion arose, gradually, and took care of what he had. As a consequence his stable now boasts the finest assortment of leather trappings and bits to be seen anywhere. Those who read of it imagine its owner a man of great wealth, whereas, discrimination has been his strong point. The fastidious may remark here that styles in horse gear change as they do in one's clothes, and that one's turnout cannot be properly rigged if the harness is old fashioned. These changes are largely

imaginary, and almost wholly unnecessary.

Now for the arrangement and management of this remarkable little stable. In the first room one enters from the street the vehicles are kept. It has space for six. I might say parenthetically, that in buying carriages, traps, brakes, etc., Mr. Thomas pursues the same course he follows as to harness. He has a brougham that is fifty years old, a stanhope twenty-four years old, and a tandem cart that is nearly thirty, and none of them looks odd on the avenue. This room is never heated. The carriages are washed in a shed in the rear and only cold water is used. Mr. Thomas believes every vehicle should be overhauled once a year, and laughs at the idea that cold weather cracks the paint. He says if one were to go on that theory he would have to give up winter driving altogether, as the real harm comes from cold mud, snow and ice. There are six stalls in the rear of the carriage room, separated from it by a sliding door. Only two horses are kept ordinarily, and they are always as fit as a show ring entry. Just above the stalls are feed and harness-cleaning rooms. In the latter, every strap, every trace, every saddle is thoroughly cleaned and greased, and every buckle, bit and chain is burnished immediately after being used. Then they are carried into the harness repository which occupies one-half the space just above the carriage room. Here every set has its own rack, every extra bridle, collar or saddle its own hook or hanger, and there is never any mixing up. Three walls are lined with harness for every conceivable turnout, and every piece of it looks as if it had just come from the maker's. On a small section of one wall are hung all the bits and stirrups that Mr. Thomas has bought since he first owned a horse. They are of every size and shape, and shine like silver. In one corner of this room are arranged riding saddles, bridles, martingales, surcingles and bands almost innumerable. In a side room are kept, well packed in camphor, blankets, horses' suits for day, night and full dress, liveries, etc. Adjoining the harness room is a comfortable and appropriately decorated office. Not an essential detail is overlooked in this entire stable, and it is all cared for by one man—the coachman. There is never any need to clean a bit, a set of harness or a vehicle except after using it, because everything is

so arranged there can be no rusting, no rotting or accumulation of dust. This establishment is a striking example of what can be done with moderate means by a master of details. It can be duplicated, in time, by many a young man who is ambitious to own a stable and smart turnouts, but who feels that his modest income will always force him to patronize a public livery.

New York's largest and most pretentious private stable is that of Louis Stern, in East Eighty-fourth street. It should be catalogued as one of the sights of the city. Externally it is pleasing to the eye. It fronts fifty feet on Eighty-fourth street, runs back one hundred and fifty, and the ground floor is divided into three squares of 50x50 each. The first of these is devoted to vehicles, there being space for twenty; the second to fourteen stalls, two of which are box; and the third to an arena where Mr. Stern's children jog their ponies, and where the horses are exercised in bad weather. The second floor of this great stable is devoted to spacious quarters for the coachman, feed rooms, a reception-room, dressing-room and gymnasium for men, and parlor, bedroom and bath-room for women. In the rear and overlooking the big arena is a balcony for spectators similar to that in Mr. Work's horse haven. On the third floor are the quarters of the grooms and footmen. This hasty and brief description gives small idea of the size and elegance

MR. H. O. HAVEMEYER'S STABLE AND WASHING COURT.

ENTRANCE TO MR. FRANK WORK'S STABLE.

of the building. Everything about it is costly and ornate. The doors and wood-work are mahogany and oak, the windows and skylights are stained glass, the walls are glazed brick, and the harness room is as finished and well appointed as a drawing-room. Five men are at work in it all the time, and it is ever ready for inspection. Under this entire building are huge heating pipes, fed by a furnace. There are radiators in every room and in all departments. The carriage room is heated on all damp and chilly days, and in very cold weather the stalls are warmed also.

This brings me to a question that has long been discussed by stable experts. The preponderance of opinion is against the use of artificial heat in the horses' quarters under any circumstances, and many are op-posed to it even in the carriage and harness rooms. Yet most of the private stables of New York and other cities are equipped with it, and the results are far from disas-trous. One will inspect Mr. Stern's estab-lishment and conclude that it is indis-pensable; he will visit that of Mr. Thomas and change his mind. The fact is, heat can be used advisedly in the room where vehicles are dried and stored, and, occa-sionally, in the harness repository, but never should it be in horses' quarters. A deep straw bed, made on a well-drained floor of oak or white pine, and a good blanket are all the average riding or driving animal needs. He should have plenty of light and good air, and should always be protected from chilly blasts of wind. I have a friend who is an expert on stable construction and recently he was the guest of a rich Philadelphian who had just finished having a very elaborate heating plant put into his stable. He was very enthusiastic and told how many thousands it had cost him.

"Could it be removed for that much," was the expert's only comment.

I recall several magnificent establish-ments whose carriage room walls are piped fully two feet from the floor, and their owners complain that the paint on the wheels of the vehicles kept in them cracks and chips off. Of course it does, and for the same reason that one could sit in these rooms and suffer from cold feet while the upper part of his body was uncomfortably warm. If one is bent upon heating, the pipes should be on a level with the floor. The carriage maker realizes how important is this department of a stable, as he is pretty sure to be blamed for any damage caused by its imperfection.

The stables of Messrs. W. D. Sloane,

Albert C. Bostwick, W. C. Whitney, H. O. Havemeyer, Alfred Vanderbilt and Frank Jay Gould stand out among the most costly and elegant of the latter day city establishments, and each is noted for some unique feature. That of the first named is the most satisfactorily lighted in New York. It is the perfection of neatness, its wood and metal work glisten like ebony and gold. This stable is designed primarily for the horse, and not the smallest detail is overlooked. From top to bottom it is as clean as Kipling tells us the Maharaja's museum at Amber is. It is in Fifty-sixth street and is really one of the sights of the city.

For completeness and all the luxuries that a lively imagination can suggest, the stables of H. O. Havemeyer and Col. O. H. Payne, in East Sixty-fifth street, are second to none. The walls are highly polished, the floors tiled, the woodwork is hard and is tastefully carved, the wrought metal used is beautifully burnished, and the stalls are trim and well kept. Then there are the carriage houses; always as clean as a new pin, with space enough for every style of pleasure vehicle that a gentleman's fancy can picture; and the harness rooms and bit closets have plate glass doors and windows. The quarters for attendants are spacious and elegant.

Frank Jay Gould's stable in West Fifty-eighth street was built two years ago, but even at this early date it fails to meet its owner's demands. Mr. Gould is passionately fond of the horse, and though he drives or rides comparatively little when in New York, he has planned a most extensive establishment. Quite a large addition is being made, and the stable will eventually be more spacious than that of Mr. Stern. The building has a frontage of only twenty-five feet on Fifty-eighth street, so the carriage room and horse apartments are necessarily cramped. Mr. Gould keeps twenty vehicles, ranging from a two-wheeled cart to a brougham, and they form the smartest collection in New York. The harness room is unique. It is fifteen feet long by five feet wide, and is enclosed in glass. The racks, hangers, etc., line the rear wall from floor to ceiling. The young millionaire is new in the business, so his collection of trappings is as yet modest, but if he utilizes the space he has set aside for that purpose, he will soon have a greater assortment than Mr. Thomas has. In the rear of his stable and connected with it only by single doors, is the much talked of academy in which Mr. Gould, his sister, Miss Helen Gould, and their friends ride horseback on winter days. It is fifty by one hundred feet—just twice as large as the Stern arena—has a very

GENERAL VIEW OF MR. W. D. SLOANE'S STABLE,
SHOWING STALLS AND HARNESS CLEANING ROOM.

high ceiling, with liberal skylights, and on one end has the usual balcony for spectators. In this balcony is a magnificent automatic organ which furnishes music while the horses are prancing around the ring. The surface of this big academy is covered with a deep layer of tan-bark, and the horses attain a speed and make sharp turns on it that really startle the spectators. In other respects Mr. Gould's stable does not differ radically from at least a hundred private stables in New York. He uses heat everywhere except in the horse stalls,

Gerry, but descriptions of them would be mere repetition. I have told of the various kinds; of their striking features and of their management; I have endeavored to give a general idea of the money, time and care that are lavished on the horse of every day use in the city. The subject is an extremely interesting one. For nearly twenty years architects, with the aid of expert horsemen, have given much time and study to the perfection of the stable, and it is hard to see where any improvement is now to be made. Mr. W. H. Moore, recently of

THE HARNESS ROOM OF MR. F. C. THOMAS.

and these are as well lighted and as carefully ventilated as any I have seen.

I could write volumes about the many private stables of New York, and would mention in particular those of Messrs. August Belmont, Walter Watson, John D. Rockefeller, W. Seward Webb, and Elbridge T.

Chicago, is building in Fifty-eighth street, a home for his horses that will cost nearly $200,000. Many rich men who own private stables are interested in this establishment, as they are afraid it will surpass theirs. think they need have no apprehension, it can only equal them at best.

New York City
Post Office
(1871)

NEW YORK CITY POST-OFFICE.

COLLECTING LETTERS.

THERE seems to be no preserved evidence that for very many years after the settlement of what is now known as the city of New York there was any officially recognized post-office. The population was small in numbers, and there were no business inducements which would lead to much correspondence. The very first ships which arrived after the primitive settlement of course brought letters to New Amsterdam, and the commencement of our local office was naturally coeval with the foundation of the city; but it was many years before there was a population which called for any system looking toward revenue.

On the arrival of the vessel those letters relating to the cargo were delivered to the merchants; the members of the exulting, expecting crowd which welcomed their friends received their letters from hands warm with the grasp of friendship. If a solitary epistle found no owner, it was left in the possession of some responsible private citizen until called for. In time the intercourse with Holland increased, and there gradually developed a system of voluntary distribution which became eventually known as the "coffee-house delivery," which maintained its popularity and usefulness more than a hundred years.

This system grew out of the custom of masters of vessels, and the people from the settlements of Breucklyn, Pavonia, and the distant Hackensack, leaving at some agreed-upon popular tavern letters intrusted to them which they could not personally deliver. Here these "waifs" were kept in a small box, conveniently placed within the reach of all, or gibbeted ingeniously upon the surface of a smooth board, by means of green baize, tape, and brass-headed nails, the "composition" displayed the while, like some choice picture, in the most conspicuous part of the public room. There were hangers-on at these popular resorts who unconsciously acted as agents for this arcadian post; for they acquired temporary importance, and sometimes a bit of tobacco or a glass of Schiedam schnapps, by circulating information regarding the "letter list." It was a curious sight, these old depositories of commercial speculations and homely friendships. Many were the neglected letters which were taken and examined by the simple-hearted old burghers, until the superscriptions were entirely defaced by the handling. Crabbed writing must, under the best circumstances, have made the characteristic and familiar Holland names of Guysbert van Imbroecken and Ryndert Jansen van Hooghten appear very much like an imitation of a Virginia fence; but when these same letters became here and there defaced and stained by soiling fingers, the superscription must have been a jumble indeed. It is asserted, however, that the possible contents of these "literary orphans" were sources of infinite gossip to the loungers at the tavern, for they would sit silently and smoke for long hours thinking over the important matter, occasionally uttering the vague speculation that they "were written by somebody;" and after this severe effort of conjectural thought would lapse again into dreamy somnolency.

The tradition, however, is doubtful that the earlier Dutch governors received their official dispatches through the coffee-house delivery, and continued so to do up to the time of the testy and resolute Stuyvesant, who conceived the idea that more rapid communication with the gubernatorial head-quarters might be had by sending these important documents, without any circumlocution, to his official residence.

For many years, even after the English took possession of New York, the coffee-house delivery was really the people's institution for the distribution of written information. The custom continued with the population of the seaport towns of turning out and greeting the arrival of every important vessel, and there followed the consequent exchange of congratulations, inquiries, and letters; and even after a more comprehensive and responsible system was demanded it was difficult to get the people to wholly change their old and confirmed ways, to depart from habits associated with so many pleasant traditions.

But this simple style of conducting business gradually became inefficient; and the "mother country," after England assumed the maternal position, turned its attention to the establishment of post-offices throughout the few densely settled portions of the colonies. At this period, toward the close of the seventeenth century (1672), New York boasted of five thousand inhabitants. Both Philadelphia and Boston were her superiors in population and commercial importance, and their citizens entered upon the new arrangements with actively expressed zeal. But New York in spirit remained a mere village, for its old population was quite satisfied with things as they were, and resolutely maintained its correspondence, whenever it was possible, through private means. An innovation on this custom was evidently made by an official order, issued in 1686, that ship-letters *must* be sent to the custom-house; and we presume that the municipal government came to the rescue in 1692, by passing an act establishing a post-office.

In the year 1710 the Postmaster-General of Great Britain directed the establishment of a "chief letter office" in the city of New York, Philadelphia having been previously made the head-quarters of the colonial organization. In the succeeding year arrangements were completed for the delivery of the Boston mail twice a month, and propositions to establish a *foot* post to Albany were advertised. The New York *Gazette*, for the week ending the 3d of May, 1732, has the following interesting advertisement:

"The New York post-office will be removed tomorrow to the uppermost of the two houses on Broadway, opposite Beaver Street.
"RICHARD NICHOL, Esq., P. M."

In 1740 a complete road was "blazed" from Paulus Hook (Jersey City) to Philadelphia, over which road, without any stated intervals of time, the mail was carried on horseback between Philadelphia and New York.

Twenty-one years (1753) after the notice we have quoted of the removal of the New York post-office to Broadway we find it still in the same location, but designated as being opposite Bowling Green, and that it would be open every day, save Saturday afternoon and Sunday, from 8 to 12 A.M., except on post nights, when attendance would be given until ten at night. Signed, Alexander Colden, Deputy Postmaster, and Secretary and Comptroller.

Dr. Franklin must have been very active in the establishment of postal facilities throughout the colonies; for in the year 1753, much to his personal satisfaction, he was appointed Postmaster-General, with a small salary, which, it was quaintly added, "he could have if he could get it." But in spite of the establishment of a city post forty years previously, New York

did not attract any special attention, and the revenues derived therefrom are not mentioned, while those of Boston and Philadelphia have frequent notice. It is probable that the municipal and the colonial authorities carried on much of their correspondence through agents, who were left to their own ways, the habits of the mass of the people confining them to their old notions of volunteer distribution, which was also encouraged by the high rates of postage. So long, indeed, did the coffee-house delivery maintain its popularity, that we find "the constituted officials" complaining of the fact as injuring the revenue, and finally an attempt was made to break up the custom by the publication of severe penalties.

In Dr. Franklin's celebrated examination before the House of Commons Committee on the situation of the colonies we find the following questions and answers, evidently aimed at the coffee-house distribution of letters:

COMMITTEE. "Do not letters often come into the post-offices of America directed to inland towns where no post goes?"

DR. FRANKLIN. "Yes."

COMMITTEE. "Can any private person take up these letters and carry them as directed?"

DR. FRANKLIN. "Yes, a friend of the person may do it, paying the postage that has accrued."

But for many years, in spite of this governmental opposition, New York city kept up the custom. The coffee-houses maintained their popularity. To them resorted the chief men and the wits of the town. At them were to be met the sea-captains and strangers from abroad, and gossip answered the place of the daily paper; and there was kept up the "card-rack," sticking full of letters and business notices; nor would public opinion severely condemn this custom, so peculiar to New York. Even the first Tontine Coffee-house, as it was called, had its place for exchanging letters. It was not until it was found out by experience that a well-regulated city post was safer, of less trouble, and more expeditious, that the coffee-house letter distribution came to an end.

The oppressions of the colonies by the British government occasioned a novel form of indignation, which expressed itself by the decided patronage of what appears to have been a "continental post," which was carried on in opposition to the one under the control of the English Postmaster-General, for we find a notice that the deputy of the British government was vainly endeavoring to keep up a post-office.

Alexander Colden remained postmaster up to the breaking out of the Revolution, for in the year previous (1775) his name appears in the *Gazette* in connection with the office, and with the additional one of agent for the English packets, which sailed once a month.

Upon the British troops taking possession of New York, the old record of the post-office disappears. For seven years it was abolished by the exactions of the provost-marshal, and little

THE OLD POST-OFFICE AT 29 WILLIAM STREET.

correspondence ensued not connected with the movements of troops. William Bedlow was the first postmaster after the close of the war, as his name appears in that connection in 1785; but in the succeeding year (1786) Sebastian Bauman was postmaster; and in the first directory of the city ever published—in which we find 926 names of citizens, the members of Congress, etc., John Hancock, Esq., President—is the following advertisement:

ARRIVALS AND DEPARTURES OF THE MAILS AT THE POST-OFFICE IN NEW YORK.

ARRIVALS.

FROM NEW ENGLAND AND ALBANY.

From November 1st to May 1st.

On Wednesday and Saturday, at *seven* o'clock P.M.

From May 1st to November 1st.

On Tuesday, Thursday, and Saturday, at *eight* o'clock P.M.

FROM THE SOUTHWARD.

From November 1st to May 1st.

On Monday, Wednesday, and Friday, at *nine* o'clock P.M.

DEPARTURES.

FOR NEW ENGLAND AND ALBANY.

From November 1st to May 1st.

On Sunday, Tuesday, and Thursday, at *ten* o'clock P.M.

From May 1st to November 1st.

On Sunday, Tuesday, and Thursday, at *ten* o'clock P.M.

FOR THE SOUTHWARD.

From November 1st to May 1st.

On Sunday and Thursday, at *two* o'clock P.M.

From May 1st to November 1st.

On Monday, Wednesday, and Friday, at *four* o'clock P.M.

*** Letters *must be in* the office half an hour before closing.

Congress in those early days was more considerate of the personal comforts of the post-office clerks than at the present time; for, with busi-

ness that was scarcely worth noticing under the head of "labor," that deliberative body found heart to pass a solemn act directing "that all letters left at the post a half hour before the time of making up the mail must be forwarded therein." Therefore, advertised the sagacious Sebastian Bauman, all letters left at the office not conformable with this act will be left over until the next post! The income of the New York post-office the first year (1786) of this most excellent red-tape official was $2789 84; and from this amount, as a starting-point, can be correctly estimated the annual increase of the postal business of New York city.

On the 30th of April, 1789, Washington was inaugurated President, and the establishment of the General Post-office as now organized immediately followed. Samuel Osgood was appointed Postmaster-General, and assumed his duties in the city of New York under the tuition of Sebastian Bauman. What should be done with this important official was evidently a subject of Congressional discussion; for we find officially recorded, that "the Postmaster-General shall not keep any office separate from the one in which the mails arriving in New York are opened and distributed, that he may by his presence prevent irregularities, and rectify mistakes which may occur." In fact, this now most important officer of the general government, and his solitary assistant and one clerk, then had nothing to do; so they took their first lessons in the service in the post-office of the city of New York. At this time there were throughout the United States seventy-five legally established post-offices and one thousand eight hundred and seventy-five miles of post-office routes.

In a very short time the national capital was transferred to Philadelphia, which had three penny-post carriers when New York had one—suggestive data of the comparative importance of the two cities at that time. The Southern, or Philadelphia, mail left New York daily, the Eastern mail tri-weekly, special mails for New Jersey and Long Island once a week. Mails to Albany were carried on horseback, contractor's remuneration, "postage collected."

"Colonel" Sebastian Bauman disappears in 1803; and his successor, Josias Ten Eyck, after what was to the public probably an uneventful year, gave way to General Theodorus Bailey, who received his appointment January 2, 1804, and who satisfactorily performed the duties of his office for nearly a quarter of a century. General Bailey was a gentleman of high standing in the community. He was a member of the House of Representatives two sessions, and a United States Senator in 1803, which position he held one year, and then resigned to assume the duties of postmaster.

The post-office was removed from Broadway by General Bailey, who established it in a house he had purchased, 29 William Street, corner of Garden, now Exchange Place. The building, even at that early day, was considered and spoken of as an "old-fashioned house." The windows were wide apart, and between the two on the lower story was a narrow door, the entrance of which was protected by a stoop lined with the usual wooden benches. A single dormer-window broke up the monotony of the peaked roof. The window-frame on the left of the door was divided into the novelty of small boxes (now for the first time introduced), one hundred and forty-four in number. The office occupied was twelve feet in width and fifteen deep. The room was so small that it soon became overcrowded, and the increase of the newspaper mail became so great that William Coleman, publisher of the *Evening Post*, who kept a bookstore corner of William and Wall streets, used to take the accumulated newspapers, generally of an entire week, over to his store, and assort them at his leisure, tying up each distribution with a string, and then sending them back to the post-office to be distributed through the mails.

General Bailey occupied the upper part of the house with his family. In accordance with the custom of those times, between twelve and one o'clock he closed up the lower part of the door and joined his family at dinner. If any parties were delayed by this attention to refreshments, they would, if strangers, reach around, and, seizing hold of the huge lion-headed knocker, make a clatter that could be heard a block away. If the solitary clerk answered this clamor, he generally remarked that the banks closed between twelve and one, and why shouldn't the post-office? and, with other evidences of dissatisfaction, would dismiss the impatient citizens. But if General Bailey was forced to reply, he would answer the call with the courtliness of an officer of the army associated with General Washington, and he would dismiss the inquirer after written and sealed information with the same old-school bow with which he would have delivered an order from head-quarters or a bouquet to a lady. If any of General Bailey's personal acquaintances happened to call in an unpropitious hour, and no one was in attendance, they would help themselves, carefully leaving the money for postage on the table, which occupied almost the entire interior of the room.

The establishment of the "embargo" in the year 1807 paralyzed all business, and, of course, seriously affected that of the post-office. From this time onward for several years there was little that occurred of general interest. It was not until the agitation of the right of the British government to impress seamen sailing under the American flag that New York was aroused from what seemed to be a chronic apathy, and the name of General Bailey, the postmaster, suddenly appears, among others, attached to certain resolutions resenting this monstrous assumption on the part "of the self-styled mistress of the seas." The war of 1812 followed, and the post-office business continued to suffer. The clerical force, in consequence, was reduced one-third by the dismissal of a junior clerk;

Archibald Forrester, one of the two retained, acting occasionally as a volunteer in throwing up earth-works "above King's Bridge," and again in superintending laborers engaged in constructing the round fort which still adorns the Battery. Jimmy Mower, the junior clerk, was drafted, but saved his place by hiring a substitute. Thus the post-office took a front rank in the patriotic efforts made to save the national honor. This war excitement had a healthy action on the country; the post-office business began to increase, and from that time steadily developed in importance.

In the summer of 1822 the city was desolated by the yellow fever, and was almost absolutely deserted by its population. The infected district was separated from the outer world by a high board fence, which ran across the city through the line of Duane, and what was then known as Harrison Street. Persons who had the temerity to climb to the top of this barricade relate that in the height of the plague not a living person could be seen. The post-office, for the public accommodation, was moved to Greenwich village, the desks, mail-bags, and all making hardly enough to overcrowd a modern furniture cart. The building temporarily appropriated was a handsome two-story frame house, erected for a bank but not occupied, situated corner of Asylum, now Fourth, and what was subsequently known as Bank Street. The magnificent trees which surrounded the house still have representatives standing in Hammond Street. Between Greenwich village and New York at that time was a vast tract of unoccupied and broken land. Woodcock and snipe "from the Jerseys" still found shelter in the marshes, the waters of which drained through old Canal Street.

When the yellow fever was raging, the rural population of the village, much to their annoyance, found their houses filled with people flying for their lives; these inflictions were borne with patience, since any fears were quieted by liberal pay for shelter; but when the post-office arrived, followed by the fear-stricken clerks, they concluded that disaster had indeed fallen in their midst, and that the letters and those grim road-worn mail-bags were but seeds and depositories of pestilence. With the sharp, biting frost of the latter part of November the post-office was removed back to its old quarters.

In the year 1825 there was an imperative demand for better, or rather for more roomy, accommodations, and the government leased the "Academy Building," opposite Dr. Matthew's church in Garden (now Exchange) Street. The free school which had been its occupant for many previous years was under the control of the "Reformed Dutch Consistory." It was a two-story wooden building, and familiar to the youthful population, and especially "the rising young men," for they had one and all within its inclosure been more or less severely disciplined in the principles of a useful education, and had

OLD POST-OFFICE IN GARDEN STREET.

been physically invigorated by the virtues of a sound thrashing.

The front of the building had some pretensions to novelty by slight attempts at ornamentation, and the unusual covering of a flat roof. On one side was a small pen, through which was the entrance into the yard, and underneath was a sort of dungeon for the confinement, if so ordered, of fractious boys, whom reason, mingled with Scripture, worldly advice, and birchen rods, had failed to reform. On the opposite side was Postmaster Bailey's residence, a narrow two-story house, with a single dormer-window, and a cellar in the basement, protected from observation by doors, which, from their propitious angle, formed the "summer sliding-pond" of Young New York.

In this new location two windows were knocked into one, and the acquired space was filled up with nine hundred letter boxes, and, to the astonishment of many, they were soon leased for business purposes. To make every thing satisfactory to the public, General Bailey obtained permission from the government to build a wooden shed over the sidewalk, so that people waiting at the delivery window were protected from the snow and rain. At this time there were eight clerks — W. B. Taylor, Joseph Dodd, George Abell, Courter Goodwin, W. S. Dunham, James Lynch, James Mower, and Charles Forrester. On the 1st of January, 1871, three of these clerks, after forty-five years of faithful service, were still at work, viz., W. B. Taylor, Joseph Dodd, and Charles Forrester; the two last named are all that are left of those who were on duty in the first quarter of the century.

In those days the prevailing spirit was one of quiet. There was not apparently even a foreshadowing of the "lightning speed" which is characteristic of every event of this generation; for, thirty or forty years ago, a voyage from Liverpool to New York was "rapid" if accomplished within two months, and quite satisfactory if not prolonged to ninety days. Even after the lapse of this last-mentioned time, there was no anxiety in the minds of self-possessed friends. The vessel, they would say, has met with some accident and put in at Fayal, of Azores or Western Islands, then a sort of half-way station, where ships and passengers alike rested from their fatigues. After repairing sails and cordage, and supplying the exhausted stores of provisions, the good ship and easy-going passengers would renew their slow progress westward, possibly consuming a third of a year in the voyage. It was after one of these "long-drawn-out events," when the skipper probably consumed more time to get his craft from Sandy Hook to the "Dover Street dock" than is now necessary to make the entire voyage across the Atlantic, that a passenger, evidently born out of his time, so fully realized the misery of the programme that he indignantly, and with some tendency to hyperbole, asserted, "that if all the trees in the world were pens, and all the men in the world scribes, and all the water in the sea ink, they couldn't explain the calamity of such a voyage."

There were no telegraphs, no speedy movements by the aid of steam, and consequently nothing of what is now designated newspaper enterprise. As a consequence, the people, even like their Knickerbocker predecessors, depended upon, and were quite satisfied to wait upon, chance for information. A well-known citizen "from the interior," now designated the "rural districts," was button-holed ("interviewed," we would say) under the post-office shed regarding the corn and potato crop of his section. A "Southerner," or a live sea-captain, or a passenger "just from Europe," were severally perfect magazines of news. Information thus obtained—if used with spirit—would frequently appear within a week or ten days. Here at the post-office was to be met, every pleasant morning, Charles King of the *American*, Redwood Fisher of the *Daily Advertiser*, and the pleasantest man of all the press, Major Mordecai Noah of the *Courier*, and other distinguished editors, who, having exchanged the ordinary courtesies of the day, would in an oracular manner give utterance to startling political or social observations, the pleasant interlude very likely terminating in a practical joke, profanely indulged in by an irreverent bank clerk, or valuable assistant of a popular auctioneer.

But the post-office had among its clerks Jimmy Mower. He was a smart business man, of wonderful capacity for work, and of the most equable good-nature. In addition, he was pretty well read; he boasted that he got his information in connection with his business of distributing the newspapers. One of his jokes grew out of the fact that in the war he was drafted, but, to avoid the responsibility, hired a substitute, who was killed at the famous sortie on Fort Erie, Canada frontier, and consequently that he (Jimmy Mower) had been killed in the service of his country, and that his bones were absolutely whitening on the battle-field. His efforts to get a pension for his heirs and get his post-office pay at the same time proved a puzzler to the best legal minds. The fashion of the times was rather "stately," but Mower, dead as he was, had life enough in him to amuse his fellow-clerks by sometimes joining in the conversations held under the shed outside of the post-office, and turning what was serious into ridicule. He generally hallooed his remarks through a broken pane of glass, at the same time making his hands almost invisible in the distribution of mail matter.

He was popular with the crowd, and if he could give the erudite Charles King, or the subtle Redwood Fisher, or the worthy Major Noah what the "boys" termed a "side-winder," it would set the post-office congregation in a roar. If Jimmy was turned on by some indignant individual who didn't see his joke, the light-hearted official retreated to the interior of the post-office, leaving the vehement eloquence intended for his head to be expended against the obtruding glass. Colonel Dodd and Charley Forrester, who are still clerks in the post-office, were great admirers of Jimmy Mower, and they still insist, after forty-five years of serious reflection on the subject, that Mower was the smartest man they ever knew, and that in his fights with "the editors and the big-bugs" he always got the advantage.

The post-office now began to be an institution, and this growing importance was pleasant to General Bailey, who, with more enlarged quarters and a private house entirely at his disposal, seemed to grow more courtly than ever, and dispensed his pleasant hospitality of conversation from the benches of his front-door, where he could often be seen side by side with the Clintons, the Willetts, and Schuylers, indulging in mutual congratulations upon the growth of the city and country, both of which they had assisted to rescue from colonial dependence and place on the high-road to national greatness.

At that time there were six letter-carriers, the extreme up-town boundary of their field of labor being a straight line crossing the island at Catharine and Canal streets. Colonel Reeside was now becoming of national importance by his connection with the Post-office Department. He carried the great Southern mail through from Washington, Baltimore, and Philadelphia, delivering it by contract at Paulus Hook (Jersey City). Here it was taken possession of by Colonel Dodd, who brought over the bags in a skiff, and then trundled them up to Garden Street in a wheelbarrow.

At the foot of Rivington Street, in the year 1825, was an important spot of high ground, known as "Manhattan Island"—a place where were located the ship-yards, among them the large one belonging to Henry Eckford. The proprietors of these yards had an extensive correspondence with the South, especially with Georgia and Florida, from which States they obtained their fat pine and live-oak used in ship-building. Mr. Charles Forrester, more than forty years an employé of the post-office, and who still performs his daily and arduous duties, then a boy, lived in the suburbs, and he would bring up the letters directed to these ship-builders, carry them across the wet meadows that lined the eastern side of the island, and deliver them to their owners.

The year 1825 was made memorable by the fact that Colonel Reeside obtained the contract to carry the mails from Boston to New York, the route being over the old post-road. Reeside's stages were very showy, drawn by four blooded Virginia horses, and driven by the most accomplished "Jehus."

On pleasant summer afternoons the people confined to the lower part of the island would purposely walk up the Bowery to see the "Boston mail" come in. Some time before the vehicle reached the old hay-scales, just where the Cooper Institute now stands, the driver would herald his approach by a melodious winding of his horn; then, laying aside this vulgar instrument, he would assume his legitimate sceptre, the whip, which he would harmlessly crack over the heads of his spirited steeds with a noise that, on a clear day, could be "heard a mile."

On Saturdays the jolly school boys and girls would gather together under the tall poplars and button-wood trees, and as the stage dashed along they would wave their hands as a welcome, and the most venturesome would catch hold of the straps, and thus have the glory of riding a few yards under the overhanging "boot." The characteristic gamins of that period would evince their enthusiasm by following the coach and rollicking in the dust of its revolving wheels; would cheer it and its passengers to the end of the route; and especially was this the case when the driver would purposely abortive attempts to drive these human flies away with his whip, or a jocose passenger would bandy wit with the boys, and make them crazy with delight by the scattering of a few pennies in the road.

In the winter these gay coaches were put aside, and in their place was a huge box on wheels, the combination not unlike a hearse, in the heart of which was deposited the load. The practice then was to abandon passengers, when the roads were heavy from mud and rain, and carry the mails; but nowadays, if the reports from many of the existing stage routes be true, under unfavorable circumstances the drivers abandon the mails to carry the passengers. Amos Kendall, the indefatigable Postmaster-General, by his industry and good management, reduced the carrying time between New York and New Orleans from sixteen to seven days. The event was celebrated at the Merchants' Exchange and the post-office by

COLONEL DODD.

the raising of the national standard, and there was a general rejoicing in Wall Street. Jimmy Mower had his joke by gravely asserting, that all newspapers delivered at the office from New Orleans less than sixteen days old were printed at the *Advertiser* office.

Progress was now perceptible in the whole city in the evident growth of wealth and population. The merchants (1825) were suddenly inspired with the ambition to have an Exchange worthy of their increasing importance, and an honor to the growing metropolis. To realize this idea they purchased a lot of seventy feet fronting on Wall Street, and at that time practically between William and Pearl streets. The foundations of the building were laid with imposing ceremonies, and its gradual erection, joined with the promising grandeur, was to the citizens a source of daily surprise and self-congratulation. In due time the structure was completed, and to give proper importance to the event, and a characteristic recognition of one of New York's greatest financiers and lawyers, a marble statue of Alexander Hamilton was placed conspicuously under the dome.

The "solid men" went from this stately pile around to the humble post-office in Garden Street, and the board front and "shanty" shed became distasteful to their eyes and unworthy of the city. This public sentiment was utilized into well-written articles for the newspapers, and the people grew suddenly ambitious for a better and more convenient post-office. The merchants favored the idea, and a part of the basement of the new Exchange was leased to the federal government, and in the year 1827 the post-office was established in its new and excellent quarters.

Wall Street at this time presented a picturesque mingling of the highest social life with churches, banks, and business stores combined. That it was in a transition state was apparent, yet we much doubt if the fact was fully realized by even the most sagacious citizens. The monetary institutions had a solid, unpretentious look, and the buildings in which they were lodged, in some instances, were occupied in their upper stories by the presidents, or cashiers, with their families. Then our most solid merchants did not find it inconsistent to live over their stores, and have at their tables their confidential clerks. Large trees still shaded the sidewalks, and private residences were to be seen, at the windows of which, after business hours, the ladies of the household presented themselves, or, standing at the front-door, according to the early custom of New York, chatted with neighbors. "Wall Street Church" and grounds occupied half the block that reached from Nassau to Broadway; while over the whole towered the venerable pile known as "Old Trinity," its grave-yard adding to the rural aspect, and giving an air of quiet to the surroundings. The Merchants' Exchange occupied only the eastern half of the square on which it was built; and directly adjoining it was a little candy shop, where they sold spruce-beer and "taffy" by the penny's worth. Then came the shop of a fashionable haberdasher, and on the corner was Benedict's well-known watch establishment, the regulator of which governed Wall Street time.

In the rear of the eastern corner of the basement of the Exchange was located the celebrated lunch-room of Charley King. How his restaurant would compare with the more pretentious ones of modern date we will not assert; but for hearty good-will, substantial fare, high respectability, and unquestioned manners, the proprietors of this now almost forgotten lunch-room have not, since its destruction, been surpassed. In the basement corner of Wall and Hanover streets James Buchanan, British consul, and David Hale printed a paper with the happily selected name of *Journal of Commerce*. It was at the commencement an unpretending sheet, and from the fact that it was semi-religious in its tone, and refused advertisements for the sale of liquors, was assumed to be a "temperance sheet." Among the well-known characters then living in New York was one "Johnny Edwards, scale-beam maker." He lived "up town," in the vicinity of what is now known as Fourth Street and Second Avenue. He was a man of the most harmless eccentricity, dressing himself in a Quaker garb, and riding about in a rickety old gig. He used sometimes to come down to Wall Street in business hours, and, taking advantage of the crowd in front of the Exchange, would proceed to harangue the "thoughtless generation" on the virtues of his patent scale beams, and the necessities of temperance. As he clinched his arguments regarding temperance with the distribution of tracts, he took great umbrage at the assumptions of the *Journal of Commerce*, pronouncing it a rival sheet on the great subject of temperance. The crowd enjoyed these interruptions of the usual routine of the street, to the great annoyance of David Hale, who considered the whole thing an undignified travesty on his gravely attempted efforts to bring about a moral reform.

Even at this dawning era the spirit of New York was unambitious, and the people, with few exceptions, were evidently unconscious of the changes in its character which were impending. One mail delivery a day was all the merchants demanded. The newspapers were rarely excited about the receipt of their exchanges. The hurry and bustle and anxiety which now pervades Wall Street were totally unknown. Groups were constantly in and about the Exchange conversing upon trivial matters; the merry, hearty laugh was heard time and again through the day, expressing admiration of harmless jokes uttered by persons at the time enjoying the hospitality of Charley King's lunch; while the clerks, less able to pay, made merry at Billy Niblo's, or Clark and Brown's, where for a sixpence they commanded a plentiful dish of Fulton Market beef, and trimmings to match; and, if extravagantly inclined, they would pay another sixpence for a cup of coffee and a kruller, to make the equal of which has ceased to be possible outside of the "kitchen-houses" belonging to our old population.

The Exchange had a narrow front on the street, and ran through to Garden. The entrance to the basement was under a circular opening, which was made of the arch which supported the steps that led up to the rotunda. The post-office was established in the rear eastern half of the basement, where it had ample room and much to spare. Two delivery windows were established, and three thousand boxes for the accommodation of the merchants; and so seemingly enormous had now become the business that twenty-two clerks were employed, and twenty-two letter-carriers, whose routes now reached up as high as Houston and Ninth, now Fourth Street. Now for the first time was found a demand for the assignment of a clerk wholly to a special duty, and "little Sam Gouverneur" was appointed to the exclusive care of the money department, and dignified with the title of "cashier."

To facilitate the arrival and departure of the mails, and give light to that part of the basement occupied by the post-office, what is now known as Hanover Street (which had, thirty years previously, been used by foot passengers as a short-cut to Hanover Square) was cleared out and made a street, and a small court on this side of the Exchange conveniently opened itself for the accommodation of the wagons and other vehicles employed by the post-office.

General Bailey, who had been an acceptable and honored postmaster almost a quarter of a century, full of years and honors, on the 4th of September, 1828, passed away. The veterans of the Revolution, as they now began to be called, State and city soldiery, the various civic societies, and representatives of the army and navy, vied with each other in paying to his memory every possible respect. General Jackson, in compliment to ex-President Monroe, who was then living, appointed his son-in-law, Samuel L. Gouverneur, to succeed General Bailey. With this event the old-times history of the post-office of New York may be said to have passed away.

RUINS OF MERCHANTS' EXCHANGE, WALL STREET.

The business of the post-office steadily increased, and the public grew more and more satisfied with its location in the Exchange. The newspaper press centred in its vicinity; and even the sad summer of cholera (1832) did not altogether destroy a certain air of vitality, that maintained itself in spite of the most unhappy surroundings.

On Wednesday night, December 16, 1835, a fire broke out in a building in the rear of the Exchange, and in fifteen hours destroyed an area of fifty acres of the most valuable business part of the city. In this dreadful calamity the Merchants' Exchange, after resisting the surrounding fire for some time, was involved in the general destruction; and the post-office, of which the people were so proud, no longer existed. Through the almost superhuman energy of the clerks—for no volunteers could be obtained to help them—*all the mail matter* and most of the furniture were saved. This result was largely due to the fact that the fire made at first slow progress in penetrating the brick walls, but more especially to the plentiful supply of mail-bags at hand, which were filled and instantly removed, by United States soldiers from Governor's Island, to what was then the new Custom-house, now the Sub-treasury, corner of Wall and Nassau streets. Jimmy Mower, who had charge of the newspaper department, was exceedingly disgusted when he subsequently discovered that the oil-cans and inkstands were promiscuously mixed up with his printed documents.

On the morning of the 18th of December, a day after its destruction in the Exchange, the post-office was extemporized in two brick stores in Pine, near Nassau Street. The destruction of such an enormous number of buildings made it impossible, even if economy was no object on the part of the government, to obtain a suitable building in the vicinity of the burned district. In this strait the city authorities offered the Rotunda in the City Hall Park, erected in the year 1818 by Vanderlyn, the artist, for a studio and the exhibition of panoramic pictures. When it was understood the government proposed to accept the Rotunda, busy as the merchants were in re-establishing themselves and counting up their losses, they found

THE ROTUNDA, CITY HALL PARK.

time to get up very demonstrative indignation meetings and protests against locating a post-office so far up town.

The post-office was, however, installed in the Rotunda, and the commercial pressure of 1837, which followed the great fire, diverted the public mind from the location of the post-office. Illustrative of the pecuniary disaster of the period may be mentioned that, in the "collapse," many of the merchants of the day owed the letter-carriers various sums, ranging from fifty to one hundred and fifty dollars, much of which money was never paid, the debtors being irretrievably ruined. This year the mail time between New York and New Orleans was reduced to six days and six hours. But the people, nevertheless, were impatient for more rapid communication, for we find in a Chicago paper of the time this notice:

"Highly Important.—By a foot passenger from the South we learn that the long-expected mail may be looked for in a week."

Fortunately for the interests of commerce and the unity of the country, rapid transit of news, cheap postage, and facilities for traveling were approaching consummation in the erection of railroad lines, with which private enterprise was threading every section of the country. One triumph announced seemed only to create a demand for another, and when Amos Kendall carried out the idea of connecting the non-continuous lines of railways by pony expresses, there was added a new value to the post-office of New York. It began to assume its present

central importance, and the promise of its brilliant future was almost realized, when the firing of guns from our national forts and vessels, with the ringing of bells, and cheers of thousands of exultant men, all joined in welcoming the first appearance of steam merchantmen in our harbor —the ever-to-be-remembered *Sirius* and *Great Western.*

The event which revolutionized the commerce and business enterprise of the world seemed to be most thoroughly appreciated; for, besides the incidents of welcome we have alluded to, crowds of curious spectators surged day by day at the foot of Clinton Street, where the vessels were at anchor, to admire and wonder; and even long journeys were taken from distant cities to behold the daring innovators. "Daddy Rice," the father of negro minstrelsy, then reigned supreme at the Bowery Theatre, and called forth his greatest shouts of applause when, as Jim Crow, he sang:

"And while they were discussing,
  And making mighty talk,
  The steamboat *Great Western*
  Came to New York:
    So turn about, and wheel about," etc.

The inconvenience of having the post-office so far from the centre of business was still complained of, and, to quiet dissatisfaction as far as possible, a letter delivery was established in the new Merchants' Exchange, where the Custom-house is now located, and placed in charge of Jemison Cox, an alderman and ex-chief-engineer. For letters two cents, for papers one cent, extra, was charged, which sums were paid without complaint by the merchants, and the amount thus collected paid the letter-carriers' charges.

In the year 1836 Mr. Gouverneur had been removed, and James Page, Esq., postmaster of Philadelphia, commissioned to take charge, which supervision was maintained for six weeks, when Jonathan J. Coddington was commissioned postmaster. When the latter assumed the duties of his position the post-office was in the Rotunda building and in the house of a hook-and-ladder company adjoining, and a "hose-house on the opposite side of the way." Nothing could have been more inconvenient, contrary to good discipline, and injurious to expeditious business operations. To remedy these evils Mr. Coddington built a handsome extension facing toward Wall Street. With this important addition, and other improvements, he brought the entire business (now constantly increasing) under one roof. The mails were received in Chambers Street, the box delivery was on Centre Street, while the interior of the Rotunda was devoted to the general delivery.

The location of the post-office in the Rotunda seemed to be unsatisfactory to citizens living in every part of the city. An application was therefore made for the establishment of a branch post-office for the receipt and delivery of the mails in the upper part of the city. The reply was that such an office could only be a branch of the one already existing, and that no compensation could be allowed for services beyond the two cents per letter paid the carriers. It was also doubted if the extent of New York demanded such an addition to its postal facilities. The proposition was also submitted to Mr. Coddington, and was opposed by him and his clerks. The subject was finally referred to the Chamber of Commerce, which recommended that there be established a sub-post-office for the reception of letters at Chatham Square, but not any place for the delivery of letters other than the existing arrangements at the post-office and by the penny post. Such was the origin of the Chatham Square post-office, which maintained its popularity and usefulness until its occupation was destroyed by the present iron boxes now so familiar on the street corners.

So much esteemed was Mr. Coddington by the officials at Washington that the Postmaster-General, under General Harrison's administration, informed him that, though a political opponent of the administration, he might retain his position. One week after this notice President Harrison died, and his successor, John Tyler, promptly requested Mr. Coddington to renew his bonds. On this hint, after some hesitation, he did as requested, and forwarded them to Washington in June. The reply was promptly returned, in the form of a commission creating "John Lorimer Graham postmaster of New York, in place of Jonathan Coddington removed."

Mr. Coddington is still remembered among the old clerks of the post-office, and the old merchants of the city, as one of the best of officers. He tried to learn the details of his position, and took pride in making every improvement that would render his department efficient. He was a man of great personal independence, and though a decided politician, he would not allow his bias that way to affect his official conduct. On one occasion a committee of ward politicians called upon him, and stated, through their chairman, that he had been assessed fifty dollars for partisan purposes. Mr. Coddington heard the proposition with patience, and then rising from his seat, said:

"I refuse to pay any such assessment as this you speak of. I'd have you understand that I am postmaster of New York city, and not postmaster of a ward committee."

The pressure to get the post-office "down town" still continued, and advantage was taken of the fact that the "Middle Dutch Church" was for sale to procure it for a post-office. There was nothing in the world so unsuited as the building for such a purpose; but the location was desirable, and the merchants went to work to press the matter upon the government. The property was offered for $350,000, but the Postmaster-General decided not to give more than $300,000. Lest the purchase might not be consummated, the merchants in a few hours raised by voluntary contributions the additional $50,000, and the old church was secured for secular purposes.

The extravagance and folly of the federal government in buying property erected for a church, and attempting to alter it to accommodate a post-office, or in leasing any kind of private property and fitting it up for public service, finds an illustration, but not an exceptionable one, in this "high old Dutch Church post-office of New York city." It may not be out of place to mention to the general reader that this old church was dedicated, in 1732, as a house of Christian worship. Until the close of the century its services were carried on in the "Holland language;" after that it was alternated with the English language. In the year 1776 the British tore out its pews, and (with the adjoining building, the old sugar-house) used it as a prison for American patriots, taken and treated as rebels. When no longer needed for this purpose, it served in rainy weather as a school-house for cavalry. When the British evacuated New York the congregation again took possession, removed the pulpit and altar from the eastern side to the northern end, and erected the heavy formidable galleries, destined eventually to become so conspicuous in the economy of the post-office.

Perhaps no building could be invented more unsuited for the purposes to which it has been appropriated. John Lorimer Graham, who had the responsible and difficult task of making it available, commenced by expending on the attempt what was then the large sum of $80,000.

He then issued a printed circular, surmounted by a picture of the old church, dated New York, January —, 1845, which read :

"The postmaster has great pleasure in announcing to his fellow-citizens that the *new* post-office building (112 years old), in Nassau Street, will be ready for occupation in a few days, and respectfully invites etc., etc., to view the interior arrangements of the establishment."

It was a grand time when the citizens crowded into this old church to look for the post-office. The eighty thousand dollars had made no material change ; to be sure, the altar railing was gone, but the pulpit and its ornamentation remained ; and the galleries, left intact, resembled great overhanging amphitheatres, from which to witness a gladiatorial display. But the post-office was finally installed, and then commenced that era in its business history that has made it a sort of visible standard, or gauge, of the mighty growth of old Manahatta toward the honor of being one of the mightiest of metropolitan cities.

The inconvenience, the necessarily miserable arrangements, the total unfitness of the place—inherently so by the original design of the building—has been a source of constant discomfort and annoyance, and made the labors of the clerks, and the supervision of the executive officers, onerous to the last degree. During the first year of the occupation the space immediately around the building was still covered with the tablets of what should have been the truly honored dead ; for there lay the representatives of a large part of our ancient and best population. The vaults under the church and the vaults around the church gave up their dead when the profane feet of the busy multitude pressed forward toward the church, not for prayer, but from absorbing interest in the living, active, bustling world. For a long year the spectacle was presented of coffins and mail-bags, of carts and extemporized hearses, jostling each other while engaged in their allotted work ; but at last this incongruous mingling of the dead population and the living ended ; but the forbidding look of that old castellated church remained.

The tower, bountifully made of stone, continued, and still continues, to look

NEW YORK POST-OFFICE IN THE DUTCH CHURCH.

THE RAT-IFICATION.

down sullenly on the bustle beneath, while the strong walls of the church, inside, announcing, in Dutch, that "My house shall be called a house of prayer," and the rough plastered walls, outside, speaking of the wasting storms of nearly a hundred and fifty years, repudiate all harmonious minglings and sympathies with the secular business of distributing the mails.

But the place is not without its living defenders of old traditionary possession. The mynheers are gone; the Knickerbockers know the place no more; but the rats, descendants of the original stock, keep high revel still, and continue to dispute possession with Uncle Sam and his salaried cohorts. And they, the rats, have had a queer history—these old Low-Dutch-Church-post-office rats.

For many years they lived a hard life, suffering starvation and dyspepsia under the preaching of Dominie Bogardus; but when the old sugar-house was erected adjoining the church, they felt that their trials and tribulations had brought them great reward, for the sweets of the Indies were at their disposal, and they reveled, until, in an evil hour, the sugar-house and church were filled with sad men, who starved and suffered and perished under a prison discipline that made the bodies of its victims not even passable fare for famished rats.

Then came the jolly times when the church was turned into a stable, and oats and hay and profanity were abundant; again another change, and the old-fashioned times returned, and the rats went into mortifications and fastings as a punishment for the good fare of the past. And tribulation was not soon to end; for, to their discomfort, the sugar-house, even as a place to hide their sorrows, disappeared, and the old church itself was finally consigned to the evil doings of the post-office.

Under this new administration even the dead bodies in the vaults underneath the church were carted away, and nothing, for the time being,

was left to prey upon but the poorly paid post-office clerks. But this resource, together with brown soap, the paste-pots, bits of apples, and the lunches of the night watchmen, left matters even worse than the most solemn times, when they heard sermons without any refreshments six hours long. But relief was to come to these historically interesting and brave old rats.

The Agricultural Bureau at Washington commenced an annual distribution of "choice seeds" through the mail, and good times dawned again for these old Dutch-Church rats. Once possessed of the secret of the rich contents of the plethoric mail-bags, the rats soon became such experts that they could smell a paper of marrowfat peas buried in newspaper walls as solid as an iron safe. In the pursuit of an honest living they have sharpened up their teeth until they can bore through a pile of compressed mail matter with the precision of an auger. They revel in cutting into leather pouches, laughing at the tough exterior, and treating the "patent, compound, burglar-proof padlocks" with infinite scorn. It is asserted by some of the old clerks, who have been hidden away for a quarter of a century in the damp vaults of the church until they are as gray and as sharp as the rats, that these rodentia read the agricultural papers; and the annual announcement in the *Tribune* of the distribution of seeds is celebrated in the lower vaults by a grand "rat-ification."

From this era onward the New York post-office becomes of too much magnitude to permit individuals to figure prominently in its history. Its leading characteristic, from the time it was established in Nassau Street, has been a constant increase of business. Robert H. Morris, W. V. Brady, Isaac V. Fowler, John A. Dix, William B. Taylor, succeeded each other as postmasters without any marked change in the routine except the employment of additional clerks. Abraham Wakeman accomplished a long-desired reform by abolishing the independent offices of Washington Heights, Bloomingdale, Manhattanville, and Yorkville, making the whole island one postal district. The names of James Kelly and P. H. Jones bring the succession down to our day.

The hard-working employés, who have carried on the department with such marked success that they have made its leading features the rapidity and correctness with which the mail matter is received and distributed, seldom appear above the surface. There are a few whose efficiency, knowledge of details, and unvarying faithfulness have secured them against the unhappy law of removals, which is especially an evil in the post-office. Among these "permanents" we must mention Colonel John Dodd, regularly in service for fifty-four years, and now the oldest clerk in the department. Fifty

INTERIOR OF THE POST-OFFICE IN THE DUTCH CHURCH.

years ago it was his business to carry the Southern mail on his shoulder down to the Cortlandt Street landing, transport it by skiff to Paulus Hook (Jersey City), and receive the Southern mail in return. The change may be vaguely realized when we consider that it takes four stout horses each day to draw the same mail to the "Washington train." In spite of the infirmities of advancing years, at eighty the colonel was faithfully at his post in the letter-delivery department. A year or more ago his desk and its business, when he was absent from duty, were moved up stairs. The old colonel, after this change, went to his accustomed place, and found it occupied by another; where there had been letters were piles of newspaper packages—all was changed. He was shown where was in future to be his desk, but he ob-

THE LADIES' WINDOW.

jected, and wanted to be put on duty in his old location; the spot and its surroundings had become necessary for his happiness. This, of course, was impossible, and he has never recovered from the disappointment. In the month of June, 1869, when the foundations of the new post-office were laid in the Park, he was a prominent actor. When all had been concluded the old government officer observed, "Now let me live to see this building completed, and I will die content."

The windows of the post-office for the distribution of letters and the selling of stamps, "in sums less than one dollar," are interesting places to study the cosmopolitan character of our busy population. It is not uncommon to witness people of every nationality "in line," waiting for their turn to inquire for correspondence. The ladies' window is especially a centre of observation; and the appearance of the sex dressed in gay colors and wreathed in smiles lightens up the otherwise care-worn, pell-mell, rushing, and sombre-looking crowd. Here the "young lady of the period" contrasts with the old crone whose undutiful son is "off at sea." The widow in her weeds throws sly glances at the dashing clerk; her hopefulness of the future contrasting strongly with the face of the suffering wife, who, sad and discontented,

turns abruptly away because her absent spouse "had failed to write."

During the rebellion the post-office clerks, by virtue of their duties, were often made unwilling participants in many sad scenes and associations. There was a terrible significance in the hymn or prayer book *returned* "from the front," often saturated with blood or marred by the bullet. Then there were the packets of unclaimed letters, dictated by loving, patriotic hearts, returned to the mother, wife, or sweetheart of the soldier, bearing the formal but terrible indorsement of the adjutant of the regiment, of "William Brown, killed in battle." It was often almost like stabbing the recipients to the heart to hand them such a fatal gift, and the look of unutterable anguish that sometimes followed haunted the day musings and midnight dreams of the sympathizing official. But there sometimes, nay, often, came a letter that conveyed to wife and family a respite to agonizing suspense, and then the old post-office was for the moment bright, and the dangers of war for an instant were forgotten. Lessons of human nature are taught at the delivery window of a post-office in the classified peculiarities of the universal patrons of the "republic of letters," among which are developed the common facts, that "clergymen, as a class, and women, universally, are the most difficult to please;" certainly they seem to complain the most.

Romantic incidents are not unusual in the history of specific mails. When the Japanese empire was opened to the outside world, the first mail from that legendary country was sent to New York in a sailing vessel *via* San Francisco, Panama, and Aspinwall. By a coincidence a mail from China *via* England arrived at the post-office simultaneously, and the written ideas and wishes of these two Oriental nations for the moment reposed side by side. In their route of destination they separated, and made the circuit of the world, to meet again in our great Western city of "mushroom barbarians." But speculation is brief in the post-office when work is to be done; the words, "Who separates?" are heard, the "travelers" are "broken up," and piecemeal sent to their various destinations.

Some years since a steamer running between Liverpool and Quebec was involved in a terrible storm that swept over the mouth of the St. Lawrence. The stanch ship was lost, and all living creatures on board perished. Two months afterward the divers, among other things, recovered from the wreck the New York city mail, and it was promptly forwarded to its place of destination. When opened the contents were found comparatively safe; the letters were carefully dried and duly distributed; and these frail, delicate, paper memorials of thought remained intact, while the iron-ribbed ship and the brave men who commanded her still repose in their ocean grave.

No service in any department of the federal government is more exacting in hours of labor and hard work than the post-office, and no government service has more enthusiastic and faithful officers. On a recent occasion a ward politician was appointed to a place in the post-office. He was set to work "killing postage stamps"— that is, defacing the stamp on mailed letters. He worked away from 8 o'clock A.M. until noon, then deliberately quit his table, went up to the postmaster, and drawled out, "Look here, gineral, I wanted an app'intment, not hard work; and ef this is the best thing you can do for me, I'll quit." And the "wielder of powerful political influence" quit, and departed to the more genial quarters of a drinking saloon up town.

The pay of the post-office clerk is exceedingly small, and, however earnest he may be as a partisan, the political tax annually levied is by no means a bright spot in his hard fortunes. We have mentioned how Mr. Coddington treated this custom; another example may not be out of place. When General Dix was postmaster he was approached on the subject of allowing a subscription to be taken among the clerks for party purposes. He appeared to promptly coincide with the idea, making only one condition—that it should be taken up in his own way. He accordingly took a small blank book and wrote the following:

"This book will be handed to you by Mr. ——, who is authorized to collect moneys of the clerks for political purposes; but I wish each clerk distinctly to understand that giving funds for such a purpose is at his own option. Those who give will not be helped by it, and those who refuse will not be injured."

Possibly it is necessary for us to state that while the clerks saved their money, and the party wasn't injured, the "grand central committee" was deprived of nothing more nor less than the means of indulging in a Champagne supper.

A post-office clerk, under the most favorable circumstances, has a delicate and responsible position to hold, for he is constantly subjected to suspicion. Money letters can be robbed before they reach the office, and can be robbed before they reach their owners after they leave the office. One day a person called on the postmaster with a letter written by a lady of great respectability, in which it was stated that "inclosed you will find ten dollars in liquidation of your bill against me." But the letter had apparently been opened, and the remains only of the edges of the remittance, sticking to some paste, were left behind. The bill, save the remains of the slight mutilation alluded to, was gone. By examining the fragment still adhering to the paste the word *one, one, one,* oft repeated, presented itself. Thus this base attempt to swindle an honest creditor and defame the credit of the post-office was exposed.

People who come to the post-office and make complaints of being robbed, when they discover that they were mistaken never call and make reparation, or relieve the department of the charge made against its employés. A merchant, much excited, complained that a letter sent to him "by a most responsible house," containing $500, had not been received. This charge was fortified by showing a letter from the postmaster who mailed the missing letter, certifying that it was forwarded, and contained the $500. Detectives were at once set to work to unravel the iniquity, but all efforts proved unavailing. Finally the post-office authorities, after weeks of hard work, called on the complaining merchant and asked if he had heard any thing about the missing money. "Oh," replied the gentleman, with great vivacity, "that's all right; by mistake that letter was thrown into the safe, and remained unopened nearly four weeks. Funny, wasn't it?" Not even an apology was made for charging the post-office with purloining the money, or for giving its officers so much unnecessary trouble.

Charges of dishonesty against the post-office are made where nobody but "extraordinary circumstances" are to blame. A letter containing two $1000 bills in it was delivered by the carrier, who, according to custom (ignorant of its contents, of course), at the house of its owner, shoved it into the hallway, under the door. The letter was missing. Complaint was made at the post-office; evidence was produced that the money had been forwarded. The detectives were set to work to trace out

POSTMASTER'S OFFICE.

the robbery. The poor carrier, and the clerks in the office who handled the letter, were placed under surveillance. The clerks where the letter was mailed were "shadowed." Every dollar they expended after the probable robbery was secretly inquired into, to see if any of them had been at any given time, after the letter was lost, unusually "flush;" but all signs failed. After a long time the floor covering of the hall was taken up, and there was the letter, "safe and sound:" the unfortunate carrier had thrust it *under*, instead of over, the oil-cloth.

The misdirection of letters is the cause of serious charges against the post-office. A letter containing $700 was mailed from Albany to New York. It was sent from a well-known person, and the package which was supposed to contain the letter, made up in Albany, was not opened until it reached New York. Both ends of the line were under suspicion. It was stated that the letter was addressed Mr. —— ——, Broadway, New York. After a long search it was found that the letter had never left Albany at all, being directed by mistake Mr. ——

——, Broadway, Albany, and the faithful clerks had thrown it into their own city delivery box instead of forwarding it to New York. The confusion in the mind of the writer of the letter grew out of the fact that there is a Broadway in both cities, and from force of habit he wrote the wrong address.

Miserable chirography is one of the most prolific causes of post-office inefficiency. It is safe to say that unmistakenly written directions would remove nine-tenths of the complaints. What is a nonplused clerk to do with letters addressed to "Mahara Seney," "Old Cort," or "Cow House," when Morrisania, Olcott, and Cohoes were really intended?

One day, possibly four years ago, Mr. Kelly was sitting in his private office opening his *personal* letters, and enjoying the delusion that every thing was working satisfactorily, when, to his surprise, he found one letter from Washington calling his especial attention to the "inclosed editorial," cut from the *Tribune*, in which the carelessness of his clerks, and the generally unsatisfactory manner with which he carried on his business, were dilated upon, ending with

DELIVERING LETTERS.

At the post-office, when they distribute letters, those on which the direction is not instantly made out, to save time, are thrown in a pile for especial examination; if a second and more careful study fails, they are consigned to an especial clerk, who is denominated the chief of the bureau of "hards." To this important functionary the envelope of Chappaqua was at last referred. He examined it a moment, and his eye flashed with the expression of recognizing an old acquaintance. "This thing," said he, holding up the envelope with the tip ends of his fingers, "came to me some days ago along with the other 'hards.' I studied the superscription at my leisure a whole day, but couldn't make it out. I then showed it to the best experts in handwriting attached to the office, and called on outsiders to test their skill; but what the writing meant, *if it was writing*, was a conundrum that we all gave up. Finally, in desperation, it was suggested, as a last resort, to send it to Chappaqua," which happened to be its place of destination. Such is the *literal* history of the reason of an earnestly written denunciation of the inefficiency of the city post.

We have traced the growth of the post-office of New York from the time when it found but partial employment for one postmaster and a single assistant to the present, and what a change! Language fails to give an idea; statistics pall on the ear in unmeaning sounds, and only confuse the mind. A few random illustrations must therefore suffice.

The discipline and efficiency of the city post is shown in the reminiscence that, twenty years ago, before there was a postal treaty with England, people in that country, according to their caprice, indorsed on the outside of their letters by what line of steamers they desired them to be sent. By some accident neither of the two composing the American line crossed from England in six months! The consequence was an extraordinary accumulation of letters indorsed "by American steamer;" and when the *Washington* did reach this port, having "broken her shaft, and been frozen up in the harbor of Bremen," she had a six months' mail on board. This enormous collection of letters was taken to the post-office, and the clerks, without neglecting their daily routine duties and working "overtime," distributed this ac-

the startling announcement that, under the present management of the department, it took *four days* to get a letter from New York to Chappaqua, distance about thirty miles, and made literally no distance by a fast railway! Consternation ensued, and Mr. Kelly, to commence examination into these serious charges, sent a special agent to Chappaqua for the envelope of said delayed letter. At the place named the official fortunately not only found what he went after (the envelope), but also Mr. Greeley and "Miles O'Reilly." After due explanations the envelope was handed to Miles O'Reilly, with the query of what he thought was the meaning of the superscription.

"Why," said that genial wit, who had once been a deputy postmaster, "the devil himself couldn't make it out."

The envelope was then brought to the attention of the berated clerks, who looked at it with glazed eyes, the hieroglyphics suggesting somewhat the same intellectual speculation that would result from studying the foot-prints of a gigantic spider that had, after wading knee-deep in ink, retreated hastily across the paper.

cumulation in *ten days!* The same number of letters, without interfering with the daily business of the office, would now be distributed in *one hour!*

Large publishing houses and newspaper establishments afford great assistance to the post-office by making up their own mails according to printed lists and instructions furnished by the Post-office Department. If this were not the case, the facilities afforded would not be adequate to perform the required service. To illustrate: If it were not advantageous to publishers to aid in the prompt circulation of their papers and magazines, and they should send their daily distribution to the post-office in one indiscriminate mass, that institution would be literally "avalanched;" floors, desks, clerks, and every available place for storage would be buried under one vast pile of accumulated mail matter.

Instead of there being as formerly only a few straggling letters, two hundred and fifty thousand postage stamps are, on an average, daily canceled, and that is a representation of the number of *domestic* letters delivered at the post-office every twenty-four hours.

It costs the government sixty thousand dollars annually for cartage to haul this vast amount of mail matter to the stations and railway lines.

One comparative statement more. The city of New York is divided into twelve postal stations, each one having its distinct officer and clerks. Station A, situated in the heart of New York, does a larger business than either of the cities of Buffalo, New Haven, Hartford, Hudson, or Troy.

Such is the epitomized history, illustrated by the post-office, of the growth and prosperity of the city of New York.

The New York
Produce Exchange
(1886)

THE NEW YORK PRODUCE EXCHANGE.

BY RICHARD WHEATLY.

THE New York Produce Exchange is one of the most conspicuous buildings on Manhattan Island, the seat of the most influential mercantile corporation within its limits, and the market in whose exchanges the entire national commonwealth is most deeply interested. "Like a beetling cliff commanding the eye of the home-bound mariner," it challenges the notice of travellers approaching through the Narrows, or crossing the Hudson from the further shore. Its massive campanile shares with the lace-like Brooklyn Bridge, the spire of Trinity Church, the tall tower of the *Tribune*, and the ambitious altitude of the Equitable and Western Union structures the admiration of the stranger.

Comparatively few of the busy multitudes that swarm about its base have any knowledge of the exceeding beauty visible from its summit. The White Tower of the Conqueror, the Colonne Napoléon, or the Monument on Bunker Hill offers nothing equal to the urban, rural, and marine scenery presented to the vision. East, west, north, and south the view is comparatively unobstructed. About its feet cluster the Field Building, on the site of Washington's head-quarters, Castle Garden, the United States Sub-Treasury, Assay Office, and Custom-house, the Stock, Produce, Cotton, Metal, and other exchanges, and the stately edifices in which the marvellous operations of commerce, finance, insurance, banking, railroading, and telegraphing are carried on. If Washington be the cerebrum, New York is the cerebellum of the American body-politic. Governor's Island, the pedestal of "Liberty enlightening the World," the civic municipalities of Brooklyn, Hoboken, Jersey and Long Island Cities, the distant heights in the receding country, and the shimmering waters of bay and river, mottled by craft of every civilization, invite delighted inspection.

The New York Produce Exchange stands near the spot where the boats of the adventurous Hollanders first touched the shores of Manhattan, and where the first rough ventures of commerce were made with the children of the unexplored wilderness. The courage, perseverance, and faith of the earliest European traders have lost nothing in transmission to their descendants. This massive and beautiful structure convincingly testifies that the sons are worthy of the sires, and indeed superior to them by so much as the theoretical and applied science of the present transcends that of the past. It is a speaking monument of that wise self-appreciation proper to the guardians of New York's commercial supremacy. It fully provides for present mercantile needs and for those of the near future; yields revenue from outlay sufficient to continuously advance the commercial interests of city and State, and by its architectural effects refines and educates the thinking toilers who manipulate so many of our material exchanges. The builders have evidently learned to look beyond themselves into the possibilities of the future. But little more than half a century ago the value of American exports aggregated about seventy million dollars; in 1885 it reached the sum of $742,189,755, and in 1881 the much larger amount of $902,377,346. Then thirty miles of imperfect railroad hinted at the more than 128,500 that now compose the sinews of the body-politic, and gave occult promise of the hundreds of thousands of telegraph and telephone nerves that connect the sensorium with every member.

In view of the purposes this edifice is designed to serve, it is architecturally unrivalled by any in this or any other country. Of the modern Renaissance in style, and marked by symmetrically beautiful lines, its general effect is imposing, and imparts the idea of strength and permanence. The Building Committee knew what they wanted, and were fortunate enough to find in George B. Post, the architect, a trained artist abundantly able to unite their original designs with the graces of elegance and uniformity. Begun on May 1, 1881, it was finished on May 1, 1884. Fifteen thousand and thirty-seven New England pine and spruce piles, driven through the yielding primitive soil to a solid bed, and cut off below the level of tide-water, insure the safety of the superstructure, and by their uprightness are supposed to harmonize with the mercantile men and morals they uphold. The building is fireproof throughout. Granite, brick, terracotta, and iron are piled above the corner-stone—bearing in lasting bronze the word

251

VIEW OF THE TOWER LOOKING SEAWARD.

"EQUITY," that was laid with imposing ceremony on the 6th of June, 1882—and compose an edifice 300 by 150 feet in superficial area, and, with tower and terrace, of 53,779 square feet. One hundred and sixteen feet measure the distance from sidewalk to roof, 225 feet to the coping of the tower, and 306 feet to the top of the flag-staff. Of course we are not surprised when told that the flag, 50 × 20 feet, is the largest ever made. The tower clock has a face twelve feet in diameter, each number measuring a foot in length, and weighs 1500 pounds.

Entering the Exchange from Beaver Street, Broadway, the terrace, or Stone Street, the visitor finds himself in corridors from which open the doors of private offices, of the Produce Exchange Bank, a branch United States post-office, the Western Union Telegraph Company, the Pennsylvania Railroad Company, and the bustling Maritime Exchange. Four elevators near the Stone Street and five near the Beaver Street entrance facilitate passage to all the upper parts. One of the latter leaves him in a hall opposite the cloak-room, whence a sharp turn to the left leads through hurrying brokers, and men lunching at counters, or investing in fruits and confections dispensed by a typical jarl's daughter, into a series of offices devoted to the uses of president, cashier, superintendents, and the Gratuity Fund.

Retracing the path just trodden, the hum of multitudinous voices, broken by explosive jets and measureless yells of noise, allures into the Exchange Hall. Admission is contingent on member's ticket or escort. Once inside, the amplitude of space—220 × 144 feet, with height of 47 feet 6 inches to the ceiling, and 60 feet to the skylight—compels notice. Light and ventilation are perfect. Seven thousand men would not overcrowd the 31,680 square feet of surface. Should the future bring a larger number, provision is made for adding 8000 square feet to the area, and also for the erection of other accommodations on contiguous ground owned by the corporation. On the right, attached to pillars, are black-boards reporting the prices of refined petroleum at London, Antwerp, and Bremen; and of naval stores, turpentine, and resin in London and Liverpool. Eight long tables, provided with drawers and distinct compart-

ments on the surface, afford conveniences to the flour merchants, and command a yearly rent of $10 per drawer. A premium of $200 was paid for the first choice at the opening of the Hall. One similar table supplies the needs of dealers in lard, grease, tallow, and oils. Booths belonging to the Western Union, Postal, Baltimore and Ohio, and Metropolitan telegraph and telephone companies furnish necessary means of communication to brokers; and wires, rented of different corporations, connect the telephones of private owners with their respective offices. Fifty dollars per year is the price of this privilege. The melancholy oval ring around which mercurial dealers in

MANIPULATING FLOUR.

petroleum used to gather has been removed since our illustration of the Main Hall (page 197) was prepared.

Tables scattered over the room for the use of commercial reporters accelerate the speed with which they make known what prices obtain at the tables whereon samples of barley, wheat, oats, corn, and feed are placed for examination. Not

C. M. VAIL, PRESIDENT OF THE PRODUCE EXCHANGE.

to their contents. They present the official cable report of the day's prices of provisions, naval stores, grain, flour, corn, and oils at Liverpool, and of hops in London; the bid and asking prices in the adjoining Call Room; the Beerbohm cable report of prices at London and Liverpool of 1,900,000 quarters of wheat and flour and 220,000 quarters of corn in passage to the United Kingdom, and of 280,000 quarters of wheat and 210,000 quarters of corn in passage to the European continent; the bids at call sales in the principal marts of the United States; the movement of wheat to the chief ports of the country, and the receipts on the corresponding day of last year; the receipts and shipments of grain and the stocks in store at the same points in the previous business twenty-four hours; the receipts of grain at lake and river ports, and also at Atlantic ports, during the last week, previous week, and corresponding week in 1885; the visible supply of grain in the United States and Canada in the last week, and in the corresponding weeks of 1885 and 1884; and also the grain in sight on sea and land. Thus, on January 16–17, 1886, the

here, however, are the prices of all cereals determined. In that corner oval, consisting of wooden steps, rising from inside and outside one above another, and technically known as the "Pit," the prices of future deliveries, at the option of buyer or seller, are decided. Back of the "Pit" is the Call Room, in which provisions and grain are sold through the medium of the presiding callers, William L. Eichell and Edward Patterson. Five hundred seats, arranged in amphitheatrical form, ascend in concentric rows from the floor. Each bears, when so desired, the name of the owner. Five dollars per annum, plus the premium bidden at the annual auction sale in January, is the price of each seat. Those not sold are free to members of the Exchange.

Emerging from the Call Room, the little crowd of daily reporters gathered in front of the bulletin-boards calls attention

	Bushels.
Visible supply of wheat in the United States and Canada was	57,108,286
On passage to the United Kingdom	14,424,000
On passage to the Continent	1,584,000
	73,116,286
The week before	73,046,176
Two weeks ago	74,237,325

The figures representing corn are also given, the quantities of wheat and maize

HERMAN O. ARMOUR.

at the Atlantic ports, and the quantities and destinations of weekly exports of corn, wheat, and flour from the chief seaboard ports.

While on the floor a buyer may receive from Europe a cable order for a cargo of grain, flour, or provisions, may purchase what is ordered, charter a vessel for shipment, engage an elevator to load the grain, or a lighter to move provisions or flour, effect insurance, sell exchange, cable back the fact of his purchases, and write and mail his letters.

Returns of exports are obtained from the shipping offices sending out vessels, and the daily and weekly receipts of flour, grain, feed, high wines, hops, oil-cake, provisions, etc., etc., from railroad companies, steam-boat and steam-ship lines, express companies, canal lines, river boats, and barges. The collecting employés begin daily work about 7 A.M., and report to the collector of produce receipts, who collates their returns, and posts them on the bulletin-boards at 11.40 A.M.

Ascending to the third floor, and calling at the office of the statisticians, so famous for accurate and exhaustive reports, the visitor passes from thence into the elegantly furnished Reception Room, where two upright pianos stand ready to beguile the tedium of waiting hours, and for which the ladies of the trade lords are dutifully bound to be truly grateful. One door of this spacious apartment leads into the office of the Complaint Committee, and another into the Board-Room of the managers. Interior arrangements correspond with the functions exercised in them. Similar provisions for the Arbitration Committee, whose duties are of a judicial character, furnish out their chamber. If wishful to sustain æsthetic reputation with the scores of stalwart, vigorous, and efficient merchants whose portraits adorn the pictorial representation of "Laying the Corner-Stone," by Carl J. Becker, it is well to study it in the clear gas-light that floods one end of the Reception Room. Preëminent among many whose names are lustrous in the commercial annals of the United States are David Dows, "the present patriarch of the grain trade in this city," whose "transcendent mercantile genius" has made his whole life "a prolonged story of the progressive development of this wonderful country"; Edward Hincken, who "has introduced the foreign commerce of this port into every country and almost every harbor in the world"; Herman O. Armour, whose patronymic is allied to daring commercial enterprise; Franklin Edson, thrice president, and ex-Mayor of the city, whose highest honor is held to be the fixed desire "to do the right as he had the ability and opportunity to see the right"; and others, whose energies have been reënforced by the conviction "that the sense of having lived up to the standard of the Golden Rule is better than being the objective point of a fickle fame or of popular laudation."

The Library, looking down upon the historic Bowling Green, and amply provided with leather-covered cherry furniture, offers a long list of foreign and domestic periodicals—the *Bangor Rustler* of Dakota included—to the choice of the reader. Seven portraits of former presidents invite criticism. The written and framed agreement, dated July 14, 1863, of many signatory members of the Produce Exchange to serve as minutemen, under command of officers of the Seventh Regiment, for the maintenance of law and order and the protection of life and property, awakens painful memories of the dark and bloody draft riots. Foreign market reports, prices current, freight reports, and shipping circulars evidently possess more interest to *habitués* of this institution than the scanty collection of volumes hidden behind the opaque glass of the cases.

A large colony of offices, in four stories of rooms devoted to mercantile uses, rises above the Exchange Hall, surrounds the entire edifice, and lends massiveness and grace to the exterior. Lavatories minister to the comfort of the occupants. Letteropenings in a conduit or "run," costing $1500, placed on each floor by the managers of the Cutler Mailing System, save weary steps to the postal depository.

In the basement are the offices of the New York Produce Exchange Safe Deposit and Storage Company, with entrance from the interior, and also from Whitehall Street. The neat and commodious Reading and Reception Room, the Ladies' Room, with parlor, toilet, and coupon-cutting conveniences attached, Trustees' Room, and thirty-seven apartments for secluded handling of documents, are all that could well be asked. The doors of the money vault, which contains 1300 safes, and has capacity for 7000 or 8000, are models of mechanical

THE WESTERN UNION BULLETIN-BOARD.

ingenuity and mathematical perfection. They have time locks set to any number of hours up to seventy, and are said to be the largest of the kind ever made, and also the safest. Each of the two outside doors weighs 7000 pounds, and each of the two inner 6000 pounds. Each outer door, hung on crane hinges, is forced bodily into position by an eccentric lever, and is thus made air-tight and powder-proof. Should the combinations of the lock be forgotten, it is said that the manufacturer's men, using all available means, would require from three to four days in which to force ingress. Seven alternate layers of steel and iron encompass the vault, and 3500-pound barred window-guards intercept the sunlight. The electric watch-clock, recording faithful guardianship, is an additional surety. In other strongly constructed vaults are stored silver plate, bulky packages, paintings, precious merchandise, books and records of firms and corporations. All are under seal, and reveal no secrets to the curious gazer.

In the Engine Room, whose presiding genius is an intelligent graduate of the Cooper Institute, are an Edison dynamo-machine of 250 light capacity, three Worthington engines for operating the elevators, two pumping engines for forcing water into tanks on roof and tower, three pneumatic engines for despatching messages from the Exchange floor to the main offices of telegraph companies by means of aerial currents generated here and driven through tubes, and a battery of three sectional boilers of 750 horse-power, which supplies motor force to the pumping engines, and also heats the building. Two thousand tons of coal annually, and 66,000 pounds of water diurnally in summer, but not in winter, owing to the peculiar method of heating, are here consumed.

The Produce Exchange, costing with land and furniture a grand total of $3,178,645 14, is a valuable index of progressive wealth and civilization. It includes 12,000,000 bricks, 15 miles of iron girders, $1\frac{3}{4}$ miles of columns, 2061 tons of terra-cotta, $7\frac{1}{2}$ acres of flooring, more than 2000 windows, nearly 1000 doors, $7\frac{1}{2}$ miles of sash cords and chains, over 47 tons of sash weights, $\frac{1}{5}$ of an acre of skylight over the Exchange Room, 29 miles of steam-pipes, nearly a mile of panelled wainscoting, and weighs over 50,000 tons. Four thousand separate drawings were required for its construction. The nine hydraulic elevators carry an average of 21,500 people daily, or 6,500,000 every year. The pumping capacity is sufficient to supply water to a city of 175,000 inhabitants, and 1,194,133 horse-power is utilized annually for heat and force. All these items are of less practical interest to the members than the fact that the 190

offices rent, together with privileges, for about $180,000 per annum, not including premiums of over $24,000 paid for choice, and return about six per cent. on the entire investment. With the rents and annual dues there will be in 1886 a net surplus above interest and expenses of $40,000. This income will, of course, increase as the bonded debt decreases. When the latter is liquidated, the Exchange will enjoy a net income of about $200,000 a year, which may be applied to the reduction either of dues or of gratuity assessments.

The history of the New York Produce Exchange is far more interesting to many readers than the dry details of its structure. As an organized corporation it is of yesterday; but its beginning was in the ruggedly picturesque traders who met for the transaction of business at the "Company's store-houses" in the weekly Monday markets established by the redoubtable Governor Peter Stuyvesant in the autumn of 1648.

Rude and primitive, with sides open to the weather, and roof covered with thatch and Dutch tiles, was the edifice that housed the embryonic trade of New Amsterdam. The insignificant Marckt-velt Stegie, on which the splendid temple of trade now stands, was the cradle in which the giant American commerce was rocked.

Increasing population swept away the old market, and the dislodged merchants next met "on a bridge over a small stream at Exchange Place—the Rialto of the New World." The Broadway Shambles, situated on the present Bowling Green, were used as a market from 1658 to 1707, and again from 1720. In or about 1675 was built the Custom-house Bridge Market, almost, if not quite, on the site of the old Produce Exchange, at the corner of Pearl and Moore streets. Thence, in May, 1684, the traffickers removed to the Bowling Green. The industry and homely wealth of the period were both fitly symbolized by the figures of a beaver and a flour-barrel engraved on the seal of the colony, and representing the most important interests of the colonists. In 1690–91 the first Exchange in New York was erected. Located on the edge of the water at the foot of Broad Street, it served for a market-house as well as a business meeting-place for merchants. In January, 1727, the first authorized corn exchange, or market, was exclusively established by

THE LIBRARY.

corporation ordinance at the water front foot of Wall Street, "for the sale of all sorts of grain, corn, and meal." In 1739 a market-house, 42 by 25 feet, arose in the middle of Broadway, on the site of the old wagon stand opposite Liberty Street, and was also declared to be a grain and meal market in November, 1741. This hideous deformity was followed in 1754 by the New or Royàl Exchange, a building raised upon arches in the middle of the street and over the canal near the foot of Broad Street. In this the merchants congregated for some years, and thence migrated to the Merchants' Exchange, now the United States Custom-house, in Wall Street.

In the fourth decade of the present century the flour trade was chiefly conducted at the foot of Cortlandt Street and at the corner of Broad and South streets, where the merchants ordinarily remained until 11 A.M. The sky was their "azure roof," and the street pavement in front of Weeks and Douglas's store, No. 19 South Street, their "tessellated floor." Colonel Edward Hincken, late of the Fourth New York Artillery, and one of the oldest veterans of the Produce Exchange, was one of the number. One day, in or about 1846, he was accosted by Alfred Barrett with the curt demand, "Hincken, give me a dollar." "What for?" was the prompt inquiry. "Buy an awning for the front of Weeks and Douglas's store," responded Barrett. The awning was bought, and under it, shielded from sun and rain, the grain and flour magnates met. There they became a "nuisance" to the occupants, whose office, pens, and paper they freely appropriated. To the credit of William H. Newman be it said, this unwarrantable intrusiveness was ended by his hiring the store No. 19 South Street from Weeks and Douglas. Like-minded associates supported him, and subscribed fifteen dollars each to defray the necessary expenditure. Organization under the title of the Corn Exchange, with Joseph Ketcham as chairman, followed. Incorporation was received from the New York Legislature in the spring of 1853, Nathaniel H. Wolfe being the presiding officer. Gatherings were informal, but grew in numbers as provision dealers, shipping merchants, and ship-owners joined them, until it became necessary to provide larger room. No. 19 South Street was purchased, and the refusal of the corner and of other property obtained. The owner of No. 17 South Street, by extravagant demands for his property, caused the Board of

Managers to select the corner of Whitehall and Pearl streets for the location of a new building. On this, in 1860, the Produce Exchange was erected. Thither about seven hundred merchants removed in 1861, leaving malcontents in the old quarters, and assumed the title of the New York Commercial Association, with John B. Wright as the first president. The new organization was incorporated by the Legislature in 1862. Under the prudent management of Vice-President James P. Wallace, the entire cost of the charter, including counsel fees and several journeys to Albany, was only $96. In this new structure the two parties were reunited. Some of the opponents to removal held out until only two members — of whom Edward Hincken was one—met in the old Corn Exchange when it was last opened. "As neither could make money out of the other," the gallant colonel and his army gave in their adhesion to the new order, and were "gladly welcomed" with "loud applause" at headquarters.

Two bodies were now organized. The Produce Exchange Building Company owned the edifice, charged $20 per annum to each subscriber of the Commercial Association, and $5 per annum for other expenses; but allowed a committee to control and pay for news, police, etc., out of the proceeds—pocketing all remainders. In 1868 the title of the New York Commercial Asso-

ciation was altered to that of the New York Produce Exchange by action of the Legislature.

The arrangement between the two companies—so decidedly objectionable to the tenants—under which business was carried on came to an end in 1872, by the purchase of the building for the sum of

VAULTS OF THE PRODUCE EXCHANGE SAFE DEPOSIT AND STORAGE COMPANY.

$265,000, which was raised by an assessment of $200 on each member of the Exchange.

Rapid growth required larger accommodations, and in 1880 the present site was bought. The three years intervening between conception of the new edifice and laying its foundation-stone on the 6th of June, 1882, were crowded with

FORREST H. PARKER.

"Three thousand men with one purpose, built into a living temple, whose corner-stone is integrity and equity, are here gathered to-day to inaugurate and dedicate this our visible temple of commerce." Brave words, good words, these be, and should guide judgment on what comes hereafter. They accord with those in which the charter expresses the purpose of the corporation, viz., "To inculcate just and equitable principles in trade; to establish and maintain uniformity in commercial usages; to acquire, preserve, and disseminate valuable business information; to adjust controversies and misunderstandings between persons engaged in business; and to make provision for the widows and children of deceased members."

anxieties and untiring labors. The name of Forrest H. Parker, the president, who officiated on the latter occasion, together with those of Franklin Edson, chairman, and Alexander E. Orr, secretary of the Building Committee, and of their colleagues, will always be significant of the prescience, faith, energy, and millioned liberality which, in the teeth of multitudinous discouragements and trials, wrought out so magnificent an enterprise.

On the 6th of May, 1884, possession of the new quarters was taken. Before quitting the old, Mr. James McGee delivered a valedictory address to the members.

Assembled in the main hall of the new Exchange, the members listened to speeches by Mayor Edson and President J. H. Herrick. The latter insisted that the elements of all progress are physical, intellectual, moral—and preëminently moral.

The membership of the New York Produce Exchange is limited to three thousand. To these large proportions it has grown within the memory of living and still active merchants. The lively crowd which congregated under the awning of Weeks and Douglas's store had increased to about 1000 in 1860, when they frequented the dark, dingy, and badly ventilated Corn Exchange. In 1863 the New York Commercial Association boasted 1238 members, each of whom annually paid $20 as dues. In 1870 the members of the Produce Exchange had risen to 2023, and the dues to $25. In 1872 the initiation fee rose to $300, in 1873 to $500, in 1880 to $1000, and in 1882 to $2500. Since then certificates of membership have been sold at $4800, and are now in active demand at $2750. In 1873 the members numbered 2469; in 1880, 2700; and in 1882, 3000.

What they will number in future is difficult of conjecture.

Most of the Produce Exchange traders are of American birth. The youth of the land, and especially of New England, take very kindly to commercial pursuits. But portation, finance, etc., are more frequent. All are, of necessity, keen politicians, and could supply a respectable Congress on the shortest notice. Good-humor, cordiality, and even courtliness are generic characteristics. Here and there may

DAVID DOWS.

here are many names on the roll which denote Celtic, German, Scandinavian, French, Spanish, and Slavic parentage. In *personnel* the corporation is cosmopolitan as its commerce. All grades of intellectual culture are represented in it. Men of college breeding are not infrequent. Men of bold, pushing, aggressive character, whose mental powers have been mainly employed on the facts and theories of statistics, demand and supply, trans- be one of whom the French *savant's* report on the customs and manners of the South-sea Islanders—"Customs bad; manners none"—is true; but of the overwhelming majority it may justly be said that they are exponents of the best elements in our national life. In the noisy activities of Call Room and Grain Pit the effervescent energies of younger members are amusingly apparent. Older participants, sobered by hard conflict in the

EDWARD HINCKEN.

out through the door. His back vanishes to another tremendous non-symphony: "Put—out—that—pipe!" followed by applausive laughter from the gallery.

As now constituted, the property affairs—to an amount not exceeding five million dollars—business, and concerns of the corporation are controlled by a president, vice-president, treasurer, and twelve managers, who together constitute the Board of Managers. All are gentlemen of high commercial character and standing. Vacancies are filled by the board, of whom the majority constitutes a quorum. Charles M. Vail, president, 1885-6, is a member of the firm of John S. Martin and Co., butter and cheese merchants. *Ex officio*, and with the approval of the board, he appoints a standing committee for each of the trades, to which all disputes arising in it may be referred for arbitration, at a cost of from $15 to $25 to the losing party. Parties at variance may, however, settle their differences by private arbitration. The president is a member of all committees excepting that on arbitration, presides at meetings of the Exchange and of the Board of Managers, and annually, or oftener, as he deems proper, communicates to either such matters and suggestions as will, in his opinion, conduce to its usefulness and prosperity. James McGee, vice-president, is at the head of the Devoe Oil Company; Richard O. Veit, identified with the Standard Oil Company, is secretary; and John P. Townsend, of the W. J. Wilcox Company, oil refiners, treasurer. Neglect of duty vacates office.

The expenses of the Exchange are defrayed by means of an assessment of not less than $10, nor more than $30, on each certificate of membership. Non-paymen

changeful years, look on with complacent, half-contemptuous indifference. Boisterous play is never carried to the extreme of insult and outrage. At the Christmas festivities tooting performers on tin horns, mock traders in options, mock glove-fights with wondrously attentive seconds, practical jokers with violent animosities against straw hats, and sundry terpsichoreans whose physical force explodes through flying feet, manifest their share in the general joy.

Nicknames, mock calls, waving hats, shouts, and catcalls are concomitants of the annual sale of choice of seats in the Call Room. The surging crowd in the Wheat Pit is occasionally inspired by wild desire to emulate the sports of Crow Indians, when fair feminine faces beam upon them from the gallery. The added presence of a cockney, "just come hover, ye know," lighted pipe in mouth, and quizzing-glass screwed into one eye, evokes stentorian shout in chorus: "Put—out—that—pipe!" A second shout shoots the pipe, with strutting stranger behind it, is punished by suspension from all privileges, which are only restored when the delinquent foots the bill.

Under the direction of the Board of Managers eighty-four employés diligently fulfil specific tasks, graduated in importance from those of Superintendent

the building and bulletins, nominates his assistants, organizes their service, and is an administrative Briareus.

Any respectable applicant for membership, duly proposed and seconded, may be admitted if approved by the Committee on Admissions, and elected by the Board

J. H. HERRICK.

William E. Fletcher, down to those of assistant porters, coal-passers, and closet attendants. During the fiscal year ending May 16, 1885, $58,322 65 was paid for salaries, and $1330 87 for uniforms. The superintendent, aided by an assistant, L. B. Howe, records the proceedings of all meetings of the Exchange, managers, and committees; collects all moneys due to the corporation; receives, deposits—either in the Corn Exchange, Central Trust Company, Fourth National, Hanover National, Mercantile National, New York Produce Exchange, or Seaboard Bank—and pays over margins on contracts; has charge of

of Managers. Prior to this he must present a properly assigned certificate of membership, and a written application stating the nature of his business and such other facts as may be required, and must also sign an agreement to abide by the organic and statutory laws of the Exchange. Certificates of living membership are transferable only to elected persons, on payment of a fee of $5, and of any unpaid assessments. The certificate of a deceased member is transferable by his legal representatives. Nine applicants were rejected for satisfactory reasons in the year ending June 1, 1885.

WILLIAM E. FLETCHER, SUPERINTENDENT.

An Arbitration Committee, consisting of five members, not managers, elected by ballot of the board, and sworn to faithfulness in duty, hear and decide disputes between parties who have voluntarily bound themselves to acquiesce in the decision. Any controversy which might be the subject of an action at law or in equity, excepting claims to real estate, is within the jurisdiction of this committee. Judgments of the Supreme Court of the City and County of New York are rendered upon the awards made. Attendance of witnesses is compulsory. Appeal is not permissible unless fraud, collusion, or corruption be alleged against some portion of the arbitrators. The costs of these proceedings— $5 per member for each sitting—are certainly moderate. Alexander E. Orr is chairman of the committee. Hundreds of very important cases have been adjudicated. Within the past few years it is said that not a single business difference between members has sought our law courts for settlement.

The Complaint Committee is a mercantile grand-jury, which hears accusations against members, endeavors to conciliate disputants, or to induce them to arbitrate. Failing in both, the controversy is referred to the Board of Managers, whose action is final. They may censure, suspend, or expel the accused. If the accused be the scape-goat of impenitent, guilty principals outside the Exchange, they are boycotted, but he is excused.

Duly notified failures are posted in the Exchange, and all contracts of the failers, so far as may be, are closed by purchase or sale at public call, or by the Finance Committee. The law of "survival of the fittest" applies with merciless rigor. The Finance Committee audits all bills and claims against the Exchange, also the treasurer's accounts, and directs all authorized disbursements. The Floor Committee supervises the rooms used in 'Change hours, and preserves seemly order. Together with the president, treasurer, and trustees of the Gratuity Fund, they compose the Committee on Admissions. A House Committee has general supervision of the employés. That on Information and Statistics supplies all news affecting the value of articles dealt in by the members of the Exchange, and records all the useful facts of movements, prices, and transportation of products. To the Law Committee is confided all required legislation, the nomination of legal counsel, and proposed amendments to the charter or the by-laws. The duties of the Committee on Rooms and Fixtures are explained by its title. The Committee on Trade is charged with the formulation of useful regulations.

Such an organization is entitled to profound respect as the best creation of commercial genius, instructed and fructified by the experience of centuries.

Under the charter and statutes of the New York Produce Exchange, a vast and various commerce, in whose materials and methods all modern civilization is interested, is conducted. The rooms of the building are opened for business at 9 A.M. and closed at 4 P.M.—on Saturdays at 3.30 P.M. The tops of grain and provision tables freely welcome the first comers, each of whom may occupy the space over a single sample drawer for his own use. Loud and boisterous conversation, throwing of dough, corn, or other articles, is forbidden, and subjects the offender to discipline, and on very rare occasions to an imminent charge of bayonets. Smoking before 2.15 P.M. costs fifty cents for each offence, and swells the treasury of the Committee on Charities. Substitutes for sick or absent members, who are responsible for their doings, may be admitted to the floor on thirty-days renewable passes. Failure to fulfil contracts excludes both the "posted" principal and his substitute. Daily sessions, announced and ended by the deafening clangor of a soulless bell,

Exchange charges itself. Seated at the point on the Atlantic coast where all lines of travel and traffic converge, whither cereals from the boundless prairies and pastoral products from the Pacific coast are forwarded by Western merchants and packers to New York dealers and commission firms for distribution among the manufacturing millions of Europe and the several commonwealths of the American continent and archipelagoes, it presents as

THE PIT.

of the grain, lard, and provision trades are held from 10.30 A.M. to 2.15 P.M., and from 3 to 3.30 P.M. All contracts are legally enforceable. They must express the facts of transactions, and if they do not, expose the parties to penalty. Washed or fictitious sales, or false reports of sales, are also penal offences.

What shall we eat, what shall we drink, and wherewithal shall we be lighted? are the three questions with whose pleasant solution the New York Produce

various aspects as its busy traffic. This last changes characteristics with the current years. Inbound freight trains, bearing lowing cattle, bleating sheep, and disgruntled hogs, do not disquiet Bergh philanthropists as in former years. Abattoirs in Chicago, Kansas City, Cedar Rapids, and other cities silence the vocal complaints of the unwilling transports; packing-houses transfer their edible remains to boxes, barrels, and refrigerating cars for safe transit to the regions whence they pass into human consumption. Transportation of live stock, intended for export or domestic use, has not ceased, but is of smaller dimensions. Changes in the provision trade are not less noteworthy. Twenty-five years ago the multitude of drays engaged in drawing barrels and tierces from railroad termini to civic warehouses, where they were inspected and recoopered, and thence to the docks of steamers and sailing vessels, excited passing wonder. Now they are shipped at once from the railroad sidings to the holds of sea-going vessels, and sent on to foreign buyers or consignees. But enough of demand for domestic supply and export remains to sustain a vigorous trade at the Produce Exchange. Southern markets are satisfied directly from the West; those of the West Indies by New York jobbers.

Merchants either purchase in the West, or send from their own packing-houses in that region, or receive consignments, on which they make advances often equal to three-fourths the market value of the provisions here offered for sale. In the first and third cases, bills of lading accompanied by sight drafts are mailed to purchasers or consignees while the goods are on the way. Before the arrival of the latter, parties in interest not unfrequently attempt to guard against loss from fluctuation of prices by selling short in the Chicago market—a process perfectly intelligible to the "hedger" on the turf. In New York, consignments or purchases of provisions pass into the custody of licensed and responsible paid inspectors and warehousemen, of whom there are seven; and by whom the condition, quality, standard, and weight of the different lots are duly certified, or declared to be insufficient to fulfil the requirements of the contract. Each warehouse receipt must be for 250 barrels, containing an average of 200 pounds per barrel, unless otherwise stipulated. All sales contemplate merchantable meats. If 10 per cent. of a lot of dry salted meat, or 20 per cent. of other meats, be defective, they are excluded from this category. Packer's name and location, number of pieces, and weight, together with the inspector's brand, must be marked on each package. Sales, in agreed lots of any size, if for export or domestic consumption, are made upon the Exchange floor, and deliveries from warehouse or from the dock, as the goods arrive. Speculative sales are in lots of 250

barrels, or their multiples. Less business than formerly is now done in options, but the jobbing trade retains its old proportions. Official but not private sales are recorded. Receipts of provisions at New York in 1880 and 1885 were as follows:

1880.

Beef	24,478 tierces.
Beef	25,067 barrels.
Beef	713,939 cases.
Beef Hams.......	18,663 tierces and barrels.
Pork	186,419 barrels.
Cut Meats.......	42,338 tierces.
Boxed Meats	1,000,851 boxes.
Hams	54,954 tierces and barrels.
Tongues	11,138 tierces and barrels.

1885.

Beef	17,567 tierces.
Beef	31,518 barrels.
Beef	435,247 cases.
Beef Hams.......	20,536 tierces and barrels.
Pork	182,744 barrels.
Hams	66,888 boxes.
Tongues	13,827 tierces and barrels.

Lard, "made from hog round, say head, gut, leaf, and trimmings," is mainly in demand by lard-refiners and oil-pressers, and passes through the hands of five inspectors and weighers of lard and provisions for delivery on sale or contract. The better grades are ordinarily sold from the packer's brands upon the tierces, and but seldom from samples. The receipts at New York during the years 1880 and 1885 were as follows:

	Tierces and Barrels.	Kegs.	Cases.
In 1880....	733,119	171,343	25,449
In 1885....	393,040	163,288	55,906

New York and Chicago are the principal markets for farm and pastoral products in the United States. It is difficult to determine which of the two exerts the greater influence upon the values of these commodities. Formerly, under the pressure of pecuniary necessity, Chicago bent her head in respectful obedience to New York's commercial dogmatism. Now that she is financially independent she insists on leading where she was wont to follow. New York gracefully declines the leadership, listens with a spirit of maternal pride to her daughter's assumptions, and braces herself to maintain supremacy. With a population that has grown from seventy in 1830 to seven hundred thousand in 1886; with nearly twenty-three million bushels of inspected grain in her mighty elevators at one time; with an average of over 22,000 head of live stock arriving within her precincts on every day of the year; slaughtering 1,188,154 cattle in 1884, and packing 4,222,780 hogs in 1883; studying in minutest detail the wants and tastes of foreign buyers, and receiving direct orders from them—Chicago is a friendly rival that it is impossible to despise. She neglects no scientific means for facilitating business,

of Chicago are represented on the floor of the New York Produce Exchange. No black-board in the elegant hall of the Chicago Board of Trade is so eagerly watched as that which, every five minutes, records the prices current in New York. New York reports only on the material of actual trade. Whatever of grain or provisions

ALEXANDER E. ORR.

saving labor, multiplying transactions, and bringing the markets of the world to her doors. Of this intense vitality, alertness, and sagacity, the splendid edifice of the Board of Trade (the interior of which is represented in our illustration on page 212) is an impressive embodiment. In design, material, and adaptation to mercantile requirements, it meets every want, and is the pride of Chicago, and indeed of the whole Northwest.

The commercial interests of these two great marts are so identified that the one is absolutely necessary to the other. All the prominent grain and provision firms

passes through Chicago to various destinations is reckoned among her receipts and shipments. ("All is fish that comes to her net," even though many pass through the meshes.) This usage swells the totals of both, but does not convey an accurate idea of her trade. The following table of statistics* exhibits the amount of receipts and shipments at Chicago, in 1880 and 1885, of flour, wheat, corn, oats, rye, barley, beef, pork, other cured meats, lard, butter, seeds, live hogs, cattle, and sheep.

* Supplied by Statistician's Department of the New York Produce Exchange, and by the secretary of the Chicago Board of Trade.

	Receipts, 1880.		Shipments, 1880.
Flour......................	3,215,389 barrels	....	2,862,737 barrels.
Wheat......................	23,541,607 bushels	....	22,796,288 bushels.
Corn	97,272,844 bushels	....	93,572,934 bushels.
Oats	23,490,915 bushels	....	20,649,427 bushels.
Rye	1,869,218 bushels	....	1,365,165 bushels.
Barley	5,211,536 bushels	....	3,110,985 bushels.
Beef......................	6,282 packages	....	117,203 packages.
Pork	39,091 barrels	....	367,324 barrels.
Other Cured Meats............	164,437,225 pounds	....	958,036,113 pounds.
Lard	68,387,204 pounds	....	333,539,138 pounds.
Butter.....................	67,337,044 pounds	....	59,970,601 pounds.
Seeds.....................	245,930,484 pounds	....	195,616,050 pounds.
Liquors and High Wines........	127,468 barrels	....	218,582 barrels.

	Receipts, 1885.		Shipments, 1885.
Flour......................	5,385,772 barrels	....	5,240,199 barrels.
Wheat......................	18,909,717 bushels	....	13,975,032 bushels.
Corn	62,930,897 bushels	....	58,805,567 bushels.
Oats......................	37,678,753 bushels	....	32,426,462 bushels.
Rye	1,892,760 bushels	....	1,216,961 bushels.
Barley	10,760,127 bushels	....	5,583,003 bushels.
Beef (Dressed)	295,960 pounds	....	484,051,428 pounds.
Beef......................	6 packages	....	14,649 packages.
Beef......................	312 barrels	....	101,934 barrels.
Pork	34,959 barrels	....	393,216 barrels.
Other Cured Meats............	162,540,742 pounds	....	705,365,709 pounds.
Lard	61,054,257 pounds	....	255,121,101 pounds.
Butter	92,275,988 pounds	....	96,816,686 pounds.
Seeds (Grass)	67,673,084 pounds	....	52,626,856 pounds.
Live Hogs..................	6,940,841	....	1,792,681
Cattle.....................	1,906,408	....	747,983
Sheep.....................	998,888	....	259,310

The receipts of domestic cereal produce in New York for the years 1880 and 1885 were as follows:

1880.

Wheat	59,492,246 bushels.
Corn....	61,076,810 bushels.
Oats	13,997,690 bushels.
Barley	3,929,517 bushels.
Malt...................	2,815,853 bushels.
Rye...................	2,045,758 bushels.
Buckwheat	19,747 bushels.
Pease..................	497,896 bushels.
Beans..................	111,122 barrels.
Grass Seed..............	124,897 bags.
Flaxseed...............	1,020,526 bushels.

1885.

Wheat	24,329,458 bushels.
Corn...................	38,257,144 bushels.
Oats	26,236,970 bushels.
Barley	4,260,713 bushels.
Malt	4,264,786 bushels.
Rye....................	700,290 bushels.
Buckwheat	29,626 bushels.
Pease..................	305,116 bushels.
Beans..................	406,652 bushels.
Grass Seed..............	243,946 bushels.
Flaxseed...............	1,715,588 bushels.

Trade in these immense quantities of cereals begins with purchase from the producers, and continues in sale or consignment by purchasers to New York dealers. On arrival at the city they are sampled by means of a hollow iron sampling-rod, whose valve opens to admit the grain as the rod is thrust into the hatches of a vessel, or the interior of a car, and closes so as to retain the sample when it is drawn out. This process, repeated several times by responsible inspectors, in different parts of a car or boat load, secures reliable samples, which are placed in boxes on the Exchange tables. Cards affixed state the name of the seller and the quality of the cereal, and facilitate business with the miller or exporter who wishes to buy.

The relative declension of the cereal traffic at New York and its corresponding growth at other ports between the years 1866 and 1875 necessitated changes in the methods of business at this point. Vessels with incoming cargoes naturally sought ports where outgoing cargoes could best be obtained, and found them elsewhere. New York had no elevators; manual labor handled the grain; and each consignment was kept separate on canal-boats and barges, which were towed from one place to another in the harbor until all were discharged. Waste, delay, disputes between merchants and railroad companies and between buyers and sellers, followed by loss of trade, were the inevitable result. New York was the last important mart —under the lead of Franklin Edson and others—to adopt, and that in the face of

THE CALL ROOM.

FRANKLIN EDSON.

The grain trade proceeds under the supervision of a committee of five —an inspector-in-chief, a registrar, and a committee of three on the delivery of warehoused grain. The Committee on Grain, of which at the time of this writing Mr. C. R. Hickox is chairman, annually establishes the several grades, supervises the inspector-in-chief and his assistants, and fixes the fees which (below $20,000) constitute the Grain Inspection Fund, out of which salaries, audited expenses, and claims for damages are paid. Of the grades of grain established in 1884, ten were of white, amber, and red winter wheat, eight of spring, and one of State wheat. More or less of brightness, soundness, dryness, plumpness, and cleanness determines the grade. The word "Steamer" prefixed to "grade" denotes slight softness or dampness. Corn has eleven grades, oats eight, rye three, barley sixteen, pease three. Heated or unmerchantable grain is not graded at all. Standard samples of all grades of grain are kept at the Produce Exchange. The duties of the chief inspector and his deputies are to inspect, grade, and ascertain the weights of all parcels going into store as graded grain (at the owner's risk), and for which transferable warehouse receipts are given; also to inspect and ascertain the weights of all deliveries from warehouse or from railroad depot. A daily copy of his record is furnished to the registrar, and returns in duplicate to warehousemen and railroad companies of all receipts and deliveries of graded grain.

fierce opposition, the Western system of grading grain. This enables the Western buyer who has accumulated as much wheat in his warehouses as he wishes to carry, and who knows daily and almost hourly the market prices in New York, to telegraph to any broker, and through him to sell for future delivery the amount and grade of wheat he may have on hand. He then ships it so that it may arrive in time to fulfil his contract. Certainty and precision are thus given to his business movements. He is relieved from the compulsory speculation attendant upon consignments of whose sale, price, and delivery he is perforce ignorant. The present terminal facilities for handling grain are so complete that they have restored to New York, probably for all time, the control of the grain trade on the Atlantic seaboard. True, option dealing and some objectionable practices have come in with the new system, but that is only in harmony with the universal fact that every solid good is abused by unwise and greedy men.

Of these warehouses, conveniently approachable by ocean vessels, having customary shipping facilities, including seventeen elevators and proper cleaning apparatus, the collective capacity is 14,110,000 bushels. The rates of storage, including weighing, are $\frac{1}{2}$ cent per bushel for 10 days, and $\frac{1}{4}$ cent per bushel for each succeeding 10 days. Elevation from canal-boats costs ½ cent, screening and blowing ¼ cent, mixing on delivery ¼ per cent., per bushel. Consignors may have their grain kept separate if so desired, but the practice is to mix parcels of grain of the same grade together, without regard to ownership. Warehoused grain heated, but not through fault of warehouseman, is posted upon the bulletin-board of the Exchange, and made deliverable to depositors of longest date, the logical presumption being that it belongs to them. In the year ending June 30, 1885, no less than 586,699 bushels were posted as being out of condition.

The registrar keeps an exact account with each warehouse firm, and every Monday morning reports to the superintendent how many bushels of each grade of grain remained in store on the previous Saturday evening. In case of damage by fire, provision is made for the cancellation of warehouse receipts affected, and the issue of new ones covering the amount of grain injured. The tender of railroad guaranteed certificates, railroad elevator receipts, or regular warehouse receipts of the grade sold constitutes a delivery of the grain, as between buyers and sellers, in the regular course of business. Each delivery from store must be of 5000 bushels or more of oats or barley, 8000 bushels or more of wheat or corn, of 5000 bushels on boat or barge, and from cars of 500 bushels per car of all grain except oats, which must be of 900 bushels. Inspected and certified grain afloat in the port may also be delivered under the superintendence of the inspector. Demurrage at specified rates is charged to parties who fail to take pos-

session of property within defined periods. Graded grain sold on time contracts is transferred by order drawn on himself by the seller, who must issue a specific order for the delivery of the quantity named to the last receiver at the maturity of the contract. Grain bought at buyer's option is deliverable on the day or day after it is called for, and certainly at maturity of contract. Minor rules, too voluminous for notice, guard the rights of all participants in the grain trade.

Grain and feed delivered from railroad

C. R. HICKOX, CHAIRMAN OF GRAIN COMMITTEE.

tracks are under the supervision of the Produce Exchange board of weighers and measurers of track grain and feed. These furnish consignees with samples, weigh and measure the materials, issue returns in duplicate to owners (whose endorsement is needful to pass title to buyers), and also a triplicate return to the railroad company delivering the property, for the adjustment of freight and charges.

An original margin of ten cents per

bushel on wheat, rye, and barley, and of five cents on corn and oats, may be called on all sales or purchases of grain on the spot, to arrive, or for future delivery, upon deposit of an equal amount by the caller. On all contracts for future delivery a further margin may be called to the extent of any variation of the market value from the contract price. Calls may also be made of one cent per bushel above or below current quotation, when no original margin is deposited.

The Call Room daily presents an impressive spectacle of the traffic in grain. The first call is made at 11.45 A.M., the second at 1.30 P.M. In January, 1886, the successive calls are for oats deliverable in quantities of 5000 bushels, or multiples thereof, in March, April, or May; of No. 2 corn, steamer corn, or No. 2 red winter wheat, deliverable in lots of 8000 bushels, or multiples, for cash, or in February, March, April, May, or June, at the option of the seller, unless otherwise stated. Deliveries are ordinarily made on the 1st of the month, but may be on any subsequent day. About 350 brokers are present. William L. Eichell, caller of grain, presides. In rapid, monotonous voice, drawn out at the close of each sentence, he announces: "No. 2 oats, January. What are they offered at?" A seller, in loud, explosive tones, replies, "At $34\frac{3}{4}$" (per bushel), or, "At $\frac{3}{4}$." "At $\frac{3}{4}$," jerkily echoes the caller. "What is bid? $\frac{1}{8}$ bid, $\frac{1}{4}, \frac{1}{2}, \frac{5}{8}$ bid." "I'll take 'em," shrieks an excited individual. "Sold by Jones to Smith at $\frac{3}{4}$." Another lot is offered "at $33\frac{3}{4}$." "$\frac{3}{8}, \frac{1}{2}, \frac{5}{8}$," bid. "Sold," growls the seller. "Sold by Thomson to Johnson at $\frac{5}{8}$." No breath is wasted. "What is offered?" (oats). "35," says one; "$\frac{7}{8}$," another. "At?" queries the caller. If so, $\frac{7}{8}$ replies, "At;" if not so, "Give." "At $\frac{3}{4}$—any part of 5, 10, 50, 100 loads," is another offer. This holds till all are taken. Any part sold at a different rate vacates all previous bids and offers. The first offer to buy or sell at a price is accepted before subsequent offers at the same figures may be placed. If doubt arise as to whether the caller has awarded the purchase to the proper bidder, appeal is made from his decision. "Sustained or not!" is, in substance, his pithy submission to the members present. "Aye" sustains, "Nay" does not. Which is in the majority he decides, and in case of doubt, like a wise man, gives himself the benefit of

it. The call lasts ten or fifteen minutes, and occasionally has the accompaniment of callithumpian discord, blended with the fiendish screeches of a dozen frenzied locomotives. All speculative transactions are not improperly such, to be settled by the payment of differences. For example, a buyer may have an order from Liverpool for the delivery of a certain quantity of grain in three or six months' time. He buys what he wants in the Call Room. Then, chartering ship or steamer, he presents his claim at maturity to the seller, and demands the warehouse or other receipt, specifying the place where the property will be delivered. The first call in grain was on May 14, 1879. Steamer and No. 2 corn only were called; wheat and oats were added afterward. In this feverish spot the "young Napoleon of finance," Ferdinand Ward, began his meteoric career.

Speculative sales of lard in lots of 250 tierces of 320 pounds each, or multiples thereof, are also made in the Call Room, at 11 A.M. and 2 P.M., the caller of provisions and margin clerk presiding. Provisions are not now called. The original margin of $2 per tierce of lard is seldom called where parties are of known financial solvency, but margins corresponding with the fluctuations of the market may be required. Deliveries are not held to be necessary, and speculative contracts are usually settled by the payment of differences. The sales on call for the year ending June 30, 1885, were of 60,384,000 bushels of wheat, 32,597,000 of corn, 5,360,000 of oats, and 130,250 tierces of lard; in the previous year 53,480,000 bushels of wheat, 31,304,000 corn, 13,875,000 oats, and 295,750 tierces of lard. No pork was called in 1884 or 1885. Margins to the amount of $24,398,215 were deposited in the fiscal year 1885.

Option sales in the "Wheat Pit" are quite as magnetic and quite as electric as those in the Call Room. The "Pit" is the scalper's delight. He has an idea that the market is going up, buys a boat-load, or any quantity of grain that may be offered, sells it at an advance of $\frac{1}{8}$ cent per bushel, thus scalps the market, and is prouder of the exploit than a Comanche after successful pursuit of hair.

Business begins in the "Pit" at 10.30 A.M. Buyers and sellers are indiscriminately blended in the compact, throbbing, surging mass. All offers and bids are on a unit basis of 8000 bushels. Winter wheat is the only grain in mind. "I'll give 4½ [94½ cents per bushel] for May wheat," is the bid of a nervous, active broker, emphasized by uplifted hand and moving fingers. "I'll sell at 5," is the quick rejoinder of a neighbor. "I'll give ⅝." "I'll sell you at ¾." ⅛ is the only obstacle to a bargain. Long and furiously, or short and sharply, the conflict rages around that ⅛. The tug of war on the part of the seller is to pull the buyer up ⅛, and on the part of the buyer to pull the seller down ⅛. The contest is quite as exciting as aught in the intercollegiate games. But seldom is the battle drawn. Victory, hesitant in the vocal hurricane, decides for one of two parties. Bids and offers are usually regulated by telegrams from Chicago. The difference in prices between the two marts should be the cost of transmission from the latter to New York. Manipulation, or, in other words, gambling, at either point, defies all criteria of value. A "corner" in Chicago may raise wheat there above the normal price at New York; or a broken corner in New York may depress wheat below the healthful standard at Chicago.

Corners in commercial staples may be either good or evil, according to circumstances. Those of accidental character may come from the unforeseen failure of goods to arrive at New York in time for delivery. Such an event temporarily throws the command of prices into the hands of dealers who have an ample stock on hand. Corners, protective in design, may be made by persons or cliques who accept the offers made by gambling speculators on the market. These sell for future delivery what they do not own, in order to depress prices below what they sell at, and to make profit by the transaction. The protective corner arrests these "commercial pirates," and mulcts them heavily for release. Caught in their own traps, the bears howl horribly against the wickedness of corners in general. "Serve 'em right," is the only just remark. An accidental or protective corner may develop into an aggressive one; but this last is usually a conspiracy from the outset, born of cunning and overreaching, repulsive to honesty, denounced by all honorable merchants, and very injurious to commerce.

The facility with which sales and purchases for future delivery are made has enormously augmented the volume of trade. Foreign merchants avail themselves of it to provide for the prospective needs of different markets. It gives to the farmer a ready home market for his products at their full value, and affords to traders the opportunity of selling at a reasonable profit and at a moment's notice, and to deliver at option within specified times, as may be agreed. The exports of grain and grain products from the United States in the fiscal year 1885 were valued at $160,370,821. Seventy-five per cent., or more, of the whole was probably sold ten or twenty times over before it was finally shipped. Sales and purchases, charter of ships, bills of exchange for payment, sale of latter—all contemplated "future" delivery. Similar remarks are true of oil, tobacco, cotton, and other commercial staples. The system is a device of necessity, the judicious adaptation of prospective supply to probable demand, the work of foreseeing prudence. It may be, and is, abused by gambling speculators, or prostituted to assist aggressive corner conspirators, and in all such instances is shamefully demoralizing.

Settlements without actual delivery are not always obnoxious to strict probity. When honestly effected, as in the Bank Clearing-House, they are wholly concordant with it. Besides, they save much needless trouble and expense.

The Committee on Flour appoints a chief inspector and his assistants, keeps for reference a standard sample of each of the various grades of flour and meal, furnishes duplicate samples to the inspector, and causes flour and meal to be classified according to these standards. Extra No. 1, Extra No. 2, Superfine, and Fine are the established grades of wheat; Superfine and Fine, of rye flour. The committee also guards the sacredness of flour or inspection brands, provides for the inspection of barrels and bags, and designates the manner in which charges for service shall be collected. These charges, to an amount not exceeding $20,000, constitute "the flour-inspection fund," in custody of the treasurer, out of which salaries and expenses are paid.

Agents of metropolitan merchants buy of Western millers, or solicit consignments, on which advances are made. The West India, province, and general export demand is met through samples drawn by the inspector. Elasticity, color, dryness, and body in the dough are tests of quality. Much depends on the skill of the miller in dressing and cleaning the wheat. The neat, cleanly, deft manipulation of the flour expert will soon detect the quality of the work. Putting some of the flour on the palm of his hand, he applies the magnifying-glass, or the smoother, that he may examine the color, purity, and granulation. If the first and second be satisfactory, and the third sharp, there will be life in the sponge and dough. This is proven by pouring water from a handy little teapot upon the flour, mixing it, pulling it, breaking it. If the dough be short and inelastic, it is best adapted for crackers and pastry. Flours are mixed for ordinary bread, and for special purposes of the bakers.

Receipts in New York, 1880.
Flour............5,422,252 barrels.
Corn Meal........ 261,522 barrels and sacks.
Oatmeal .... 112,650 packages.
Buckwheat Flour... 72,201 sacks.

Receipts in New York, 1885.
Flour............5,970,627 barrels.
Corn Meal........ 477,196 barrels and sacks.
Oatmeal .... 99,581 packages.
Buckwheat Flour... 83,692 sacks.

Exports from New York, 1880.
Flour....................4,215,415 barrels.
Corn Meal................ 203,716 barrels.
Oatmeal .... 62,902 barrels.
Rye Flour................ 5,204 barrels.

Exports from New York, 1885.
Flour....................3,696,149 barrels.
Corn Meal................ 152,670 barrels.
Oatmeal .... 56,079 bags.
Rye Flour................ 3,811 barrels.

The Committee on Distilled Spirits licenses six inspectors and gaugers, who must make their returns of "proof," "just proof," "above proof," or "below proof," in accordance with the straight gauge rod, wantage rod, the hydrometer used by the government in the ascertainment of the tax on distilled spirits, or the Gendar hydrometer conforming in all respects to the government standard. Of whiskey 57,325, of high wines 58,247, and of alcohol 220,977 barrels were received at New York in 1880. In 1885, of whiskey 134,318, of high wines 74,304, and of alcohol 68,257 barrels arrived.

The Committee on Naval Stores licenses inspectors in New York and other cities, decides prices as a basis for business settlements, and holds a standard sample of spirits of turpentine with which all sold in shipping order must agree. Settlements of contracts are on the basis of 310 pounds for a barrel of rosin, and 43 gallons for a barrel of spirits of turpentine. Speculation follows the usual channels, and is in quantities not less than 25 barrels of the latter, or 100 barrels of rosin or tar.

Receipts, 1880.
Turpentine, Crude........... 2,871 barrels.
Turpentine, Spirits .... 99,789 barrels.
Rosin ....389,125 barrels.
Tar....................... 21,706 barrels.

Receipts, 1885.
Turpentine, Crude........... 3,241 barrels.
Turpentine, Spirits .... 76,139 barrels.
Rosin ....318,656 barrels.
Tar....................... 23,849 barrels.

Exports from New York, 1880.
Turpentine, Crude........... 4,263 barrels.
Turpentine, Spirits .... 36,624 barrels.
Rosin ....189,419 barrels.
Tar....................... 6,883 barrels.

Exports from New York, 1885.
Turpentine, Crude........... 173 barrels.
Turpentine, Spirits .... 13,600 barrels.
Rosin ....155,123 barrels.
Tar....................... 5,714 barrels.

Connected with the natural oil industry is the Committee on Petroleum, which appoints the Petroleum Quotation Committee to quote prices for business settlements, and administer the rules of this traffic. The Committee on National Transit Certificates of crude oil is composed of members dealing in these documents. Transactions are in 1000 barrel lots, or multiples thereof; and are for Cash, Regular, or Future Delivery. The bulk of the business, whether real or fictitious, in this comparatively new but enormously valuable product, is done at the New York Consolidated Stock and Petroleum Exchange.

Its marvellous growth may be estimated by comparing the production of 82,000 barrels in 1859 with that of 21,500,000 in 1885. The computed product between and inclusive of the two years is 287,000,000 barrels. Speculation therein is rampant. There is, of course, a solid, or rather fluid, basis for the National Transit Certificates, but much of the pretended dealing in them has as little real relation to them as to the outflow of caoutchouc in Brazil. Of the production of 1885 about 70 per cent., mostly refined, was exported, partly in barrels and partly in cases. Of the latter, about 10,000,000, containing two cans of five gallons each, were shipped to China, Japan, India, Java, and Singapore. Many large cargoes are sold on the floor of the Exchange, owing to the facilities it affords for bringing buyers, sellers, and shipping agents together.

The trade in animal, vegetable, and mineral oils is supervised by the Committee on Oils, under rules which define qualities, quantities, and weights of materials; basis and price of contract settlements; size and place of deliveries; condition of packages; tares, etc.; manner of call of oils, margins, contracts, transfers, etc. Six inspectors and testers of oils are employed in conducting this department of trade. The receipts in 1880 at New York were: of lard oil 9075, of lubricating oil 34,714, of cotton-seed oil 44,084 barrels. The exports were: of lard oil 734,569, and of cotton-seed oil 1,340,709 gallons. In 1885 the receipts were: of lard oil 9234, of cotton-seed oil 67,438, and of lubricating oil 27,757 barrels. The exports were: of lard oil 579,580, of cotton-seed oil 1,351,015, and of lubricating oil 12,217,873 gallons.

The Committee on Lighterage acts under rules defining the duty of lightermen, rates of demurrage, pecuniary liability for extra towing, etc.; that on Butter consists of three receivers and two exporters, who recommend to the Board of Managers for license as inspectors of butter three members of the Exchange, whose duty it is to pass judgment on lots of real or imitation butter referred to them, and to brand such lots accordingly. An official weigher of butter is also licensed on their recommendation. The Committee on Cheese, assisted by an inspector and weigher, who is also inspector of rejections, is charged with supervision of trade in this manufacture. Two brewers and three dealers compose the Committee on Hops. These vegetable products are subject to inspection, weighing, and sundry regulations interesting to those who are engaged in dealing in them. Receipts and exports of the last three articles at New York for the years 1880 and 1885 were as follows:

Receipts, 1880.

Butter	1,479,014 packages.
Cheese	2,672,759 packages.
Hops	66,759 bales.

Receipts, 1885.

Butter	1,733,643 packages.
Cheese	2,191,531 packages.
Hops	146,209 bales.

Exports, 1880.

Butter	29,030,908 pounds.
Cheese	129,524,180 pounds.
Hops	28,798 bales.

Exports, 1885.

Butter	11,307,005 pounds.
Cheese	91,770,106 pounds.
Hops	60,642 bales.

To the Committee on Maritime Affairs is confided the enforcement of the rules relative to the chartering, loading, unloading, and demurrage (or charges for delay and extra service) of sea-going vessels.

Complaint is frequently made of misrepresentations emanating "from the romancing brains of newspaper reporters, who sometimes look upon the New York Produce Exchange and the New York Stock Exchange as only a little more magnificent and a little more legalized gambling houses than some uptown"; whereas "there is more of personal honor in the keeping of contracts and engagements involving losses and profits of thousands, without regard to legal liability or compulsion, than can be found in any other equal territory on the face of the earth." That the opinion of reporters is largely that of the general public there can be no question. To what extent is it in harmony with the facts?

All business transactions are the outgrowth of intention to fulfil contracts according to terms, or not so to fulfil them. The first series is legitimate; the second illegitimate, because speculative in the gambling sense. The first necessarily accepts the risks incident to undoubted and continuous demand for consumption: the second, from motives of cupidity or love of excitement, unnecessarily accepts risks contingent upon the operation of known and unknown forces that do not essentially differ from those of the gambling table. In every legitimate business transaction each of the parties to it parts with something that he esteems of less value to himself than that which he receives. Mutual interest and obligation are essential to it. Business is not the getting of a maximum for a minimum; neither is it "the art of getting whatever you can without any consideration of equivalents." This may be the definition of "Sam'l of Posen," but never of true philosophy. Values ought to determine prices, not prices values. The fundamental consideration is what a thing is worth, and not what it can be bought or sold for. True business and gambling are opposed to each other as light and darkness; different from each other as a nursing mother from a cannibal. "Two years ago," said Chauncey M. Depew to the members of the New York Produce Exchange in 1884, "the speculators of Chicago, acting upon a theory which might have been well enough if food products could have been purchased by Europe only from America, by gigantic corners and other artificial processes drove the price of wheat up to fabulous figures." This feat awoke the slumbering energies of other nations, who became anxious to share in the wealth accruing from unusual harvests. The world went to wheat-growing. The result, in the United States, was the exportation of gold instead of grain, and the accumulation of debts instead of dollars. The orator added: "In the Wheat Pit at Chicago in a single year was buried more of the future prosperity of this republic than the sum of all the traffic which flows through that great city in a decade." This bold statement, uttered with characteristic courage, gave no small offence to the Chicagonese, and has been challenged with a boldness and force of reasoning—that of Alexander E. Orr — not inferior to his own. All parties agree that the "Wheat Pits" of Chicago, New York, and other cities have, at times and under certain circumstances, been injurious to commercial interests; but their defenders claim that these injuries are but as "a drop in the bucket" compared with the universal benefit to all interests secured by the ability to make "future" sales of merchandise. The injury done by the Chicago operations denounced by Mr. Depew lies in the loss of control—for some time at least—of the European markets. Whether the magnitude of that injury be so large as he asserted is matter of grave doubt. The daily bank deposits and withdrawals may be accepted as representative of the traffic flowing through that city. A low estimate of their amount would be four million dollars. This sum, multiplied by 300 (business days in a year), equals $1,200,-000,000; and by 3000 (ten years), $12,000,-000,000. Gambling greed kills the geese that lay golden eggs. The damage done at the epoch in question may not amount to twelve billion dollars, but still it was enormous.

The rules of any exchange may ordain that the seller *must* deliver and the buyer *must* receive, unless the contract can be legitimately cleared in some other way. There never was a law, human or divine, but some men would try to break it. Just as there may be thieves in a church, so—and with more likelihood—there may be gamblers in a wheat pit. A million bushels of wheat at a certain price, deliverable at option in the future, may be offered in the "Pit." Some one may cry out, "I'll take it." The contract is closed. Both parties are bound by it. Both join in the declaration, "We are not gamblers—no, never." Are they not gamblers when there is no *intention* on the part of the seller to deliver or of the buyer to receive the wheat when the contract expires, but only to settle the difference between the price current when it is sold and that when it is deliverable by payment of the loser to the winner of the bet? The margin, judiciously designed to guard the interests of honest parties to equitable contracts, is converted into an instrument of gambling by those who do *not* intend the exchange of values or of their representatives. Speculative options are detrimental to beneficent business, inasmuch as they enable insufficient capital to operate largely on small margins, and thus to cause fictitious markets and deranged prices. "The American option is the curse of the world," is a *dictum* of the *Mark Lane Express* that may find some justification in this fact. All laws against washed sales and fictitious sales are inoperative where option gambling is common. Extravagance and dishonesty attend it; financial if not moral ruin is a very frequent sequence. Unwilling to accept consequences, the pallid victims—uncanny as Banquo's ghost—often reappear amidst activities where their presence is not joyously welcomed. The fact is that while legitimate business is attended by inseparable risks, much of the so-called trading in stocks and products is unmitigated gambling. It is a consuming parasitic growth on otherwise healthy commerce.

"Puts" and "calls" are subjects of so-called trading in and around the Wheat Pit from the close of business at 3.30 to 4 P.M. Brokers of all ages excitedly engage in it. Some of them may be acting in behalf of firms or persons who wish to remain unknown. He who sells a "put" collects $10 from the man to whom he sells the privilege of "putting" or selling to him 8000 bushels of wheat at a specified price on the next day, or at any period within a designated time, if he (the purchaser) wishes to do so. The price specified in the put is lower than the market price at the time the put is sold; e. g., Cornheimer sells to Jackson a put—always of 8000 bushels, or multiples thereof—for one or two days at 93 when the ruling rate is $93\frac{3}{8}$, and pockets $10 whether Jackson does put the quantity to him in that time or not. Or Cornheimer may have sold "short" 80,000 bushels at 94. He must fulfil his contract, or pay the difference between that and higher rates at maturity. He sells ten puts of 8000 bushels each at $93\frac{1}{2}$, and pockets $100. He is perfectly willing to have the 80,000 bushels put to him at $93\frac{1}{2}$, for thereby he will make $\frac{1}{2}$ cent per bushel on the quantity he has contracted to supply. Whether it is put or not, he has received $100, and to that extent certainly has "hedged" himself against loss.

A "call" is the reverse of a put, and is the privilege of calling for 8000 bushels at a given price within a definite time, the price being higher than that of the last market-day. The cost of a call is also $10. The whole put and call business is simply betting on prices going up or down. It has grown to very large proportions. One dealer has been known to buy or sell to the extent of 400,000 bushels in the half-hour of active operations. The rules of the Exchange take no cognizance of the practice. It is said that it cannot be eliminated because of the difficulty of drawing a hard and fast line between the right and the wrong. A repudiating bettor may be boycotted, but cannot be disciplined.

Nothing human is physically or morally perfect. Evitable evil is to be denounced wherever it may be. But in speaking of men and of corporations just criticism requires that the good as well as the evil that is in them shall receive due recognition. The New York Produce Exchange has done immeasurable good to the commerce of the United States by simplifying and establishing its laws, gathering and disseminating all knowledge related to it, preventing its concentration in the hands of a few men of enormous wealth, and equalizing the chances of individual success. The average daily value of its business exceeds ten million dollars. The greater part of the farm products exported are handled by it. To the transportation of agricultural and mineral staples from the interior to the seaboard at minimum cost and maximum speed it has been no less serviceable. Whatever favors this, it has advocated; whatever would hinder, it has opposed. More than any other organization it contributed to the absolute freedom of the State canals from the exaction of tolls. In the development of indigenous resources it is one of the most potent factors. Its accumulations have helped to cover the land with a net-work of railways and canals. The debasement of the currency by means of the 79-cent silver dollar receives its hot condemnation. In defence of the purity of exported food products, of reciprocally beneficial commercial treaties, and of maritime rights, its stirring voice has often been heard. "The men who continually hold their fingers upon the commercial pulse of the nation are best able to detect injurious influences, and to suggest the necessary legislative remedies," is the just assertion of its members.

The Sickles Brigade—4000 strong—volunteer hospital corps, patriotic members enlisting or forming relieving committees, were the practical response of the Produce Exchange to the appeals of the heroic Hancock and others during the agony of the civil war. Organized to deal in the products of the country, it is patriotic by doing so—piratical only as some of its members gamble in them. It is one of the strongest cohesive forces of the body-politic, one of its most effective ethical teachers, and—by its system of arbitrative jurisprudence—one of the most hard-headed illustrations of corporate good sense. "We search our records in vain," said ex-President Herrick, "for one appeal of the sorrowful and suffering unheard, one cry for help unanswered."

Each of the 2900 subscribing members to the Gratuity Fund—which bears the stamp of ex-President Parker's genius—pays $3 on the death of any one of the number. Out of the proceeds a regularly increasing sum is paid to the widow, or divided among other heirs by just regulations. It is a gift, and therefore free from all legal claims—a just provision for helpless wives and dependent children. After the Exchange is freed from debt, part of the surplus revenue will swell the Gratuity Fund, which now amounts to between $800,000 and $900,000. In or about 1891 the appropriation payable to heirs of each deceased member will be about $9000. This sum, with $1000 added from the Surplus Fund, will then constitute the maximum payment of $10 000.

The Brooklyn Navy Yard (1870)

HARPER'S
NEW MONTHLY MAGAZINE.

NO. CCXLVII.—DECEMBER, 1870.—VOL. XLII.

THE BROOKLYN NAVY-YARD.

MAIN AVENUE, BROOKLYN NAVY-YARD.

COMMANDER SIMPSON, lately inspecting the broad and spacious Ordnance Dock of the Brooklyn Navy-yard, complained to the officer in charge that the grass grew unclipped between the great pyramids of shot and shell, and spiders masked with their silken webs the great batteries which lay unmounted and in confusion about the grounds. It was not precisely in these words that the complaint was uttered, for Inspector Simpson is less poetical than practical; and the presence of growing grass in a navy-yard was as grievous, in his official eyes, as would have been the absence of tar from his ship's rigging. When he had first begun his inspection, and was walking through the broad avenue by which one escapes from the noisy and dirty York Street of Brooklyn into the cleanliness, the quiet, and the strict discipline of the Ad-

miral's Office, he had observed the offensive green things growing all around him, and had given a true naval reason for his grumbling mood.

"This road must be cleared of grass," he had said, "or it will look as though there was nothing doing here."

It is the common error of sailors, and soldiers too, to believe that the people do not delight in their idleness. It is all a mistake to suppose that, because moralists generally, and political economists especially, deplore the examples and expense of the idle soldiers and sailors, the people also object to them. On the contrary, they are sights the unreflecting soul delights in, because their idleness is the present proof of peace—the positive assurance of prosperity. The shady spots, and the green slope of the forts where no sentinels challenge, are welcome resorts; and there is a grateful quiet in the broad, high ship-house of the navy-yard, where no workmen's children snatch great chips from under the edge of the swift-descending adze. The lazy fortress and the idle war-ship are emblems of peace in which the nation delights, after all that is said to the contrary; and, exhausted from a great struggle, the American people join heartily in the sentiment of Buchanan Read's prayer for peace:

"Oh! that some sweet bird of the South
Might build in every cannon's mouth,
Till the only sound from its rusty throat
Should be the wren's or the blue-bird's note;
That doves might find a safe resort
In the embrasures of every fort!"

But the people go even further than the poet. It is not in the nature of the American people to be content with the idleness of any element of power. No sooner was our late war ended and peace declared than, as will be remembered, the people demanded that the war forces should be utilized, not merely reduced. Without ceasing to love peace, or forgetting to be grateful to the soldiers and sailors who maintained the unity of the nation, the American people insisted that peace should not be a wholly idle season, and that the army and navy should be employed, not merely in preventing possible mischief, but in performing positive good. They would not wish a single veteran dismissed unwillingly—their deep sense of gratitude prohibits that; and, in spite of all that has been said and written by partisans for political effect, there is no authenticated instance of government neglect of its veteran soldiers and sailors. The people can not consent to see a single navy-yard dismantled uselessly—their sense of economy prohibits that; and all that has been published in the papers, all that has been said in Congress of reduction and economy, expresses simply the earnest desire of the people that in peace army and navy and armories and navy-yards shall be utilized. Very earnest at present is this demand with respect to the navy and the navy-yards and stations. The latest national experience has demonstrated that, though we possibly have too large a navy and too many naval stations for peace, we have too few ships and not enough dock-yards for time of war such as the nation has lately passed through. The assertion will not be disputed that, but for the then-existing navy-yards of the North, there could have been no blockade of the Southern ports completed and recognized as effective before the end of 1861. Shall a power such as this, though developed by war, be destroyed in peace? It is not against our present argument to admit, as the rebels claimed at the time, that the surrender of the extensive naval dépôt at Norfolk, with its immense supplies of munitions of war, gave the Confederates their means of resistance. Better to utilize for the purposes of peace than to destroy such agencies as these.

It should not be forgotten that the navy-yards of the North not only created, during the war, an entirely new navy, built on original principles of naval construction, but that they fitted more than six hundred merchant vessels to perform blockading duty as men-of-war. Is not that organization which thus converted peaceful ships of commerce into sturdy men-of-war powerful also to transform men-of-war into merchantmen? The rapidity with which the alterations of vessels for the war was effected was, at the time, the wonder and admiration of the country. Merchant ships, coming home from Southern ports, in more than one instance returned on their regular advertised trips as ships of war. It is related that the steamer *Monticello*, of the Cromwell line, had been making regular trips, for mercantile purposes, from New York to the Southern ports, and in April, 1861, was thus running between New York and Washington. It was rumored that the rebels had made preparations for its capture. The Government bought the steamer, and sent it to the Brooklyn Navy-yard to be fitted out. The largest force that could work upon the vessel was employed in the work of alteration. The elegant fittings of passenger service yielded to the stern exigencies of war, and the hand-saw tore its way through silken tapestry and velvet cushions which there was no time to remove. Within forty-eight hours from the time of purchase, and twenty-four hours from her arrival at the navy-yard, the *Monticello* was on her way to the Potomac, a war steamer, armed and equipped, carrying a large pivot-gun and four 32-pounders. In the darkness of the night she ascended the Potomac; the rebels made their attack, and the great guns roared out their reception. The *Monticello* reached Washington; it was never ascertained what became of the attacking party.

Similar alterations of the merchant marine for warlike purposes was a chief service of the navy-yards during the war, and that experience has suggested to national economists an idea which is only just now being impressed upon public attention, in connection with the schemes for reviving American navigation interests. The war which created the American navy destroyed the American merchant service. Scores of merchant ships were then changed to men-of-war; hundreds of sea-captains entered the naval service for the war; and thousands of sailors, trained to the free life and simple duties of the merchantman, voluntarily submitted themselves to the strict discipline and dangerous duty of the man-of-war. As the chief dependence of the navy, in time of war, was on the merchant service, it is now proposed to rely on the navy-yards and the naval service to aid in reviving American navigation. The idea proposed is the employment of the national dock-yards, in time of peace, in the construction of a merchant marine, which shall do service, in time of war, as a national navy. The various measures for reviving American navigation and reducing the American navy, which were agitated during the last session of Congress, had this result; and, as yet, no other. The plan is still merely a suggestion of that debate, and, not yet having taken shape, remains to be considered in its details. Such a proposition, it is understood, will be introduced during the coming winter session of Congress, in a bill which will encourage the building of iron ships at American navy-yards, and the manning of the merchant marine with American seamen and American naval officers. That the nation must resort to some plan like this seems indisputable in the face of the experience of other countries. Instead of selling the national navy-yards, they should be utilized, and employed no less vigorously in arts of peace than in those of war. It has been by permitting her naval officers to engage in it that England has made her merchant service the finest in the world, and fitted her every sailor for instant duty as a man-of-war's man when occasion requires. Her naval stations are public ship-yards, at which merchant ships and men-of-war alike are built, and her iron ships are built alike at private and national ship-yards. It is to this resort we are urged by our experience and the advice of our leading officers. It seems a wiser one than that other suggestion, to sell the stations and reduce the navy, which, in an emergency, might be indispensable to national safety. Since it is simply a question of destroying or utilizing a great power, there can be no hesitation in choosing, and the Ameri-

can Congress can hardly refuse its consent if a plan shall be devised to convert our idle naval stations into busy dock-yards, nor fail to extend every aid of legislation for the consummation of that desirable achievement. "Ships and naval organizations," says the letter from Secretary Robeson, of May 30, to the House Committee on Naval Affairs, "can not be extemporized like regiments, but are the growth and product of long-continued industry and skill." And this, which is true enough of ships, is pre-eminently the fact in respect to their birth-place, the navy-yard. Its growth is inevitably slow. The dismantling of any one of those already completed is not, therefore, to be hastily resolved upon.

Among the navy-yards which it has been proposed to sell is that at New York, commonly but erroneously called the Brooklyn Navy-yard. Officially it is the New York Navy-yard, and is so described in the almost forgotten parchments by which the State and city of New York transferred to the General Government their right and title in the Waal Boght, or Fallow Bend, of the old Dutch settlers, which has since, by a curious corruption, been transformed into Wallabout Bay. And since Chancellor Kent and Robert Tillotson examined and attested the deeds, who shall doubt the correctness of the title? Its locality is one hallowed by revolutionary memories. It was in this bay that the British prison-ships were moored; and on the surrounding shores, then only salt marshes, growing with each tide that overflowed them, twelve thousand American

SALUTING BATTERY.

ORDNANCE DOCK.

patriots, who had perished in that dismal confinement of hunger and malaria, were hastily and but partially interred. Years afterward those mouldering bones were collected with pomp and imposing ceremony, and removed to a temporary receptacle in Jackson Street, then adjoining. There they still remain, though during more than half a century their removal to a suitable mausoleum has been from time to time agitated; and a structure was to have been erected for this purpose upon the summit of Fort Greene, now an ornamental park in Brooklyn.

Very curious reasoning first directed the attention of the Government to this site as a suitable one for a navy-yard. At least, such arguments would be thought curious enough if made in the interests of the metropolis, as at present existing. In the official correspondence preceding the first purchase, in April, 1801, it was announced that the selection was resolved upon because of the desire of the Government to bestow a proportion of its patronage on New York, and that New York might benefit by the employment which her citizens would receive at the proposed navy-yard. We smile at these things now; and whether the navy-yard, in an emergency, hires double or treble its usual number of laborers, or whether, upon the motion for retrenchment of the gentleman from Buncombe, or some Western Congressman who never sniffed salt-water breezes nor knows the importance of a navy, it dismisses a large number of men in a single day, there is no perceptible change in the vast labor market of New York city. But if this naval station were transformed into a national ship-yard, its location in the chief port, the largest and cheapest market, and the most populous city of the country, would assume an importance, aside from mere considerations of labor, not to be disregarded in the interest of commerce.

Another reason for selecting this site for the navy-yard was, that it would afford a defense to the metropolis. By the terms of the sale it was distinctly stated that the site was to "be used and applied to the defense and safety of said city"—meaning New York. It has never been in any military sense, however, a part of the defenses of the port. A battery exists on Ordnance Dock, and its mortars, looking south, are trained to drop hot shot or bursting shells into the Narrows and the lower bay, two miles and more seaward; but as a means of defense it would not enter largely into any tactician's calculations. It is rather a collection of relics than a formidable array of powerful mortars. Some of them did service in opening the Mississippi, at Forts Jackson and St. Philip, under Porter. Others aided to make night hideous at the bombardment of Vicksburg; and still others bowled their fiery missiles at Mobile. But, situated as they are, they are as powerless to protect New York against the approach of a modern fleet as would be the handsome but ineffective guns of the Saluting Battery, which stands at the other side of the same dock, or as the dismounted monsters near by, which, in spite of their size, are objects of curiosity rather than weapons of defense in their present position. These guns, seen in the illustration of the Saluting Battery, have been named Satan, Lucifer, and Moloch. There was a fourth of the same pattern called Beelzebub; but it has since been mounted in the tower of some Monitor. They are the largest cannon ever cast. Each weighs forty-two tons. The diameter at the breech is nearly six feet. A man can easily crawl in and out of the muzzle, which admits a 20-inch shell. Mounted on a trunnion, they are easily handled by experienced gunners.

As a means of defense for New York city the navy-yard is, therefore, useless; and that consideration which influenced its establishment need not embarrass any proposition to change its character. The transfer of the water-front of Wallabout Bay was made on the considerations above noted, and the payment of $40,000 in money. There was a rumor to the effect that the Government had paid too much for it, whereupon one of the agents employed to purchase the site, determined not to be considered a party to a fraud on the Government, offered to take the bargain off its hands. The water-front alone is now valued at $20,000,000. But it must not be supposed that, in case of the sale of the yard, the Government is to profit by this advance in the value of its real estate; nor will the city of Brooklyn, of which the yard is now a part. On the contrary, the State of New York will be benefited, and it only. By the terms of the deed the transfer of the water-front to the General Government is for such time only, and "so long as the same be used and applied to the defense and safety of the said city and port of New York, and no longer, and revert to the people of the State of New York when not applied to the purpose aforesaid." A hasty resolution of Congress to sell the yard would, therefore, transfer $20,000,000 of government funds to the State of New York, a proceeding to which Western Congressmen, at least, are not disposed to consent.

The Brooklyn Navy-yard is approached through one of the least attractive parts of the City of Churches, and the contrast between the yard itself and the locality immediately outside its walls can not but strike an observant visitor. There is to be seen a certain naval aspect in the adjacent streets; but nothing of the cleanliness and the order of the yard is visible in the neighborhood immediately beyond its high walls. Inside, "Poor Jack's" fondness for the appurtenances of his calling is gratified by collections of old figure-heads which have gone dozens of times round the world, and which grace or disfigure various lawns within the yard. Outside, this love of the sailor for his vessel and its representations is traded upon by "the land-sharks" who prey upon his generous nature. Weather-beaten signs over dilapidated taverns, or dusty prints in small shop windows, disclose the portraiture of red-faced naval dignitaries, resplendent in gold lace. In front of tobacco shops the conventional figure of the Indian graciously presenting, not the aboriginal pipe, but the modern rolled cigar, is superseded by that of a sailor, with unlimited breadth of hat-brim and trowsers. Instead of popular packages of chewing tobacco, "navy-plug" is displayed. There are shops whose glass fronts boast of attractions in the shape of models of ships, with masts and rigging complete. The ordinary Dutch corner grocery announces that it keeps "naval stores;" and a liquor saloon steals the great name of one who detested its traffic, and styles itself the "Farragut House."

There is visible in this part of Brooklyn none of those immense warehouses and magnificent dock-basins which commerce has built in the southern part of the same city. Although there is a pier and a dry dock in the navy-yard superior to any like structures in this country, and the latter of which is not inferior to those of Liverpool and London, their use has been confined solely to vessels of the navy. Merchant ships have been excluded from them, though pier and dock are for the most part

MORTAR BATTERY.

OLD FIGURE-HEAD.

to be full of water. After the vessel that is to be docked is floated in, this caisson, which contains an upper and lower compartment, is brought from the outside and set against the open end of the dock, which it closes, and in grooves which fit its bow and stern. Water is then let into the lower compartment of this caisson, and it sinks so as to hermetically seal up the dock, which is then pumped out. As soon as water is removed from the dock, the pressure of the water of the East River upon the caisson holds it in place as firmly as though it were part of the granite walls. When the dock is to be opened, a steam-engine and pump in the upper compartment of the caisson are set to work in pumping out the water in its lower compartment, and the caisson, rising in its grooves, allows the East River to flow beneath its keel and fill the dock. The strain on the gates is thus greatly relieved, as they are only used to break the intervening movements of the water. Success in shoring a vessel properly in dock depends largely upon its management in giving it its first "set." The dock, which contains 610,000 gallons, can be emptied within two hours and ten minutes. The whole height of its walls is 36 feet; its least depth, measured at high-water over the mitre-sills, 26 feet; and its least width, similarly measured, 66 feet. Its main chamber is 30 feet wide at bottom, and 286 feet in length; at top, 98 feet, and 307 feet long; and 52 feet can be added to its length by using the vestibule between the doors and the caisson.

idle from year to year. The consequence is, that commerce has been driven from the vicinity of the yard. The devotion of these parts of the yard to mercantile purposes would, without doubt, attract commercial and manufacturing enterprises to the city, and they would form the nucleus of a system of docks and piers and warehouses of great advantage to the metropolis. The pier alluded to is known as Ordnance or Cob Dock, and was completed in 1866, at a cost of $1,900,000. It is built on an old island in Wallabout Bay, shaped on the old maps not unlike the Mikado's famous fan-shaped refuge for the Dutch apostates in Japan. It covers an area several times greater than that of any other pier in the port; but its vast space is devoted to the storage of shot and shell and artillery, instead of the rich products of industry and agriculture.

The Dry Dock is an immovable basin of solid granite. More than ten thousand piles were driven to bear this vast mass of masonry. It was begun in August, 1841, and was ten years in building, costing not less than three millions of dollars. Its bottom is at least 23 feet below the surface of the East River at high tide. When its gates are open, the dock fills with water, a vessel is floated in, the gates closed, and the water pumped out. Ingenious devices aid in accomplishing these ends. The gates, or doors, are immense structures—their hinges alone would make several good-sized portals for ordinary dwellings. The gates are supplemented at the entrance of the dock by the most singular of all doors or portcullises, leaving a vast vestibule between. This outside door is an iron boat, called a caisson or pontoon, shaped much like an axe-head, with the edge for a keel, being 66 feet long, 16 wide, and with 30 feet depth of hold, supposing the dock

The growth of a navy-yard, like that of a city, can be traced by the different styles of architecture of successive periods. In earlier years, continuous blocks of buildings seem to have been the rule, single structures the exception, in the Brooklyn yard. First of all were old-fashioned houses, fronting as if on the street of a city, with gables at either end of the row, and looking at the present day like what a New Yorker would call a row of tenement houses. After these, separate lofty buildings grew, but these now seem old-fashioned, but far more pretentious, with vast roofs, double and hipped, reaching more than half the distance between the ridge-pole and the ground; strangest of all, they are not unfrequently built with sides sloping inward, as if the architect's ideas were derived from the tent, or the Indian wigwam. However inferior in architectural beauty, it is quite certain that these older buildings excel more modern structures in the element of strength. "These are none of your balloon frame houses," said an old attaché of the yard, one George Washington Lee, who has watched its growth for more than fifty years, and who in that long period has been absent from duty —think of it, oh gentlemen who represent us, in the intervals of holidays and excursions and "pairings off," in Congress!—only forty days. "These are houses such as they don't build nowadays. There are beams in them, Sir, like the timbers of a seventy-four." Near the entrance, on the left of the main avenue, and obstructing the view of several of the most magnificent of the warehouses in the yard, is an odd specimen of architecture, called the Round House, probably from the fact that it is octagonal in form. Set in its tower is a great clock, by which the yard is ruled, as far as time is concerned. Within the building is the mustering office, where, twice a month, the workmen receive their pay. On one semi-monthly pay-day only round sums are paid; on the other, the account is closed with fractions, if any. Even on the day when only round sums are paid, a sister of charity may be seen sitting in the hall waiting to receive alms; and it must be inferred that either the workmen bring with them some remnant of previous pay, which is very improbable, or that they contribute legal tenders of not the smallest denomination.

Perhaps, however, the surest index of the architectural dates is yellow paint. Until within ten years at the furthest, every permanent structure in a navy-yard had to be painted with yellow ochre. But the more recent buildings are allowed to retain the natural beauty of brick and stone; and massive warehouses, elaborately trimmed with hewn granite, mark an improved era of taste, and better adaptation in construction. There are about fifty of these immense buildings in the Brooklyn Navy-yard, each suitable for commercial or manufacturing purposes. The Brooklyn yard is considered as the chief naval *entrepôt* for the receipt and delivery of the materials required at other navy-yards. At almost every hour of the day, in the busy times of the yard, vast coils of rope may be seen going in at one door, while immense chain cables are issuing from another. There is even a "pepper-and-mustard" building, where spices and condiments are ground, prepared, and packed for ships' use. In other buildings are stored specimens or samples of naval stores, from the latest style of the tin dipper to the newest form of explosive missile. In the store-room of the Ordnance Department may be found numerous articles, or patterns of articles, of this kind, and various illustrations of newly developed principles in construction, naval warfare, and mechanics. There is exhibited there, for instance, a plank upon which the experiment was made, by Admiral Farragut, of shooting with a tallow candle as a projectile. It is an oak plank of at least an inch in thickness. One candle has torn a hole through the plank. Another has splintered it at the place of impact, but not actually passing through, and pieces of the candle are still 'sticking in the clefts. The distance was

ROUND HOUSE.

DRY DOCK.

five paces. In the Naval Lyceum or Museum, an apartment of the Admiral's Office, are numerous other naval curiosities which repay examination. The Lyceum was started in 1833, by prominent citizens of Brooklyn, and chartered by Congress in 1835. Chief among those who labored for its establishment was Captain Matthew C. Perry. The honor of belonging to it seems to have been the inducement for the annual subscription. Citizens sent books and paintings, some of which are of unquestionable value; among the latter being good portraits, in oil, of several of the naval heroes of our first wars, and a series of portraits of the early Presidents of the Republic. Naval officers afterward sent many contributions. An elegant coral formation, about two and a half feet high, is designated as the *Alexonia Gigantea*, or "Neptune's Cup," and was obtained in the Bay of Bengal, from a depth of sixty feet below the surface. There are models and plans of various naval structures. Two links of a chain are preserved, with a certificate that there were fifty-one links in all, fished out of "Hudson's River," between Fort Montgomery and West Point. The links weighed from thirty to thirty-five pounds apiece, and there can be no doubt that this massive product of Revolutionary forges was originally stretched across the river to prevent its ascent by invaders. An ecclesiastical chart, hung against the walls, reminds the visitor that he is yet within the boundaries of the City of Churches.

In other buildings sails are manufactured. It must not be supposed that the mere stitching of the canvas forms the chief part of this labor. The proportioning of sails to ships, and devising their outline for each vessel, are matters requiring mathematical calculation and measurement, as well as the knowledge that is acquired in nautical experience or developed in practical skill; and these require large apartments or floors on which to test the calculations by diagrams, as on a blackboard. And as every vessel, preparatory to a voyage, must have two or three suits of sails, their manufacture becomes an important branch of industry. Other floors are devoted to the making of "patterns." Before it became customary in navy-yards to build a house for laying out "moulding" lines by which vessels are shaped, they were simply traced in the sand of the shore where the construction was to take place. And this was by no means in those ages of antiquity when school-boys learning to write traced their "copies" in tablets of sand, but quite within the present century. Now there is no neater exemplification of the technical methods and scientific calculation by which all such works must be performed than the pattern-shop, with its "moulding-room." Here the lines of every vessel that is constructed in the yard, and those of many that undergo extensive repairs, are drawn upon the floor to the full size of the proposed vessel. These lines are taken from perhaps half a dozen different points of view of the hull, sectional and otherwise; such as might be obtained by looking from either end, from the deck downward, from the keel upward, etc. From these geometrical lines, which thus present in accurate and flowing curves the ou-line of every stick of timber or frame of iron in a vessel, "patterns" are cut to correspond. These patterns, representing solid timbers, themselves are cut in thin boards, bearing the same relation to the ship which is designed that a tailor's paper pattern does to the garment it is proposed to cut.

There are also immense work-shops, where the forge glows, and the steam-hammer falls on the glowing iron with a

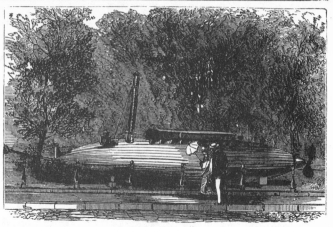

REBEL TORPEDO BOAT "MIDGE."

heavy thud, cutting it with wedge-shaped blades as though it were a fresh cheese under a case-knife. It is commonly supposed that the wedges or knives used for cutting red-hot iron are of the hardest steel. This is a mistake. The hot iron that is to be cut would heat a steel knife, and draw its temper before ten minutes' work could be done. The knives are of iron, and illustrate, as the experiments with the candle do, the rule that sufficient momentum may force a soft substance through a hard one. In other shops the timbers of a vessel undergo singular treatment in receiving the shape that fits them for their uses. A remarkable planing-machine handles these immense masses in a very easy way. The planes are what in other machinery are known as "routers," and revolve with high speed in a horizontal direction, each being suspended by

a perpendicular axis of revolution. The planes of course sweep off a circular surface as the timbers pass beneath them. Such is the toughness of the timber, and such the speed of the planes, that a stream of fire as well as of chips flies from the outer edge of the circle, while the plane is itself invisible on account of the rapidity of its motion.

The change from the use of wood to that of iron in naval structures has effected prominent changes in the requisites of this as of every navy-yard in the country. The machines which handle that metal are, of necessity, formidable. Hideous monsters, mechanical ogres, stand ready with savage jaws to bite out mouthfuls of solid metal. The metal shrieks as chisels pare it away while sliding under the planing tools, held down on a bed twenty or thirty feet long, where

SAIL-MAKING.

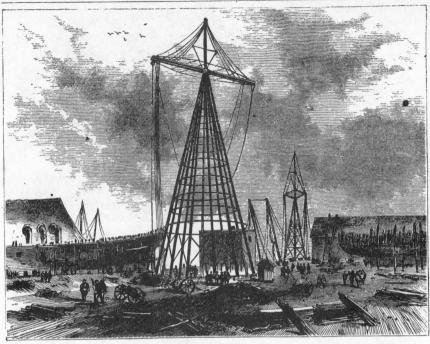

IRON DERRICK.

it can not writhe, no matter what its agonies. Or it is twisted around by ponderous lathes, which whirl these enormous masses as lightly as if they were shillalahs at Donnybrook Fair. Some of the largest piston-heads ever turned have been required for the steam-cylinders which operate the guns in the turrets of the Monitors. The steam in the cylinder also acts as a buffer, or, rather, constitutes a "steam-cushion," that receives the recoil of the gun. The diameter of one of these piston-heads, probably intended to operate a 20-inch gun, and manufactured in the Brooklyn yard, measured within a small fraction of eleven feet, and compared to but little disadvantage with the piston-head of the great caloric engine of the *Ericsson*, the experimental ship driven by hot air, whereon admiring members of Congress sat in enjoyment of a strange ride, which seems destined never to be repeated.

Perhaps the culmination of the growth required by the use of iron would have been in rolling plates for iron-clads. A building was constructed in the Brooklyn yard for this purpose, and received the title of the "Iron-clad Shop." The shafting was introduced, and a variety of preparations completed, but Peace spread her white wings over the land, and the nest was never used that was to have hatched out, Minerva-like, men-of-war in full armor.

Among the most perfect machines which ingenuity has devised for the economy of labor in naval construction is the derrick, of which one of the finest specimens in the world is to be seen in the Brooklyn Navy-yard. These singular structures, taller than the masts of frigates, moved and actuated by steam in performing their labors, surpass even the genii of the Arabian tales in the prodigious facility with which they stretch out their long arms, seize vast masses of material, lift them in air, and deposit them where required. Sometimes, however, their fingers slip. Absolute skill, only acquired by practice, is required to safely "sling" a marine boiler or a main shaft. A heavy gun did once slip from the derrick slings in the Brooklyn yard and fall into the hold of a vessel; it, however, happily occasioned little damage. In 1863 a 15-inch gun was carried to the same yard from a distant foundry. It was destined to form part of the armament of the United States Monitor-turreted steamer *Roanoke*. The armament of that vessel was to be the heaviest afloat. She was intended for the protection of the harbor of New York. This gun, weighing about 50,000 pounds, was lifted out of a vessel that brought it at night, and gently deposited by a derrick on the shore end of one of the docks. Next morning no gun was visible. It had sunk, carrying with it the portion of the dock on which it rested, down into the quicksand, and was quite out of sight. The derrick was again brought into requisition. A hole was dug around the monster; it was "slung" again and lifted into the air. The gun, however, slipped from the slings, and this time going down into the hole breech foremost, was once more lost to view. To raise it again it became necessary to sling it behind the trunnions. So troublesome was the quicksand that this was only eventually accomplished by sinking around it iron plates and building them into a cofferdam, from which the sand was extracted, and at length the gun.

Among the practices which the navy-yards have outgrown is the old-fashioned one of building ships in the open air. It would seem so manifest an improvement that a structure which requires months or years for completion should be

MARINE BARRACKS.

built under cover, that it is quite surprising that "ship-houses," in which ships are built preparatory to launching, should rank among recent improvements. There are several of these in the Brooklyn yard. Some idea of their size may be inferred from the dimensions of a ship now in process of construction in one of them—a vessel formerly known as the *Kalamazoo*—before Indian names were abolished—now to be called the *Colossus*. She is intended as an iron-clad, and has two turrets in Monitor style. Her extreme length, over-all is nearly 350 feet; breadth, about 57; depth of hold, 19. Within her vast wooden frame a truss-work of iron, composed of long girders and cross-pieces more frequent and heavier than those of any bridge of equal size, bolted and braced together and through her timbers, gives her an indescribable appearance of absolute and permanent strength. She contains a vast ventilating apparatus, which is itself a curiosity, and six steam-boilers, each more than twenty feet across the face. There are six furnaces to each boiler—36 in all, giving a heating sur-

face of more than 23,000 square feet, which may be regarded as a small Gehenna, capable of consuming 84 tons of coal per day. Her four engines have each cylinders of nearly four feet diameter, the stroke being a little over four feet—calculated to give to two fifteen-feet propellers sixty revolutions per minute, and a speed for the ship of ten and a half knots per hour.

The only buildings in the Brooklyn yard which it would be impossible to utilize for the purposes urged are the Marine Hospital and Barracks. These are, however, in a part of it remote from the water-front. The Barracks form one of the most attractive resorts for visitors, and are built on an elaborate plan and maintained at liberal cost. There is always a squad of marines drilling or pacing the green before their otherwise desolate-looking domicile. The United States Naval Hospital is near by. It is a splendid building in the Doric style of architecture, surrounded by the heavy foliage of full-grown trees. Beside the long corridors, which 230 feet of frontage and 125 feet depth

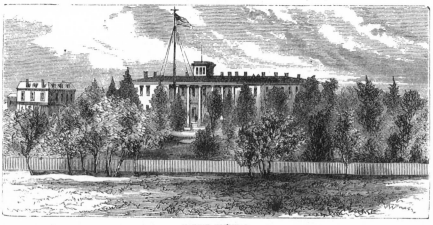

MARINE HOSPITAL.

A RELIC OF THE "ONEIDA."

67 Brs., 1755." Near by is a gun which is all that remains of the ill-fated United States war steamer *Oneida*. It was taken off that vessel just before she sailed on her last cruise. She was originally built in the Brooklyn yard, being one of twenty-three vessels entirely constructed there during the war. This gun, an 11-inch, passed through all the great actions on the Mississippi, and bears the marks of several engagements during which it was struck by the missiles of the enemy. The heaviest blow by which it was indented was received in Mobile Bay during the passage of the forts from a shot fired by the rebel ram *Tennessee*. Perched up in a dock, not far from this gun of the *Oneida*, are now lying the bones of the famous old *Hartford*, which led in the famous battle in the bay. After she was sent to the Brooklyn yard some improvement was contemplated in her. Her wales were removed, exposing her to top-timbers like the ribs of some vast fossil skeleton. Then the appropriation was stopped, and the work was suspended.

Several torpedo-boats, among others the *Midge*, captured in Charleston Harbor, are scattered about the yard, and are objects of great interest. The importance of the torpedo in modern marine warfare is only beginning to be appreciated. Attention has been called to it in a recent letter from the Secretary of the Navy. After the war was over, as well as during its pendency, the obstructions in most of the Southern rivers had to be cleared and blown up by means of torpedoes; in fact, when the existence of torpedoes among the obstructions was suspected, torpedoes were the only safe things to attack them with, as though one should fight fire with fire. The Northern vessels used for dicharging torpedoes are not so gracefully constructed as those built at the South. A torpedo-boat of New Bedford construction, preserved in the Brooklyn yard, looks about as beautiful in outline as a stiff, dead lamprey-eel, except that a smoke-stack stuck in it, like a pin in an insect, gives it a somewhat different effect at first sight. But each and all of these torpedo-boats impress the beholder with the belief that size is not the true test of force. Massive iron-clads as well as mighty frigates are not invulnerable when attacked by these enemies, whose proportions are to theirs like those of a wasp to an elephant, but carrying a more fatal sting.

provide, are arranged rooms for one hundred invalids. There is accommodation, however, for twice that number; and during the war the space between the wings of the building was filled by a temporary structure, and several hundred patients were admitted. The sick of the navy from all parts of the world are sent to this hospital; for, although there are many other naval hospitals, the rule is to transfer the sick of the navy, when in foreign ports, to any United States vessel going home, and they are sent to the hospital of whatever yard or station the vessel is ordered to. It happens that in many cases there would be too long delay, for the welfare of the patient, in waiting for such a vessel, and he is sent by the quickest lines of travel, which inevitably bring him to New York, and therefore to this hospital.

Visitors to the Brooklyn yard will find many curious objects, other than those named, to interest and attract them. Emerging from the Admiral's Office, where it is first of all necessary to go to obtain passes, trophies are seen on every side. At every corner of the numerous streets of the yard there is a "great gun," planted with the breech in the ground and a ball two or three sizes too large, so that it can by no possibility enter the bore, stuffed part way into the muzzle. At the doors of the Admiral's Office are guns captured during the Mexican war, some of which, of brass, undoubtedly contain a percentage of the precious metals. One of these, captured at San Juan de Ulloa, is a 30-pounder, and is covered with ornamental engraving. Various inscriptions are interspersed. Its title is "*Le Robuste*," which its appearance does not belie. The motto "*Ultima Ratio Regum*" ("The last resort of kings"), twits upon facts after a manner akin to sarcasm. "*Nec pluribus impar*" ("Not an unequal match for numbers") did not apply at the time of its capture. There are names, titles, and a date upon it, as follows: "Louis Charles de Bourbon, Comte D'Eu, Duc D'Aumale," and "A Douay par Berenger, Commissaire des Fontes,

The receiving-ship of every navy-yard is always attractive, for it is the residence of the sailors. The *Vermont* is the present receiving-ship, which is anchored off the navy-yard at Brooklyn.

The first receiving-ship employed in the United States Navy was built at the Brooklyn Navy-yard. It was an immense steam floating battery, called. *Fulton the First.* While fastened to the dock as a receiving-ship, on the morning of the 4th of June, 1829, the magazine on board exploded. Thirty-three persons were killed and a large number wounded. Among the killed was the commander, Lieutenant Breckinridge. The vessel sank at the dock. The ship which succeeded to the unfortunate *Fulton,* the *North Carolina,* became, we had almost said, a landmark, and it was popularly believed that she was aground; at all events, she was a fixture associated with the early memories of the people of Brooklyn. There was a school for naval apprentices on board. The vessel had been launched after the war with Great Britain, and, before being thus stationed, had made cruises to the Mediterranean and Pacific. During the rebellion she was sold at public auction, and probably at a mere tithe of her original cost, as no purchaser could have had any use for her except as so much wood, iron, and copper, for which she was broken up.

What has been said of the Brooklyn Navy-yard applies, in almost every particular, to the other seven yards and six stations of the country. The yards are at Portsmouth, New Hampshire, Boston, Philadelphia, Washington, Norfolk, Pensacola, and Mare Island, California; the stations are at Annapolis, League Island, Sackett's Harbor, New London, New Orleans, and Mound City, Illinois. The number of men employed at these is now about the same as just before the breaking out of the rebellion. The number which may be employed if a national scheme for reviving American shipping is devised can be imagined by the statistics which have been preserved of the operation during the war of the Brooklyn Navy-yard. In 1860 there were about 1200 men, and there was paid in all about $200,000 during the year. In 1861 the largest number was about 3700, and the total year's payments were about $680,000. In 1862 the corresponding figures were 4800 men, and $2,000,000; in 1863, 5000 men, and nearly $3,000,000; in 1864, 5900 men, and $3,750,000; in 1865, 6200 men, and $4,000,000; the culmination being in August, 1865, when the payments for that month were a little above $400,000.

The great difficulty to be encountered in the effort to restore American shipping, it is evident, will not be the lack of materials, workshops, and workmen. It remains for statesmanship to devise a policy which will give them use and employment.

RECEIVING-SHIP "VERMONT."

Bowery, Saturday Night
(1871)

BOWERY, SATURDAY NIGHT.

INFANT GERMANY.

THE more noticeable features of the growth of New York city, from its grotesque and singular germ in the little Dutch village on the southern end of Manhattan Island, have been to a certain extent forced upon it by topographical peculiarities, both of land and water; but social and national groupings have also exercised an important agency. Like has sought and clung to its like, and as strenuously shunned and avoided its unlike or its opposite, until now, speaking within limits, different classes and nationalities have assumed and occupied their different "quarters" almost as distinctively as if assigned to them by despotic edicts of the Middle Ages. Neither has the city's growth been at all subservient to the prophecies or plans of those who have sought to direct or control it. Nothing has gone as it was meant to go, nor is any thing where, according to map and calculation, it should be. The men who fondly looked upon Chatham Square as the future centre of trade are not more hopelessly "out" than those who pinned their faith to Pearl Street, or settled themselves for life within sight of the City Hall clock.

If, however, we resign the doubtful task of prophesying what and where the city will be, there is a good deal in the study of the city as it is. Some one has put on record the remark that "New York is not by any means an *American* city," but he would have been nearer the truth if he had said, "Hardly any of these New Yorks, scattered on and around Manhattan Island, are distinctively American." Some of them have developed curiously composite characters of their own—constantly changing of course—not to be mated elsewhere in the world; and one of them, quite a large "city within a city," is sufficiently German in its characteristics to merit an especial description.

Turning off to the right, or easterly, from the City Hall, is a street of varying width, irregular direction, and no great length, destitute of all pretensions to beauty, architectural or oth-

erwise, always dirty, crowded, and busy. This is Chatham Street, the main connection between the technically "down-town" districts of New York and the swarming "east side." It terminates in a very irregular open space on what was once a pretty steep hill-side, known as Chatham Square, being about as far as possible from that shape, or, indeed, from any whatsoever. Here, also, terminate or begin, as you please, a number of other streets. New Bowery, an attempt at a short cut down to the "Swamp" and the leather-men; Oliver, East Broadway, and Catherine, running to the banks of the East River; Division, stretching away toward Corlear's Hook; Worth, newly opened through from Broadway and the west side, by way of letting in the daylight of a broad business thoroughfare upon the darkness of the intervening "Five Points," and thereby destroying all the sombre and filthy romance of that once famous locality. Mott Street, running nearly parallel with the Bowery, is but a tenement-house lane, and Doyer but a *cul de sac*, while all the others are legitimate and more or less important feeders of the Bowery—the great artery of the eastern side of Manhattan Island and the Broadway of Germantown.

Let no unlettered rustic win derision to himself by calling this great thoroughfare Bowery *Street*, for it is "The Bowery," and nothing more. In the good old days when the memory of Hendrick Hudson and due reverence for "their High Mightinesses" of Amsterdam had not yet departed from Man-a-hatta, stout-hearted and hard-headed old Governor Peter Stuyvesant had his *Bouwerie*, or country seat, out this way, and the highway thereto, out of proper respect, derived its imperishable name therefrom.

In some of the earlier maps, to be sure, prepared by presumptuous Yankees or usurping Englishmen, the Governor's drive is degraded to "the high-road to Boston," as if New Yorkers cared what settlements bordered on their highway after it had departed from the incomparable island. In the maps of 1766 a better spirit is manifested by the superscription "Bowery Lane;" and in 1806 it was noted as the "Bowery Road," connecting near what is now Union Square with the "Bloomingdale Road," and continuing its career higher up as the "road to Boston." On most of the later maps there is no attempt to add useless appendages to the simple and sufficient cognomen.

In those ancient and excellent days of pastoral simplicity, on the left, as you went north from Chatham Square, lay the estates of the De Lanceys, and above them the broad lands of Dyckman and Brevoort, while on the right the old records give us the historic names of Rutgers, Bayard, Minthorne, Van Cortlandt, and others; and beyond and exceeding these were the Bouwerie and other possessions of the Stuyvesants, who have left more traces of their ownership and occupancy than all others put together—partly because the family yet retain much of the property, but more because of the bad temper of the old Governor, and the preposterously long life of the "Stuyvesant pear-tree," at the corner of Thirteenth Street.

There can be little room for doubt in the mind of any devout antiquarian but that the spirits of the sturdy old burgomasters of Nieuw Amsterdam continue to tutelize their old haunts, and have exercised a material influence in determining the character and nationality of their successors; nor would it be altogether difficult at the present day to find, on some pleasant summer evening, sitting with his "vrauw" or gossip in front of some Bowery *halle* or *garten*, the modern representative of "Hard Koppig Peter" and his bellicose neighbors. Solid and sturdy men were they—sturdy and solid men are these good and honest citizens, and as eager for news of father-land and the stirring deeds of "unser Fritz" as were their prototypes for the slow-coming tales of the prowess of Van Tromp and De Ruyter. Not even the news by telegraph and the street railways can deny to the properly constituted mind the privilege of recognizing the flavor of the old times in what we assume to be the new.

If nowadays we leave behind us the busy and rattling slope of Chatham Square, with its "old post-office" and its vanished hopes of centralization, we find ourselves at once entering a region which has not its exact parallel on this side of the Atlantic, or the other either. There are no gradations except a few "old clo'" shops. Chatham Street is itself, and has a character of its own, which it seems to have been unable to push beyond the corner of Division. Various lines of street railway converge from different directions toward the Bowery; some, as the Third Avenue and others, entering it here, while others still, as the Fourth and Madison avenue lines, come in at points higher up. The very cars with their passengers have something special for the eyes of him who would see. If observations are begun early enough in the afternoon, it may be possible to "stratify" the successive loads to a certain

OLD CLO' SHOPS.

extent, and study the uses of the Bowery as a main artery and thoroughfare. It is so on all days, but more especially on Saturday, when the hours of labor terminate somewhat earlier than usual. Let us begin our researches between three and four o'clock, and pass from car to car, as the pickpockets, who are plenty here on Saturday night, are accustomed to do.

The Madison Avenue and Fourth Avenue lines hardly belong to the Bowery; they get their loads nearer the City Hall, and carry them through, not taking up or putting down many hereabout.

Their cargoes are largely made up of spruce Wall Street men and down-town clerks and merchants, with here and there an economical lady from "above Fourteenth," who has been shopping at low prices in the Bowery. Such, too, at this hour, is in a great measure the case with even the closely packed cars of the Third Avenue—which is but an extension of the Bowery—for a surprisingly large number of our down-town men have their homes on the east side, as far up as Yorkville and Harlem.

Thanks to the early-closing movement, the hard-worked attachés of the wholesale and shipping houses in the lower wards begin, a trifle later, to furnish their quota; but they, too, are for the most part through passengers, and we have little to do with them. Then, at various intervals, from four until six, with belated exceptions, lingering along till seven, or even after, come swarms of weary and grimy mechanics and other workmen, with bevies of

THE BOWERY SHOP-GIRL.

walls, and the newspaper and concert bulletins, are Teutonic in type and language.

It is after six o'clock now, but the cars that pass are still densely packed. They might be likened unto human sardine-boxes, but that no living being ever yet saw the little oily fishes clinging that way on the *outside* of their portable sarcophagi. The workmen with their tools, of manifold shape and use, are on the front platforms, while inside are women with their arms full of finished work, or babies, while every inch of standing room, and every last hope of holding on, are utilized to the uttermost. It is hot to-night, and how that mass of over-packed humanity manages to catch its breath is a problem for the philosophers.

There are some few manufacturing establishments in and about the Bowery; but except these there are no "wholesale" concerns, the business carried on being for the most part strictly "retail." As a consequence of this, one of the first things to strike the eye of a wanderer from Broadway is the multiplicity of small, narrow-fronted shops, none of them deep, and, as a general thing, squeezed uncomfortably into sections of the lower stories of queer, antiquated little edifices of wood or brick, whose total elevation would hardly reach the second-floor of an average Broadway palace of trade. Lager-beer, the most intensely retail of all commodities, seems alone to aspire to the dignity of full fronts and extended area. It is evident at a glance, however, that during

laughing shop-girls and factory operatives, tired enough, all of them, but buoyant for the moment, at least, with the sense of relief from labor, and the certainty that the week has reached an end, and that rest is before them. This, too, is almost a universal pay-day, and it is easy to discern in the countenances of these children of toil the traces of that peculiar feeling of satisfaction which is the sure effect of money in the pocket. No matter if the sum be small, or how soon it is to vanish before the demands of the evening's necessities, for the moment the well-earned wealth is there, and they are rich. If Astor's income is ten dollars a minute, and I have ten dollars, then for one minute I am as rich as he.

The evening ride of a very large number, especially those of German birth, terminates in the Bowery, while, even of those who are to be carried beyond, many pause briefly here, to transact their modest shopping and marketing.

But here we are at the lower terminus of the Bowery, and as yet there is nothing very brilliant about it; something rather of gloom seems to pervade the atmosphere; and so it will be later in the evening, in spite of the street lamps and the glare from the windows, as if shadows floated out from the over-crowded tenement houses that loom in the darkness on either side. Here, in the dingy beer-shops and dirtier cellars, lurk some of the worst specimens of our foreign population, and uncanny forms of varied evil stop a moment to stare at you before they dive down dimly lighted stairways or slink around the corners. "The exile," omnipresent in America, does not always present to us a more fascinating shade of character than that which he was moulded into by his transatlantic circumstances and career.

Hereabout are multitudinous drinking-shops, and "hotels" of limited proportions; but their broad sign-boards are almost invariably decorated with German or Franco-German names and emblems. The very posters on the dead

UNATTRACTIVE EXILE.

the more active hours of the day the retail commerce is expanding, for it overflows upon the sidewalks, and furniture, boots and shoes, crockery, hardware, and unlimited "notions" confine to a strait and narrow way the ample space theoretically allotted to foot-passengers. Here and there the merchant, male or female, paces seductively up and down among or in front of his heaps of wares; and among these may be discerned numerous representatives of the "absentee landlords" of Judea, to many of whom the Bowery has proved indeed a land of promise, overflowing with mercantile milk and honey. The larger part of these shops, it is worth while to notice, are thoroughly family

FRUIT STAND.

affairs, containing both home and warehouse, and frugally employing the time and energies of all the generations gathered under the humble roof. The father, spectacles on nose, may be plying his trade in the far corner; the mother, baby on arm, may be chaffering with hard-to-please customers within, while keen-eyed youngsters of either sex watch from the threshold over the safety of the wares on the sidewalk. Keen-eyed, indeed, for they seem to discern, with an unerring instinct, the pause of the probable customer from the mere stare of curiosity, and the field of *their* survey is a poor one for the "shop-lifter." Most assuredly the business interests of the house will be well served by the coming generation.

On the left, as we slowly make our way northward, is the Old Bowery Theatre, the news-boys' elysium, and undisputed realm of the "yellow covered" drama. Here "The Red Robber of the Blue Hills," "The Pirate's Daughter," and all the old-time glories of the sensation stage survive to draw crowds of enthusiastic admirers, whose taste is yet above Shakspeare, if it has not attained the level of "The Black Crook." Just at this present, however, the ample front and the tall bulletin-boards are placarded with the announcements of that unchained hero who "has sworn to liberate Ireland or die," and whose portraits here are enough to make any one believe he will do it. Where *could* George Francis Train be so utterly and appropriately at home as on the boards of the Old Bowery? His foot

is on his native heath in the home of tragic farce.

A few doors further up are the open portals of the Atlantic Garden, but it is too early yet to witness the evening resorts of the Germans in all their glory; we must wait till supper and marketing are over for that. The streets are full, but the crowds are doing no strolling—they are for the most part hurrying homeward. Almost any body looks in place on Broadway, but more than half of the frequenters of that thoroughfare would have an exceptional appearance here. There is very little flash, and an immense amount of genuine respectability. Even the work-girls have a solid and wholesome look, as if their toil sat lightly on them, while not a few of the rosy-cheeked lasses from over the Rhine would evidently sit heavily enough on toil or care. Not much beauty. No, you must wait till the next generation has somewhat Americanized their type; only let us hope that they may retain their robust constitutions.

These German friends of ours have brought with them—let America be thankful for it—a genuine Teutonic love of home and family, but in this overcrowded city life they are compelled to gratify it under difficulties. On either side of Bowery, for its entire length, the parallel streets are given up to tenement houses, while the transverse streets to the eastward, on which side the population is more German in its character, are lined with long rows of unpretending two and three story dwellings, relics of an

OLD BOWERY THEATRE.

pied with its Saturday-evening meal. In thousands on thousands of narrow and humble homes, up endless stairways, in secluded "back-buildings," over half-deserted shops, where even the wide-open windows afford but slight relief from the stifling heat and the varied fumes of German cookery, the hard-worked and hungry multitudes are busy with the food which the Giver has sent them; and it may be there is less of dissatisfaction and querulous discontent to be recorded against them on this Saturday evening than disgraces the luxurious tables of those whose pride ignores the very existence of such as they. Be it known, however, that such of these Germans as are able to boast of a house and home of their own, for all their careful frugality, are no starvelings, and know how to base their goodly proportions on solid foundations of good fare.

We have already purchased three dailies and as many weekly papers, as we came along, one of them illustrated, but all in the German tongue; nor have we found a news-boy with any thing else. How they cling to their language and traditions! but how quickly a sort of queer Americanism creeps over and modifies, externally and internally, not only themselves but these their publications! Not a single German news-boy, however, has yet made his appearance. The infant Teutons do not take kindly to Bohemianism.

It is getting along into the dusk of the evening, and on the street corners the fruit wagons and other "stands" are beginning to show their flaring torches of smoky kerosene, while their salesmen are shouting forth their descriptions of wares, and the wonderful cheapness of their prices. Here are the remnants of stocks of oranges, lemons, etc., left over from the day's business in the down-town markets, closing out at sacrifices alarming enough, in view of the fact that few of them would keep safely till Monday; and here are eloquent peripatetic soap and patent-wonder vendors, each with his little knot of curious customers holding up their motley faces in the glare of the kerosene.

earlier and less crowded era in the city's history. Many of these tenement houses offer commodious and decently arranged apartments, but the greater number aim only at packing the largest possible aggregate of humanity into the smallest possible modicum of space. "Store-room" there is none, even for those whose thrift would otherwise enable and incline them to purchase housekeeping materials by larger quantities, and the poorer sort are, therefore, one and all, driven to the petty, vexatious, and uneconomical "shopping" and marketing, which, in their turn, sustain these multitudinous small traders.

An employment of the trite similitude which likens these swarming tenements to bee-hives suggests at once the further likeness, and with it the vast improvement to be gained by adopting the "co-operative principle," which is the world-old key to success in honey-making. Co-operation will come some day, in some shape, because in the nature of things it is one of those future births which *must* come.

The broad street is now but little lumbered or obstructed by vehicles, almost the only ones in sight being the crowded street cars that follow one another in such quick succession. There seems to be even a sort of lull or temporary thinning out of the crowds upon the sidewalk, for the Bowery world is at this moment largely occu-

But before Bowery does any thing extensive in the way of promenading, or otherwise enjoying itself, it will make its purchases of supplies, and otherwise settle its commissary department, for over Sunday. Let us begin at Tompkins Market, an institution which is largely patronized by the Bowery, though not the only source of its supplies, by any means. It is a building of very respectable size, the upper part of which is occupied as the armory of the famous Seventh Regiment, and it is located just where the Bowery is split by the Cooper Institute and Bible House into Third and Fourth avenues. It will at once appear that both "education" and "piety" were required to effect any material change in the prevailing characteristics of the great thoroughfare.

The butchers and other dealers of Tompkins Market have brought down from other days an excellent reputation for their wares; and they have aristocratic customers who come from far, but not the most prosperous of them disdains to cater for the humble needs and limited purchases of their nearer neighbors. Every thing is light and pleasant and clean, nor is it difficult to assure one's self that there must be a good deal of mild pleasure in the providing as well as in the consumption of our daily food.

The family party nearest us on the right is one to gladden the heart of a dealer in solids, if not in liquids. Behold a burgomaster worthy the pencil of Rembrandt, and a pipe worthy of

A VERY LOW LIVER.

its bearer! The boy, half grown as to height—if middle-aged laterally—will one day come here with a dame as keen and sprightly, in spite of her avoirdupois, as the motherly vrauw, whose fat forefinger is deciding which of the lordly cuts on the block shall go into his capacious basket. Others may weakly have their meat sent home for them; but she prefers to *take* it, and Wilhelm is content, for his round eyes testify that he will dream of his burden all the way home as being already tabled; for "tabled" it will be on the morrow as surely as a "peace petition" to Congress.

Hold your string tight, little girl; it is a region of but doubtful comfort for dogs with that expression of countenance, and he does well to cower close to your skimp little skirts. It is your turn now.

"Vot you vants, eh?"

The reply is all but inaudible, but it is listened to kindly enough.

"Shoost a little liver? Vell—"

And though we know that the rates for liver are low, we judge that something of Dutch liberality went with the knife in separating that generous "chunk."

"Ant dere's a pone for de leetle tog."

That's thoughtful. Where's Mr. Bergh? We should have been apt to have forgotten a dog so pretercaninely meek as that.

PATENT SOAP VENDOR.

THE HERO OF THE BOWERY DRAMA.

possible, as those of Broadway, though not nearly so numerous. Time was, if we may trust tradition and the police records, when this region was the peculiar hunting-ground of ruffianism, and the "Bowery Boy" has received an established place in the local drama and flash literature; but the worst of that passed away with the Volunteer Fire Department, and now, except toward the lower end, which is liable to the incursions of the Chatham Square Comanches and other barbarous tribes that roam over the howling municipal wilderness south of Division Street, the Bowery, until after the orthodox German bedtime, is as orderly for its numbers as any other portion of the city. Not as much can be said for its auxiliaries and feeders; for there is a great deal of human nature in this part of the city, and mixed multitudes have their fermentations, especially after eleven by the clock.

Travelers in the German father-land have for many generations—Julius Cæsar being the first, though his account is dry and unsatisfactory—brought back with them marvelous stories of the German breweries and beer gardens; and though our lager factories are situated in Newark and other suburbs of New York, we are not without one or two gardens that would do credit to any university town in all Deutschland. These and their multitudinous small imitators solve for us the evening recreation problem. The stoops and window seats in the side streets are not so densely peopled now as they were an hour ago, and we may as well follow the crowds that have left them.

This is the "Atlantic Garden." A constant stream of people is pouring out, and we must take our time with the other torrent that is pouring in. Through a sort of huge vestibule, lined with busy "bars" and lunch counters, and we are in an immense hall, somewhat airily roofed with wood. Over the vestibule, at this end, is a capacious gallery, and away yonder, at the other, is a raised platform, while midway, on the left, is the "bureau of supplies,"

and over it the orchestra. In shape it is a parallelogram, with another smaller one jutting out from it there on the right. No matter for the exact dimensions; but they are huge enough, and all this space is closely occupied with narrow tables, flanked on either side by high-backed benches capable of seating four or five each, according to physical development.

There is hardly a table or a seat vacant, and yet not many are compelled to stand long, for the thirsty multitudes come and go with a sort of irregular regularity. It is of no use to ask for strong liquors, for "ve does not geep visky," and the waiter will only scowl at you. Very good light Rhine wein, very good lager, however, and in unlimited quantities—hundreds of casks on any warm and pleasant night like this. But we must not fill our eyes with mere statistics, for this is a representative German institution, thoroughly national, and it is also, in more ways than one, a political power, for the beer garden has its distinct and audible voice in the answers of the November ballot-boxes. It has done a great deal in the way of forcing our too hasty politicians to recognize important moral facts.

"Moral facts?"

Yes, think of the stifling tenement houses and the uninviting streets, and then look carefully around you.

Germans all, and our own exceptional nationality is promptly and good-humoredly noted by the crowd. On every side are family groups, father, mother, and children, all merry, all sociable, all well-behaved and quiet. There is not the remotest danger of insult or disturbance, or need of the presence of any policeman. The Germans are proud to keep up the respectability of the place to which they bring their female friends and relatives, and we hope they may fully succeed in maintaining it. Here and there are couples from whose appearance not even the crowd, the laughter, and the lager can drive away the sheepish romance; for this is a great place for courting. Let us go forward to the platform, if we can get there, and take a seat at the edge, where we can have a look down upon these thousands of Bowery Germans.

You wish they were not drinking lager-beer and Rhine wein?

Your superior wisdom and philanthropy is to be bowed to, but what if it were whisky, or even the strong beer of old England, would that better the case?

"There should be no compromise?"

Well, lager may fairly be viewed in that light, but it is a compromise up, not down; and then what about the tenement houses this hot night? It is doubtless true that Croton is a healthful, sociable, and stimulating beverage of a Saturday night, after a week's labor, and there are better places than the beer gardens, but also there are worse. And do not let us moralize over what we perhaps do not altogether understand. You think there is a crowd here

CELEBRATING THE CAPITULATION OF SEDAN AT THE "ATLANTIC GARDEN."

to-night; and so there is, and a crowd so quiet over its beer and wine as to seem almost stupid; but you should have been here on Saturday night, September 10, 1870, when the details of the great French overthrow at Sedan were being brought in here from the telegraph offices, and you would have seen what a heat of intense enthusiasm slumbers under this calm, stolid, Teutonic surface. They made a sort of human pyramid there in the centre, and a big-voiced German shouted out the news, but no one could hear him at twenty paces. There were flags and portraits on the walls; and how they did cheer, and how the band up there, doubled for the occasion, did bang and work at the national airs!

They sang the "German's Father-land" and Luther's Hymn, and patriotic choruses of a dozen lands, until they were hoarse, and hardly could get breath to drink the health of "unser Fritz" and Von Moltke, and every body else. They even tried to waltz, and nearly brought the platform down, but desisted out of regard for the ladies; and nobody was drunk, as they would have been if they had been, let us say Patagonians; and one could not help feeling that a part of "Father-land" was here, for they had brought it with them in their hearts.

One more brief walk on our way up town through the still crowded street, for it is yet early. Not much extravagance in dress about us, and an endless stream of oddities in face and form and apparel, but very little noise, or nonsense, or glaring vice—that is, much less than you would naturally expect.

It is wonderfully easy to collect a crowd, for every body is out to be amused, and an excitement is an especial windfall. A dog-fight or a broken window would gather a thousand in a minute; but there are no fights or broken windows, and we are compelled to admit that Bowery has a respectability of its own. Two or three hours later things may have changed for the worse, but then these throngs who are passing us now will be at home and abed; for their week's work is over, they have had their Saturday evening, and every soul of them is honestly and reasonably tired.

Picturesque New York
(1892)

PICTURESQUE NEW YORK.[1]

I.

IN the last century, Sir Uvedale Price, preaching the new gospel of reaction against formality in gardening art, tried through a whole volume to explain picturesqueness. By dint of piling up descriptions, in very pretty phrases, he succeeded. But he nowhere hit upon a good quotable definition, and I do not think that any writer since his day has found one. However, many writers have tried to define beauty with no better

natural man. Its charm — if I must attempt a bit of defining myself — is made up of harmonious and alien elements. It must have some elements which speak to the esthetic sense, and also some which speak to that love of sharp and telling contrasts, to that delight in the fortuitous and surprising, which is equally innate in our souls.

Thus the essence of picturesqueness is variety; and the charm of variety is more easily appreciated than the charm of simple and pure perfection. More attractive to the average tourist than even the cathedrals, which

THE BATTERY.

ENGRAVED BY C. A. POWELL.

success, and yet most people know, although they cannot tell, what beauty and picturesqueness are.

Of course, with the one as with the other, individual estimates differ. But divergence in taste is greater, I think, as regards beauty than as regards picturesqueness. Only that long practice of the eye and mind which we call cultivation can fully reveal the higher kinds of beauty; but picturesqueness instantly appeals to the

stand undisturbed, are the ruined abbeys of England — those abbeys to which the destroying hand of the Reformer and the decorating hand of Nature have given a greater amount of variety, a larger element of the unexpected, a higher degree of picturesqueness. There must be many persons who would rather look at the Parthenon in fragments than see it as it was before the Turkish bomb exploded. I am sure that a quite naïve, untrained eye would rather see its fragments picturesquely overgrown with ivy and sprinkled with wild flowers than beautifully naked under the un-

[1] With nine etchings by Charles F. W. Mielatz, reproduced by wood-engraving, and three pen-and-ink drawings by T. R. Manly, on page 174.

COENTIES SLIP.

ENGRAVED BY A. GAMM.

clouded sun. And such an eye would admire Alcibiades more in the peaked cap, scalloped jerkin, and pointed shoes of the fifteenth century, than draped in the straight folds of a chiton, or passing unclothed from the wrestling-ground to the bath.

Nevertheless, not all eyes can appreciate picturesqueness wherever it occurs. While esthetic cultivation leads one gradually to rank the beautiful above the picturesque, at the same time it opens the senses to many forms of picturesqueness hitherto unperceived. It is a truism to say that a landscape-painter finds a hundred things paintable, pictorial (and this comes very near to meaning picturesque), which the Philistine finds absolutely uninteresting or actually repulsive. Why should this be? It is because, as I have said, some elements of real beauty must enter into the picturesque, and the artist's eye is so trained to seek out beauties that it finds them, very often, where the untaught eye sees unmitigated ugliness.

Among the things it has learned to value are beauties of light and shadow. Ordinary folk seldom notice these. To them a landscape is the same landscape at dawn, at noon, and at dusk. To the artist it is three different landscapes at these different hours; and at one hour, perhaps, is totally uninteresting, at another exquisitely lovely. Again, the artist notes charms of color with especial keenness. And, again, he has trained himself to see things as a whole, when they look best that way, without being disturbed by their details, and, in a contrary case, to forget the whole in admiration for certain features or effects.

Thus the artist sees more in nature, and sees it better, than the ordinary man. And as it is with the spontaneous products of the earth, so

of New York, which seems to sparkle with Atlantic salt, also stands by itself to the eye. Even the air of Philadelphia seems duller and less vital, and the air of Boston colder and more raw.

The quality of the atmosphere influences not only the aspect of sky and cloud, the in-

ON THE EAST RIVER.

ENGRAVED BY T. H. HEARD.

it is with those huge artificial products we call cities. The painter will agree with you when you say that Paris is beautiful and New York is not, or that, compared with Nuremberg, New York is prosaic. But, whether you assert or deny the fact, he will insist that there are many picturesque things and places in New York, and that, under certain conditions, it presents many broadly picturesque effects; and he may even tell you that it is a picturesque city in a queer New World fashion of its own.

II.

ONE great influence determining the aspect of a city is the quality of its atmosphere. This quality is not alike in any two large towns unless they are geographically and industrially very near akin. Doubtless the atmosphere of Birmingham is quite like that of Manchester. But the smoky air of London is not the same as the smoky air of Chicago. The delicate, grayish atmosphere of Paris can nowhere be matched. And the clear, pure, crystalline air

tensity of sunshine, and the look of long street-perspectives, but every minor fact of color, and of light and shadow. Put our party-colored New York buildings in London, and we should hardly recognize them, even while their surfaces were still unstained by soot; the thickness of the air would effectually disguise them. Put the dull-looking buildings of London in New York, and they would be transfigured to something new by our brilliant sky, our crisp lights, and our strong, sharp shadows.

Ugly as the American tourist thinks the smokes and fogs of London, they have a great attraction for the artist, lending themselves to the most powerful effects of chiaroscuro, and removing the need to draw details with prosaic accuracy. The fact that London has so seldom been portrayed by English artists simply shows that there have not been many sensitive artists in England. On the other hand, the much thinner, purer, but still slightly misty air of Paris, has had a thousand devotees. It subdues without shrouding facts of local color, and softens details into manageable shape without conceal-

A RAINY NIGHT, MADISON SQUARE.

ing them. The transparent, almost metallic air of New York is more difficult to deal with. It keeps our city incomparably clean, and cleanliness is not so artistic as it is godly. I am glad of this chance to celebrate the cleanliness of New York, for we are always being told how dirty it is. It is certainly very dirty underfoot in many of its streets. But the eye which is looking for beauty or picturesqueness — the eye which is really seeing a city — does not care chiefly about pavements. And above our pavements we are so extremely clean that an artist of any previous generation would have declared us impossible to paint. The modern artist, however, is not afraid of subjects which lack "tone." He has washed the old traditional palette, and set it anew with

fresh, cheerful colors; he has learned how to portray the brightest sunshine; and he can rejoice in a place where he must paint sunlight falling on clear whites and yellows, bold reds, bright browns, and vivid greens, no less than one where, as in London, he can confine himself to neutral tones, or where, as in Paris, he can veil his whites, his pale light blues, his soft greens, and occasional notes of a more brilliant kind, with a delicate gauze of airiest gray. Indeed, the more modern in temper he is, the more he is attracted by the "toneless" problem; for it is the more difficult one, the newer one, and, therefore, the one with which he has the best chance to do something that was not hackneyed long before he was born.

So our young artists are beginning to draw

and to etch and to paint New York, and here and there they find corners and vistas of delightfully novel flavor. They are excited by those frank, big irregularities of form which drive an architect to righteous despair, and which tune the Philistine tongue to less discriminating contumely. They are stimulated by our high, clear notes of color. And they take particular pleasure in seeing how finely an occasional stream of black smoke from a chimney, or billowy rush of white steam from an elevated train, cuts into and contrasts with the crystal air and the azure sky, and then dies away, leaving them unpolluted. They do not say that New York is beautiful, but they do say that it is "most amusing"; and this is the current studio synonym for picturesque.

The most picturesque of all the sights that New York offers is its general aspect when seen at night from a boat on the water. The abrupt, extraordinary contrasts of its sky-line are then subdued to a gigantic mystery; its myriad, many-colored lights spangle like those of some supernally large casino; and from the east or ward, the big islands in mid-stream look much too pleasantly varied and bright to be the abodes of poverty, illness, and crime. And there is nothing in any land which, to the searcher for broadly picturesque effects, can be more satisfying than the southward outlook from the bridge itself, when the afternoon sun is shining on the gray-and-silver bay.

One of the most beautiful views I have ever beheld, one far too nobly beautiful to be called picturesque, is the view of Paris, seen from the top of the towers of Notre Dame. None of New York's towers can show us anything which equals this panorama of pale gray and verdant tones, slipping away to the encircling hills, and cut through the middle by the shining line of the many-bridged Seine. Yet we get a very entertaining panorama of ruddy architectural irregularities, spotted by the more aggressive tall white or yellow irregularities of recent years, from the tower on Madison Square, while the desirable element of beauty is supplied by the distant boundary-lines of water and further

EAST RIVER AT GRAND STREET.

ENGRAVED BY A. HAYMAN.

south we see one element of rare and solemn beauty — the sweep of the great bridge, defined by starry sparks, as though a bit of the arch of heaven had descended to brood over the surface of the waves.

In the daylight the city's sky-line, all along the western shore, is much too pronounced and yet prosaic to be picturesque. But on the more winding eastern shore there are many picturesque points of view, with the bridge always playing its part. When we get further north-

shore. And from the top of the "World" tower down-town, where the adjacent buildings are loftier and the wide waters are much nearer, the prospect is astonishingly picturesque, astonishingly beautiful even, although in a wilder, cruder way than the one from the towers of Notre Dame.

III.

WHEN we walk through our streets we want to appreciate all the picturesqueness they con-

THE TOMBS.

ENGRAVED BY J. CLEMENT.

tain, we must cultivate the artistic faculty of seeing only just as much at a time as we ought to see. We must sometimes note the general effect without considering special features, and sometimes contemplate a special feature to the exclusion of its neighbors. And we must put all rules of enjoyment learned in other towns out of mind, and all respect for ancient architectural canons.

For example, we may walk a long way upon Fifth Avenue without finding a truly picturesque feature. But do you want to see a finely picturesque general effect? Take an hour toward sunset, stand near Thirty-fifth street. Look to the southward, first down the slope of the long, gentle hill, and then down the longer level reach beyond, and let your eye rest on the far roseate mist and the crimson southern sky. This is more than a picturesque sight. It is a beautiful sight, and there are so few of its kind in New York that it ought never to be offered to unheeding eyes.

Continue your course down the avenue, and perhaps you will be lucky enough to round the shoulder of the Brunswick while the shadows lie heavy on the trees in Madison Square; but the sky is still vivid overhead, and a strong beam of sunshine still lingers far up on Diana's saffron tower. This too is a beautiful sight, if you look only at the tower. But, seen from a more southerly point, with alien buildings around it, and a mat of foliage at its feet, the tower is eminently picturesque even at noontime, still more at sunset, and especially at night when it is wreathed with flashing lamps. But it grows purely beautiful again in a clear midnight, when there is no light but the stars' light, yet this suffices to bring out its pallid grace against a sky which, being the sky of New York, is, even at midnight, definitely blue.

A little further to the southward still, and you stand at the corner of Twenty-third street. Here you will be happiest in winter, for then a carpet of snow may give a key-note of color repeated in the white fronts of certain big shops, and again in the clouds which mark the flight of an elevated train at the end of the vista. This is not a beautiful view, but it judge them collectively as an element in a tangled street-perspective. Our elevated roads have certainly "spoiled" many of our avenues; yet they bring numerous picturesque notes into the vistas of our cross-streets; and when we

ENGRAVED BY J. F. JUNGLING.

ELEVATED RAILROAD STATION.

is a picturesque one, and picturesque in a bold, careless, showy way quite characteristic of New York. For in other American towns where architecture is as audacious and irresponsible as here, there are not the same high colors distributed in the same effective large masses, and bathed in the same almost yet not quite metallic air. Chicago uses more different kinds of building-material than do we; but even if her smoke did not subdue their tints, she would still lack the coloristic decision of New York; for we make a much larger use of white and pale-yellow stone and brick and terra-cotta.

Twenty-third street is a good place in which to learn that there are two sides to many optical questions. Our women, for instance, clothe themselves much too gaudily outdoors if we judge them individually by the standard of good taste in dress; but they do not if we

travel by them, especially at night, they delight our eyes with striking effects never seen until they were built. And it is the same with our flaunting sign-boards. Architecturally criminal, and destructive of that look of dignified repose which may be even better in a city than picturesqueness, they add to the accidental contrasts which a painter of modern temper loves.

The whole of Madison Square is picturesque to a painter of this sort, by day and night, in summer and winter. Or it would be if only some one would build, on its sharp southern corner, another tall light-colored tower to challenge Diana's across the trees. Even this same shabby corner, as our etcher shows, is not unpicturesque when veiled by night and a rainstorm; and there are many other places in New York which assume a surprisingly pictorial aspect under these conditions.

But these are not our characteristic conditions. They do not show our picturesqueness as most distinctly different from that of any other town. Our atmosphere and our light are our chief glories, with the splendid sapphire sky they give, and the sumptuous masses of white clouds they allow to brood or fly above us. Therefore we have been wise of late years to run so decidedly to architectural whites and yellows. And therefore a shining spring day is the one on which we prefer that a stranger shall first behold us; or a snow-clad but equally shining winter day — the sort of day which

filthy water-streets show touches of it, and from the water itself there unrolls a perpetually new grouping of those many-sized hulls and tangled spars and cordages which, in every century and every maritime land, have been the artist's joy. Queer, sordid and ramshackle are many of these waterside pictures, but often good to paint, and still more often very good indeed to draw.

New York has nothing, alas, to recall the clean, stately quays which are a distinctive feature in most European seaports. But around the Battery there is a dignified promenade, and

TWO BRIDGES ON THE HARLEM.

ENGRAVED BY T. H HEARD.

comes rarely now, as regards the snow, but, if we may believe veracious elders, used to come by months at a time. Then, when the sleighs are out, and every note of color in house or dress is keyed up to a double intensity by the white background, and the sleigh-bells do not ring more gaily than the brisk wind greets our cheeks, it must be a dull eye which finds the upper part of New York dully prosaic.

IV.

But it is not only up-town, in the central, respectable streets, that the picturesqueness of New York resides,—not only and, in one sense, not chiefly,—although here our color-effects are most brilliant. Picturesqueness of detail is unending along the river-fronts. Even the grimy,

the prospect it offers of restless water and protean craft need not fear a rival. South street is more respectable than most of our water streets, and seems distinctly picturesque to me But perhaps this is because, as a child, I used to sit there in my grandfather's office and marvel at the giant bowsprits which almost came in at the window. Farther north lies Coentie Slip, with some rare remaining bits of old-time architecture—"stores" whose quaint, Dutch bourgeois quietude is emphatically brought ou by the self-assertiveness of the big square rec tower of the Produce Exchange behind them

Then, as we penetrate toward the center of the down-town district, there are picturesque glimpses of verdure, lighted up by flaming flower-beds, at Bowling Green and near the City Hall; and there are the varying reaches now straight, now curving, now narrow, and now broad, of the teeming business streets. Here is the famous slant of Wall street, made almost tunnel-like in recent years by the height of its reconstructed buildings. And from it we get another of New York's best sights—the sight of Trinity Church, and of that peaceful graveyard which looks doubly peaceful amid this riot and roar; church and graveyard impressing not only the eye but the mind as witnesses that beauty and righteousness have their claims no less than money-making and architectural display.

But we cannot appreciate the picturesqueness which New York wears to both mind and eye unless we go immediately from the stately commercialism of its down-town streets to the adjacent tenement-house districts. Pest-holes to the sanitarian and the moralist, loathsome abodes of filth and horror to the respectable citizen, many parts of these districts gratify the eye that seeks pictorial pleasure. I have seen Grand street at Christmas-time when the East-siders had on their best clothes, and were wandering in crowded groups along the booth-lined pavement, and the big shops seemed to have disgorged half their contents outside their windows; and Grand street was almost as picturesque as a German *Jahrmarkt.* I have seen Hester street on a Friday afternoon in May, when it swarmed so thickly with Jews of a dozen lands—hucksters and buyers inextricably mixed—that there seemed no room for another, and all were as little like Americans as though they had never left their outlandish homes, and not a sound in their loud Babel was a recognizable part of civilized speech; and Hester street was amazingly like those foreign ghettos which traveling New-Yorkers take such pains to visit. I have seen Mulberry Bend on an October day, when it was just as full of Italians, lounging, eating, working, gossiping out of doors, with faces as beautifully brown and ruddy, teeth as white, smiles as quick, speech as voluble, jewelry as profuse, and garments as party-colored, as though they were at home in their Naples; and the New York sun gilded them as radiantly as though it had been the sun of Naples. I have seen the Bowery at night, when it is not a Parisian boulevard, but is something the like of which one could not see in any Paris; and a Chinese theater filled with Chinamen as absolutely celestial as though they had come through instead of around the globe. And while of course I know that there are many other odd sights to be seen in New York, these have been enough to prove that he who says it is unpicturesque has never looked at it at all.

Even yet we are by no means at the end of it. We must not forget the City Hall Park, which, with the giant newspaper buildings around it, would be so fair a center for the down-town districts had not Uncle Sam seen fit to truncate it and shut it in with his great ugly Post-office. Still, however, it is shady, flowery, and attractive, as the newsboys always know, and as scores of tramps daily discover. And it still holds unchanged that old City Hall, which is perhaps the most beautiful of all our buildings, and which ought never to be changed, no matter how much money and how many other alterations it may cost us to preserve it. A couple of miles up-town is Washington Square, where, again, there are many tramps, but, instead of the newsboys, a sprinkling of baby-wagons and white-capped nurses; for this is the boundary-line between very poor and crowded and very well-to-do and roomy streets of homes—South Fifth Avenue, with its teeming French, German, Irish, and negro population, ending against one of its sides, and the true Fifth Avenue starting from another. This square shows at its best, perhaps, when from the window of some tall apartment-house we look over its crowding tree-tops at the flushing morning or evening sky. But even at the street-level its foliage gives a double interest to the University building, which, architecturally, is a poor imitation of English collegiate structures, but pictorially has considerable charm; to the neighboring gray church whose qualities are of a similar sort; to our new white Washington Arch; and to the beautiful Italianesque campanile of the new yellow-and-white Baptist church. This arch and this tower have made Washington Square really picturesque, especially when, standing near the one, we see the other against a sunset sky, and its great crowning cross begins to glow with electric flame—a torch of warning and of invitation alike to the outwardly righteous dweller on Fifth Avenue and the openly sinful dweller on South Fifth Avenue.

Buildings which are pictorially, if not architecturally, very valuable can here and there be found in every quarter of New York. The Tombs is one of them. Jefferson Market is another. Grace Church is a third, when we stand so far off to the southward that it seems to finish Broadway once and for all. And still another, very different in character, is the Quaker Meeting-house on Stuyvesant Square, which, with its simple shape, big trees, and little plot of well-tended grass, looks as though it had been bodily transported from some small Pennsylvanian town.

Picturesqueness is hardly thought of when we go miles to the northwestward and find the Riverside Drive. It is beauty that greets us here, in the drive itself and the quite matchless river-view. But both beauty and pictur-

IN CENTRAL PARK.

ENGRAVED BY T. H. HEARD.

esqueness can be found by him who seeks along the Harlem River, and, still further away, along the Bronx. And if he has time to search out here and there those scattered, fringing spots which go by the general name of Shanty-town, he will find perpetual picturesqueness in their tottering, pitiful, vanishing, yet often greenly environed, relics of bucolic days.

But even if all that ought to be said could be said about every other quarter of Manhattan, how should one describe the Central Park? I shall not try. You, across the bridge, who own Prospect Park, may say you have a more beautiful pleasure-ground. But scarcely any other people in all the world can say this, and no one can say that he has a more picturesque pleasure-ground. Out of the nettle difficulty Mr. Olmsted, great artist that he is, plucked the finest flower of achievement in this especial line. Out of the most unpromising park-site that men ever chose, he made the most picturesquely lovely park that men

ever created. Few New Yorkers know it; few know more of it than its eastern and western drives. But the artist is finding it out; and whether or not he cares to bring into his canvas bits and glimpses of adjacent streets, he will not soon exhaust its capabilities of pictorial service.

v.

PERHAPS the most characteristic trait of our city is the quick and thorough way in which it makes good New Yorkers of its immigrants, foreigners or Americans, and the tenacious way in which it retains its hold, no matter how far off its sons may stray. The New Yorker who lives abroad may fancy himself a cosmopolite; but he always remembers he is a New Yorker, and can never even fancy himself a simple American, much less a semi-German or a semi-Frenchman. But the Berliner who lives here is not a Berliner, a simple German, or even a mere German-American. He is a New York

German, and this, as a florist would say, is a well-marked subvariety of the German species. And I need not speak of the Irishman who so instantly identifies himself with his

feeling in the sense of historic vanity, municipal self-respect, local public spirit. But they love their city so well that they shudder at the thought of living anywhere else. They are deeply hurt if a stranger is dull enough to question where they belong. And if they were born here, they never pay any other city the compliment of discussing how it would seem to have been born there, while the proud Bostonian is apt to show his pride by declaring he is glad he is not a native of New York. We are all good New Yorkers, I say, whether we were born on Fifth Avenue, in a far European village, at North Granite Ledge in Vermont, or near the head waters of the Yellowstone. And yet there is a dif-

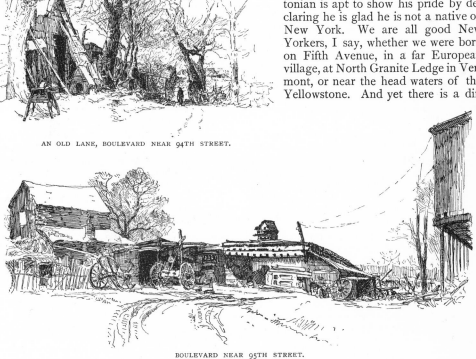

AN OLD LANE, BOULEVARD NEAR 94TH STREET.

BOULEVARD NEAR 95TH STREET.

new home that he instantly thinks it ought to belong altogether to him. Then, if one of us removes to Boston, he or she remains, to the end of the chapter, a New Yorker who happens to live in Boston; but a Bostonian who comes here is transformed at once into a New Yorker who happens to have been born in Boston. Manhattan is for all the world, and all the world has taken possession of it; but Manhattan retaliates by taking possession of every man who comes, and marking him with earmarks which no one can mistake.

This is partly, of course, because we who were born here care so little where our neighbors were born. We care only what they are, and they are all good New Yorkers. They are not proud of their city, perhaps, as Parisians are proud of Paris, Bostonians of Boston. At least it is the fashion to say that they have no filial

IN SHANTYTOWN.

ference between the merely good New Yorker and the true, or born, New Yorker.

John, who came by rail from Buffalo three years ago, feels in the same way about his present home as James, who came forty years ago, by an older path, trailing his little clouds of glory straight from heaven. But he does not see this present home in the same way. He sees our actual, visible New York. But James —

even if he came only thirty years ago — sees this and an earlier, vanished one as well; and his constant perception of the vanished one vastly increases the picturesqueness of the actual one.

As I, a born New Yorker, take my walks abroad, I note a series of composite pictures, much more striking in their contrasts, unexpected in their variety, than any which you, a recently adopted New Yorker, can behold. My mother's composites are more picturesque still, for often she sees three bits of New York mistily standing together on the same piece of ground. And if my grandfather could come back,—I am proud to say he was born in New England, but I am sure he thinks less of this fact now than of the fact that he lived nearly seventy years in New York,—if he could come back, he would behold, as a setting for his composites, the open fields and gardens upon which most of our New York has been built since he left Connecticut; and so their picturesqueness would be green and flowery.

There is a city in the West which, within twenty years, has sprung up, new in body and feathers, from the ashes of its predecessor. And there are younger cities in the farther West which have been born, and have grown to architectural maturity, within the same brief period. But the deliberate hand of man has, during this period, done for New York almost as much as flame did for Chicago. Old New York has been torn down, and another city has arisen on its site, since the days when our streets rang to the tread of the returning armies of the Union. For a parallel to what we have done with this city of ours, we must look far back to some English cathedral where the still sturdy work of earlier generations was destroyed simply that living men might rebuild it bigger and taller and more in accordance with their own ideas of architectural excellence.

To realize what this change means to the true New Yorker, we need not examine those districts within a mile of the City Hall where transformation has been most audacious. We need only look, I will say, at Union Square, and only with the eyes of one who holds the day of Lincoln's assassination among her earliest clear memories. Union Square is a lively place now and an amusing; and when we see it from upper Broadway, with, over the trees, the tall Domestic Building in the far distance, it is not an unpicturesque place. But this is how I behold it: Tiffany's store stands on a certain corner, and it is commonplace and prosaic enough. But on this same corner I see

a pale-gray stone church with a square tower, plausibly like that upon some English parish-church, and with a thick mantle of ivy exactly like an English one. There are no sky-scraping business buildings anywhere, and not a single shop, and no horse-cars except along the Fourth Avenue side. The tallest structure is the Everett House, and elsewhere there are merely rows of modest high-stoop dwellings, with vines on their balconies and trees along their sidewalks. The trees in the square itself are much more numerous than you think, and spread out much farther, so that there are only narrow streets between them and the houses; and they are mingled with dense thickets of shrubs, and inclosed by a high picket-fence. Under their shadow all of us—all the boys of the neighborhood and one or two bad little girls as well—are playing "I spy" among the bushes, digging shallow pits in the earthen paths for our game of marbles, and drawing circles out of which we hope, with our pet lignum-vitæ top, to drive the tops of the other fellows, perhaps—oh, bliss!—splitting them in two in the act. There are no tramps or other doleful figures on the benches; there is only a rare policeman, who takes a fatherly interest in our sport; and there is a stall at one corner, where a fat Irishwoman in a red shawl dispenses pinked-out gingersnaps of a heavenly essence which, cannot be purchased, even by bad little girls, within a mile of the sophisticated Union Square of to-day.

Now, this quiet old Union Square that I see, lying like a pretty cloud over the variegated and noisy one that you see, makes with it a very picturesque composite scene. And picturesque, too, is the Broadway I see, looking northward from the square; for there, mingling with the lofty stone and iron shops, are the ghosts of rows of little two-storied shops, with broad wooden platforms in front of them such as still exist in small New Jersey towns. And high up, before one of these shops (*the* toy-shop of my youth, kept by a Frenchman named Phillipoteaux, for whose sake I have always liked to praise the painter of panoramas), stands the ghost of a life-size figure of Santa Claus, picturesquely promising next Christmas while the trees are still in their budding season.

Even you, young artist, born on the Pacific slope and now fresh from Parisian boulevards, can see that your New York is picturesque. But I wish that I could show you mine—mine, which is not mine of my infancy or mine of to-day, but the two together, delightfully, inextricably, mysteriously, perpetually mixed.

M. G. Van Rensselaer.

Coney Island
(1896)

SCRIBNER'S MAGAZINE

VOL. XX   JULY 1896   No. 1

CONEY ISLAND

By Julian Ralph

ILLUSTRATED BY HENRY McCARTER

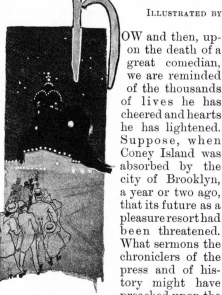

NOW and then, upon the death of a great comedian, we are reminded of the thousands of lives he has cheered and hearts he has lightened. Suppose, when Coney Island was absorbed by the city of Brooklyn, a year or two ago, that its future as a pleasure resort had been threatened. What sermons the chroniclers of the press and of history might have preached upon the good it had wrought—not to mere thousands, and not in the simple, unplanned ways in which other resorts have scattered their benefits, but in unique ways, by means better and more varied than the masses knew of or enjoyed anywhere else on the continent. For Coney Island was not only the pioneer with modern improvements for giving the crowds a good time ; it still remains *sui generis*, enthroned, the king of all the popular resorts of America.

The drama which it daily provides for the delight of its patrons, is declared to freshen the souls of so many millions annually that in order to comprehend the bulk of the multitude we must fancy gathered together all the inhabitants of London, all the people of New York, every soul in Chicago, and every man, woman, and child in Brooklyn. And even then, we would be assuming that the largest boasts of those cities were truths, for one year's crowd on Coney Island was composed of eight million souls !

No painter has perpetuated its bewildering scenes, and no poet has sought to immortalize its wonders. It is doubtful whether the foreign world — the " outer barbarians " as the Chinese call the others — has heard of the place ; certainly the Atlantic Garden, in the Bowery, is tenfold farther and better known. And yet eight millions of fares were paid by travellers to it in a year— by travellers who journeyed only the time that a cigar lasts. It no more wants or depends upon better fame than grass needs painting, or fresh air needs a rhymer. It is New York's resort almost exclusively ; our homœopathic sanitarium, our sun - bath and ice-box combined, our extra lung, our private, gigantic fan. All our cities, except Chicago, have such places, and we are content that they should. Boston may keep little Nantasket ; Philadelphia may continue to reach across New Jersey for her beaches ; New Orleans is welcome to all of Lake Pontchartrain, and San Francisco may monopolize her opera-glass spectacle of the Seal Rocks, if she pleases. We do not want their resorts or need their patronage. In this we are as narrow and provincial as every stranger delights in saying that New Yorkers are in all things. Certainly, New York and Coney Island are sufficient to each other —whether they are sufficient in themselves or not.

I had pointed out to me, the other day, a man who discovered Coney Island; some two decades later than most of us, to be sure, but none too late for his own satisfaction. Mr. Shelley of the Oriental Hotel was exhibiting him.

"I ah—saw the place from—ah the deck of the ah—steamer coming ovah," said he, "and I ah—thought I'd see what sort of a place it was, don't you know? And, upon me word, I find it most astonishing at the ah—cheaper end, you know, and doosid comfortable heah."

His formal and deliberate manner of putting his *pince-nez* glasses up to his eyes, after much bother with the chain to which they were attached, suggested a perpetual alertness for discovery. He never merely looked at anything. One cannot call the work of an astronomer "looking at things," and this Englishman brought the same effort and aid of glasses to his simplest visual action. When a newsboy rushed at him

with a paper, meaning to sell it like lightning, before it became old and worthless by the arrival of a later edition, the Englishman went through the same serious preliminaries with his glasses and ended by making the little arab feel that he, also, had been discovered; that no one had ever looked at him before. Indeed, the startled lad shot his own eyes all over himself as if he suspected that he had been seen all over and might find himself naked. Thus the Englishman looked at Coney Island, after it had grown ancient under Indian, Dutch, English, and American rule, and discovered it and brought to it a case of Apollinaris and a bathtub, so as to be sure to have those luxuries while he was there. And yet, in a sense, he was more right in his position than I am in making sport of it, for he was one of comparatively very few strangers who have been to Coney Island and who, if they were able to analyze their surroundings, would see that they were marked objects among such crowds of New Yorkers as to suggest the idea that they had unconsciously invaded a private park — or perhaps a better simile is a backyard — to the myriad houses of the city.

The Light-house and Fog-bell at Norton's Point.

I have spoken of the age and changes of nationality of the little island. It is so new in its present character and so youthfully vigorous in its spirit that we are apt to forget how aged it is. The very earliest history of the place— after the Canarsie Indians ceased to own it—is slender, but it proves that it was known to the only hallowed New Yorker — Petrus Stuyvesant, the Dutch Governor who was our sternest, bravest, and yet most picturesque magistrate. He is immortalized and enthroned as our patron saint under the title of Father Knickerbocker; at least, our minds conceive no other single personality than Stuyvesant's when, in penitence or triumph, we invoke the guardian-spirit of the city. Stuyvesant is declared to have held fast to the right to the fisheries off Coney Island on behalf of the government. As we think of what the island must have been in the middle of the seventeenth century it is likely to occur to us that the governor cannot have conceived the land to be of any value as compared with that which the waters around it possessed. But that is not so.

Land's End.

Mere sand strip as it was, it was even then a bone of contention between ambitious settlers who carried their quarrel into the courts. The records of that litigation were principally written by a shrewd lawyer of that era named La Chair, who was retained by the schout and magistrates of Gravesend, now part of Brooklyn. His memorial is not only historically valuable and interesting, but it is written in a style so simple, vigorous, and clear, as to shine among the records of that time. It may be that some New York lawyers of to-day might profit by a study of it. He says that "in the year 1643, the first founders and inhabitants of the said town (Gravesend) came there with the Lady Deborah Moody, deceased, and their cattle, and with the express consent, order, and approbation of the Right Honorable Director General, William Kieft, of laudable memory, and Council, of New Netherland, from the very first time down, enjoyed and made use of Coney Island as a pasturage for cattle, together with the valleys adjacent to mow their hay." He says that two years later, in 1645, the Governor and

Council granted letters patent to the Lady Deborah and her associates wherein they granted Coney Island and dependencies as a pasture and the lands on which Gravesend lay for planting. And the Lady and her associates had possessed the same, freely and peaceably, "without molestation or gainsay of anyone — except some trouble with the Indians." (How perfectly modern and commonplace that contemptuous reference to the real owners—the red ones—sounds.) "And," goes on the lawyer La Chair, "though no one in the world hath any right or title to the above mentioned Coney Island, . . nevertheless so it is, that one Mr. Evert Pieters and Harman Vedder have, in the name of one De Wolfe, merchant at Amsterdam, caused to be erected, this summer, a salt kettle on said island." For peace' sake, though unwillingly, the petitioners permitted this, but when the trespassing salt boilers gave written notice afterward that the cattle of Gravesend must be driven off Coney Island at twenty-four hours' notice, then they thought it time to protest. The lawsuit that followed was decided by the Right Honorable Peter Stuyvesant and Council in favor of the settlers of

Gravesend, of which town Coney Island is a part to-day. This was in 1662. It is surprising to find that the little sand-bank was known then by the same name, spelled in the same way, as to-day. There have been many ingenious definitions of the word "Coney;" but the simplest one—that it means "rabbit" and was conferred upon the island because rabbits abounded there —is the definition that seems always to have been popularly accepted.

Coney Island lies in the mouth of

New York Harbor. It is part of the broken reef that faces the ocean side of Long Island, and it is just around the corner from the Narrows. It is like a tooth in one jaw of the harbor mouth and opposes Sandy Hook, the single tooth in the other jaw. Those whose memory looks longest back upon it can remember it as a wind and water tossed collection of low sand-dunes bearing coarse grass, a few gnarled and twisted trees, and some little road taverns or excursion inns that, before, had been farm-houses. It is cut off from the bulk of Long Island by Gravesend Bay and Sheepshead Bay and little Coney Island Creek, between the two. Sheepshead Bay is behind the eastern end of the island, back of Manhattan Beach, and there on the Long Island shore is the ancient village of Sheepshead Bay, which was a resort longer ago than our grandfather's days. Early settlers and small communities seem never to get the best of what is around them. We see that everywhere. They begin the establishment of cities by building on the low land and, in the natural course, it is their grand-kin that mount the hills and bluffs of the background and enjoy the breezes and the good drainage and the views. And so it is with the first resorts of a new cityful. It sometimes happens, if a city grows too madly fast as Chicago has, that a place assumes great size before it has any resorts at all. In the case of New York, the early Dutch set-

HENRY McCARTER

Brighton Beach.

tlers built country houses back upon Manhattan Island, and their successors followed them—to parks and picnic grounds upon the sites of the old farms and gardens. Only a very few, who were the richest and most leisurely burghers, sought the sea. They went by much tacking periaugers, to the Navesink Highlands, still undeveloped and still the very choicest site for a summer settlement within the same distance from the city.

But, by the time of our grandfathers and great-grandfathers, we had begun to reach the sea, first at Sheepshead Bay and Long Branch and Deal, in New Jersey, and then in genuine crowds at Rockaway, Far Rockaway, Islip, and other places. Sheepshead Bay commended itself to our ancestors as the seat of a spring of such magical waters as those kings and princesses who were always wanting offspring, in the old fairy tales, would have been glad to have known about. Coney Island was ten strokes of an oar farther on, but the crowds stopped at Sheepshead Bay. They went there to fish and shoot ducks and snipe, and to put up their horses and eat fish dinners, at the turning point of a lovely drive from New York and, more generally, from Brooklyn. Judge Tappan's road-house at Sheepshead Bay is still there and just as it used to be. It is so Hollandishly immaculate, so picturesquely whitewashed and green-painted among the bowery trees around it, and so rich in the few and simple resources of its bar and kitchen that, when I think of

it, I do not see how I am going to be able, presently, to tell the reader how mean and clumsy and musty and primitive used to be the water-side resorts we patronized before Coney Island was transformed into the exemplar of what all such places should be. I must tell it, and therefore the reader will please do with the exceptional Judge Tappan's as the millions of New Yorkers behave toward the magical spring in the same village — rush by in a swift train and forget it. The fact is, though, that at times modern humanity in the cars does seem to remember that spring and then its locomotive engineers send it a high-pressure, ninety-ton shriek—one that amuses the villagers who know that there is no

cause for a panic since they bricked up the spring so many years ago that, now, they have forgotten where it was.

In the days of the glory of Sheepshead Bay there used to be other drives and road-houses and resorts on the way to Coney Island, and at last there sprang up one or two little taverns, transformed out of farm-houses, on the island itself. That of William Wheatley, a theatre manager, whose place was the resort of the leading actors and wits of the period of the Rebellion, was the best known. Early in the '70s Mike Norton took Wheatley's house and enlarged it, and several lesser places sprang up around it on the western end of the sand strip. Then it was that Coney Island began to be widely known, but in a way that brought it no credit. The eastern end, where immense capital has reared the great palaces and modern improvements of to-day, was still a waste of sand-dunes when the excursion boats began to take crowds to the western end, to drink and dine in the flimsy frame taverns, and to use the two-score ramshackle bath-houses that offered their wretched shelter to those who took surf baths. The crowds got drunk before the steamboats started back for town, and the steamers became travelling battle-fields upon which few orderly folk ventured more than once. But more and more carriage passengers went there for clam-bake dinners and fresh air, and among them went Mr. Austin Corbin with his invalid son, upon a visit that began in a search for health and led to the making of Manhattan Beach and Brighton Beach and the marvellous Coney Island of to-day. A little railway called "Gunther's" had been extended to the island from its earlier terminus at Bath, and still in the

early seventies Culver's railway and Cable's Hotel led in the transformation of the island. Thomas E. Cable's little hotel, with its spreading verandas, its glory of fresh paint, its showy white napery and attentive waiters, and its wide open restaurant, confronting the smooth white beach, seemed to us New Yorker's to typify the apex of excellence in a seaside hostelry, and with its foundation the rise of Coney Island really had its beginning. But the resort still kept its raw side. It remained a place to drive to, a place for the pursuit of fiddler crabs by bare-legged boys, and a place for the enjoyment of clams and fish above all other forms of food. Disorderly crowds still gathered there. At the now magnificent eastern end men still hunted yellow-legged sand pipers, and at the western end, among the barracks on the sand, the burglars and ruffians, who were then permitted to maintain an aristocracy among the criminals of the city, hid and spent their plunder in debauchery.

It was in July, 1877, that the great modern hotel at Manhattan Beach was opened ; but as we look back upon the evolution of the eastern end of the island we know that it was not until two great corporations had spent more than a million and a half of dollars and erected the three great hotels that are now there that Coney Island became what I have called it, the pioneer in the provision of seaside pleasure with modern improvements. The development is part of the progress of our centennial era. The Manhattan Beach Hotel was opened in 1877, and Brighton Beach is one year younger. The palatial Oriental Hotel at Manhattan Beach was put up at about the same time, being built and completely furnished in ninety days.

When all three were opened and, in time, the original sand was covered with a garden of grass and broad walks of cool gray coquina, when the bath-houses gave place to "bathing establishments," and the best band-masters of the time led grand orchestras by the surf side, we began to enjoy that to which we now refer when we speak of Coney Island.

The Oriental Hotel from across the Meadows.

That was the first made-to-order resort in America ; the first resort which, instead of developing its own capital, had capital brought to it and lavished upon it in the manner in which so many great nineteenth century enterprises, banking upon certain prosperity, have leaped from nothing into full-fledged perfection. Up to that time our summer resorts had begun with single roadside taverns and grown into villages, the first tavern growing, usually, a few feet wider, a few feet longer, and a few feet higher each year. A white frame house, a wide veranda, a sanded barroom, and a long line of carriage-sheds were the outward, visible signs of such a place and the internal comforts were such as we might get from a negress in the kitchen, some country maidens in starched calico to serve the fried chicken, the cheese, and the pie, and in our bedrooms from musty ingrain carpet, startling wall paper, and painted pine furniture. This pattern of place has not yet been relegated to history. It dies hard. Long Island and New Jersey still know it in abundance.

If such a place was by the seaside, there was but one form of bathing apparatus at the beach—a row of tumbledown sentry boxes standing in drunken lines upon the sand, each as hot as a Mozambique shanty, each one fretted with rusty nails for clothes hooks, and each appointed with a pail which you

were lucky not to have to fill with fresh water for yourself. If a bather had not left his valuables at home he hid them in the toes of his shoes or in the dark crannies of the bath-house. All along the ocean side of Long Island to-day these collections of ramshackle boxes serve a few visitors, and deter the majority from bathing. They are in almost every resort the property of a bare-legged rustic, tanned the color of plug tobacco, who has preëmpted the beach, who charges more for his mediæval accommodations than the best would be worth, and who even sets up disreputable arbors of tree poles and dried evergreen, precisely like the burial places of the wildest savages, and collects toll for the shade they cast upon the sand.

Until Manhattan and Brighton Beaches were established we knew no better than this. We knew no assurance of protection from thieves or rowdies, no way to dodge the drunkenness of excursionists, no hope of faring better than upon chowder, fish, or ham and eggs, and no possibility of bathing without coming away dirtier than we went in. Luxury and elegance—except in the forms of fresh air and foliage—we expected to leave behind us, intelligent service we supposed to be confined to the capitals of commerce, and we did not miss good plumbing and policemen because we had never given them a thought in connection with natural attractions.

We can scarcely carry to the distance of to-day the remembrance of the full shock of delight with which we enjoyed the new sensations at the new beaches. How wonderful the railways seemed, with their long and almost perilously swift trains of coaches that were built like our summer horse-cars, open on both sides to the view of the ancient Dutch villages and farms whose names we had been reading, ever since we

Old Raven Hall Road-house.

were born, upon the quaint-covered wagons that bring our fresh vegetables to market in the height of each summer. We had seen the Dutch farm wives and daughters jolting into town on their canvas-covered loads, and now we saw them again picking the pease and the lettuce and cabbage in the fields, in a way that seemed, as it was, more European than home-like. And, presently, we rattled across Coney Island Creek

and its adjacent marsh, and found ourselves at a brand new sort of seaside, platted with fine grass, set with aloes and palms in huge vases, crowded by orderly battalions of smartly dressed city folk and with only the blue, sounding sea unchanged and natural. All this we saw from the noble porch of an immense latter-day hotel, substantial, costly, and excellent in every way. One of these houses offered dining accommodations for thirty-eight hundreds of persons at once, and the other was almost as generously ordered. All about us were people refreshing themselves in a vast room of which the veranda formed a part, for it, too, bore tables equipped with milk-white napery, and sparkling glass and heavy plate. We ventured to test the restaurant, and instead of receiving a visit from a bullet-headed country girl in calico were waited upon by a professional waiter from France or Germany, bearing a bill of fare that we presently characterized as "like Delmonico's." And so, from a wide variety of necessaries and delicacies, we chose a delicious dinner and ate it under the spur of good service, fresh, cool air, a merry crowd of neighbors, and that best of all sauces, agreeable novelty.

There, many of us first saw an abundance of electric lights, newly popularized at the Philadelphia Centennial and, as if to impress upon us the part which that world's fair played in enlarging all our comforts and elegances, there rose above our heads on Coney Island the tall skeleton tower which had been the highest object at the Centennial, and we were pulled to and fro, on the Marine Railway, by locomotives from the same exposition. Sooner or later we joined the crowd in bathing. Thousands used to stand in line awaiting their turns to enter the great bathhouses, so that it was evident to the dullest mind that for some reason surf-bathing, just then and there, was more popular than it had ever been anywhere else in America. We know now that, under the most favorable circumstances, sea-bathing is a great deal of a trial and a bore ; that it is those who live farthest from old ocean who bathe most in her billows, and that, wherever there is a fixed sea-side community of cottages, there is very little surf-bathing indeed. Even at Coney Island, the surf-bathers form a very small minor-

ity of the visitors in these years, but at that time this was not the case. Long cues of hundreds of men and women and children tailed along the coquina walks that led to the impressive buildings enclosing the dressing-rooms. The reason for this new enthusiastic interest in the old sport was that here, also, there had been a great bound from savagery to modern convenience. The dressing-rooms were larger than those to which we had been used, and in each was a looking-glass, a seat, clothes hooks, a grated floor, and a faucet for the release of running water. But the approach to these compartments was what most pleased us. The roomy outer building was at least as fine an example of carpentry as we had seen in any country hotel, and the conveniences for the bath with which we were served went delightfully beyond our experience and expectations. Take the item of dry towels alone : We had been accustomed to ones that were damp if not actually wet, but now we got them dry and sometimes hot and sweet from the steam laundry. So it was with the bathing suits. We had fancied it essential that they should be clammy and certain to strike a chill to our spinal columns when we put them on, but these also were dry and clean and sweet ; all woollen suits, in those days, if I remember right.

"A safe is provided, free, for your valuables," several signs announced ; and what a safe it was ! Even now, many of us have seen no larger treasure-box, than the enormous casket of steel that we saw through a barrier of coarse net-work, attended by nimble clerks. These used to climb upon the face of the great steel closet to reach the upper tiers of the hundreds, perhaps thousands of little drawers, into which were stored our watches and larger or smaller rolls of

Lower End of Culver's Park, West Brighton.

surf, and sought our sentry-box, lo! the door pushed open with a slight pressure as readily as if we had not locked it. But, now, at Brighton and Manhattan Beaches we locked up our clothing soundly and tight, and went jingling to the surf with two rubber collars and several kinds and pieces of metal hung proudly round our necks, as full of conscious elegance and up-to-date-ativeness as ever a

A West Brighton Concert Hall.

greenbacks, our studs and pins and bracelets and brooches— all of which we first sealed up in baglike envelopes and ornamented with our signatures. We had come to the safe with a bath-house key, which had a numbered brass disk attached to it, the key, in turn, being fastened to a long loop of rubber to be worn around our necks, in the water. And now the custodians of our valuables presented to us another key and disc and rubber necklace—astonishing novelties to us who had been accustomed to stowing our watches in our shoes, and then leaving our door-key with the beach-comber who seemed to own the ocean, until, when we emerged from the

Pawnee belle set out for a sun-dance. We were treated as persons of some distinction as well, for the bathing beach was walled in against the idle, the curious, and the unclean, and that was a grateful novelty after having bathed in the presence of all New Jersey or all Long Island wherever else we had been.

Those were delightful first sensations, and the fact that we know better ones now does not rob us of the pleasure of these recollections. We have since seen beautiful dressing-rooms, with a chair in each, and a brush and comb, and varnished walls and a rug, and a separate

Morning on the Bowery.

tub and shower, beside a cool and airy assembly room set with madras chairs, with places in them for glasses full of cool drink—but that is so exceptional that we would still be satisfied if all the surf resorts were as well appointed as the eastern end of Coney Island was fifteen or seventeen years ago, and is to-day.

I went there at midsummer when this article was written, and found that the novelty had worn away like thin plating off a restaurant spoon. Only 3,030 persons had bathed in one of the best establishments on the Fourth of July, and on the preceding Sunday only 2,050, so that not above ten or twelve thousand can have sought the surf on the entire island on the "biggest" day. What is that for a crowd where eight millions of persons gather during the ninety days of the season? The once triumphant rattle of the bath-house jewelry upon my neck sounded vulgar instead of *fin de siècle*, and whether it was that the water was chilly, or whether it was due to the unpleasantness of soaking one's apparel with brine and sand, it was a fact that few of us went into the billows for more than a ceremonious plunge. Instead, we lolled in the sun upon the hot, dry sand, and chatted with the girls and women and embanked their limbs in grave-like hillocks the while we anticipated in our chatter the delights of the music and the dinner that were to come. I noticed, too, a very strange fact strongly indicative of a popular sharing of my own pessimistic opinion of surf-bathing, and that was the general habit of smoking in bath uniform on the part of the men. Nearly all of them had brought cigars or cigarettes out of their dressing-rooms to enjoy as they lounged in the sand. One very tall youth, I recall, carried a

I came away with the new idea that what brought my neighbors into that bath enclosure was the barbarous but natural desire to free themselves from the fetters of prim modern dress and revel, loose and free, in the sunshine and the sand.

After the bath there was a choice of concerts. One was by Seidl's orchestra straining to be popular, and the other was by Sousa's band straining to be classical. Both sets of musicians were prettily housed in airy pavilions of great capacity and it was noticeable, that half as many persons as paid to sit in the pavilions lingered close by on the verandas and the stone walks drinking in the beautiful strains that escaped to the outer air. It is said, that persons whose blood is strongly European abound in the audiences at these concerts. To them these concerts seem in thorough keeping with the rest of the attractions of a great resort, for we borrowed this feature from Europe, but to us Americans of

A Sidewalk Café.

cigarette between his lips and two over each ear, where, I suspect, he was more used to putting pens and pencils. It needs not to be said that men who enjoy bathing do not court the sea-nymphs with fire in their mouths, and

the third to the tenth degree Coney Island introduced them as a novelty. We had heard Theodore Thomas in an uptown summer garden, but at the seaside resorts our only music came from the rheumatic instruments which a danc-

The Old Clam-boat.

amusement annex of such a fair, at least and on a scale so large as to make the hodge-podge seem a novelty. The principal avenue through it is well called "the Bowery," a title which is at once amply and minutely descriptive to the born New Yorker, who has all his life called that which is cheap and yet pretentious, that which is loud, that which is beer-sodden, and that which is "faked" or made-up or make-believe—all by the comprehensive term "Bowery." There is not a thing (except the fireworks), on the higher-priced end of the island that cannot be obtained or witnessed at the cheaper end, but there are scores of attractions at the hurly-burly end that the more exclusive region does not hold forth. The peculiar theory of some religionists that we shall have differing heavens, to conform to our mundane ideas and tastes, gets some confirmation from the fact that ten go to the Bowery where one frequents the better beaches. Most excursionists who set apart a day for Coney Island put aside a generous sum to spend there—to "throw away" as we say. The resolution is eloquently expressed in the manners of the men, whether they are rotund old fellows in fine cloth ordering "the best" for their exquisite wives at Manhattan Beach, or wide-eyed mechanics clutching the arms of pallid sweethearts and pushing them through the perspiring mob around the elephant. And some, near the elephant, have set aside money sufficient for a day within sound of Seidl's orchestra, yet they prefer the oom-pah bands of rusted brass. They would rather have a luncheon of Frankfurters and lager and a dinner of

ing master marshalled for his nightly dances in the hotel parlors. On Coney Island, at the outset, the great bands played to the crowds free for all who cared to listen, but the season is so short and the cost of the music (something like $40,000 in a season) is so great that it became necessary to house the players and charge an admission fee, against which, I think, there never has been any protest. At night, the concerts compete with a grand fireworks exhibition — a London diversion, the like of which we never saw anywhere else than here, and still believe to be as splendid and dazzling a sight as the hand of man can create.

These were the novelties and triumphs for whose delights we owe gratitude to Coney Island. It will be noticed that they confine their territory to the newer or east end of the island, for it is a fact that the house in the shape of an elephant and, possibly, the iron steamboats and the first iron pier into the ocean were the only innovations that the older or western half of the resort brought forward ; and yet, it seems to me, that if we were to die to-day and take our memories to another planet, much of that recollection would carry us back to that transplanted Old World fair. For a transplanted Old World fair is what the older portion of Coney Island suggests—the

Beach Hotel at West Brighton.

roasted clams and melted butter, than the finicky food and precise surroundings away from the hurly-burly where nostalgia eats up appetite. And the queer thing is, that each sort of persons makes his cast-iron, habitual choice and calls it "seeing life;" whereas if the masses sent a deputation to Brighton and Manhattan and a few of the few spent an occasional day in the Bowery, they would really see life and learn a great deal, and alas! be more or less unhappy.

Even now, that the political baron who sowed vice in western Coney Island, and fattened on it, has gone to jail and his bailiwick has become a part of Brooklyn, that end is the most bewildering, noisy approach to bedlam that we know of in America. The singers in the concert halls and the variety shows have lengthened their dresses and abbreviated their misbehavior, and the worst criminals who swindled the people or pandered to their weaknesses have been banished, so that the place does not reek with evil as it did; but it is still the seat of a delirium of raw pleasure. Physically, the place is a sort of Chinatown of little frame buildings set about, helter-skelter, like a cityful of houses in a panic. Aurally it is a riot of the noises of roller-coasters, from two to six stories high; of test-your-lungs and test-your-strength and test-your-grip machines; of shooting-galleries and "see-if-you-can-hit-the-nigger's head" contrivances; of those

McPherson's Hotel—from the Sand-dunes.

strange merry-go-rounds which seem to be manufactured exclusively in New Utrecht, L. I., of animals designed by a baker of ginger-bread; of razzle-dazzle rings that go all ways at once, like a ship's compass; of a band of howling Sioux; of the yells of the shouters in front of the freak museums; of rocking-boat devices that would make Neptune seasick if he rode in them; of "ring-the-cane and get-a-cigar" layouts; of hand-organs, of yelling sea-bathers; in short, of pandemonium.

I like to go there, once in a while, to see the iron steamboats and the steam and trolley cars fling their loads of the poorer city folk upon the sands, complacent and at ease, beside the nervous, uncertain country people who come, a thousand at a time, upon the irregular excursion boats. What Barney and Julia, from the tenements, go to "the Bowery" for I do not know, unless it is to enjoy the triumph of their own sagacity in not ever, by any chance, being victimized by the museum men and the fakirs who prey upon the unsophisticated. Barney looks on, from the outside, at all the clumsy traps for the unwary, and loves to guy the touts, who stand without, coaxing the people in.

"Say, cully," he says when he catches the eye of a roper-in, "is de fish bitin' good to-day?"

And Julia says of him proudly, to the other girls in the tenement at home: "Dere was a man tried to git Barney to take a chance on a watch, but Barney don't buy gold bricks an' he never blows out de gas."

What Barney and Julia like at Coney Island is the bathing in the afternoon when Barney "berhaves terrible—" by endeavoring to duck his sweetheart; wherefore he chases her, screaming, all through the crowds—and at night the dancing. There are what are called dancing pavilions at the western end, where the music scarcely pauses between seven o'clock and that hour which is invariably called "de las' boat." It is when we see Barney and Julia dancing that we realize the feelings of the Oriental potentate who said, "I never dance myself; I hire it done." The city boys and girls described their own fashion of dancing when they gave the name of "pivoters" to the thousands of girls who are seized with such a madness for dancing that they spend every night in the dance halls and the picnic parks. Julia stands erect, with her body as rigid as a poker and with her left arm straight out from her shoulder like an upraised pump-handle. Barney slouches up to her, and bends his back so that he can put his chin on one of Julia's shoulders and she can do the same by him. Then, instead of dancing with a free, lissome, graceful, gliding step, they pivot or spin, around and around, within the smallest circle that can be drawn around them. The expression of Barney's face is usually that of grim, determined effort, like that of one who is taking part in a trial of endurance; but Julia's eyes are uplifted, like those of a maid at her devotions, and a settled, almost sanctified calm is upon her features. On the last boat a great crowd of these honest young people is apt to gather on the upper deck, aft, where the young men practise that repartee which is quite a sharp and vastly more kindly than the wit of the London street folk. And before the Narrows are reached Julia has taken off her hat and gone to sleep on Barney's breast, held there by the arm that he puts ostentatiously and defiantly about her waist ; and he smokes in a silence that is only broken by the tuned breathing of one of the younger Barneys, who has brought his mouth-organ along and has glued it to his lips.

This glance at all parts of Coney Island shows us that while it has some of the main features of the great watering-places of Europe, it is yet different from all of them in being purely and wholly an excursion resort. It is true that the Oriental Hotel at Manhattan Beach is

tenants see the tip-ends of the fireworks and they hear the tooting of the railway locomotives, but these things are, to them, like seeing Saturn and hearing the distant guns of a man-of-war in New York Harbor. What is peculiar to Coney Island is that no one lives there. It embraces practically no cottage settlement — none at all, except a few homes of those who are in business there—and from one point of view, all its tenements, halls, hotels, and houses are temporary, like its delights, all being wooden, however costly some may be. Other resorts offer change and rest, but Coney Island offers only change. A reporter having to announce the formal opening of one of the beaches there, put the case of Coney Island in a verbal nutshell in this brief sentence, one day: "Manhattan Beach has opened, and now New Yorkers have a place by the seaside where they may go for

Manhattan Beach Hotel.

the summer home of hundreds, but the secret of that hotel's success and the charm of it is, that it is not at Coney Island at all, nor even at Manhattan Beach, as its proprietors say, but is, of and by itself, cut off from all the neighborhood, with its own beach and, I was going to say, its own ocean. Its

dinner, spend an evening enjoyably, and get home at a reasonable time."

That is true, and since that is all Coney Island is for, we understand why it is peculiar among the really crowded resorts in the absence of summer costumes among its votaries. What we call the typical "summer girl" is seen there,

Old Tappan Road-house.

looks like a tatter torn out of Broadway and when, after the races, it bursts upon the verandas of Brighton and Manhattan Beaches, it fits into the multitutle there precisely as if it was of the same web and woof.

Another bit of evidence that Coney Island's crowds are made up most largely of those who are town-stayed all summer, lies in the color of the crowd's hands and faces. From the waxen whiteness of the women and

now and then, in sailor hat and thin white gown, but her champion in white flannels, yachting cap, and tennis shoes never, perhaps, set foot on this glistening strand. In his place we see the costumes of Broadway and the Stock Exchange, of Tompkins Square and Central Park. On summer Saturdays the clerks and merchants and the professional men who are kept in town, take an early luncheon in the city and catch the Bay Ridge boat for the races at Sheepshead Bay, across the creek from the island. Such a crowd, dressed as this is, would look out of place in Saratoga or Narragansett Pier, but on the boat it

girls whose waking hours are spent amid gaslight, to the pinker hue of the men who have leisure to walk to and from luncheon—if not to business—every morning the color of all is the same and only the shades of it differ. How much more admirable, how almost blessed, Coney Island seems in the light of these facts! How grand an acquisition it is for us to possess a beach to which we can go in an hour at the cost of a quarter of a dollar, to get a new environment and have old ocean's pure tonic breath blow the cobwebs out of our brain—and then, as the chronicler saith, "get home at a reasonable time."

Riding in New York
(1887)

HARPER'S
NEW MONTHLY MAGAZINE.

Vol. LXXV.　　　　　SEPTEMBER, 1887.　　　No. CCCCXLVIII.

RIDING IN NEW YORK.

BY A RIDER.

THE Central Park had been open for pleasure some years before it became evident that its bridle-path had not been made in vain. Even yet, astonishing as the progress of the last decade has been in the diffusion of knowledge about the uses of the bridle-path, there is no reason to believe that riding in New York has by any means reached its limit. Each new riding-school finds itself full of business without perceptibly diminishing the business of its older rivals. Fifteen years ago there was but one riding-school. Now there are four considerable, not to mention the Riding Club, which includes among its functions those of an academy.

There were horsemen in New York before the riding "fad" set in. One well known and now venerable physician has ridden in the suburban roads for fifty years, and may even yet be seen of sunny afternoons in the Park, or of stormy afternoons in the ring, taking his constitutional on a cob that is quite capable of throwing younger horsemen. He informs the present writer that when he began to ride in New York, during the remote thirties and under the consulate of Van Buren, at least one of his fellow-physicians made his professional rounds on horseback. It was a good many years after this, early in the fifties, in fact, that a riding-school was established "opposite the Hay Scales." How many of the readers of this paper know as much about the site of the Hay Scales as about the site of the choragic monument of Lysicrates? Yet the Hay Scales stood where the Cooper Institute now stands, and opposite, at the foot of Fourth Avenue, was "Disbrow's," which migrated twice afterward, and in its latest habitat subsisted until the war, when it was merged in another school that again migrated and still flourishes. The late William B. Astor was a rider in those days, and built a riding-hall on his own grounds for his use in bad weather. In good weather, though the Park was not, the unpaved roads were more accessible than now from the heart of the town, and along the Bloomingdale Road, now the dusty Boulevard, horsemen might have been seen as regularly, and in about the same numbers, as in the opening chapters of the then famous G. P. R. James.

Before the Park was fairly opened, and while its main lines were laying through a region of rocks and shanties, compounded of a goat pasture and a mining camp, the equestrian pioneers were exploring its untrimmed surfaces, and making the goal of their rides one of the road-houses to which the trotting men, then as now, resorted in much greater numbers. One little band of these was known to the keeper of the hostelry they frequented as the "literary cavalry." Mr. Charles A. Dana is, I think, the sole survivor of this informal club, which included, besides, Mr. Henry J. Raymond, whose white pacer was known to his companions as "The Little Villain," in allusion to an amenity of journalism current in those days, Mr. Frey, remembered as the stalwart and emphatic musical critic of the *Tribune*, and Edmond O'Flaherty, known then and long afterward in New York as William Stuart. There were already women who rode also, though for the most part they had learned to ride elsewhere, and there was the same scarcity of well-broken saddle-horses for ladies of which Fanny Kemble had complained years before, upon her first visit to these shores. Even after the Park was completed, the ordeal of riding to it attended by a company of grinning and hooting boys was very trying to the nerves of the weaker sex. Now the riding-schools have all been moved to the immediate neighborhood of the Park, and "a lady on horseback" is so familiar a sight that even the most excitable of the circumjacent small boys is not moved to make proclamation of it. Perhaps the strongest proof that riding had not become a fashionable amusement until a good many years after the facilities for it had been provided by the Park Commissioners is that the late Horace Greeley addicted himself to it during his latter years. Of course he rode in a sad sincerity, and because he thought it was good for him, but he submitted himself to a regular course of instruction, and he proved so plastic in the hands of his riding-master that those who have seen him ride declare that, if he did not precisely witch the world with noble horsemanship, he looked at all events considerably less irregular on horseback than he did on foot. Another candidate for the Presidency was an even earlier and a much more constant horseman. Twenty years ago, at least, Samuel J. Tilden used to disport himself in the Park on horseback, and he continued his riding until he was forced to abandon it by physical infirmity. Most of us remember among the cipher despatches the admonition, "Tell Russia saddle Blackstone," and this was in the crisis of November, 1876. When he was Governor of New York it was Mr. Tilden's habit to do his official reviewing on horseback, and once or twice this practice led him into perils from which it was a feat of horsemanship to extricate one's self. Nevertheless there are those who disparage his horsemanship, and not on political grounds. "He rode single-footers," says my informant, more, in sorrow than in anger.

It is only fair to say that my informant is a German, and that in Germany, as for the matter of that in England, the walk, the, trot, and the gallop (the latter subdivided in England into the canter and the gallop) are the only gaits permitted to a well-regulated saddle-horse. The single-foot and its variant, the rack, are cultivated only in regions, like our own Southern States, of which the horsemanship is ultimately derived from Spain. So that it is perhaps a piece of too Teutonic stringency to put a man out of court altogether as a rider because he prefers the languors of

the single-foot to the strenuous joys of the German trot. For Germans there be who despise him who rises in the trot even as him who rides single-footers, and are prepared to maintain that he only rides who merely bobs and bumps. This view prevails chiefly, it is true, among those Germans who immigrated some years ago, and before rising in the trot had been enjoined upon the German cavalry as a proved preventive of sore backs. It is none the less held as an article of faith, and as it is well known that there is no other being on earth quite so uncompromising as a German professor of anything, it is inculcated by those who hold it in all its rigor.

This leads me to remark upon the vulgar error that riding in New York is mainly a phase of Anglomania, an error which appears in the scornful treatment of the equestrian dudes of the metropolis by a fearless Western press. In point of fact it is quite as much an importation from the land to which we owe our culture in beer and Beethoven, if not rather more. The proportion of Germans who ride for pleasure is at least as large as that of natives. Three of the four principal riding-schools are owned and managed by Germans, and at one of them German is the prevailing language. At another there is a Reitclubb, composed mainly of Germans, who pursue equitation with a German thoroughness, and have attained in it, perhaps, a greater proficiency than any other like body. Even in horseflesh German ideas have made their way, and horses imported from the great Prussian breeding establishment at Trakene, or their progeny, are preferred by many riders, Americans as well as Germans, for the work of an all-round saddle-horse, to the weight-carrying hunter or the half-bred Park hack which is the ideal of the Anglomaniac. In its effect upon horsemanship here the German influence is distinctly greater than the English. The German teachers outnumber the English probably three to one, and leave their impress upon their pupils, while the land of Baucher and the *haute école* is scarcely represented at all. Even at "the Club," which is commonly supposed to be the centre and citadel of Anglomania, the head riding-master is, or lately was, a German. Along with the vigor and rigor which, according to Mr. Matthew Arnold, characterize the German professorial mind in general, go the systematic and exact methods of German instruction. Apart altogether from the much-discussed question of the superiority for general purposes of the military seat or the hunting seat—a question not to be mooted here—the superior-

thus has his disadvantages in teaching and in training. It must be owned that he is apt to have his revenges also when there is "a downright nasty brute" to be mounted, or an obdurate refuser to be jumped. As for American riding, one

DER REITMEISTER.

ity, for the purposes of teaching, of the systematic instruction which the Germans have received, over the more or less happy-go-lucky way in which Englishmen learn to ride without knowing how they learned, is scarcely to be disputed. Inasmuch as almost all the German teachers "have served," and transmit the military seat which they have learned, it is not surprising that their pupils should sit rather like German cavalrymen than like cross-country riders, notwithstanding the English hunting man's sneer that the three men who cannot possibly ride horses are "a sailor, a tailor, and a cavalry officer." The Englishman who has learned to ride by riding, and not by being taught to ride,

may occasionally see in the Park the actual cow-boy in his deep saddle astride of his loping broncho, but he does not commend himself as a model for Park riding. The West Point seat, again, may be seen as exemplified not only by casual graduates of the Academy taking their pleasure, but also by the mounted policemen, many of whom are old troopers. Seats, however, as the excellent and entertaining Major Dwyer has shown, depend upon saddles, and as it is only with stirrups hung well forward that the characteristic hunting seat can be attained, so it is only in the McClellan saddles that are used by the mounted Metropolitans out in Seventh Avenue and the region beyond Macomb's Dam, but have been discarded for the Whitman by the Park police proper, that the fork seat and the straight leg with the toe rather down than up can be seen in perfection. The cross-country man and the *Reitmeister* agree in disapproving this seat, though they are both aware that men may ride horses well in many ways. Their disapproval rises to frantic intolerance when it is transmitted to their respective disciples, who are not aware of this important truth. The well greaved and buttoned Anglomaniac, whose own person makes a violent angle at the waist, whose feet lie out on his horse's shoulders, and between whose legs, when he trots, the following horseman gets really panoramic views of the landscape, declares that the policeman "cawn't ride." The vigorous and rigorous and procrustean German, who would rather fall off by bumping than stay on by rising, will tell you that no man with the policeman's seat "gan mannitch" a horse. Whoever has seen a mounted policeman in the act of catching a runaway, and noted the skill, the coolness, and the perfect command of his animal which the performance involves, could not help wishing to subject his critics to the same test of horsemanship, were it not that capital punishment is somewhat too severe for the offence of rash and incompetent criticism. It is not to risk committing this offence to say that, whether the hunting seat or the military seat be the better, the former lends itself the more readily to exaggeration, and that German riding cannot be so successfully caricatured as the riding even of an English groom is unconsciously caricatured by his complacent disciple when he takes a "kenter in the Pork."

These differences of horsemanship are very much softened when the question becomes of horsewomanship. They are not enforced by so widely different theories and practices of saddlery, and the male German who insists upon bumping for himself concedes to the weaker vessel the privilege of rising. The Kentuckian or Virginian equestrienne reveals her training mainly by holding her left hand with the reins in it level with the elbow and across the body, cavalry fashion, while the fair Anglomaniac can testify her devotion no otherwise than by exhibiting a crop instead of a whip, and by carrying both elbows as nearly as may be on a level with her shoulders—a posture which,

she will be pained to learn, is regarded by British horsemen as characteristic of the British cad. To Anglomania used to be imputed the banging of horses' tails, which has no longer anything distinctive, since a long-tailed saddle-horse has become an exceptional object, either on the road or in the ring. Where a long tail is seen, unless its beauty be its own excuse for being, it is commonly brandished as a patriotic protest against the manners and customs of the English.

It cannot be denied, however, that Anglomania has had its influence. The hunting in this country is, of course, English in its origin, and the humorists of the press hold it up to ridicule by pointing out that it is an anise-seed bag that is hunted—as if fox-hunting were anywhere a cheap and expeditious method of destroying foxes, or anything beyond a means, like "steeple-chasing," in its literal sense, of getting a gallop across country. The ridicule, however, is gradually ceasing as it is coming to be understood what riding across country involves. A man risking his neck for the sake of an exciting exercise may be reprehensible, but he is not properly ridiculous. Young men of the increasing class that is devoted to "high living and plain thinking" might make a much worse use of their abounding leisure, and be infected with much more injurious phases of Anglomania. In Boston the cross-country riders avowed Anglomania and anticipated ridicule by boldly calling themselves the Myopia Hunt Club, and possibly by glazing an eye each when they rode to the meet. There is no need of such an avowal on the part of the gilded youth who ride to hounds in Long Island and in New Jersey, and whose dock-tailed horses and pink coats and buckskin breeches and "hunt balls" to the neighboring yeomanry so excite the risibility of one class of patriots and the wrath of another. It is not quite true, by-the-way, that all fox-hunting, even in the Northern States, is imported. In Chester County, Pennsylvania, there is an indigenous hunt, with a pack of hounds and horses of native breed. The farmers ride after foxes as their fathers before them rode, and they would be as astonished to hear that they were imitating the English as was Molière's hero to learn that he conversed in prose. Nevertheless they have what to the scorners is one of the chief "notes" of

Drawn by T. de Thulstrup.

A TAILOR-MADE GIRL.

Engraved by Lindsay.

Anglomania, in that they do not pretend to hunt for the sake of the game, but only for the sake of the hunting. With them, as with the gilded youth of the suburban hunts, it is "not the conquest but the battle" that allures. "We cannot afford to kill foxes," said one of them to the present writer, implying, of course, that a fox that is hunted and runs away may live to be hunted another day, but explaining that early in the season it was customary to give one fox to the hounds in order to encourage them thereafter. But for our immediate purpose fox-hunting may be regarded as an importation, with all the modifications it has induced in horses, seats, and equipment, and these are many and considerable.

The seasons for riding in the Park are the spring and the autumn, and year by year the habitual rider notes the progress of riding by noting the increasing throng in the bridle-path. Mr. Olmsted, in his notes on the proposed suburban park of Boston, observes that by the opening of the Central Park, among other things, the number of saddle-horses kept in New York has increased a hundredfold. If we limit the statement to horses kept exclusively or mainly for the saddle, it is doubtless literally true. The Club alone houses 250 saddle-horses. The four principal riding-schools have together about 700 more. There is also another school, which is scarcely in the competition, being as yet but a small beginning, though it testifies in a powerful and pathetic way to the steady growth of the interest in riding, having a ring the size of a large drawing-room, in which sensitive persons may take secluded lessons and have their initiatory contortions veiled from the unfeeling and critical experts who lie in wait for them in the more frequented schools. Here we have a total of not far from a thousand horses, and to this is to be added the number of saddle-horses, not so easily ascertainable, kept in the private stables of their owners. In all, it seems safe to estimate that there are 1200 saddle-horses in New York, and it is not likely that there were a full dozen before the Park was opened. To help the reader realize how considerable this number is, it may be pointed out that the entertaining author of *Living Paris* cites as a proof of the luxuriousness of that city of luxury that there are at least 8000 private horses kept in Paris—meaning kept for pleasure.

Comparing the number of those who drive and those who ride in New York, rapidly as this latter number increases, it seems likely that in this article of luxury the American "metropolis" surpasses the capital of the world. The number of riders, at any rate, like the expenses of one of the departments in Washington, according to a memorable report of its chief, has "exceeded the most sanguine anticipations." The projectors of the bridle-path were censured at the time of laying it out for allotting so much space to so little purpose. Since the Park was opened the bridle-path has been extended across the foot of it, and has already become in some respects inadequate. Experience has shown that some of the turns are dangerously sharp, and to avert the danger, so far as possible, signs are now put up to forbid "running or galloping" on the bridle-path, except around the reservoir, where the road has long straight stretches, and a horse approaching can be seen around the turns. Frightened horses, however, pay no heed to these warnings, and reckless horsemen, whether boys or "Sunday riders," pay little more, and there is an evident necessity that some of the sharper turns shall be straightened and made gradual against the increased chances of accident that increased numbers bring. The number of riders apt to be encountered at any point is not as yet so great as in Rotten Row during the London season, where the equestrians are often brought to a walk. If the suggestion made a short time since in the press for the establishment of a Rotten Row in Central Park were carried out, there might before long be danger of a like engorgement. This suggestion, it is not unfair to suspect, emanated from those equestrian visitors to the Park to whom their own visibility is an important consideration, but it is not likely to be carried out. In spite of the "Carriage Concourse" that was provided in the original plan of the Park, it is fortunate for the comfort of visitors in general that there is no one point in the circuit of it, as there is in Hyde Park, that is consecrated by usage to a general assembly. Both "carriage people" and equestrians can be conveniently observed from Mount St. Vincent, where the bridle-path joins the East Drive, which thence becomes the common highway to the upper end of the Park. The most eligible coigne of vantage for

THE HUNTING MAN.

seeing the riders alone is perhaps the east side of the reservoir, where fast riding is permitted, and where from five of a fine afternoon there is for nearly an hour a passage of horsemen and horsewomen so constant as to assume the character of a procession. The procession includes many men whose names are known throughout and beyond their own country—men eminent in all the professions and in nearly all the great industries. There are physicians, whose profession notoriously induces a fondness for horseflesh, and who here at least show a creditable willingness to take their own prescriptions; there are lawyers, men of letters, artists, "railroad men";

> "Sometimes a troop of damsels glad,
> An abbot on an ambling pad"—

for riding is so far from being regarded as an unclerical recreation that among many clergymen who ride there is at least one prelate, by no means recognizable from the poet's description, but apt to be seen bestriding an animal much less

episcopal of aspect and action and much less easily manageable than "an ambling pad," which I take to be mediæval for a single-footing cob.

It is no disparagement to these dignitaries to say that they do not compose the most attractive part of this daily procession. The "troop of damsels glad," under escort of a riding-master, or the family party of the same, personally conducted by paterfamilias, or the solitary horsewoman followed at a respectful distance by a belted groom, or accompanied by a more interesting male—these are the objects which the judicious spectator deems it worth while to retain his perch alongside the reservoir to see. The fashion in riding-habits abjures anything that suggests romance. The trailing robes and sweeping plumes of the last generation of horsewomen are banished to remote rural parts of the Southern States. A "silk hat" on man or woman seems the negation of romance, and nothing can be more prosaic and severely business-like than the habit which it surmounts, the absolutely plain garment in dark monochrome, of which the requirements are that it shall be without ornament, and that it shall fit and hang without a wrinkle. It is a fact as familiar as it is consolatory that no fashion can make a pretty girl look otherwise than pretty. The looker-on is inclined to believe, as Simplesse Munditiis passes him at a canter, that there was never any equestrian costume so exquisite, and that Queen Guinevere, with her gown of grass-green silk and her golden clasps and her light green tuft of plumes closed in a golden ring, was dressed very inappropriately for the sad-

dle compared with his tailor-made vision of loveliness. If of a romantic mind, he may drop again into Tennyson:

"As she fled fast through sun and shade
The happy wind upon her played,
Blowing the ringlet from the braid;
She looked so lovely as she swayed
The rein with dainty finger tips"—

we need not go on, though we may have every reason to suspect that the young man who escorts her has "gone on," under the friendly shade of the grove at the turn, where it is the custom of young couples of assorted sexes to pass at a walk before they come into the unsheltered straight stretch and break into a canter.

Around the Park, or twice around the reservoir if one keeps to the bridle-path, is the usual "promenade on horseback," and is about an hour in duration, if taken at a judicious alternation of gaits, and six or seven miles in extent. The more ambitious extend it out Seventh Avenue, along the broad road kept soft for the speeding of trotters, to the bridge two miles beyond the Park, or leave the Park at Seventy-second Street for the macadamized Riverside Drive, at

ANGLOMANIACS.

MOUNTED POLICEMAN.

the upper end of which there is half a mile or so of straight bridle-path. If the project is executed that was authorized by the last Legislature to connect the upper end of the Central Park with the upper end of Riverside Drive, by paving the connecting streets like the driveways in the Park for pleasure traffic, there will be a continuous driveway of some nine miles. To complete the felicity of the riders it will be necessary only to carry the bridle-path along the whole extent of the Riverside, for which there is ample room.

When one has more time than the hour or hour and a half to which most riders of the male sex are restricted for their constitutionals, there is a choice of suburban excursions, though the choice is not so large as it should be, and as it

is to be hoped it will be when it comes to be recognized that people who ride or drive for pleasure have rights as to the paving of a limited number of streets which drivers of drays are bound to respect. The bridging of the East River at Blackwell's Island, if it ever comes to pass, will make Long Island accessible, as it can scarcely be said to be now, with four miles of block pavement between the Brooklyn Bridge and the lower end of Central Park. The lower ferries to New Jersey are impracticable for a like reason, but the ferry to Fort Lee is at the upper end of the Riverside Drive, and a short climb brings you to a road through the woods at the top of the Palisades. Jerome Park, too, at the end of another stretch of soft road which the riders owe to the trotting men, is the goal of a pleasant afternoon's ride.

In the summer, of course, the Park and the city are deserted by them that drive in chariots, although they sometimes leave their chariots behind in the keeping of their charioteers. In that case John Thomas drives Mary Jane daily in the Park, and excites the wonder of the mid-summer pilgrim from the country concerning the manners and customs of rich New-Yorkers. It was one of the annual absentees who opposed the planting of a shrub that was fragrant and beautiful upon the ground that in midsummer nobody ever went to the Park. Such of the horsemen as cannot get away take their constitutionals as usual—in the early morning, if they be of heroic mould and able to do things before breakfast, or otherwise in the late afternoon. For the most part the riding-schools are deserted, and some of them establish colonies at the watering-places as an alternative to turning their horses out to grass.

In winter the owner of a saddle-horse is the object of a commiseration of which he does not stand in the least need. Some horsemen, indeed, defy the season, and

A FAMILY GROUP.

THE CONSTITUTIONAL RIDER.

ride out-of-doors all winter long, although in midwinter it is to less hardy souls and bodies an abuse of language to call such riding riding for pleasure. At least one horsewoman there is who pursues the same courageous practice, and for whom no weather that a man can ride in is too severe. Most riders, after the winter has fairly set in, and until it has fairly broken, know the bridle-path only once or twice a month, when the weather relents for a day and the ice disappears from the roadway. But these enjoy their exercise little less for being compelled to take it under cover. This is the season for teaching, and the "rings"—the rectangles of riding-schools are always rings—are at their busiest. The timid and awkward girl who is hoisted upon a horse for the first time in December, and totters there in a state of highly unstable bodily equilibrium and of keen mental anguish—this

autumnal grub bursts the chrysalis of the ring in April, and appears upon the bridle-path as a fully developed horsewoman. All the morning is given over to lessons, but at the usual riding hour, between business and dinner, in the afternoon, the ring is shut against them, and opened for class riding. There are so many horses that some order has to be observed. At least everybody must ride in the same direction until a change is ordered by the ring-master. Even with this minimum of order riders going each his own gait are sure to obstruct one another, and it is for the general comfort that the riders shall form a line, and ride at the same gait by the word of command, the tedium of walking being relieved by the performance of such simple manœuvres as require only a moderate horsemanship. This is the daily practice during the winter in the larger schools. In addition to this daily ride, there is once a week, or oftener, a "music ride" in the evening, and last season one of the schools set the excellent example of a daily music ride—an example that will no doubt be followed.

Those riders who are ambitious to carry their horsemanship beyond the standard required at the music rides associate themselves in clubs for that purpose, and one of these clubs has for several years made an excursion of a fortnight on horseback. It is not defamatory to suggest that "The First Hussars," an independent military organization recently founded, with its head-quarters at one of the riding-schools, is in the nature of a riding club, and that its objects are rather equestrian than warlike.

Of course these clubs are not to be confounded with *the* Club, the objects of which may be said to be equestrian and social, and which, though not yet five years of age, has had a very powerful influence in developing the practice of riding and in giving it a status in "society." The New York Riding Club was founded by a few owners of saddle-horses who constabulated, so to speak, at one of the riding-schools, and to whom it appeared desirable that there should be a school in which they could select their own associates. No sooner was the project formed than it became evident that it met that long-felt want to which the projectors of new enterprises invariably appeal. Already it has nearly five hundred members, and one honorary member, I know not by what merit raised to that lonely eminence. Of the active members more than half are actual horse owners and riders, and all of them may be supposed to cherish more or less definite aspirations toward horsemanship. The actual membership is much larger than the figures indicate, since by the constitution of the club the ladies of a member's family and his minor sons are entitled to its privileges, the daughters forfeiting their privileges when they marry, unless they marry into the club, as it were. There must thus be quite twice as many virtual members of the club as appear upon the club list, and it is to these unenrolled members that the club is most nearly indispensable. Its male members might find their own requirements very nearly as well met in all essentials at one of the public riding-schools. But a place of instruction and exercise to which ladies

and children can resort unattended, and about the associations of which they may be quite secure, has the same advantage over even the most carefully conducted public school that an ordinary club has over a restaurant. As has been hinted, the club is regarded by outsiders as a citadel of Anglomania, nor is the charge without some plausibility. The attendants are habited in plush and small-clothes, and exhibit those balustraded calves that are the trade-mark of the British flunky. When the visitor has got over his aversion to this grewsome spectacle he will find little else to offend his patriotic sensibilities, unless he considers a high degree of luxury in the living-rooms of the club, and an absolutely flawless neatness in the stables, corrupting to the simplicity of republican manners. The club-house is within a few hundred feet of the Fifth Avenue entrance to the park. Its area is about 200 feet by 125, and gives room for a ring in the centre 107 by 94, with a range of rooms along the street front, and spacious stables for some 300 horses in the rear. The dimensions of the ring, when it was built, were the largest in New York, though they have since been exceeded by one or two of the public schools, and of course by such a monument of capricious extravagance as the famous subterranean riding-hall of the Duke of Portland at Welbeck Abbey. It is proposed to enlarge it still further, but it is now ample for the music rides, or, as they are called at the club, the "drills," which occur during the winter twice a week in the afternoon, and in which some sixty or seventy horsemen and horsewomen usually take part. There are few prettier sights to lovers of horseflesh and horsemanship than one of these drills, exhibiting practised riders, on the best and best-looking saddle-horses that can be bred or bought, executing more intricate evolutions than the schools for the most part venture on, with admirable precision, and upon occasion at a smart pace. There is not one of the riders who is not deriving physical benefit from an exercise for which very few of them would find any substitute if this were not at their command. If riding in New York be, as with many of its votaries it must be owned to be, a matter of fashion mainly, the philanthropist may be well satisfied if fashion inspires nothing less useful or less delightful.

The Little Laborers of New York
(1873)

THE LITTLE LABORERS OF NEW YORK CITY.

LITTLE TOBACCO STRIPPERS.

ONE of the most touching facts to any one examining the lower strata of New York is the great number of young children toiling in factories and shops. With the children of the fortunate classes there are certain years of childhood which every parent feels ought to be freed from the burdens and responsibilities of life. The "struggle for existence," the labor of money-making, the toil for support, and all the cares and anxieties therewith, will come soon enough. And the parent is glad that the first years at least should be buoyant and free from care, with no shadow of after-life upon them. He knows how heavy the burden must be which the child will soon be forced to carry, and he is pleased that a few years can be left cheerful and happy and free from anxiety. But the father of the poor child can indulge in no such sentiments. He is compelled to harness the little one very early to the car of labor, or if he be not forced to this, he is indifferent to the child's natural growth and improvement, and believes that his boy ought to pass through the same hard experience which he had himself. He is struggling with poverty, and eager for every little addition which he can make to his income. The child's wages seem to him important, and, indeed, it requires a character of more disinterestedness and a mind of more scope of view than we usually find among the laboring class to be able to forego present profit for the future benefit of the little one. The laborer sees the daily earnings, and does not think much of the future advantages which the child may win by being educated now. The father, accordingly,

ENVELOPE MAKERS.

way to rouse the public feeling and conscience. They had against them the indifference of the poor parents themselves, and an enormous factory interest which made rich profits out of the toil of these unhappy children of poverty. Every where the specious arguments were brought forward that the poor themselves most of all needed the labor, that the earnings of the children supported the families of the laborers, and if these were excluded from factories they would all come upon the unions or the public almshouses. It was claimed that it was better to support the children of the laborers even by their own overwork than to keep them in poor-houses. It was urged that it was an oppression on the parents, who had brought these children into the world, not to allow them to use their earnings. The production of England would be diminished, it was said, and she would lose in the markets of the world, if this great source from children's labor were dried up. Even the education of the factory was lauded, and it was claimed that the incessant labor on one object was better for a poor child than the training it would get in the streets. To direct the manufacturer where to procure labor and where not was an interference with "freedom of trade." Capital and labor, even child's labor, should be left to natural laws.

of a poor boy is found in all countries to be willing to neglect his education, if he can put him at profitable work. Neither his affection for his offspring nor his unselfishness can be relied upon as guarding his child's future. The law is forced to protect the minor.

In Great Britain the evils of this great army of infant workers had, a few years since, increased to an alarming extent. Hundreds of thousands of little ones were found growing up without any education, except the petty practical experience of the small branch of factory labor in which they were engaged, without any full development of body, their little forms bent and rickety, their countenances pale, their growth stunted by premature labor, and arriving at manhood utterly unfitted either to be citizens or the heads of new families. Vast numbers of them also died under this youthful slavery; and the mines and factories were discovered to be an immense slaughter-house for these unfortunate children. At length a band of devoted reformers and philanthropists arose, who were determined that this burning shame of their country should be wiped out, who felt that the wealth and culture of England rested on a hideous foundation when the labor of oppressed children built up the structure. They began an incessant agitation against the overlabor of factory children. They wrote for the press, printed documents, held public meetings, petitioned Parliament, and sought in every

Against all these sophistical arguments, however, the great humanity of England asserted itself. It saw it was the manifest duty of the state to guard the children of the poor and unfortunate against the greed of capital and the indifference of their own parents. It felt that these little beings were the wards of the public; that they ought not to be dwarfed in body and cramped in mind by the covetousness of others; that they had a claim on the protection of the fortunate. It was more and more seen, also, that it was not for the interest of England that a great multitude of human beings should grow up among the people ignorant in mind, weakened in body, and unfit for the duties of manhood. There were "dangerous classes" enough in the English cities, whom no reformation or legislation could reach, without adding to them this immense mass of children, enslaved, as it were, in their early years. The interest of the state was evidently in education, even if production were diminished. A greater evil than poverty was widespread ignorance. It was clear, too, that this great class of children would produce all the more hereafter if their minds could be trained in childhood. The best condition for popular wealth is popular education. Moreover, it was not believed that

GOLD-LEAF WORKERS.

the exclusion of the children from the factories would drive the families to the almshouse. There was no difficulty, evidently, in arranging half-time schools and half-time work. The one would help the other. The young laborer would be better for his school, and the young scholar for his toil.

After incessant discussion and a long contest, the English "Factory Bills" were carried through Parliament, were repeatedly amended, improved, and enlarged, until they form now a ponderous Blue-Book.

These acts have been rigorously executed, and their effects have been that hundreds of thousands of little " white slaves" have been redeemed from slavery, saved from premature toil and sickness, and that a new class of English laborers are growing up, better educated, healthier, happier, and of more value to their employers. The reform was one of the most glorious and beneficent ever carried out in Great Britain.

This terrible evil of the overwork of children was early felt in the State of Massachusetts. A great manufacturing population had concentrated there, and some of the economical conditions of the Old World were repeated. Children were found in various parts of the State enslaved to labor from their earliest years, without proper education, and weakened in bodily power. No thorough effort, however, was made to check the evil till 1866, when the Legislature passed an act "restraining the employing of children of tender years in manufacturing es-

tablishments." This was subsequently repealed, and a more thorough and stringent law passed in 1867 (Chapter 28). By this act no child under ten years of age could be employed in any manufacturing establishment in the State. Of children between the ages of ten and fifteen years no one was allowed to be thus employed unless he had attended a day school at least "three months of the year preceding," or a "half-time school" during the six months. And if this amount of education be not secured, the employer is obliged to at once dismiss the child. It is necessary also that the school should be a suitable one, and approved by the school committee of the town where the child resides. The "ten-hour provision" is also made applicable to children, and no child under fifteen can be thus employed more than sixty hours per week. If ever the "Eight-hour Act" was reasonable, it would be as applied to children, and forty-eight hours per week seems to us quite enough for any working boy or girl. The penalty for the violation of this act in Massachusetts is fifty dollars both to employer and parent.

The phraseology of the Massachusetts law does not seem as careful as would be desirable, and is not made sufficiently yielding in cases of hardship among the poor; neither is sufficient power given to the executive officer to enter manufacturing establishments, and no sufficient school certificates or forms of registration for the factory children are provided for.

THE LITTLE BURNISHERS.

educational reform. Her citizens early saw the terrible evil from children's overwork, and the Legislature passed acts against it as early as 1842. The final and most stringent law, however, passed on this subject in Connecticut was in 1869 (Chapter 115). This law includes agricultural as well as manufacturing labor, and it throws on the employer the responsibility of ascertaining whether the children employed have attended school the required time, or whether they are too young for labor. The rules, too, in regard to school attendance are exceedingly strict. The age at which three months' school-time is required is fourteen. The penalty for each offense is one hundred dollars.

The law, however, is defective in that it does not establish the lowest age under which a child may be employed in a factory, and does not limit the number of hours of labor per week for children in manufacturing establishments.

The manufacturers of Connecticut seem to have co-operated with the law with the utmost good sense and humanity. One of them writes to the State executive officer: "We do not dare to permit the children within and around our mills to grow up without some education. Better for us to pay the school expenses ourselves than have the children in ignorance." Others have followed the example of Massachusetts manufacturers, and have opened night schools and half-time schools for their little employés, while others have permitted the division of the children into alternate gangs, of whom one is in school while the other is in the factory.

It is difficult to obtain minute or accurate information in relation to children employed in factories in New York city, and more difficult still to gain access to the factories, owing to the reluctance of employers to admit strangers. The manufacturers naturally suspect some sinister motives on the part of the inquirers. They are jealous of one another, and desirous of keeping their various patents and modes of work secret from

It is evident, however, that, with all its defects, the law has brought about a great alleviation of the evil of children's overwork. The officer appointed for the execution of the act has been in correspondence with all the manufacturers of the State, and has visited their works. This has at once called the earnest attention of the employers of Massachusetts, who are a very intelligent and philanthropic class, to the extent of this great evil. They have immediately sought for themselves to remedy it. Some of them have established half-time schools, which they require all the children in their employ to attend; and their experience here is similar to that in England—that they secure thereby a much better class of workers. Others arrange double gangs of young operatives, so that one set may take the place of another in the factory while the latter are in school. Others, again, have founded night schools, and great numbers of the young factory laborers are trained in these. The law is considered throughout Massachusetts as having been the commencement of a great and much-needed reform.

The act passed in Rhode Island (Chapter 139) is very similar to that of Massachusetts, except that no child under twelve can be employed in any factory, and no child during the nine months of factory-work is allowed to be employed more than eleven hours per day. The penalty for the violation is only twenty dollars.

Connecticut is in advance in matters of

their competitors. There have been not infrequent instances of covert attempts by the members of one firm to get possession of the secrets of another, and they are consequently all somewhat suspicious of strangers making inquiries.

It is estimated on trustworthy grounds that over 100,000 children are at work in the factories of New York and the neighboring districts, while from 15,000 to 20,000 are "floaters," drifting from one factory to another. Of these the envelope factories employ about 8000 children, one-quarter of whom are under fifteen years of age. The average earnings of the little

MAKING PAPER COLLARS.

workers are $3 per week. The ventilation in these factories is generally good. The gold-leaf factories employ a large number of children, though the exact statistics of the number can not be given. This occupation requires much skill and delicacy of touch; it is not severe, but demands constant attention. The outside air is carefully excluded from these factories, owing to the fragile nature of the material used. The girls employed are mostly over fifteen years of age. The burnishing of gold, silver, and china-ware is mostly done by girls, some of whom are under thirteen years of age. Singularly enough, it is said that men in this business require to wear breastplates, in order to prevent injury from the steel instruments employed, while the girls who labor at it sit at long tables, their undefended breasts · pressing against the handles of the frame.

Paper-collar factories are a very important branch of

MAKING PAPER BOXES.

TWINE MAKERS.

children's labor. Fully 8000 girls from twelve to sixteen years of age are employed in it. A girl can count and box 18,000 collars in a day of ten hours.

Paper-box factories, embracing all sorts and sizes, from a match to a work box, employ at least 10,000 children. These become very expert, and often invent new patterns. The material being cheap, the children are permitted to take home enough to do extra work, and are thus, in fact, excluded from night school.

In regard to factories for making artificial flowers it is extremely difficult to obtain trustworthy information, as access to the shops is rigidly refused. After considerable investigation, it seems to us that from 10,000 to 12,000 children are engaged in them, of whom nearly 8000 are under twelve years of age. Many are only five and seven years old. The latter are employed preparing and cutting feathers for coloring. Employers claim this to be a healthy business, but, judging from the pale and sickly countenances of the girls, we doubt the assertion.

Another important industry employing children in the city is the manufacture of tobacco. The tobacco factories contain fully 10,000 children, of whom 5000 at least are under fifteen years. The youngest child we saw employed in them was four years of age. He was engaged in stripping tobacco, and his average earnings were about one dollar per week. Many laborers work all their lives in these factories. We saw per-

sons as old as eighty years in them. A man seventy years of age told us he had spent thirty years in one factory. His two boys had entered the factory with him at the age of ten and twelve years, and were now at work as men in the same shop. Another, the foreman, and general workshop manager, had entered that factory thirty-five years ago, when a boy ten years of age. In some of these factories boys under fifteen years are employed in dusky cellars and basements, preparing, brining, and sweetening the weed preliminary to "stemming." The under-ground life in these damp, cavernous places tends to keep the little workers stunted in body and mind. Other boys from ten to twelve years squatting on the floors, whetting the knives of the cutting machines with a mixture of rum and water applied with a sponge. The rapidity with which the girls work is wonderful. A girl of sixteen years can put up thirteen gross of packages of chewing tobacco in tin-foil, and twenty-two gross in paper, in one day. Girls and boys from twelve to fourteen years earn in this business from four to five dollars per week. Some little girls only eight years of age earn $3 per week. The fact is that these children are often able to perform the same amount of this light labor as adults, while they only receive a portion of the pay given to older laborers. Thus the children who ought to be in school are made to deprive older laborers of their employment and remuneration.

THE NIGHT SCHOOL.

Still another branch absorbs a great number of children—the twine factories. No accurate estimate can be obtained of the number of little laborers in these, but it is known to be very large. In one up-town factory alone, 200 children, mostly girls, are employed. This work is dangerous. The "hackling machines" are generally tended by boys from ten to fifteen years of age. Their attention must be riveted on the machinery, and can not relax for a moment, or the danger to life or limb is imminent. The "twisting machines," attended to by girls, are equally dangerous. Many have lost their fingers, or joints of them, that were caught in the twine. Only great presence of mind has saved many of these girls from losing the whole hand. We knew in one instance, in a single night school in New York, five factory girls who had each lost a finger or thumb. It is evident that strict legislation is needed here, as it has been in England, to protect these young workers from dangerous machinery. The air of these twine factories is filled with floating particles of cotton and flax, and must be exceedingly unhealthful.

It will be seen from these condensed statistics what an immense population of children in this city are the little slaves of capital. How intense and wearying is their daily toil, and how much of their health and education is sacrificed in these early years and premature labor! The evil in New York is evidently enormous, and most threatening to our future. These children, stunted in body and mind, are growing up to be our voters and legislators. There are already over 60,000 persons in New York who can not read or write. These little overworked operatives will swell this ignorant throng. Fortunately this great abuse has not escaped the attention of humane men.

There is one well-known benevolent organization in New York which has been especially the friend of working children—the Children's Aid Society. This has established in various parts of the city "industrial schools," where the children of the working classes are taught habits of industry, order, and cleanliness, together with common - school lessons and some industrial branch, and are then forwarded to places in the country. Besides these well-known institutions, which contain now during the year some nine thousand children, they have also founded night schools in destitute quarters, where boys and girls who labor all day can acquire a little education at night. The eagerness of these hard-working youths after a day of severe toil to obtain the rudiments of education is one of the most pathetic experiences in the field of the society's work. In one school, the Park School, near Sixty-eighth Street, young girls and lads, who have been working from seven o'clock till six, have been known to go without their supper in order not to miss the evening lessons. The stormiest weather and the worst

SEWING-MACHINE OPERATORS.

walking do not keep them from these schools. In the various night schools of the Children's Aid Society will be found hundreds of little ones from six to thirteen who have been working very hard the whole day, and who are now just as eager to learn their little tasks. Their occupations are innumerable. Thus we learn from a recent report from one of the society's visitors that at the school at 98 Crosby Street "there were some hundred children. Their occupations were as follows: They put up insect powder, drive wagons, tend oyster saloons; are tinsmiths, engravers, office-boys; in typefoundries, at screws, in blacksmith shops; make cigars, polish, work at packing tobacco; in barber shops, at paper stands; are cash-boys, light porters, make artificial flowers, work at hair; are errand-boys, make ink, are in Singer's sewing-machine factory, and printing-offices; some post bills, some are paint scrapers, some peddlers; they pack snuff, attend poultry stands at market, in shoe stores and hat stores, tend stands, and help painters and carpenters.

"At the Fifth Ward School (No. 141 Hudson Street) were fifty boys and girls. One of them, speaking of her occupation, said: 'I work at feathers, cutting the feathers from cocks' tails. It is a very busy time now. They took in forty new hands to-day. I get three dollars and fifty cents a week. Next, I'll get more. I go to work at eight o'clock, and leave off at six. The feathers are cut from the stem, then steamed, and curled, and packed. They are sent then to Paris, but more South and West.' One boy said he worked at twisting twine; another drove a 'hoisting-horse;' another blacked boots, etc.

"At the Eleventh Ward School, foot of East Eleventh Street, there was an interesting class of boys and girls under thirteen years of age. One boy said he was employed during the day in making chains of beads, and says that a number of the boys and girls present are in the same business. Another said he worked at coloring maps. Another blows an organ for a music-teacher.

"At the Lord School, No. 207 Greenwich Street, the occupations of the girls were working in hair, stripping tobacco, crochet, folding paper collars, house-work, tending baby, putting up parcels."

Among the institutions of this society for the education of working children should not be forgotten the Girls' Lodging-House, at No. 27 St. Mark's Place. Here a gratuitous "Sewing-machine School" was opened a few years since, the manufacturers supplying machines gratuitously, and any destitute girl, whether a lodger in the house or not, can be trained here to be an "operator." It is found often that a poor half-starved girl will enter this school, and if bright in learning the business, will in three weeks go out and earn from a dollar to two dollars a day in operating on a machine. The fact is a remarkable one in an econom-

TRAINING SERVANTS.

ical point of view, and shows that the supply of skilled machine labor is by no means equal to the demand. That such wages can be earned by utterly destitute girls, after so short a training, is one of the most hopeful signs which have ever appeared here with reference to the female working class. In this machine school, during the year, over a thousand girls are trained.

Another interesting experiment in this house is the opening of a "training school for servants." Its benevolent managers have taken pity on our housekeepers. They have remembered the troubles which every family undergoes from awkward and ignorant domestic service; the bad and unhealthy cookery, the slovenly house-cleaning, the ill-made beds, the poorly washed garments, and all the inflictions which we suffer daily from a class of workers who do not understand their business. An experiment is being

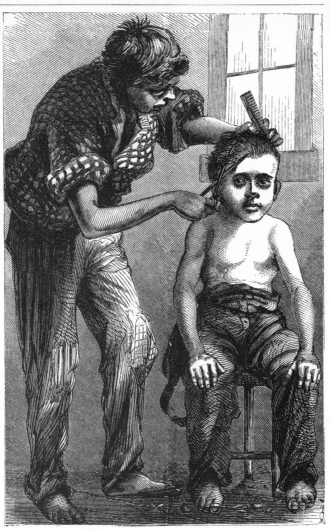

THE NEWSBOY'S FIRST LESSON.

made to remedy this evil by training a few young girls in this house as thorough and skillful servants. They are taught to cook a simple and nourishing breakfast in the morning; they then receive lessons in bed-making; they are next drilled in sweeping and scrubbing. They are instructed how to prepare a plain and well-cooked dinner, and a supper which a Christian may eat. On some days they are trained in laundry-work, on the sewing-machine, and in hand-sewing. The idea is an excellent one, and the experiment may result in producing a class, which is the greatest necessity in this country, of thorough-trained servants. The practical difficulty, however, will be that every housekeeper of the land is at the head of a "domestic training school," which will more than compete with this, as

the lady not only trains the girl, but pays her board and wages for being trained.

Besides this lodging-house are four other lodging-houses, for newsboys, boot-blacks, and other street lads. The best known of these is the Newsboys' Lodging-House, No. 49 Park Place, the first ever opened in any country, founded in 1854. During nineteen years it has sheltered 91,426 different boys, restored 7196 lost and missing ones to friends, provided 7108 with homes, furnished 576,493 lodgings, and 426,580 meals. The entire expense of all this, including rent, furniture, repairs, etc., has been $124,223 29, of which amount the boys have contributed $32,806 96, leaving the actual expense, over and above receipts from boys, $91,416 33, being only about $1 for each boy.

Still another is the Rivington Street Lodging-House, No. 327 Rivington Street, which has attached to it a beautiful greenhouse of flowers; a third is at No. 709 East Eleventh Street, and a fourth at No. 211 West Eighteenth Street. All these lodging-houses together shelter during the year some 12,000 homeless children.

Another ingenious effort for the benefit of the destitute children of the city is the "placing-out system," which has been carried out by the Children's Aid Society during the last twenty years with such remarkable success. The society early saw the immense benefit in taking advantage of the peculiar economical condition of this country in treating questions of pauperism. They at once recognized the fact, and resolved to make use in their plans, of the endless demand for children's labor in the Western country. The housekeeping life of a Western farmer is somewhat peculiar. The servants of the household must be members of the family, and be treated more or less as equals. It is not convenient nor agreeable for a Western matron to have a rude European peasant at the same table and in the same room with the family. She prefers a child whom she can train up in her own way. A child's labor is needed for a thousand things on a Western farm. Children, too, are valued and thought much of. The same opportunity is given to working children as to all other children. They share fully in the active and inspiring Western life. They are moulded by the social tone around them, and they grow up under the very best circumstances which can surround a poor boy or girl. No treatment which man could devise could possibly be so beneficial to the laboring children of this city as that offered by Western farms. Moreover, a child's place at the table in our rural households is of small account. Of food there is enough and an abundance. Generosity, and especially toward children, is the rule in our Western districts. This benevolent association, taking advantage of these great facts, early made arrangements for scattering such little workers of the city as were friendless and homeless all through the Western country. Western agents are employed who travel through remote farming districts, and discover where there is an especial call for children's labor. An arrangement is then made with the leading citizens of the village to receive a little detachment of these homeless children of the great city.

On a given day in New York the ragged and dirty little ones are gathered to a central office from the streets and lanes, from the industrial schools and lodging-houses of the society, are cleaned and dressed, and sent away, under charge of an experienced agent, to seek " a new home in the West." When they arrive in the village a great public meeting is held, and a committee of citizens formed to decide on the applications. Farmers come in from twenty to twenty-five miles round, looking for the "model boy" who shall do the light work of the farm and aid the wife in her endless household labor; childless mothers seek for children that shall replace those that are lost; housekeepers look for girls to train up; mechanics seek for boys for their trades; and kind-hearted men, with comfortable homes and plenty of children, think it is their duty to do something for the orphans who have no fair chance in the great city. Thus in a few hours the little colony is placed in comfortable homes. Subsequently, if changes should be necessary, the committee replace the children, or the agent revisits the village, while a steady correspondence is kept up by the central office with the employers. In this way something like 25,000 boys and girls have been placed in country homes during the past twenty years. Nearly 3000 a year are now sent forth by the society. Great numbers of these children have acquired property, or have grown up to positions of influence and respectability.

This association, not content with all these ingenious devices for the benefit of the working children, are now especially laboring to prevent the evil of overwork in factories. An act has been drawn up by their counsel, Charles E. Whitehead, Esq., and is now before the Legislature, designed for the protection of factory children. By this law no child under the age of ten years is allowed to be employed at all in a manufactory, and no child under the age of twelve, unless he can intelligibly read.

No child under the age of sixteen years is allowed to be employed more than sixty hours in one week, while four public holidays are secured to him. We think a humane amendment to this provision would have been the limiting of the day's work of children to eight hours. Other sections of a very stringent character secure to every factory child between the ages of ten and sixteen a certain proportion of education, either in night schools, half-time day schools, or by three months' annual schooling. Judicious exceptions are made in cases where a poor family is dependent on the labor of its children, in permitting such children to attend the night school instead of the usual day school.

Careful registers are required to be kept by the manufacturers or employers, showing the amount of schooling enjoyed by each child, the time of his labor in the factory, and other facts important for the execution of the law.

Humane provisions are also included in the act for the promotion of the good sanitary condition of the factories, and to protect the children from dangerous machinery.

RESCUED.

HOMELESS.

OFF FOR THE WEST.

THE YOUNG FARMER.

ADOPTED.

WORK OF THE CHILDREN'S AID SOCIETY.

Under the proposed law a new official has to be appointed by the Governor, to be called the "Inspector of Factory Children." Such an officer, acting under so wise and humane a law, can not but accomplish immense good throughout the State.

It is a matter deeply to be regretted that certain manufacturers in the State Legislature in Albany have not imitated their more enlightened and humane contemporaries in Massachusetts, and given their hearty support to so beneficent a measure. Instead of this, we are sorry to be informed that they are offering a factious opposition which may entirely defeat this act, and put New York in a very unfavorable position, as compared with the New England States, in her legislation to protect factory children.

The History of the Staten Island Athletic Club (1888)

THE HISTORY OF THE STATEN ISLAND ATHLETIC CLUB.

BY CHARLES E. CLAY.

Author of "A Bout with the Gloves," "Bermuda Yachts and Dinghies," "The History of the S. I. Cricket and Base Ball Club," etc.

ITS ORIGIN AND COMMENCEMENT.

STATEN ISLAND has always been looked upon as the home of the athlete. During the summer months the ranks of the resident population are very largely increased by the addition of hundreds of lusty young fellows devoted to the pursuit of base ball and cricket, of lawn tennis, yachting and rowing, who find on the grassy meads of the beautiful island the space for their favorite games that the bricks and mortar of Manhattan Island begrudge them. The Kill von Kull, or, the "Kills," as it is more familiarly known, is a broad sheet of lovely water between the Jersey coast and Staten Island, and forms one of the great arms of New York's magnificent bay, and, before the Standard Oil Works had polluted its clear and sparkling water with tons upon tons of filthy sludge acid and all the other noisome refuse from its factories, was as pretty a piece of water for the enjoyment of rowing and small boat sailing as could be wished for. Prior to the introduction of general athletics, inaugurated and so enthusiastically advanced, some ten or fifteen years ago, by the New York Athletic Club, swimming, rowing and boating were the chief amusements of the sons of the families that lived along the north shore of Staten Island, and to the Hesper and Neptune

boating clubs, two of the most famous aquatic organizations on the "Kills," most of the votaries of the sport belonged.

Several athletes of both clubs not content with seeking laurels with the oar had, during the year 1876, banded together for the purpose of keeping up other athletic exercises, such as running, jumping, walking, and hurdle-racing, and this, at that time, insignificant confederation, was known as the Staten Island Athletic Club, and became the parent of the present popular and famous club.

Among the original members of the club were such men as William Iken, Oliver T. Johnson, one of America's pioneer amateurs on the cinder path, John W. Edwards, captain of the Neptune Rowing Association, Wm. J. U. Roberts, Fred. W. and Frank G. Janssen, Robert Fiske, Fred. Rodewald, Thomas Chute, and Henry A. Cæsar. These enthusiasts, after a great deal of difficulty, succeeded in hiring a piece of ground on Bement and Henderson avenues, New Brighton, and in 1878 attempted to hold their first athletic games, but rain and want of proper experience made the opening venture but a sorry success. Nothing daunted, however, the forlorn band went hard to work; greatly improved their running track, fenced in the ground, erected a clumsy grand stand roofed by an old tarpaulin, and in the fall of the same year, gave the first successful field meeting open to all comers. The success of this event put fresh courage in the drooping spirits of the struggling club and foreshadowed the grand possibilities that were open to it in the future. In these early years of its existence the club was greatly benefited by the untiring efforts of its worthy president, Wm. K. Soutter, and the faithful and meritorious services of Messrs. D. J. H. Willcox and H. W. J. Telfair.

The year 1879 passed off rather quietly, although three meetings were held, as well as some private club events. The 100 yards "Soutter" medal, and the 440 yards "Sacks" medal being then on the programme for club members. The first competition for these medals took place in 1878, at the Fall Meeting, and early in the Spring of '79 members were in training to win the handsome trophies. First

De Garmendia and Rimmer won them respectively in 10 2-5 and 56¼ seconds, while later on the former went through the hands of Roberts three times, Beers once, Janssen three times, Fiske once, Morris once, and Rimmer five times, who finally retained the prize. The fastest races were the first and last, 10 2-5 and 10½ seconds by De Garmendia and Rimmer, while the "Sacks" medal was given up by Rimmer to Janssen, who walked over, but afterwards defeated Price, Telfair, Fiske, Morris and Stursberg, running twice in 55¾ seconds. Mr. Telfair also won this medal twice before it became Janssen's personal property.

It will be seen, therefore, that the athletic interests of the North Shore centred in three principal organizations, viz., the Neptune and Hesper Rowing Clubs, and the Staten Island Athletic Club, and most of the participants in any pastime, whether aquatic or field, belonged to two if not to all three of these associations, and paid dues to all such as they

S. I. A. C. CLUB-HOUSE.

Old Boat House

INTERIOR OF PRESENT BOAT-HOUSE.

belonged. It was more than natural, therefore, that many of those who desired to enjoy both field and water sports thought it would be advantageous both to the interests of the existing clubs and of individuals who composed them, to consolidate their forces. The first attempt towards amalgamation was tried between the Hesper and Neptune Rowing Clubs, neither at this time being in such a flourishing condition as they had been, and each falling more and more into decay as the interests of the members leaned towards the rising Athletic Club. But neither of these old time rivals would listen for a moment of merging their identity in the other, until at length a happy idea occurred to the wiser heads that both should affiliate with the Athletic Club, and that the Athletic Club should incorporate rowing as a prominent department in the new organization which would thus be formed. This consolidation was finally effected and all members

of good standing in the Hesper and Neptune Boat Clubs were admitted to membership in the Athletic Club ; the dues being fixed at ten dollars initiation fee, and twelve dollars a year for all. These amounts obtain to the present time.

The new life thus engendered bore rapid fruit. The track on Bement Avenue was much improved and the grand stand was made a permanent and serviceable structure, while underneath were arranged dressing-rooms and lockers for competitors, and comfortable lavatory accommodations were provided.

THE HISTORY OF THE OLD BOAT-HOUSE.

In the meanwhile the largely increased rowing fraternity had to be provided with a suitable boat-house and other facilities to carry on the sport. It was decided to build a new house of two stories, but a great difficulty was met in the fact that a suitable water front was not to be got. True, the Sailors' Snug Harbor authorities consented to the erection of a house on their frontage, but they restricted the building to one story. After a great deal of pains Mr. D. J. H. Willcox procured a site at the foot of Franklin Avenue, New Brighton, and very soon the members possessed a very neat and picturesque two-story structure of Queen Anne architecture with ample accommodations for boats, lockers, shower-baths, and every other requisite. The only fault that could be found with it being that it was farther from the field than desirable.

Up to this time the club was strictly athletic, that is to say, it devoted itself almost exclusively to the events of the cinder path, running, jumping and hurdle racing, and had not as yet taken up lawn tennis and baseball to any degree; but as the constantly increasing membership brought wider interests into prominence, these new departments were willingly set going by the directors, and in 1881 we find that baseball and tennis began to be taken up very generally, and the club also showed an inclination to cultivate lacrosse, as was evidenced by their sending a team to Waverley, N. J.

When, in 1879, the New York Athletic Club handed over the management of the Annual Meetings for the Amateur Championships into the hands of the National Association of Amateur Athletes of America, an organization called into existence for the purpose of carrying on the good work that the New York Athletic Club had so nobly begun, the Staten Island Athletic Club not only was one of the first to join the Association, but was of sufficient strength and importance to merit the choice of its captain, Mr. O. T. Johnson, as the Vice-President.

In the years 1880 and '81 the club colors, the famous orange and black, were carried victoriously to the front in all parts of the country. The athletes who thus gained glory for the club were Messrs. Janssen and Rimmer, while such men as W. C. Rowland, W. G. Dedrichsen, C. A. White, R. T. Fiske, John Edwards and H. Telfair upheld the fair fame of the club upon the water.

To furnish the interior of the boat-house it was proposed to hold a mammoth fair, and Messrs. Janssen, Rowland, Carroll and Davis undertook the arduous duties of managers. The lady friends of the club entered most enthusiastically into the scheme, and the fair was held on December 12th, 1881, and proved an unprecedented success, the net profits of the undertaking aggregating $975. A large portion of this sum was expended in fitting up the upper story of the boat-house. Some idea of the progress and improvements in the condition of the club at this time may be gathered from the fact that at the completion of the house on Franklin Avenue, the property was valued at thirteen thousand dollars, and the shells, boats and barges of the organization consisted of one eight-oared shell, four four-oared shells (racing), four four-oared barges, three pair-oared shells, two pair-oared gigs and twenty sculling shells, the property of private individuals.

THE BOARD OF MANAGEMENT AND REPRESENTATIVE GROUP S. I. A. C.

REMOVAL TO WEST NEW BRIGHTON.

But the boat-house was not destined to remain long at the foot of Franklin Avenue. It was rumored that the property on which the house stood had changed hands, and that the club would have to seek a new abiding place. A water front was always a most difficult thing to find, and the Directors were almost at their wits' end to know where to locate. It was most desirable that the next move should bring the boat-house nearer the ball ground and race-track, and good fortune seemed to come in the very nick of time. The President heard that the water front of the Campbell property was available, and this was at once secured. To remove such a bulky building was an arduous as well as a hazardous performance, but it was most happily accomplished without detriment to building or the precious boats that were stored within, although not a single thing was removed from the house during its transportation.

It was always the practice of the club from its inception almost, to hold two games at least in each year, the first in the spring and second in the fall, and a little while after the consolidation of the land and water interests of the North Shore the club also held an annual regatta. These regattas were the means of bringing together crews of the various rowing and boating clubs around the Kills, which were united into one common organization under the title of the "Kill von Kull Rowing Association." In the contests against Newark, Elizabethport, Bayonne and Argonanta Rowing Association the Club more than held its own.

During all these years by wise and careful management, and by a close attention to the various duties of their important trust, the officers of the club had kept the financial condition of the organization in a splendid status, and any extra strains upon the exchequer were met by the liberal efforts of individual members, and the hearty co-operation of the younger contingent in getting up minstrel shows and various entertainments of a remunerative kind.

THE CHARLESTON BLUES.

Among the minor combinations originated by this enterprising club must be mentioned the famous military organization of the Charleston Blues, who under the captaincy of W. C. Davis and his able lieutenant F. W. Janssen have ofttimes covered themselves with glory. They are uniformed in dark blue tunics with red facings, white cross-belts and white trousers, with a most imposing bearskin for a head covering. They are well drilled, and on parade look a fine soldierly set of young fellows.

THE CLUB'S BASEBALL HISTORY.

From the earliest days the club has had the reputation of possessing excellent material for forming a powerful baseball nine, and the national game was played in a desultory kind of way every season, but during the past five years the Staten Island Athletic Club Baseball Team has been recognized as one of the strongest leading amateur nines in the country. Among the first players may be mentioned the Janssen brothers, and Mr. Fiske, who founded and led to repeated victory the famous old Alpha Baseball Club, which during the years 1870 to 1877 was credited with more triumphs than any other amateur team in America. As the game increased in science and skill, so did the S. I. A. C. continue to capture many of the finest college exponents of the game, so that its nine always had the best of coaching, and with unremitting practice has continued to hold the lead it had successfully gained. The Club has been a member of the National Amateur Baseball Association since the birth of that organization, but the resignation of the Nassaus and Brooklyns of Brooklyn has virtually narrowed the Association to two Clubs—the Bergen Points and the S. I. A. C.—but it still plays against the representative nines of the country. The team never was stronger than it is to-day, and the club may well feel proud of its recent creditable performances. The leading players are James A. Tyng, a veteran pitcher of Harvard College whose wonderful dexterity in the "box" has led to his services being sought by some of the leading professional nines of the League. Besides his qualities as the best pitcher, he is a brilliant field anywhere, and a free and successful scorer with the bat. Finley and Larkin are sure and safe catchers, the former, I am told, being the best man to understand Tyng's peculiar eccentricities of curve. De Garmendia is a free hitter and reliable first baseman, while burly Arthur Cater does excellent work at right field, but can be put anywhere, being a quick and brilliant field and

THE S. I. A. C. BASEBALL NINE OF '87.

safe catch. Moore and Tyndale are excellent left and centre fields, and both may be counted on to get runs. Brush, Wyllis Terry, Shaw, Dick Halstead, and a host of others are active players, and the club can at any time turn out a couple of really representative teams.

The club has an excellent diamond and practice is indulged in every day in the week. Their principal rivals are the Bergen Points and the Young Americas, and the meeting of these teams invariably brings about a stubbornly contested game. The other teams against which the Athletic Club play with more certain hopes of victory are the baseball nine of the S. I. Cricket Club, the Newarks, the Columbia College, the various amateur clubs of Brooklyn, Jersey City and Philadelphia. In fact, from May till October, there is a match game on the card for almost every Wednesday and Saturday. Thus it will be seen that while the older and larger organization of the Staten Island Cricket Club confines itself principally to the maintenance of a high degree

of proficiency in the cricket and tennis field, the men at the Athletic Club go in for fame on the cinder path and are also more prominent with the oar and baseball. It may be well to mention just in this connection that the two clubs are now situated almost side by side, and though they are keen in their rivalry at baseball and tennis, yet the emulation is healthy and carried on in the most generous and manly spirit. Socially the two clubs fraternize most cordially and many of the men in each belong to both. There is ample room, so great the interest in all sporting matters, and so diversified the pastimes of the rising generation, for both clubs to flourish and grow yet larger, and future years will show how wrong and unfounded were the croakings of those who kept constantly saying that there was only room for one good club on Staten Island. I know that even in the two years the Cricket Club has been located at Livingston, it has already begun to show signs that more field space and more ample house accommodations must be found in the near future ; and it is exactly the same conditions at the Athletic Club, for no sooner have they got into their present elegant house than they are beginning to find that more room is needed, so rapidly is the membership increasing.

Nevertheless, it was undoubtedly the fact that at about the time the Rapid Transit Company were preparing to turn the Cricket Club out of their quarters at Camp Washington, there was a serious effort made to consolidate the two clubs. The proposed basis was that the Athletic Club should put in their field, track and boating plant and the Cricket Club should purchase the house and ground of the Campbell property. This proposition I give just as broadly as possible, because the actual details for amalgamation were never entered into. The first overture, I believe, came from an authorized member of the Cricket Club and the same club were the ones to withdraw from the negotiations without giving any reasons for so doing. The original basis for joining forces was about as fair a one as could have been made. The Athletic Club valued the ball field, with running track and grand stand, etc., at about $12,000 and their boat-house and boats at $13,000, and this was certainly a very fair as well as a moderate valuation, and the Campbell property was thought to be obtainable for $25,000. But there the matter ended.

THE PURCHASE OF THE CLUB-HOUSE.

It has always been the maxim of the Athletic Club, first to feel that certain things are needed for the welfare and prosperity of the club, and then to set to work, with every shoulder at the wheel, and the thing is put through. So it was with the purchase of the Campbell property. Once the idea of owning the house entered their minds, they were bound to have it.

Mr. John W. Edwards first ascertained that the property could not be had for $25,000, as the owners were asking $30,000; he then, I believe, made an offer of $26,000, though what amount was finally paid I am not able to state positively. This was indeed a bold measure to take, and the management might well have had grave doubts of the club being able to carry so great an' amount, but Mr. Eberhard Faber, a warm friend to the boys, and an enthusiastic lover of all sports, stood behind to help in case of need, and the club hold to this day a deep sense of their indebtedness to Mr. Faber, and would be ready at any moment to testify their appreciation of such generous conduct, by electing him to the highest office in their power to bestow, but Mr. Faber, secure in their goodwill, finds that he has all he can manage in attending to his important business engagements.

This purchase was completed in 1885, and the money was subscribed for in $10

THE S. I. A. C. DIAMOND AND GRAND STAND.

scrip payable in five years, and bearing interest at 6 per cent. How the membership of some 200 was to bear all these extra expenses was met with the energetic answer that every man must bring a friend into the club ranks, and so well did the President know the mettle of his men, that it did not cause him any surprise to find that on the same evening on which the purchase was concluded, fifty new names were on the books waiting election.

the early morning of Tuesday, October the 5th of last year. Two tugs with a number of heavily laden coal barges in tow were coming down the Kills, and before they were aware of the strength of the current setting towards the Staten Island shore, the tow had drifted into the boat-house, and torn the building from the piles and was dragging it towards St. George's Ferry, where the unfortunate structure was carelessly beached. The tide soon floated it again, and smashed

S. I. A. C. BOAT-HOUSE.

And so the good cause advanced, and by the time the boys were able to get once again onto the grounds in the following spring, there were 450 "brave men and true" that donned the "orange and black." This year learn the number is between nine hundred and a thousand, and the slogan is, "still they come."

THE DESTRUCTION OF THE BOAT-HOUSE.

The first, and I am glad to say, the only serious calamity that ever befell the club, was the total destruction of their beautiful boat-house. This occurred in

it entirely to pieces, by driving it against the jetty.

The house and every boat that it contained, including also the furniture and piano in the upper story, was completely demolished. The Pennsylvania Railroad was responsible for the disaster, and they and the company in which the house and fixtures were insured, made good the pecuniary loss, I believe; but in spite all such solid consolation, the accident was a terrible blow to the club, handicapped as it was with the expenses of improvements then in progress on their lately purchased property. However, their energy and indomitable pluck was equal to even this severe trial, and hardly had the news of the loss spread among the members, than the board of management had new plans to rebuild on a more extensive and elaborate scale, ready to lay before the members. The work was commenced at once, and last summer saw them comfortably installed in the handsomest boat house that exists in the country to-day.

fought struggle. Handsome cups and other trophies ornament the mantel-shelves. Pictures of most of the famous athletes in all the pride of their "war paint," surround you on all sides. A fine piano stands ready for use, and not a few of the boys can touch the notes with a practiced hand. Beyond, through an archway, is a smaller room, in which there is an excellent pool table. On the right of the hall are the dining-rooms,

THE LANDING STAGE S. I. A. C. BOAT-HOUSE.

THE CLUB-HOUSE.

The house is situated on Richmond Terrace, a couple of hundred yards to the west of the Livingston Rapid Transit Station, and is built on a little knoll rising gently from the road. On entering the hall a broad stairway faces you, leading to the bed-rooms and private dining-rooms, which are on the upper story. On the left hand on the ground floor is the great reception-room, a fine rectangular chamber, with bow windows. The walls are prettily festooned with flags won by the victorious crews in many a hard

capable of seating fifty to sixty of the members at a time. There are verandas on two sides, and, during the warm summer evenings, it is pleasant to dine outside, while the silvery moonbeams dance and shimmer through the whispering leaves of the surrounding trees. Beyond, through the hallway, is the bar, and in rear of that is the kitchen and the other offices. The meals are all that a hungry athlete could wish for, and the cooking and attendance excellent. If you want a more elaborate spread and the uninterrupted companionship of a few kindred spirits, there are the private dining-rooms

RECEPTION ROOM.—S. I. A. C.

up-stairs. There are ten or twelve large and airy bed-rooms on the upper story, where the belated loiterer and transient guest find comfortable quarters. In rear of the house the first of the fields you come to is the tennis courts. At present but seventeen nets can be spread, but this portion of the ground has been the last to receive attention, and is not yet put in perfect condition. Nets are up all day long, and you can play to your heart's content without fear of interruption from the ball players, whose field is divided from the tennis courts by the grand stands.

As yet there seems to be no inclination to ingraft a ladies' club onto the sturdy bachelor-stem, but the fair sex are always sure of a gallant and most cordial welcome. When relatives of members or ladies introduced by them are present, they are privileged to the use of the nets, and it is seldom that one walks along the courts without seeing half a dozen pretty girls hard at work with the racquet.

THE BASEBALL FIELD AND RUNNING TRACK.

The baseball field is a magnificent rectangular piece of beautifully green and level turf, round which a twenty-yard-wide running track is laid. The baseball field proper is about 420 feet square, but the board fence which surrounds the inclosure takes in about 500 feet every way. Along the north side are erected the grand stands—for there are two—one covered and the other not. The covered stand is for ladies and their escorts and members who will forego the luxury of tobacco while seated there, and has a seating capacity of about 550. The other stand is simply a succession of seats rising tier above tier and seats 400. The home plate is directly below the ladies' stand and the batter faces south-east. The public entrance is on Bement Avenue. The club makes a small charge of twenty-five cents admission to all their games of baseball. There is also a charge to the public for entrance to the athletic competitions, which varies according to the importance of the meeting. The money thus collected goes into the general club funds.

Beneath the ladies' stand are the dressing-rooms and lockers, and, also, shower-baths and lavatory.

THE BOAT-HOUSE

is immediately across the road from the house and is reached by a bridge crossing the Rapid Transit Railroad. It is a very picturesque and commodious two-story wooden building, with a spacious room on the top story, surrounded by broad verandas, from which the whole of the regatta course, as well as a charming view of the surrounding country, can be had. The lower story is fitted up with racks for the boats, oars and other paraphernalia, and there are also dressing-lockers, shower-baths of fresh and salt water, and every toilet convenience.

MANAGEMENT.

The interests and management of the club is in the hands of fifteen members, who form the Board of Direction. All the officers of the club are elective, but the President appoints all committees. The best praise that can be given to the wise and prudent counsels of those hard-working, self-sacrificing individuals who have guided the club into this, its noontide of prosperity, is simply to point to the gigantic results that have been achieved.

THE DECENNIAL CELEBRATION.

The crowning effort and most glorious exploit yet achieved by the club, was the successful carrying out of the jubilee celebration of the decennial games, last "Labor Day," Monday, Sept. 5th. During the . day, upwards of ten thousand spectators were present, and thoroughly enjoyed the day's programme, which included a magnificent exhibition of lacrosse, between the New York Lacrosse Club and the Niagaras, won by the former; a very fine game of baseball, between the home team, and their most persistent rivals, the Young Americas of Philadelphia, in which the visitors were victorious ; a splendid tennis tournament, athletic games of all kinds, a bicycle race, won easily by Mr. Rich, the representative wheelman of the club, an eight-oared shell race on the Kills, in which the laurels were gained by the Potomacs of Washington ; the whole winding up with a lively dance and grand display of fireworks.

YACHTING DEPARTMENT.

The latest addition to the Club's numerous interests is the establishment of a yachting department. Formal and definite action was taken last spring and resulted in the election of Mr. J. Eberhard Faber, as Commodore ; Mr. K. K. McMurray, Vice-Commodore ; Mr. A. L. Faris, Secretary, and Dr. A. L. Carroll, Fleet Surgeon. The fleet already numbers 25 or 30 sail, mostly catboats from 18 to 27 feet in length, with a good sprinkling of canoes and open sailing craft. Although not positively registered on the Club roll of yachts, the Athletic Club is proud of claiming Mr. Morgan of the *Mayflower*, and Mr. Chapman of the *Rambler*, as members. The Club has a capital anchorage, and the boat-house affords a jolly rendezvous for the boats, and I feel sure that the yachting element in the Club will flourish just as strongly as the other pastimes that have existed for longer periods.

The S. I. A. C. to-day is one of the finest in the country, in first rate financial standing, where the visiting athlete will be sure of a cordial welcome, and where he will meet as jolly a lot of enthusiastic sportsmen as can be found anywhere on the globe.

Quaint Shops in New York (1909)

OFFICE
31 JOSEPH NONAN IRON WORKS 31

QUAINT SHOPS
IN
NEW YORK.

PICTURES BY   OTTO H · BACHER ·

Drawn by Otto H. Bacher

Half-tone plate engraved by H. C. Merrill

AN OLD CLOCK SHOP

Drawn by Otto H. Bacher   Half-tone plate engraved by H. C. Merrill

A LITTLE DELFTWARE SHOP

Drawn by Otto H. Bacher   Half-tone plate engraved by H. C. Merrill

AN ANTIQUE COPPER SHOP

The Story of the
New York Yacht Club
(1901)

THE STORY OF THE NEW YORK YACHT CLUB

By A. J. Kenealy

JOHN C. STEVENS,
THE FOUNDER OF THE CLUB.

FOR more than fifty years the first home of the New York Yacht Club was a landmark of rare historic interest to yachtsmen. It occupied, when first built in 1845, a conspicuous place on the New Jersey shore of the Hudson, with the lovely Elysian Fields of Hoboken at its back, and it was the cradle of a sturdy infant sport destined to grow to gigantic dimensions. Hoboken was rural and sylvan in those days. Picturesque farmhouses of Dutch and German types dotted the green meadows, watered by purling brooks, and no prettier spot could have been chosen for a yacht club.

The devotees of the sport were then few, racing was confined to matches for a modest stake or wager and these were rare. The few pleasure craft in existence hailed from New York and Boston. One of these, the schooner *Gimcrack*, was owned by John C. Stevens, the father of American yachting, and the first commodore of the Club. This gentleman had boated from his boyhood. The first craft he owned was built by himself in 1802, and was christened *Diver*. She was nine feet long, three feet deep and three feet wide. The *Maria*, his last and most famous craft, for many years flagship of the Club, flew her pennant one hundred and fifty feet above sea level.

Mr. Stevens was the first to realize that the sport of yachting needed organization. He consulted with his friends and won them over to his opinion that the time was ripe for an American yacht club. The failure of the Boston (so called) Yacht Club, which had been founded in 1835, with Captain R. B. Forbes as commodore, but had only lasted two years, did not appear to be a case in point, for the Boston club had for flagship and fleet the schooner *Dream*, of twenty-eight tons custom house measurement, and its chief pleasure was fishing. It exercised no influence on yacht building, cruising or racing. It was only a

CUP WON BY CYGNET IN FIRST REGATTA
OF N. Y. Y. C., JULY 17, 1845.

yacht club in name, composed of members who loved to sail in pleasant weather and indulge in old-fashioned chowder and card parties. The club went quietly out of existence in 1837, a year of commercial panic.

Mr. Stevens on July 30, 1844, called a pointed: John C. Stevens, George L. Schuyler, John C. Jay, Hamilton Wilkes, Captain Rogers. On motion it was resolved that the club make a cruize to Newport, Rhode Island, under command of the Commodore. The following yachts were represented at this meeting: *Gimcrack*, John C. Stevens; *Spray*, Hamilton Wilkes; *Cygnet*, William Edgar; *La Coquille*, John C. Jay; *Dream*, George L. Schuyler;

THE FIRST CLUB-HOUSE—ELYSIAN FIELDS, HOBOKEN, N. J., 1845.

meeting of yachtsmen, which assembled aboard his schooner *Gimcrack*, anchored off the Battery, New York. Nine yacht owners responded. What happened on that occasion I transcribe from a treasured document in the archives of the Club.

" Minutes of the New York Yacht Club on board of the *Gimcrack* off the Battery July 30, 1844, 5 p. m. According to previous notice the following gentlemen assembled for the purpose of organizing a yacht club, viz.: John C. Stevens, Hamilton Wilkes, William Edgar, John C. Jay, George L. Schuyler, Louis A. Depaw, George B. Rollins, James M. Waterbury, James Rogers.

"On motion it was resolved to form a yacht club. On motion it was resolved that the title of the club be the New York Yacht Club. On motion it was resolved that the gentlemen present be the original members of the club. On motion it was resolved that John C. Stevens be the Commodore of the club. On motion it was resolved that a committee of five be appointed by the Commodore to report rules and regulations for the government of the club. The following gentlemen were ap-

Mist, Louis A. Depaw; *Minna*, James M. Waterbury; *Petrel*, George B. Rollins; *Ida*, Captain Rogers. After appointing Friday, August 2, at 9 a. m., the time for sailing on the cruize the meeting adjourned."

In this business-like manner the keel of the Club was laid. Next day the little fleet started on the first squadron cruise ever sailed in the United States, touching at Huntington, New Haven, Gardiner's Bay and Oyster Pond, known now as Orient Point, and reaching Newport on August 5th, where they were joined by ex-commodore Forbes, of the defunct Boston Club, Col. W. P. Winchester, of the schooner *Northern Light*, and David J. Sears, all of Boston. These were the first Bostonians that were elected to membership. This cruise was the forerunner of many others. Newport, at that time a mere fishing village, from its splendid harbor was naturally appreciated by seafaring men, but that it would in time become the

MODEL ROOM OF THE FIRST CLUB-HOUSE.

yachting center of the country, probably never occurred to the owners of the little fleet that anchored there in 1844.

In the light of subsequent events it is interesting to note that the flagship *Gimcrack* was a tubby craft of twenty-five tons custom house measurement, and that the united tonnage of the whole fleet was less than two hundred and fifty. *Gimcrack* in spite of her apple bows and her cockle-shell dimensions will always be famous as the prototype of the modern fin keel, for she was fitted with a fixed fin of heavy plate iron, four feet deep and fifteen feet long—lacking only the bulb of lead at the base to make it a twentieth century device.

The first election of officers took place at Windhorst's, New York, on March 17, 1845. John C. Stevens was chosen Commodore; Hamilton Wilkes, Vice-Commo-

SECOND CLUB-HOUSE—ROSEBANK, STATEN ISLAND, 1865.

dore; John C. Jay, Recording Secretary; George B. Rollins, Corresponding Secretary; and William Edgar, Treasurer.

The first club-house was built by the brink of the Hudson, on ground the use of which was given by Commodore Stevens, who also paid the builder's bill. Modest and unpretentious, it was opened in 1845, and from the anchorage off the club-house the first regatta was started on July 17 of that year. So far as I can discover after a good deal of research it was the first yacht race worthy of the name held in the United States. It was an event so unique that according to the newspapers of that time a crowd of many thousands

Schooners also set a single headsail, a gaff-foresail and mainsail and a small main gaff-topsail. Foretopmasts were rare at that date. Sometimes when the wind was dead aft or on the quarter, a squaresail of modest expanse was bent to a yard and set flying. Spinnakers and club-topsails were of a later growth. But the nine boats made the best of the brisk sou'wester and the strong young ebb. They sailed a gallant race, rounded the Southwest Spit and homeward ran, the schooner *Cygnet*, owned by William Edgar, winning the cup and gaining the plaudits of the people who had lingered in the Elysian Fields to see the victorious yacht sail home.

In this unpretentious manner the sport of

THIRD CLUB-HOUSE—STAPLETON, STATEN ISLAND, 1875. (NOW ON GLEN ISLAND.)

flocked to the Elysian Fields to see the start. There were nine competitors, the prize being a silver cup, which cost $45, the amount being made up from the entrance fees of $5 per boat.

At a signal from the club-house anchors were hove up aboard the contesting craft, sails were hoisted and amid cheers from the populace, the yachts started for the Southwest Spit, the outward boundary of their course.

In those primitive days no "ballooners" bothered the crews, and the era of professional jockeying was happily unknown. Sloops carried one headsail only—a jib with a bonnet in it. The after canvas consisted of a mainsail of moderate dimensions, and a jib-headed gaff-topsail set on a stumpy spar.

yacht racing was introduced to the inhabitants of the island of Manhattan and their neighbors in New Jersey. The growth of the glorious pastime has since been concurrent with the progress and prosperity of the Club.

Its founders and early members loved the sport for the enjoyment and pleasure it yielded. There was no society end to yachting in the youthful times I write of. People of fashion took no interest in either racing or cruising. Commodore Stevens and his clubmates generally were seamen and navigators. They handled their own craft in sailorly style. As a proof of this I cite a regatta held by the club on October 6, 1846, in which the competing yachts were manned by club members solely, the regular crews being left ashore. This was the first Corinthian yacht race sailed in America, and the prize was a cup subscribed for by the club. The starters were the sloops *Maria*, J. C. Stevens, and *Lancet*, G. B. Rollins; the schooners *Siren*, W. E. Miller; *Cygnet*, D. L. Suydam; *Spray*, H. Wilkes, and *La Coquille*, John C. Jay. The course was from the flag-ship *Gimcrack*, anchored off the club-house, thence to a stake-boat off Fort Washington Point, thence to another stake-boat in the

THE RECENT CLUB-HOUSE, MADISON AVE., N. Y.

Narrows, and back to the starting point, the whole distance being forty miles. The time allowance was twenty-five seconds per custom house ton. The wind was strong from south-west. *Maria* won with ease, beating the schooner *Siren* (the second boat) by fifty-eight minutes and fifteen seconds actual time.

The sloop *Maria* is famous among yachts-men all over the world. As the second flag-

ship of the club she is part of its history. She had as much influence on yachting in this country as the schooner *America* exerted on the yacht builders and sailmakers of Great Britain, which was vast. She came into existence in the following manner: The crack North River sloop in 1844 was *Eliza Ann*, whose skipper's veins were full of sporting blood. When he learned that the fleet of the newly formed club was going on a pleasure jaunt to Newport he decided to go also, and show them how fast a North River sloop could sail. Without going into particulars, it is sufficient to say that the *Eliza Ann* beat every yacht with much ease in each daily run from port to port. Commodore Stevens was impressed by her speed. At his request the Commodore's brother, Mr. Robert Livingstone Stevens, took off the lines of *Eliza Ann* and improving upon them, designed *Maria*, which was built in the same year by Mr. William Capes, of Hoboken. On her maiden sail she nearly capsized in a squall off the Stevens Castle. A ferry-boat steamed to her rescue and towed her to her dock, where her redundant rig was reduced and her monstrous wings were clipped. After that she beat every craft she sailed against, including steam vessels.

Maria will ever be remembered as the yacht whose owner originated many devices which at the present time masquerade as modern. Even as *Gimcrack* possessed the germ of the fin keel, so was *Maria* the mother of outside lead, the weighted centerboard and hollow spars. When Commodore Stevens formed the syndicate which built the schooner-yacht *America*, as an exhibit from this country to the World's Fair held in England in 1851, Mr. Robert Steers, her designer and builder, agreed to charge nothing for her if she did not defeat *Maria*. The reverse happened. *Maria* actually sailed round the *America* many times. The syndicate absolved Steers from his compact and paid him in full. But so disappointed were the members with the performance of *Amer-*

ica that they almost decided to send *Maria* to England in her stead. A certain notable experience of the big sloop in a nasty sea and a northeast gale, when she met with her only defeat in a race against the schooner *Coquette*, a much smaller vessel, demonstrated that she was not adapted for blue water work. So *America* crossed the Atlantic, being the first American yacht to sail over the western ocean. She won the cup which has made her name renowned among all maritime racers.

It is not generally known that the first international race between America and England was sailed in 1849. Particulars are lacking. Only the bare record remains that the Yankee keel schooner *Brenda*, flying the burgee of the New York Yacht Club, sailed against the Marquis of Anglesey's famous cutter *Pearl*, beating her by fifty-five seconds. The length of the course is not given. *Pearl* was the first yacht with the distinctive cutter rig. She was built at Wivenhoe in 1820, and was for a long time the fastest yacht in Great Britain.

The Club in its second year had 122 members, but only ten yachts in its squadron. The building of a pleasure craft in those days was quite a serious undertaking, not because of the cost, which was far less then than now, but for some other reasons which cannot easily be explained. Perhaps because yachts were considered too luxurious for the simple tastes of our forefathers. It may be concluded that the victorious visit to England of *America* had not been without a certain amount of fruition, for we find that in 1853 the membership had increased to 153 and the fleet to fourteen. Commodore Stevens remained in command of the Club until 1855, when

failing health compelled him to retire. An enthusiastic yachtsman, a generous gentleman, liberal, opulent and popular, he established the sport on an enduring basis. He suggested the visit of *America* to England, defraying the lion's share of the expenses.

THE NEW HOME, WEST FOURTY-FOURTH STREET, N. Y.

While there he tried to induce British yachtsmen to engage in other races with his schooner but the way the Yankee terror flew away from their fleetest yachts in the ever memorable race for the Royal Yacht Squadron Cup, scared off the faint-hearted English.

Commodore Stevens spent at least $100,000 —a vast sum in those days—in building *Maria* and in subsequent alterations. In every possible manner he showed his devotion to the sport. Yachtsmen mourned sincerely when he died at the age of seventy-two at his home in Hoboken in June, 1857.

The third international yacht race between America and England was held in 1852. Mr. Robert M. Grinnell, of the New York Yacht Club, commissioned Bob Fish to build him

STAIRCASE AT THE ENTRANCE.

the twenty-one-foot centerboard sloop *Truant*. The craft proved fast. She was taken to England on the deck of the *New World*. She raced against yachts double her size, winning handily seven races out of eight—four times on the Mersey, once at Kingstown, and twice on the Thames. Her only defeat was on Lake Windermere, when she lost by six seconds. In the following year the English made a rule that centerboard yachts should sail by themselves. As *Truant* was the only yacht of that type in Great Britain, her racing career was thus brought to a sudden close. The war on centerboard yachts was waged with great bitterness in England until 1893, when Lieutenant Henn induced the Yacht Racing Association to abolish all restrictions on centerboards, thus making possible the racing in British waters of Mr. Royal Phelps Carroll's *Navahoe* and Mr. George Gould's *Vigilant*.

For many years the house in the Elysian Fields was the headquarters of the Club. From its porch many exciting finishes were seen. In the model room the members met, and smoked, and spun rare yarns. There was no club uniform, no pipe clay and no red tape. There was however, a sturdy and admirable simplicity, an exact sense of honor among the old salts in every way commendable. When the war broke out in 1861, the Club had 488 members, and a fleet of 75 schooners and 22 sloops. In that year the annual regatta and cruise were omitted. The Club met with its first reverses during the years of the war. Its membership dwindled and its fleet decreased. In 1865 the Club was incorporated. Hoboken began to hum with industry. Its natural attractions were marred by the encroachments of commerce. In 1868 the Club abandoned its home in New Jersey and leased a villa on Staten Island, near Fort Wadsworth. Its fleet then numbered 42 boats and the members were 278. The old house was occupied later by the New Jersey Yacht Club. Subsequently the New York Yacht Club occupied another house at Stapleton, Staten Island. In 1871 city quarters were taken at the corner of Twenty-seventh street and Madison avenue, the Club having on its roll 452 members, 37 schooners, 14 sloops and 8 steamers.

It is violating no confidence to mention that the Club had its share of adversity and in fact that its very existence was imperilled in 1877, for lack of money. Things were so bad that the Club resolved to give up its New York quarters and its Staten Island home, meanwhile storing its models and other property until times improved. Happily this course was not necessary. Some rich men stepped into the breach and saved the day. Ever since then prosperity has attended the organization. In 1884 the Club moved into No. 67 Madison avenue, with 309 members and a fleet of 108 yachts. This was its home until 1901. Here its triumphs over Sir Richard Sutton, Lieut. William Henn, Vice Commodore Bell and Lord Dunraven were celebrated. On the occasion of its semi-centennial, in 1894, it dawned upon the Club that its quarters were too cramped for comfort. At every meeting new members were elected and when special functions were held the house was crowded so that there was standing room only. At that time there were 1,038 members and its squadron consisted of 85 schooners, 84 single stickers and yawls, 122 steam yachts and 12 steam launches. A larger house was imperative, but the Club is conservative and deliberates before it acts.

The present magnificent house in which the Club begins its second century is on West Forty-fourth street, between Fifth and Sixth avenues. It is in startling contrast to the first club house, which was demolished last year. The land on which the present building stands was a gift to the Club from ex-Commodore J. Pierpont Morgan. The members subscribed liberally to the building fund and the result is a mansion in every way worthy of the Club. In the style of the modern Renaissance of the French school it is simple, substantial

and handsome. The employment of Indiana limestone with artistic carving gives a massive appearance to the exterior. The three windows in the second story modelled after the sterns of Spanish galleons, afford the requisite nautical flavor.

The interior is superb in every way, combining all the luxuries and conveniences of this sybarite age. Two apartments are striking, the model room and the grill room. The first is a lofty room

FIREPLACE IN MODEL ROOM.

of noble space on the second floor, finished in carved oak, elaborated with representations of sea monsters. The grand marble fireplace is a work of art. The mantel weighs forty-five tons. A fine gallery runs round the north, east and west sides. And on the walls of this room is displayed the most notable collection of yacht models in the world. Some of the whole models, fully rigged, of yachts that have added luster to the Club, are in glass cases and stand in alcoves. The display shows the progressive growth of the American and the British yacht. The arrangement so far as possible is chronological in order that an intelligent study of yacht evolution may be easy. The models of *Maria* and *America* have a commanding place as well as those of *Julia*, *Rebecca* and other famous old craft.

Historic ocean races conducted under the flag of the Club are recalled by models of the schooner *Dauntless*, which when owned by James Gordon Bennett was beaten by Mr. James Ashbury's schooner

yacht-naval architecture. The models of the modern school, beginning with that epoch-making yacht *Minerva* and the equally remarkable *Puritan*, supplemented by *Gloriana*, *Vigilant*, *Defender* and *Columbia* complete the story.

With regard to steam yachts the collection is not so rich. The first steamer that flew the Club's burgee was the paddle wheel steamer *North Star*, owned by Cornelius Vanderbilt; a yacht only by courtesy. It is only within the last twenty years that steam yachts have been popular in this country, although as a matter of history the first steam yacht races held

THE GRILL.

Cambria in a race from Ireland to New York, by one hour and seventeen minutes; by models of the three schooners *Henrietta*, *Vesta* and *Fleetwing* which faced the boisterous Atlantic in midwinter, in 1866, for a purse of $90,000, which *Henrietta* won. Another great ocean contest is recalled by a model of the schooner *Coronet*, owned by Mr. Bush, which beat *Dauntless*, owned by Commodore Colt, in a race across the Atlantic, sailed in March, 1887. The model room is impressive when it deals with the glorious past. It is a neverending source of joy to the student of

in this country were managed by the Club in 1875. On the roll of the Club to-day are the largest and most magnificent steam yachts in existence. The cruising schooner on which the Club once prided itself has given way to steam. Sails are too slow for the rapid life of the twentieth century. A wise provision of the Club which makes it compulsory for a person entering a yacht in a Club race to furnish a model of the craft insures the growth of the model collection.

The grill room is built after the fashion of an old wooden ship, with beams and

EX-COMMODORE J. PIERPONT MORGAN.

drubbing, Captain Cuthbert threatened to challenge again with her the following year.

The Club on December 15, 1882, resolved to return *America's* Cup to Mr. George L. Schuyler, the only survivor of the winners of the trophy. Mr. Schuyler embodied some new conditions in another deed of gift, the principal one being a clause forbidding a defeated vessel to compete again for the cup until two years have elapsed. Thus Captain Cuthbert was headed off, and the real object of the new deed of gift was attained.

The New York Yacht Club up to 1885 had assumed the duty of defending *America's* Cup against all comers. In that year, Sir Richard Sutton challenged with the cutter *Genesta*, and the Eastern Yacht Club interested itself in the contest. Mr. Edward Burgess, of Boston, was a young ambitious naval architect with original ideas. His yachts, all of moderate size, had proved highly successful. The Eastern Yacht Club determined to be represented in the trial races. Accordingly, Mr. J. Malcolm Forbes and some of his friends, commissioned Mr. Burgess to design *Puritan*, and this he did with rare skill and judgment. To the generous beam and centerboard of the American

knees. It is plainly furnished in oak and is of the sea salty.

The library, though not large, is rich in the literature of the sport. It is added to continually. Rare old prints, engravings, lithographs, portraits in oil and yachting scenes in water colors, as well as modern photographs adorn the walls in artistic profusion.

The most precious treasure owned by the Club is the cup won by *America* sailing against a fleet of fifteen in the regatta of the Royal Yacht Squadron round the Isle of Wight on August 22, 1851. The trophy was presented to the Club by Messrs. J. C. Stevens, George L. Schuyler and Hamilton Wilkes on July 20, 1857, to be held as a perpetual challenge cup for friendly competition between foreign countries. The principal proviso was that the cup should always remain in the custody of the Club winning it, and not become the property of the members or yacht owners.

The Club accepted the trust, and subsequently assumed the control of the races sailed for it by Mr. James Ashbury's schooners, *Cambria* and *Livonia* in 1870 and 1871, and also in the Canadian challenge by Major Charles Gifford's schooner *Countess of Dufferin* in 1876, and Captain Cuthbert's challenge with the sloop *Atalanta* in 1881.

The *Atalanta* was a very inferior craft. She was signally defeated. In spite of this

CUP PRESENTED BY THE CLUB
TO MR. MORGAN.

type he added the outside lead of the British and also the cutter rig. So artfully did he combine these powerful factors that *Puritan* proved vastly superior to the New York boats in the trial races, and was chosen to defend the Cup, which she did quite handily defeating *Genesta*.

When Lieutenant Henn challenged in 1886 with *Galatea*, General Charles J. Paine, of Boston, commissioned Mr. Burgess to design *Mayflower* to beat *Puritan*. The result was that *Mayflower* did beat *Puritan*, and also *Galatea*. In 1887, Vice-Commodore Bell challenged with *Thistle*, and was beaten

ler, the sole surviving owner of the Cup, and he once more transferred it to the Club.

Divested of legal verbiage, the deed of trust conveys *America's* Cup from George L. Schuyler to the New York Yacht Club in trust as a perpetual international challenge cup to be sailed for by yacht clubs having an ocean course. Competing yachts, if of one mast, shall be not less than 65 feet nor more than 90 feet load water line; if of more than one mast, not less than 80 feet nor more than 115 feet load water line. Ten months' notice must be given by the challenging club, as well as the name, rig and following dimen-

SOME CLUB TROPHIES.

by General Paine's *Volunteer*, another Burgess centerboard.

Owing to the water line length of *Thistle* being found to be several inches in excess of the figures given by Mr. Watson, her designer, the New York Yacht Club decided that still another deed of trust was necessary to guard against a similar error in the future. Mr. John H. Bird, who was at that time secretary of the Club, accordingly drew up a legal document known as the "Deed of Trust, 1887." By this the Club again returned the trophy to Mr. George L. Schuy-

sions: length on load water line, extreme beam and draught of water, which dimensions shall not be exceeded. Challengers must cross the ocean under sail on their own bottoms. No restriction on sliding keels or centerboards.

As soon as the provisions of the new deed were published, a storm of hostile criticism burst from the British press. Complaints of "sea-lawyerism" and "sharp practise" were plentiful. The reason for the wrath evoked was the dimension clause, which was supposed to give too much advantage to

EDWARD M. BROWN.

E. D. MORGAN.

ELBRIDGE T. GERRY.

SOME EX-COMMODORES.

the club defending the trophy. Lord Dunraven was especially bitter in his denunciations. So much so that his first challenge in 1889 was recalled. The New York Yacht Club pointed out the following clause in the deed of trust: "The club challenging for the Cup and the club holding the same, may by mutual consent make any arrangement satisfactory to both as to the dates, courses, number of trials, rules, and sailing regulations, and any and all other conditions of the match in which case also, the ten months' notice may be waived."

This provision seems to be broad and fair to an unprejudiced person. Lord Dunraven was induced to alter his views. The Club agreed to accept the length on the load water line, as the only dimension required and on that basis Lord Dunraven challenged again and yet again, and was beaten twice. Under the mutual agreement clause, Sir Thomas Lipton's challenges were ar-

ranged, and yachtsmen generally admit that under the deed of trust, in spite of its reading like a mortgage, a perfectly fair and sportsmanlike match can be made.

It is certain that the keen international rivalry for the possession of the Cup has been of boundless benefit to yachting. The schooner *America* opened the eyes of the English, and wrought a revolution in the hulls and the canvas of their racing yachts. Enemies of the great ninety-foot sloops decry them because of their immense cost and their utter worthlessness after their racing careers are finished. One might as well run down a race horse for not being able to haul a coal wagon, or draw a plough, after the turf has seen his finish. Or a racing automobile for its uselessness for business purposes.

Modern competitors for *America's* Cup are racing machines, if you will, but they are the most graceful fabrics that human art has devised. The glorious memories of their achievements will live in history though their hulls are sold to the junkman after their deeds are done. The stimulus afforded to the cleanest and healthiest of all sports by the Cup races is worth more to the nation marine—in a word, of our salt water supremacy.

The growth of the sport has been phenomenal in the last decade. Society has taken up the pastime. The girls love it. The

THE MODEL ROOM.

than the money and effort expended. It induces in young men a love for the ocean. It keeps alive the glorious traditions of our navy and of our once magnificent merchant squadron cruise of the New York Yacht Club is one of the great events of the season. Few fashionable people care to miss the race for the Astor cups. Fewer the international contests; yet on the roster of the Club, figure the names of men who do not know one end of a yacht from the other. The most exalted foreign personage in the honorary list is King Edward VII. The admission of women as flag members was a popular step. The receptions to ladies are always well attended. The yachting girl is very much in evidence, and has come to stay.

The Club prides itself on its stations established at points along the coast from Atlantic Highlands to Martha's Vineyard. Each has a fine float and landing stage which does away with the old unpleasant practice of shinning up a slimy wharf when desiring to go ashore. The yachtsman finds a long distance telephone at all the stations, a comfortable room to read and lounge in, a mail box and other conveniences. The station at Newport is the largest, but all are well adapted for the purposes for which they were devised. The cost of establishing these stations was about $18,000, and the expense of keeping them up is about $7,000 a year. The Club permits other yacht clubs to enjoy the accommodations of these stations. This privilege is highly appreciated by foreigners, and also by members of American clubs, who enjoy it every day during the yachting season.

The members of the Club are more benefited by these stations than they would be if there was only one large club-house near the water front. Though it seemed wise to have a town house in the very heart of clubdom, whence a start may be made for any place on earth, and stations at Whitestone, New London, Newport, and other places frequented by members.

The Club will begin its fifty-seventh yachting season under the happiest auspices. With a handsome club-house, a magnificent squadron of 424 vessels, a membership of 1,619, and a large balance at the bank, and, above all, with a history of which it has reason to be proud, it may thus look forward with confidence to maintaining its praiseworthy prestige of being the premier yachting organization of the United States, if not of the world.

The coming summer will be a busy one, and an anxious one for members of the Club, for there can be no doubt that Sir Thomas Lipton, and his designers and advisers, have benefited by the past experience in our waters, and that in his present challenge for that time-honored trophy of the Club, the *America's* Cup, he will be represented by the best designed, and built, and equipped, and handled boat that has yet crossed the Atlantic in quest of this much-coveted symbol of yachting supremacy. All the ability that money can command will be backed by the determination of a very persistent opponent.

The preparations being made on this side, too, are marked by an equal spirit. Two boats are being built to determine which is the better to meet *Shamrock II.* One of them, for a New York syndicate headed by Mr. August Belmont, is being designed and built by the Herreshoffs; and the other for Mr. Thomas W. Lawson, of Boston, is from designs by Crowninshield, and is being built by Lawley. Nothing has been spared which money can procure or ingenuity invent to assure that either of these boats shall be capable of successfully defending the Cup. They will, in a short time, be ready for preliminary spins, and in the early summer they will contest in a series of races for the supreme honor of becoming the chosen one to meet the challenger.

Natural interest will be accentuated by the local pride of the two great yachting centers of the Atlantic seaboard, and yachtsmen are assured of a summer of unusual, indeed of intense, interest.

What the result will be never admits of a doubt within the walls of the New York Club, where the spirit and confidence which animated its founders still runs strong.

The Normal College
of New York City
(1878)

THE NORMAL COLLEGE OF NEW YORK CITY.

AT ten minutes to nine o'clock one morning last November the writer took seats
with the president on the chapel platform
of the Normal College. The vast hall was
then empty and reverberant; the day outside was cloudy, and the long Gothic win-

hall was black with seats, and the gallery
on both sides of the organ offered further
accommodations. Precisely at five minutes
to nine—not a second earlier or later—a
lady seated at the piano in front of the
platform began to play a lively march, and

THE PROCESSION INTO THE CHAPEL.

dows let in a gray twilight which gave the
interior an ecclesiastic solemnity, the effect
being heightened by the gilded pipes of a
large organ in the gallery. On the platform with us were the professors and tutors,
both ladies and gentlemen. The body of the

at that very moment the doors leading into
a wide corridor, with class-rooms on each
side, were thrown open, and what seemed
to be an endless procession of girls came in,
the patter of their feet sounding like the
dripping of a fountain, and harmonizing

prettily with the allegretto movement of the music. They were formed in single file, and stringed in with measured pace, silent and demure—girls all the way from fourteen to twenty years of age, from the farther edge of childhood to the farther limit of maidenhood; girls with every shade of complexion and degree of beauty; girls in such variety that it was amazing to contemplate the reduction of their individuality to the simple uniformity of their well-drilled movements. We looked for the last of them; the seats in the body were fast filling, without the least noise or confusion; but the lady at the piano was still beating out the allegretto air, and we could see the long lines threading in through the great corridor, and hear the steady rain of footsteps. The clock in front of the gallery marked nine, and the body of the hall was now filled, but the stream continued to pour into the gallery, until nearly every seat was occupied; and at four minutes past nine the last of the procession had entered, the doors were closed, and the piano became silent. What a triumph of system! The first thing to excite our wonder and admiration was the number —there were 1542 pupils; the second thing was the earnestness of the discipline; and the third was the suggestiveness of so many girls at work in assembly, with their own education as the primary aim, and the education of countless thousands of others as the final aim, of their toil. The latter was fascinating, and inclined us to reverie, opening long vistas of stirring possibilities, the evils counteracted by intelligence, and the happiness evoked by enlightenment. But despite its mellow atmosphere and ecclesiastical architecture, the chapel is not the place for dreams, its uses exacting intense application, and leaving no time for vagrant thoughts. When the doors had been closed, and the last footfall had died away, the pianist struck one note, and the girls, who had been standing, erect and silent, before their seats with the faces directed to the platform, turned half round; another note was struck, in response to which they unfolded the seats; and upon hearing the third, they sat down in a body, not one being the tenth of a second later than the others. If, instead of being self-willed, independent, audacious American girls, they had been automata si-

multaneously controlled by a rush of electricity, the unanimity of their movements could not have been more perfect; and with our admiration came the thought of the invaluable lessons their future husbands might learn from a philosophical study of normal school government. The inmates of a convent, with their burden of silent bitterness, could not possibly be more decorous and systematic than these untrammelled maids of the new era were, who at once vindicated their sex and set at naught the critics of young Americans.

The students being seated, a chapter of the Bible was read by Mr. William Wood, president of the Board of Education—a venerable gentleman, whose name is identified with one of the historic banking houses of the metropolis (this duty being done by Mr. Thomas Hunter, president of the college, in the absence of Mr. Wood)—and a non-sectarian hymn was sung to the accompaniment of the organ. A pause followed, and we instinctively became aware that mingled expectation and hesitation were rife in the assemblage. It was time for quotations.

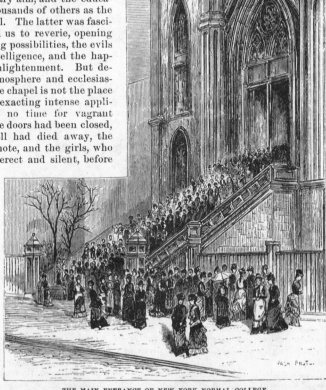

THE MAIN ENTRANCE OF NEW YORK NORMAL COLLEGE.

To exercise their memories and inspire self-confidence, the students are invited to volunteer personally selected quotations from authors, and "the multitudinous seas" of literature, from the nearest to the farthest, are explored for aphorisms, epigrams, odes, and elegies; Herbert Spencer or Emerson yielding a subtle morsel of philosophy now, and good Thomas à Kempis or Mohammed doing service then in sonorous adoration; the Attic salt of Oliver Wendell Holmes and the envenomed wit of Talleyrand, the ponderous wisdom of Dr. Johnson and the sweet piety of Jonathan Edwards, the musk-and-lavender verse of literary Ladies' Repos-

of hearing their own voices alone, and feeling that over three thousand eyes were fixed upon them—the ordeal was too much for them, and nearly a minute, lengthened by suspense, elapsed before one, with stronger nerves than her associates, ventured to rise and in a tremulous key repeat a few lines from Thomson:

"In the service of mankind to be
  A guardian God below; still to employ
  The mind's brave ardor in heroic aims,
  Such as may raise us o'er the grovelling herd,
  And make us shine forever—that is life."

That came from a girl with serious intentions; and this game of authors, once be-

NEW YORK NORMAL COLLEGE.

itories and the robust humor of Shakspeare or Sheridan—scarcely any thing is deemed inappropriate, and the selections made indicate most varied reading, with, perhaps, too great a taste for the florid in rhetoric.

The pause continued. Many of the girls evidently had quotations at their tongues' ends; but the creeping horror of rising amid that great silence and facing the president and the awful-looking row of professors and guests on the platform, the nervous dread

gun, was carried on with spirit. Following her was a self-possessed maid, with archly dressed hair and innumerable coquettish touches and twists of ribbon, who quoted a saucy speech of Rosalind's from *As You Like It* with elocutionary emphasis; and then another risked all her reputation as head of a class in French with a bold excerpt from the maxims of La Rochefoucauld. The individuality that had been temporarily obedient to the disciplinary stroke of the piano keys was now emancipated, and revealed itself in much diversity of costume and manner, in pretty faces and softly modulated voices, and in faces that were, to say the least, not pretty, and piping voices that were not modulated at all.

A pensive student, with a tight-fitting suit of black, and big, liquid, lustrous eyes in a pale face, enunciated a sagacious passage from Huxley: "The saying that a little knowledge is a dangerous thing is a very dangerous adage. If knowledge is real and genuine, I do not believe that it is other than a very valuable possession, however infinitesimal its quantity may be. Indeed, if a little knowledge is dangerous, where is the man who has so much as to be out of danger?" Another had been reading Shakspeare, and gave the following from *King Henry VIII.*:

" Still in thy right hand carry gentle peace,
　To silence envious tongues. Be just, and fear not:
　Let all the ends thou aim'st at be thy country's,
　Thy God's, and truth's."

Another had explored the profundities of Bacon, and recited this characteristic fragment: "The pleasure and delight of learning far surpasseth all others in nature; for in all other pleasures there is satiety, and after they be·used their verdure departeth. Of knowledge there is no satiety, but satisfaction and appetite are perpetually interchangeable, and therefore knowledge appeareth to be good in itself simply, without fallacy or accident." Some broke down, and we could see troubled hearts and tears of mortification behind the failures; but clear intonation, nice emphasis, and self-possession marked most of the recitations.

President Hunter next addressed the students, urging them not to miss a single lesson; and while one of the divisions into which the college is divided remained in the chapel for musical instruction, the others retired, responding to the touches of the piano with the extraordinary precision shown at their entrance, and the fountain seemed to be playing again in the patter of their footsteps.

But we have forgotten to say what takes place previous to the services in the chapel. Should the day be wet, the students leave their wraps in the drying-rooms on entering the college. The drying-rooms are provided with racks for overshoes and rails for clothing. At a quarter before nine a gong is struck, the students repair to their recitation-rooms, and all conversation is prohibited. Five minutes later the gong is struck again, the rolls are called, and marks are awarded for punctuality; and at a third stroke of the gong all the students pass into the chapel, as we have seen.

The day's work was now begun, Tennyson's "Princess" becoming almost reality to us:

" And then we strolled
For half the day thro' stately theatres
Bench'd crescent-wise. In each we sat, we heard
The grave Professor. On the lecture slate
The circle rounded under female hands
With flawless demonstration: follow'd then
A classic lecture, rich in sentiment,
With scraps of thunderous Epic lilted out
By violet-hooded Doctors, elegies
And quoted odes, and jewels five-words-long
Sparkle forever: then we dipt in all
That treats of whatsoever is, the state,
The total chronicles of man, the mind,
The morals, something of the frame, the rock,
The star, the bird, the fish, the shell, the flower,
Electric, chemic laws, and all the rest,
And whatsoever can be taught and known."

The first normal school was founded in 1681 by the Abbé De la Salle, canon of the

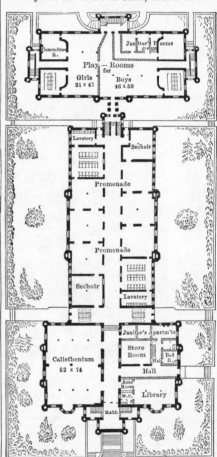

GROUND-PLAN OF NEW YORK NORMAL COLLEGE.

cathedral at Reims, and sixteen years later a teachers' class was opened in connection with an orphan school at Halle, the pupil-teachers receiving two years' training under the head-master, August Hermann Francke, under whom the system developed surprisingly, and soon received the invaluable support of Frederick the Great. Other normal schools were opened in Hanover, Austria, Switzerland, France, Holland, Belgium, and, about forty years ago, in Great Britain, whence they have extended into nearly every civilized country. The aims of the schools are well expressed in the following extract of the Prussian law: "The directors of teachers' seminaries shall rather seek to conduct the pupil-teachers by their own

DRESSING-ROOM.

experience to simple and clear principles, than to give them theories for their guidance; and with this end in view, primary schools shall be joined to all teachers' seminaries, where the pupil-teachers may be practiced in the art of teaching." There are now about 850 normal schools in Europe, the British colonies, and British India, the latter having 104.

Massachusetts was the first State in the American Union to establish normal schools, of which there now are 137, with over 29,000 pupils and over 1000 instructors, Ohio and Pennsylvania each having twelve schools, while New York State has nine, Illinois and Missouri eight each, and Massachusetts seven. The largest number of pupils are in New York, however, where there are 4158.

The necessity of such schools needs no other enforcement than a few statistics relating to education in the United States. Nearly 9,000,000 scholars are enrolled in the public schools. Nearly 5,000,000 are in attendance daily, and about 231,000 teachers are employed, including 133,000 women. The amount expended annually upon this vast scheme, which seems almost fabulous, is about $82,000,000, and the imagination is carried away by the tremendous suggestiveness of the figures.

Previous to the establishment of the present college, normal instruction was shabbily provided for in New York city. A school for teachers was opened in 1856, and closed three years later; but ample amends for past deficiencies are made in the existing institution, to which the citizen who is shamefaced in the consciousness of the political iniquities manifest in scores of ways can with returning pride direct a visitor's attention as the completest of its kind in the world. The building is one of the most attractive sights in the city; it covers, with the inclosed ground surrounding, the whole block bounded by Lexington and Fourth avenues, Sixty - eighth and Sixty-ninth streets; it is 300 feet long, 125 feet wide in front, 78 feet wide in the rear, and the principal material used in its construction is red brick, which is still fresh and glowing. It overlooks Central Park, and is within a stone's-throw of the Lenox Library, the Museum of Natural History, and the Carnivorium. A female grammar school with accommodations for about 300 and a primary with accommodations for about 500 pupils are attached to it. The corner-stone was laid on March 19, 1872—a wild, blustering day—and eighteen months later the enormous pile had risen as if by magic, and was ready for occupation, $350,000 having been expended upon it. Over 1000 girls attended the first sessions, and its great capacity is now taxed to the utmost. It has four stories above the basement, and contains thirty recitation-rooms, two lecture-rooms, an art studio, a chapel with seats for 2000, a library, a calisthenium, two drying-rooms, six retiring-rooms for instructors, president's offices, and three great corridors, each fifteen feet wide.

The best criterion of its usefulness is the fact that of the 2300 teachers employed by the Board of Education, 2100 are women, eight or nine per cent. of whom retire annually, and the college fills these vacancies with its graduates.

The faculty consists of Thomas Hunter, President, and Professor of Intellectual Philosophy; Arthur H. Dundon, Professor of Latin and English; Joseph A. Gillet, Professor of Physics and Chemistry; Charles A. Schlegel, Professor of German; Edward H. Day, Professor of Natural Science; and Eugene Aubert, Professor of French Language and Literature. Besides these, there are thirty instructors, including one tutor in methods of teaching and five in mathematics, twenty - eight of the thirty being women. The writer is particularly indebted for assistance to President Wood, of the Board of Education, whose work in its behalf entitles him to distinction as founder of the college, to President Hunter, and to Professor Aubert.

A dainty little manual, with a chocolate cover and gilt lettering, is issued for the government of the college; but the outside prettiness binds the formula of a martial discipline. Its tinted pages of creamy mildness give no idea of the severity of the text, which is both curt and imperative. Stu-

dents *must* account for every minute of lateness or absence, and after an absence of one day they *must* not be permitted to re-enter their classes without a written permit from the president or lady superintendent; they *must* maintain single files, always taking the right-hand side in changing rooms; and they *must not* run in the halls or on the stairs, nor delay in passing out of the building. Unladylike conduct of any kind in the cars or stages on the part of a student is investigated by the lady superintendent, and may be punished by expulsion.

WILLIAM WOOD, PRESIDENT OF THE BOARD OF EDUCATION, NEW YORK CITY.

Those students who are in the last or graduating year of the course are more carefully marked than the others, with a view to ascertaining their moral fitness for the work of teaching, and those who are found wanting are refused diplomas, even though the number of marks awarded to them reaches the necessary average. A Madcap Violet is not possible among the girls of the Normal College; but while strict obedience is enforced, they receive, without the smallest expense, such an education as very few other cities in the world can give at any price, qualifying them for the practical duties of life as well as for the teacher's profession; and excelling proficiency is further rewarded with medals, etc., given by patrons of the institution. A gold medal and a silver medal are annually awarded to the best students of German; a silver medal and a bronze medal for excellence in methods of teaching; a gold medal for physiology; a gold medal for Latin; two money prizes for French, and one for physics.

The catholicity and toleration crystallized in the country's Constitution prevail in the college; about two hundred of the students are Jewesses, and a black face, framed in

the other girls is refining and otherwise beneficial; the most feasible plan that occurred to him being the lengthening of the course from three to four years, an amendment that would undoubtedly advance the standard of graduates and exclude candidates who are not thorough in their aims.

The course of study is as follows:

FIRST GRADE. *First Year. First Term.*— Latin; outlines of ancient history; German or French; algebra, in simple equations, involution, evolution, and radicals; plane geometry.

SECOND GRADE. *First Year. Second Term.* —The studies are the same as in the first

DRAWING CLASS.

curly African hair, may occasionally be seen at the recitations. The capacity of the college being strained, and the directors being perplexed as to the means by which the number of students may be regulated, the writer asked President Hunter why candidates for admission are not required to express an intention to become teachers at the time of their graduation, no such engagement being now exacted, and many of the students entertaining no intention whatever of earning a livelihood in the scholastic profession. It was Mr. Hunter's opinion that such a measure would simply lead to deception, and would exclude many girls of the better classes who are now enrolled, and whose influence upon some of

term, physics, including heat, electricity, and mechanics, being substituted for algebra, and music, drawing, penmanship, and English composition being added.

THIRD GRADE. *Second Year. First Term.*— Easy selections from classic authors in Latin; outlines of modern history; French or German reader and conversation; algebra, in quadratics; physics, in light and sound; music, drawing, English composition, and botany.

FOURTH GRADE. *Second Year. Second Term.* —Latin extracts from Cæsar, Sallust, and Cicero; rhetoric and English composition; German or French conversation; mathematic and descriptive astronomy; notation, nomenclature, and atmospheric elements in chemistry; music, drawing, geology, and mineralogy.

FIFTH GRADE. *Third Year. First Term.*—Third Book of Virgil; English language and literature; German or French; electricity, galvanism, and magnetism in physics; astronomy, music, drawing, and zoology; review of subjects prescribed for the primary and grammar schools, and the methods of teaching them.

SIXTH GRADE. *Third Year. Second Term.*—Virgil continued; intellectual philosophy and the theory of teaching; English language, literature, and composition; general review of French or German grammar, with conversation and translations; general review of physics; music, drawing, and physiology; review of subjects prescribed in primary and grammar grades for common

A DEMONSTRATION IN GEOMETRY.

schools, and practice in the model school under critic teachers of experience.

As we have already said, at the close of services in the chapel, one of the great divisions remained for a lesson in vocal music, while the other passed out for review in rudimentary subjects, such as spelling, grammar, and arithmetic, and for physical training in the calisthenium.

Watching them introspectively as they filed out through the corridors on the day of our visit, we could scarcely refrain from applause, so admirably precise were their movements, several hundred behaving with the perfect unanimity before noticed, which was almost machine-like. Here were girls with latent mischief twinkling unmistakably in their eyes; girls of the mercurial volatility

INTERIOR OF THE CHAPEL.

CALISTHENIC EXERCISES.

that shakes a household; girls brimming with animal spirits and fertile ingenuity for kittenish pranks —all subdued for the present, and thoughtfully observant of college discipline. Other girls, too, there were with natural serenity and dignity of manner; girls with sweet, clear faces and quiet ways, the good angels of their homes; girls with domesticity shining through them, and girls, alas! with suspicions of the virago about them; girls that, like Miss Miggs in *Barnaby Rudge*, would rather die than go up a ladder; girls that believed in round dances and theatres, and girls that execrated both those amusements; girls with shrewish angularity of feature, and girls of suffusive amiability; prudes and tomboys, the angelic and (presumably) the devilish, the extremest differences of temperament fused into a mobile, cohesive unit, which flowed along as rhythmically as a river in placid weather. The warmest praise of the normal school government is not undeserved, for while the discipline is exacting, the idea inculcated among the students is that they must be self-governing; they are placed on their own honor, and mean espionage is carefully avoided.

The exercises in the calisthenium last fifteen minutes, and no students are excused from taking part in them, except on a physician's certificate of disability. About three hundred girls were assembled when we entered, and under the direction of a teacher, placed on a commanding dais at the end of the room, they were performing simple and graceful evolutions to the music of a piano. The tune was lively; and the lines weaving in and out, the waving of arms, the measured step of the feet, and the swaying of the body made a pretty and inspiriting sight, like a theatrical *ensemble*. Each girl held a strong elastic band, with wooden handles, which was stretched from side to side in front, from shoulder to hip, from back to breast, and from over head to chin in ways that develop muscle, expand the chest, and—let us whisper it—prevent the silly fashion of tight lacing. At the end of the fifteen minutes those students who

four hours, history two hours, English grammar and composition two hours, algebra three hours, geometry three hours, drawing one hour, and music one hour. In the Junior, or second year, the same time is given to Latin, modern languages, history, drawing, and music as in the first year, besides which two hours a week are given to rhetoric and composition, three to physics, and three to natural science. In the third, or Senior year, Latin and modern languages are allowed three hours a week each; intellectual phi-

NORMAL COLLEGE TYPES.

had been languid felt a freer coursing of their blood, and a glowing activity that prepared them for the work of the day. Their steps were lighter and their brains clearer; indeed, the advantages of these brief calisthenics can not be overestimated, and are too apparent for dispute.

At ten minutes to ten the regular recitations were begun. There are four of them every day, each continuing fifty minutes, with intervals of five minutes, during which the students have the great privilege of talking. In the Introductory year Latin is studied four hours a week, modern languages

losophy and methods of teaching, English, astronomy, physics, and natural science, two hours each; elocution, algebra and geometry, drawing and music, one hour each. The years are divided into first and second terms, and the vacations are the same as those of the public schools. Students failing at the general examination in June are reduced one year, and students failing at two consecutive examinations are expelled, seventy-five per cent. of marks being the minimum attainment recognized. On Saturday special sessions are held for the benefit of female teachers employed by the Board of Education, who are required to attend until they have had two years' experience in the schools. They are formed in classes for practice, and each in turn becomes class

how thorough an *alma mater* the Normal College is.

A covered passage, which is known among the girls as the "Bridge of Sighs," connects

LUNCH COUNTER.

teacher, subject to the criticism of her associates, the professors, and the instructors.

As we have stated, the boon of conversation is granted during the five-minute intervals between recitations, and we half suspect that to some of the students—only the feather-brained ones, of course—these are the great events of the normal school day. A whirl of small-talk is compressed into the brief space, and an eavesdropper would be deafened by the variety of verbal nothingness that flows from tongues which a few moments previously have bravely enunciated "electric, chemic laws, and all the rest." The appearance and history of the "distinguished visitors" who have been on the platform, the dress and subjects of the quotation-makers, the temper of the instructors, the state of the weather, and much besides, are discussed with a volubility that amazes. But before the last second of the five minutes has expired the girls are as demure and silent as ever, and ready to resume their studies. Half an hour is allowed for luncheon, and that makes another interesting sight, though it is one upon which a modest visitor will not intrude. The purveyor is a woman, whose counter is weighted with sandwiches, pies, and fruit, but candy is excluded on account of the president's reasonable consideration for his pupils' health—another regulation which proves

the college with the training schools. The latter consist of a female grammar and a mixed primary department, with a *Kindergarten* attached. They are perfect in their appointments, and wonderfully cheery in their appearance. In many places the Commissioners of Education have been compelled to abandon training schools connected with normal colleges, because the parents would not permit their children to be experimented upon by young and inexperienced teachers; but in the New York college this difficulty is avoided, each class being presided over by a veteran, who instructs the children three-quarters of the time. The other quarter is given to the pupil-teacher for practice, though the critic-teacher is always present and responsible; and the variety arising from the instruction under the former affords some relaxation to the wearied little ones.

KINDERGARTEN TRAINING SCHOOL.

The aim of the entire course through which the Normal students pass is not so much to burden the mind with facts as to develop intellectual power, cultivate judgment, and enable the graduates to take trained ability into the world with them. "Because teaching is intangible," says President Hunter, "and can not be weighed like flour, nor measured like muslin; because it is spiritual in its nature, and deals with the human mind, the evil influence of a weak, foolish, or incompetent teacher is not felt until it is too late—is not seen by those in authority until the helpless children have been so bent and twisted that no subsequent training can make them straight. The thirsty, tempest-tossed mariner had better not drink at all than drink salt-water, for madness and death inevitably ensue. The ignorant had better not be taught than have their moral and intellectual natures destroyed by empirics. Our great free-school system is an organized body of which the normal schools and colleges are the head, and it would be well for friends of this system to remember that a severe blow on the head is very apt to paralyze the whole body. Injury can not be inflicted on a vital part without endangering the life of the whole, and any crippling of the Normal system would react disastrously on every public primary school in the United States."

A Spring Jaunt
in Staten Island
(1878)

A SPRING JAUNT IN STATEN ISLAND.

A GLIMPSE of the country while the foliage was in the sappy verdurousness of the spring, and the earth was still fragrant with the moist incipiency of early May; before the hot maturity of summer had laid its last bud open, and the fullness of the woods could remind us of its waning toward autumn: the desire for this impelled a little party of artists and the writer down the inexhaustibly attractive harbor of New York one night, some months ago, in the late ferry-boat from Whitehall to Staten Island.

Why Staten Island? asks the reader. Staten Island is one of the unloveliest, unhealthiest, and least romantic of haunts, one of our coterie had complained. It is a reservoir of Teutonic beer, a scattering of uninhabitable villas, a humid nursery of mosquitoes, and its exhalations are blue with pestilential chills. "I confess that the North Shore is naturally pretty," the grumbler continued; "but it has been disfigured by a wild diversity of modern dwellings more frail, meretricious, and preposterously composite in style than the average suburban house. One little gingerbread cottage I know of has two colossal Sphinxes before its porch, which take up almost as much space as the house, and the galvanized iron of which they are made has been painted in fatuous imitation of a green bronze. Miserable sham! No; let us select some other place. We might as well make the tour of a back yard as Staten Island."

But he was overruled upon the testimony of another member of the party who was familiar with the many charms of the island, though not unaware of its disadvantages; and on the May night aforesaid we sat "forward" on the upper deck of the *Middletown* as she trembled and plunged against the incoming tide toward the luminous blue hills projecting in the haze far down the bay. It was one of those poetic nights that often shed a glamour on the commonplaces of the sordid city. The haze was genuinely opaline, and the path of moonbeams on the quivering water, which seemed like some lustrous quilted fabric, was golden to within a shade of orange. Now and then a lazy, heaving sloop or schooner stood out for a moment in the reflected track of the moon, and vanished; a panting tug-boat dashed the white spray in a diamond shower over her low deck, and left a milky trail behind her; and a phantom-like yacht swept past us. Robbin's Reef Light was burning steadfastly over our starboard bow, and far away through the narrow outlet to the ocean the surpassing brilliance of the beacon on the Highlands piercing the thin veil of mist sent its kindly beams to the mariner many miles away at sea. These luminous blue hills curving southwestward were the island itself, with all its superadded deformities transformed by the witchery of the night. He who had wished to seek other fields was appeased, and sat in mute enjoyment of the scene, with his little tray of water-colors burning in his pocket, and his mind busy in memorizing the "effects."

The shore came nearer, and was dotted with lights; it was very quiet, and the beat

FROM THE RICHMOND ROAD.

425

QUARANTINE—THE DOCTOR'S GIG.

of the paddles was echoed back to us as in resentment of the disturbance they made. We landed at old Quarantine, with a few other passengers, and the boat, which was the last one from the city, proceeded on her way, leaving us securely insular for the night. The tavern was closed and dark, and there was some prospect that we might continue our enjoyment out-of-doors until morning; but in response to a vigorous pulling of the bell and the loud summons of one of the artists, the landlord, in a red flannel gown, admitted us. The artist had been illustrating Shakspeare, and vastly surprised mine host by quaintly calling, "What, ho! within there!"

Our bedroom windows looked out upon the bay and the Narrows, and a fleet of vessels lay at anchor almost immediately below them. The weather was so warm that we left them open. We could hear voices on board the ships, and the striking of the bells in nautical time almost made us believe that we were afloat in the sultry quietude of a tropical ocean. It seemed impossible that we could be within ten miles of the populous city, and on the island that had been so severely animadverted upon by one of our own party. Here were solitude, serenity, relaxation, and picturesqueness. We went to sleep, soothed by the lapping of the water, and when we awoke we saw from our pillows a scene full of spirited motion and varied color—the harbor with its verdant shore was dazzling with sunshine, and

checkered by the frothy wake of sail and steam boats vanishing beyond the Narrows, and beating up to the city, which was purple in the distance. The red sandstone of old Fort Lafayette glowed with a warmth inappropriate to its vacant port-holes and deserted interior, and the waves sparkled and whitened around the reef on which it stands. The granite batteries of Fort Wadsworth gleamed opposite, with the grassy embankments, hiding portentous shot and shell in their covered recesses, rising to a wooded height. Lying within a stone's-throw of us was a massive iron steamer bound for Havre, with thick clouds of black smoke issuing from her funnel; by-and-by her propeller began to churn the water astern, and she glided seaward; but despite her bulk and power, a large bark, unattended by a tow-boat, with all sail set, overtook and passed her, and gallantly sped ahead. The activity was too exhilarating for contemplation from a pillow. The coming and going of ships stir the emotions and draw out one's heart-strings, for they are transitions which seem to give the Fates visible shape, and enlarge the sad uncertainties of life.

Our landlord appreciated the beauty of the harbor when he built his house, and he set us down to breakfast in a delightful little room with three windows that ranged up and down and across the bay. The porter-house steak and the crisp Saratoga potatoes were delicious; but the constant changes of the scene outside, the discovery of unsuspected " bits" along the shore or in the construction or management of the vessels, the effects of color, light, and shade, broke the repose of the meal by drawing the marine artist away from the table to sketch in elementary outlines some of the many objects that attracted him. When breakfast was finished a page of his book was filled with topsy-turvy, hurried, yet strongly suggestive, pencillings. Here was an old scow imbedded in the sand and mud on the beach ; two innocent urchins who were gathering mussels at the water's edge re-appeared in the centre of the page; a water-logged sloop laboring against the tide was very nearly balanced on the head of one of the boys; a floating mass of drift-wood and a shad net hung out to dry were stretched across the paper, which was covered to the corners; and should the reader visit next year's exhibition at the National Academy, perhaps he would see some of these specimens of the artist's short-hand expanded into charming pictures.

After breakfast we went southward along the shore toward the Quarantine station, shutting our eyes to the raggedness and squalid variety of shops, eating-houses, and beer saloons which unfortunately line a road that would otherwise be a lovely drive and promenade, and fixing our attention upon the water.

The Quarantine station was formerly at the first landing, where we passed the night ; but a few years ago it was removed to a point nearer the Narrows, and though the name is a reminder of disease, the institution is innocuous as far as Staten Island is concerned, only vessels from healthy ports being examined inside the Narrows, except from November until May, when all are permitted to enter the harbor. From May until November vessels from the West Indies, Mexico, Bermuda, the east coast of South America, and the west coast of Africa are detained in the lower bay and examined by the medical officer from a hospital hulk stationed near Sandy Hook. If there are any cases of yellow fever on board, they are transferred to the spacious buildings on Dix Island, and the well persons among the crew and passengers are removed to Hoffman's Island, which is provided with quarters and cooking appliances for a large number. The cargo is then disinfected. The hatches are lifted and the hold is exposed to fresh air and light for a few days. The vessel is next towed inside the harbor and unloaded by means of lighters, which are ungraceful, broad-beamed sloops with short thick bowsprits. No one is allowed to visit her except coopers, cleaners, and the men attached to the lighters, and they are required to take their meals and sleep on board a boat anchored at Upper Quarantine. When the

unloading is done, the holds are fumigated, and the ship is towed to the city. The people on Hoffman's Island are released in a few days if the disease does not break out among them, and the sick on Dix Island are sent to the city as soon as they recover. The dead are buried at Seguin's Point—a desolate spot some distance from the south-eastern corner of Staten Island. The land was chosen for its loneliness. It is malarious, and without any beautifying features. No flag-staff or landing marks it out, and the surf beats in on a shelving beach. The dead are brought here in an open boat manned by a few silent men. No burial service is read, and no friends or relatives are near. The body, in a common wooden coffin, is placed in the loamy soil, a numbered stake is driven at the head of the grave, and the boatmen leave it to the secrecy and gloom. There are many other such graves on every side. Here and there the number has been supplemented with a name and the brief record of birth and death. In a few instances a stone tablet has been provided by friends. When the cold weather of winter comes, the bodies may be reclaimed and reinterred in other ground; but until then whoever dies of an infectious disease meets with the common lot, whether or not it is a sailor, an immigrant, or a magnate.

Both Dix and Hoffman's islands are artificial constructions. Previous to their establishment the hospitals were located upon Staten Island, whose inhabitants suffered severely from the recurrent epidemics of the horrible Yellow Jack. Finding their petitions for the removal of the buildings unavailing, a mob assembled on the nights of September 1 and 2, 1858, and destroyed the four pest-houses by fire—an act which resulted in a proclamation declaring the island to be in a state of revolt, and its occupation by several regiments of militia. Some wealthy and intelligent citizens were concerned in the affair, and two were arrested on a charge of arson ; but they were acquitted, the county paying $120,000 to the State by way of restitution. The hospital buildings were reconstructed near the site of the present grave-yard at Seguin's Point; but they were again burned down, and the prejudices of the people were calmed only by the erection of the two artificial islands in the lower bay.

All that remains of Quarantine within the Narrows is the pretty houses of the health officers, which are surrounded by trees, and fronted by a greensward that slopes to the water's edge. The vessels from transatlantic ports are examined here between sunrise and sunset, and the writer has seen as many as seven large ocean steamers, with varicolored funnels denoting the lines to which they belong, gather together in the morning, besides a smaller fleet of sailing

THE AUSTEN HOUSE.

craft. The examination is a matter of form. The captain takes oath that no contagious disease has appeared on board his ship during the voyage, and a permit admitting him to the city is granted.

A short distance north of the Quarantine station stands a very old house, which was a home when Washington had scarcely reached the dignity of manhood, which has outlasted revolution and the storms of nearly two centuries, sheltering the British redcoats and the patriots against whom the redcoats fought, looking out through its quaint dormer-windows on the thousand changes that have been wrought during its existence, and remaining to this very day a secure and hospitable dwelling. Its preservation is a matter of wonder, because no crisis or event in history is associated with it. A King George's man fell in love with a maiden who lived in it, and being rejected, desperately hanged himself from a beam in the ceiling, while she, like Charlotte in Thackeray's ballad, "went on cutting bread and butter." The disembodied spirit of this soft-hearted and soft-headed warrior still visits the chamber of his folly, and shamefully disturbs its occupants by the midnight clinking of his spurs and the tread of his double-soled boots. The ample fire-place that gapes in the cellar was surrounded in the evenings of many years by the supine slaves, who were locked up for the night, and who in their entire simplicity never thought of avenging themselves upon their bond-masters by a brand from that convenient burning. A crowd of wondrous and anxious faces filled the mullioned windows of the parlor when the little *Sirius* and *Savannah* opened steam communication with Great Britain, and astonished the civilized world by their fifteen and twenty-five day passages; and from the same windows one can now see the iron levia-

thans of modern navigation arriving after eight-day runs. A few shots that missed the compliment they were no doubt intended to pay during the Revolution have been unearthed from the grounds; but the building is in sound condition, and is now known, after the family that has lived in it for some forty years, as the Austen house.

It is close upon the water, and the luxuriant lawn in front needs a strong sea-wall to protect it from the tidal encroachments. The lilacs were in bloom when we called, and the long grass rippled in the wind, and shook the golden chalices of the buttercups that opened in the sunshine. Patriarchal shade trees flickered over the shingled roof —that symbol of unfaltering protection, the shield against how many storms, the seal of how many secrets! A hardy vine interwove its twisted branches up the supports of the wide porch, under which the gentle mistress sometimes sits with her embroidery or book. Only the ground-floor is distinctly visible. The floor above merely suggests itself by three dormer-windows in the gray roof, which is bent with the weight of its years. It is a place for dreams and musings, this old house by the bay—a sanctity not to be profaned by the vulgar strifes of passionate men. The rustle of the leaves, the sibilant murmur of the long grass, the plashing of the waters against the low sea-wall, and the noiseless traffic of the vessels give Memory wings, and inspire her to flights through the pale twilight of the past.

The outer door is diamond-paned glass,

and just inside of this there is another one made of oak not a bit less than three inches thick, with an old-fashioned latch still attached to it, by which we pass into a cheerful hall. There is a bell to summon the inmates, by the way of concession to modern convenience; but who that has affection for old-time things in him would be able to resist rapping a sharp tat-tat-tat on the big knocker, whose hammer is wrought into a griffin's head? This knocker was brought from an old château near Rouen. Though the house is not itself historical, it contains numberless odds and ends that are reminiscent of momentous events in the country's progress. Cheerful is an adjective that applies to every part as well as the hall. The sunshine streams in copiously, and the bees find passage from front to rear; but the stone walls are three feet thick, forming charming window-seats; the low ceilings are beamed with ponderous oak, and the floors are of solid deal taken from the cabins of captured ships. Furnished after no arbitrary formula, the little parlor gratifies the artistic sense, and, what is more essential, adapts itself to the ease of its occupants. It is warm in color, brilliant in effect, and cozy in arrangement; it stimulates repose, and

treatment grotesque. Among a crowd of other objects upon the mantel-piece are two small candlesticks that belonged to the Van Tassel family; and who will venture to say that they are not the very ones that revealed Katrina's pretty face to the school-master of Sleepy Hollow? A centre-piece is formed of a small knocker taken from the house in Chester which was occupied by Washington, and visited by Rochambeau, Lafayette, and other celebrities; and below this is a link of the chain that was stretched across the Hudson at West Point. It was Mrs. Austen's grandfather, Peter Townsend, who forged the metal, and to her we are indebted for an extract from an unpublished manuscript concerning it.

In the early winter of 1778, Congress, upon the recommendation of General Washington, determined to improve the fortifications at West Point, and ordered the construction of a chain double the strength of that used at Fort Montgomery, which was unsuccessful. The supervision of the work was assumed by Timothy Pickering, the Secretary of War, and about March 1, 1778, he visited Townsend, who lived at Chester, Orange County, and owned the Stirling Iron-Works. Townsend was pleased with the project. and

INTERIOR OF THE AUSTEN HOUSE.

leads to meditation. The grand old fireplace, with logs ready for lighting stretched over the brass andirons, is about ten feet wide, and is surrounded by ancient tiles brought from Amsterdam two hundred years ago, the subjects being Biblical, and the

such was his ardor that he and Pickering left Chester in a violent snow-storm on Saturday night, riding over the mountains to the forge, twelve miles distant, and putting all the available men to work on their arrival in the morning. The operations were

SOUTH BEACH, FROM RICHMOND AVENUE.

continued day and night until the chain was completed; it was conveyed to New Windsor by mule teams, and from New Windsor to West Point by yawls, being delivered at the latter place within six months of the date of the order. Its weight was 120 tons, and it was extended across the river until 1783, when it was removed.

As we left the Austen house another point was scored against the grumbler, who carried a rich sketch of the interior in his portfolio, and who confessed that the island of

his objurgations had already revealed more than he had ever dreamed of.

We drove over the hill by the fort as the distant Highlands were adding warmth to their purple from the declining sun, and as the east was turning gray. The ocean was still, its surface glossed with a coppery hue, and flecked with the white reflections of a few almost motionless vessels. Then we turned into Richmond Avenue, which is canopied by foliage and bordered by handsome villas set amid croppy lawns and luxuriant woods. At the end of this road we reached the brow of a hill, and gazed upon a long, low, transcendently green plain of pasture land that quietly spread to the water, which was now crisp and cold. The view inland conveyed an indefinite feeling of isolation, and the

"HE ASKED FOR BREAD."

fields and woods had a chill and drenched look. The shades of green were multiplied by an unusual variety of trees. Here was the sassafras, the wild cherry, the elm, the poplar, and the willow. The distant hills were streaked by areas of cedars, which among the lighter foliage seemed like vast, portentous shadows. A pond of lilies scented the air for a moment as we passed, and a ripening apple-tree showered some of its snow upon us. There were few houses, and those that we saw were very old, with curb-roofs, and no doors or windows to speak of. An incline in the road and a curve showed us the ancient Perine homestead —a sturdy structure of stone, which has been crazily whitewashed instead of being left to the mellow and unapproachable coloring of time. It is very picturesque, nevertheless; the roof is softly gray, and the foliage completely shelters it. The landscape artist declared that he had seen nothing in New England to compare with it.

Our progress was slow, for a succession of objects insisted, by their quaintness, their repose, their oddity, or their beauty, on reproduction in the sketchbooks, and occasionally an amusing incident happened as one of the artists left the road to seize with his pencil some of the many irresistible "bits."

Brush, an illustrious member of the coterie, who is known, from his extreme obesity, as "the skeleton," re-appeared through a break in a fence, and demanded to know if we had not heard him calling. Being satisfied that nothing was farther from us than the intention to slight him, he told us, with the quivering risibility that belongs to corpulence, of what befell him while he was making his sketch. Sitting upon a fence and drawing a barn, he was carefully watched by the farmer, who stood under the porch, and was apparently mystified by his actions. Brush's sketches are notable for their perfect finish, and having made some mistake, he sought in his pockets for rubber to erase the error. Failing to find it, he went to the house and asked for a piece of dry bread. The farmer gazed at him stupidly for a minute, and repeated, "Dry bread?" "A small

THE TERRACE AT AUSTEN HOUSE.

piece will do," said Brush. The farmer looked at him with greater amazement, and called to his wife, who was invisible within, "Bring us a chunk of bread;" then going inside, he added, sympathetically, in a whisper just audible to Brush, "And put plenty of butter on it." So Brush came back to the vehicle with the error still in his sketch, and his faith in the kindliness of humanity fortified.

Many strange guesses were made as to our business as we rode along, or paused to give Brush and his fellows a chance to sketch. "I say it's cirkiss," said one parched and sunburned old man among some rustics who were making us the object of various surmises. "Not cirkiss at all," said another, who was evidently a born disputant; "they's attached onto that survey which is making of the new drain." A third, with the prevailing spirit of investigation strong within him, ventured to peep over Michael Angelo's shoulder, and unable to appreciate the luminous grays and blacks with which that very clever artist had washed in his pencillings, he went back to the others disappointedly, and nodding at us, said, contemptuously, "They's only artises, and don't amount to much, either."

Our day ended at New Dorp, in a great white tavern, with wide porticoes before its first and second stories, wide corridors and stairways, and low ceilings. It has a good

THE OLD MORAVIAN CHURCH AND PARSONAGE, NEW DORP.

deal of individuality about it, and the builder, whoever he was, had as generous an idea of the proper apportionment of space as a sheep-farmer in New Mexico. None of your embellishments for Mulberry Sellers, however. The glaring white walls have not so much as a faint shade of pink or yellow upon them, and the space is sepulchrally void of furniture, excepting, of course, a few debilitated chairs and a vacant table. How the establishment supports itself is a mystery as deep as that of the Pyramids, unless the little bar-room, which has an unprovoked way of making any one who enters it feel ashamed of himself, yields revenue for all the rest; and that is doubtful, because the only customers we saw were the vendors of bottled beer, who, after leaving a dozen or so on the counter, imbibed affably with the landlord and drove away. Lest we convey an unfair idea, let us say of the landlord that his house was very clean, and his supper as good as could be expected in the bower of a country tavern. The lack of adornment within was made up for by the view outside from the windows: a motionless stretch of pasture and woodland ending by the sea; and over the sea, that was elusively changing color, we could discern again the four pale lights on the black headlands of the Navesink and the low promontory of Sandy Hook. The lights were visible before the stars had dawned, and as the twilight deepened they became more and more brilliant, like the brave souls whose heroism burns the clearest in the darkness of martyrdom. From the rear windows we could see another light-house rising above sombre masses of colors near the site of an old British signal station, from which a watch was kept on approaching vessels.

However much General Howe was reviled by the patriotic Revolutionists, his presence has bequeathed historic dignity to many localities, and the inhabitants of the island point with unmistakable satisfaction to the buildings occupied by him. For some time his head-quarters were in an old tavern that stood near the New Dorp Hotel—the Rose and Crown, which was recently demolished; and during the same period his staff found accommodations in the Black Horse, which remains at the corner of the Amboy and Richmond roads—not as a public-house, but as the home of a fisherman. The accommodations must have been very limited indeed, even for that epoch. The principal thing about the Black Horse is the gable roof, which is so large that the walls under it give one the idea of a baby with its papa's stove-pipe on. Age and weather have given the shingles a silver-gray color, and a brick chimney affords the contrast of its temperate red. It is evident that the *habitués* of the old tavern were not addicted to excesses, or many a head must have been broken in tipsy efforts to mount the steep flight of steps that lead from the green in front to the tap-room, which is next to the roof in matter of space. A broad veranda fronts it, and a wicket door opens into it. There could have been no bickering for situations before the fire among the guests on the cold nights when the northeasters from over the bay were rocking the little hostelry and making the jugs of flip on the hearth-stone dance, for the logs blazed from one side of the room to the other, and made candles unnecessary. The fire-place nearly monopolizes all of the west wall, and we wonder what sportive shadows it sent in fantastic procession over the great uncovered beams in the ceiling.

The islanders were Tories, and met the British welcomely. General Howe landed early in July, 1776, with about 9000 men. His brother soon re-enforced him with 20,000, and Clinton, having been repulsed at Charleston, came North and added 3000 more to Howe's command, the combined forces on the island being nearly 33,000. The plans were formed in the Rose and Crown, and the evening conversations of the young staff officers at the Black Horse were exciting, no doubt, as they weighed the possibilities of the issue. Did they clank their spurs, stretch out their brawny legs, kiss the landlord's pretty daughter, and drink deep cups to the king? Did they ever for a moment doubt the success of their cause, and were they not as arrogant, as loud, and as unscrupulous as the local historians say? Perhaps one night when the sentries were posted, and the white tents below were spectral in the still night, they told among themselves of the chase after old Peter Mesereau, an American loyalist who refused to be conciliated by General Howe, and took an active part against him. As he was endeavoring to escape from the island, he was pursued and was almost captured, when he disappeared on the edge of a swamp, in which he concealed himself. Dogs were put on his trail, but they were misled by a miserable little rabbit, and the patriot found his way into the American lines, while the soldiers returned to camp and swore vengeance against him over a fresh bowl, for these British were as thirsty as Stephano, and never missed an opportunity to "kiss the book." On August 22, Howe crossed the Narrows from the island to a point between New Utrecht and Gravesend —an expedition that resulted disastrously for the Americans, and gave the enemy possession of New York.

The west wall and the foundations of the Black Horse are stone; the rest of the structure is wood. One uncommon feature of it is the second floor, which consists of one apartment, formerly called the ball-room. The sleeping-rooms were back of the tap. The house ceased to be an inn about twenty years ago, and until then a famous sign swung from a post at a corner of the intersecting roads, alluring wayfarers with the gorgeousness of its blue, black, and yellow. We asked the fisherman's wife what had become of it, and she directed us to a little shed in the back garden, where we found it

with weeds and wild flowers growing around its cracked and nearly obliterated surface; the iron rods from which it had swung in many a furious storm were bent and rusty, and the counterfeit of the steed in the centre was a mere shadow.

On the second day of our jaunt we travelled between the showers, rain and shine playing at hide-and-seek while the light lasted.

How are the unities ignored in rural communities! Here was a race-course, and on

SIGN OF THE BLACK HORSE TAVERN.

the brow of a hill overlooking it a cemetery —a very old cemetery, with frayed and mouldy tombstones among the later ones of white marble—that ghastly material, which symbolizes so well the awful coldness and pallor of death. Four of the earliest are half smothered under rank grass, with cedars that look like black-robed sentinels sheltering them. The inscription upon one reads:

Here lyes ye body of
COLL. NICKLAS BRITTEN,
Aged 61 years,
Deceased January ye 12, 1774.

His epitaph commemorates his benevolence as follows:

Here lyes a man of tender hart
Unto the poore in every parte.
He never sent the poore away,
Which well is nowne unto this day.

His wife, who died in 1748, is buried next to him, and in the same row are the graves of Ruth, daughter of Thomas and Rachel Dougan, who was buried in 1749, and Rachel Dougan, who was buried in 1748. The granite tomb of the Vanderbilts is in the

OLD WELL ON THE RICHMOND ROAD.

vicinity, and a faded wreath of evergreens lay at the portal of the vault, where it had been left by some mourner of the dead millionaire. The bluebirds and yellow-birds, the orioles and the robins, were busy and noisy in the trees and shrubs with spring-time blitheness, and over the green meadows the sea was turning up its flushing edges of gold.

The church and the ground are Moravian. The former is a modern structure, and previous to its erection the parsonage was used for services, the corner-stone having been laid one hundred and fifteen years ago.

Turning by the Black Horse we drove to-

"Don't you remember this?" he said, with beautiful innocence, bringing the *Queen of Sheba* out of his coat pocket and reading a passage, telling how, as Lynde rode along the lanes, a country girl would now and then steal slyly to the red gate in the lichen-covered wall when he had passed, and follow him with her palm-shaded eyes down the lonely road; "'and it as frequently happened,'" Michael Angelo continued, "'that he would glance back over his shoulder at the nut-brown maid, whose closely clinging, scant drapery gave her a sculpturesque grace, to which her unconsciousness of it was a charm the more. These flushes of subtile recognition between youth and youth—these sudden mute greetings and farewells'"—Michael Angelo paused and sighed plaintively. "Ah, they don't do it here!" and, indeed, whether there is a surplus in the male population, or the island is too near the big cities for maidens to entertain a sentimental interest in passing vagabonds, the girls in the gardens went on picking weeds, and Michael Angelo pined vainly for a reciprocal glance.

The weather did not continue the same for more than twenty minutes at a time. Now there were great mountains of black and purple clouds in the air that threatened lasting rain and wind, and drew their folds over every part of the sky; we drew up for shelter under a desolate barn, and patiently watched the rain shooting its fine silver wire in oblique strokes through the murky atmosphere; then great chasms were opened in the vaporous mountains, which

CHARACTERS AT PRINCE'S BAY.

ward Richmond. It was noticeable that Michael Angelo looked back with candid interest at the girls in big sun-bonnets who were working in the gardens or watching us from the doors of the cottages. Michael Angelo is young, tender, and unreasonably impressionable; he adores the prose of Aldrich, and is some day going to make a picture of Margery Daw seesawing in her hammock.

dissolved or went scurrying away with the wind, and the sunshine discovered diamond mines in the damp, intensely green fields, and stalactites under the branches of the cedars and the pines. From the top of Richmond Hill a wide reach of undulating country was revealed to us, with the water of Mill Creek meandering through. Upon this eminence the British built their earth-

ACROSS PRINCE'S BAY FROM THE OLD TAVERN.

works, which are still visible, although the grass is sprouting out of the reddish soil.

As we were returning to our carriage, after having made the ascent, Michael Angelo lagged behind, and we were some distance ahead, when we discovered him running with extraordinary speed for the nearest fence, over which he leaped with a sudden development of agility that surprised us. Nor was he a moment too soon in gaining the road, for an Alderney bull had been at his heels, and stood gazing at him with disappointed anger.

A railway extends through the island from the ferry at Vanderbilt's Landing to Tottenville, opposite Perth Amboy, and we availed ourselves of it to Prince's Bay Station. From the station a pretty lane, with

shrub, which is a love song in botany, and awakens affectionate memories by its delicate white flowers that are so exquisitely placid, and its tender, succulent leaves. At the settlement, off which a fleet of schooners and sloops was at anchor, salty-looking men, with red and freckled faces, were coming to and from the boats with baskets of freshly gathered clams. A Prince's Bay clam, when the shell is still wet with brine, is a delicacy not to be hastily spoken of; it is more than delicious, and we kept the captain of an old tavern by the water-side busy for some time. The captain was a tall, thin, loosely jointed man, who opened each bivalve with a constant smile, and occasional nods of the head. "There's character in that old fellow's face," said Michael Angelo;

CLAMS AT PRINCE'S BAY.

hawthorn hedges at each side, leads to the fishing settlement, which is celebrated for its oyster beds. The hawthorn was in bloom, and filled the air with its incomparable fragrance. It seemed to us that the rose itself was not sweeter than this hardy English

and he actually insisted that Brush and the rest of us should keep him occupied in opening clams as a gratuitous model until his odd face was sketched. Our satisfied appetites were mercilessly ignored to suit this cool demand.

THE WAY TO THE BILLOPP HOUSE.

Then we drove to Tottenville, the south-western extremity of the island, and a very pretty little town it is; but the inhabitants that we met were given to a rashness of statement that caused us no little trouble. We were told that the old Billopp house, which we were searching for, was at the bottom of a certain street; at the bottom of that street we were told that it was at the top; at the top we were told to follow a certain hill: and an hour was lost through these unprovoked prevarications. At last, and in despair, we asked for directions from a venerable-looking old boy in a garden. "Ah, yes, the Billopp house!" he said, and added, as though it was a particularly good joke, worthy of great emphasis, "*You* call it the Billopp house, some calls it the Bently house, and *I* call it the old *stone* house." He repeated this with much unction, and shook his head with an imbecile sort of satisfaction. This thing could not last forever, however, and we had conspired to make a hostage of some one, who should not be released until he delivered us at the Billopp house, when the patriarch's intelligence experienced a lucid interval, and he put us on the right path.

The Billopp house is one of the oldest buildings on the island. It is built of stone, on a bowery slope that overlooks the confluence of the Raritan and the Staten Island Sound. The walls are two or three feet thick, and the gable roof is preposterously high and steep. Its first owner was Christopher Billopp, and its history is exceedingly interesting. When the Duke of York had conveyed New Jersey to Berkley Carteret, a question was raised as to whether Staten Island was included in the grant, and to settle the matter it was decided that all islands in the bay or harbor should belong to New York if they could be circumnavigated in twenty-four hours. Christopher Billopp, who owned a small ship called the *Bently*, sailed around Staten Island in that time, and the duke gave him the tract of land, on part of which the house is built, in reward for his services. Another story states that

GRAVE OF THOMAS BILLOPP.

THE OLD BILLOPP HOUSE.

Billopp was rewarded by the land for gallant service in a naval action.

It was in this old homestead that Franklin, Adams, and Edward Rutledge, of South Carolina, assembled to negotiate peace with Lord Howe after the battle of Long Island. The meeting lasted four hours, and the Americans, who had been appointed by Congress, would not consent to any treaty that was not based on the acknowledged independence of the colonies. Here, too, Billopp entertained various distinguished guests, including Sir Henry Clinton, General Robertson, General Knyphausen, Major André, and others. He had a pretty wife, and was celebrated for his hospitality, but he subsequently fared roughly at the hands of the patriots, and his property was confiscated.

From Tottenville we returned to the city, each of the artists avowing his intention to come back again at a future day in search of more of the abundant picturesque materials, of which they carried numerous graphic evidences in their books.

OLD WELL AT THE BILLOPP HOUSE.

Hospital Life
in New York
(1878)

HOSPITAL LIFE IN NEW YORK.

MOST of the hospitals of New York have two beginnings. The first is in the charitable forethought of the rich men who have endowed them. Inclosed by the privacy of his chamber or study, the millionaire has pondered over the disposition to be made of his accumulated wealth, and feeling the hand of sickness upon him, has remembered the thousands of others whose pain could not to do all that it craves, the fever might be allayed now and then, and life itself prolonged. In such meditations as these some of our hospitals have begun, and the total outcome of the endowments made through private munificence is a variety of establishments for the treatment of every imaginable ailment. A stranger is struck with the number and magnificence of the

NEW YORK HOSPITAL.

know the alleviation that money can procure. The heavy damask curtains drawn in ample folds over the windows, the glowing fire, the mild light of the study lamp, the soft resoundless carpets, the ministrations of the most skillful physicians, and the attentions of trained servants — all these blessings might not take the sting away from death nor wholly disarm suffering, but they surely assuage both. Love can do more than money in smoothing the distressed pillow; the dying laborer in his attic, with his wife's hand in his, may cross the gloomy boundary with greater resignation than the millionaire, says the sentimentalist; but were the love that waits upon the laborer with tireless devotion supplemented with the means New York hospitals. Some are of the size, and have the appearance, of palaces. They are ornaments to the city, and are among the largest buildings. The newer ones are built of warm red brick, and, with their sunny windows, spacious pavilions, and galleries, are memorable objects to the city's visitors. There is no kind of physical suffering that may not find treatment in one or the other, as we have said. The penniless outcast who is overtaken by sickness, the haggard victim of hip-disease, the incurable consumptive, and the raving creatures stricken with fever, are provided for with care and liberality; the patient with means may command all the luxuries a home could give, and those who are poor enjoy comforts impossible to them in their own narrow dwellings.

All hospitals began with Christ, and belong to Christianity. The Greeks looked with contempt upon physical weakness, and other nations of antiquity thought it beneath them to make provision for the sick and infirm. But the Nazarene and His dis-

horrible spot on the pavement baptized by the blood of a man who has fallen from a scaffolding aloft, out of a window, or through one of the trap-doors by which goods are hoisted into the lofts of the stores. "Give him air!" some cry, but the crowd hedges him in with morbid curiosity, only a few of the weaker ones turning aside with pale

A STREET ACCIDENT.

ciples taught men to compassionate suffering, and as the Church increased in wealth and influence, hospitals were founded—in the first place as houses for the shelter or refreshment of travellers, especially pilgrims, according to the Latin meaning of their name; and it was only with the multiplication of inns that they assumed their distinctive character as refuges for invalids.

The second of the two beginnings to the hospitals of New York that we spoke of above is in an episode with which all who walk the city streets must be familiar. There is a crash, a scream, a dull thud, and a crowd that momentarily chokes the traffic of the busy thoroughfare, the cause being an accident. The crowd presses around the

faces. He lies there huddled up and deathly white, as though all the bones in his body were broken; his eyes are filmed and opaque, and his mouth is rimmed with blood. A telegram sent from the nearest police station brings an ambulance, which dashes up to the spot from the nearest hospital. The surgeon quickly binds the fractured limbs between splints; and while the crowd gapes with wonder and admiration at the dexterity and system, the sufferer is gently lifted into the vehicle and driven away. Such is the practical and beneficent beginning of the New York hospitals to the hapless thousands who are annually maimed in the turmoil of the city streets.

For the purposes of ambulance service

PRIVATE PATIENT'S ROOM, NEW YORK HOSPITAL.

the city is divided into three police tele-graph districts, an independent wire con-necting all the precincts with the hospitals that are provided with ambulances. These are the New York and Roosevelt hospitals on the west side, and the Bellevue Hospital on the east side. The New York has two ambulances, one stationed at the House of Relief in Chambers Street, and the other at the hospital in Fifteenth Street; the Roose-velt has one, stationed at the hospital in Fifty-ninth Street; and the Bellevue has several. When an accident is reported at a police station, it is immediately announced by telegraph to the hospital of the district, and an idea of what usually happens then may be gleaned from the following account of our personal experience.

We were loitering one morning last Jan-uary in the apothecary's shop of the New York Hospital, which, besides the long rows of shelves filled with glass jars and bottles, contains a dial instrument, whose impera-tive tinkling suddenly put an end to our conversation. "The ambulance is wanted in Eighteenth Street," the surgeon in charge explained; and though his name was Slaugh-ter—an obviously unfortunate one for an Es-culapian—he proved himself to be one of the tenderest men that ever touched a wound. The apothecary's shop is in the basement, and from it a door opens upon a court-yard, at one side of which is a stable. A well-kept horse was quickly harnessed to the am-bulance; and as the surgeon took his seat behind, having first put on a jaunty uniform

cap with gold lettering, the driver sprang on to the box, where we had already placed our-selves, and with a sharp crack of the whip we rolled off the smooth asphalt of the court-yard into the street. Our speed was only pardonable in view of its object. As we swept around the corners and dashed over the crossings, both doctor and driver kept up a sharp cry of warning to the pedestrians, who darted out of our way with haste, or nervously retreated to the curb, looking aft-er us with faces expressive of indignant remonstrance, until they discovered by the gilt lettering on the panels what our vehicle was. The surliest car-drivers and the most aggressive of truckmen gave us the right of way, and pulled up or aside to afford us passage. People in a hurry stopped to look after us, and strove on tiptoe to discover whether or not we had a passenger. We rattled over the uneven cobble-stones of West Eighteenth Street, and at No. 225, where there is an iron gate before an alley-way with a small house at the end, an old man appeared and hailed us. We alighted, and followed him into the front-room on the ground-floor, the doctor carrying his in-struments under his arm.

The case was not very serious. The oc-cupant of the tenement, an old laborer, had slipped in entering, and fractured his leg a short distance above the ankle. The room served as kitchen and parlor for him and his wife, who began to whimper as soon as she saw the doctor, and refused to be com-forted, with a determination worthy of a more reasonable cause. The furniture consisted of a few chairs, a table, some dishes, and a stove, upon which a kettle was steaming. "Where's the man?" inquired the doctor. The wife moaned, and we might have waited for an answer had not an expostulatory voice come from an inner apartment, "Hould yer noise, Mary." Obtaining a candle, we found the sufferer lying on a disordered bed with all his clothes on and a pipe

nate called out, as the doctor rolled up his trousers. "Mary, me pipe's out; give us another draw, an' be quick about it. Maybe it 'll be a long time till I get another one." The pipe was refilled with tobacco, puffed into a glow by an obliging friend, and handed to him. "Yes, I must have another draw," he went on, as he put himself in position for the doctor, who gently raised the injured limb and applied the splints to it,

DOCTOR TREATING SULLIVAN'S FRACTURED LEG.

in his mouth, the room having neither windows nor other light or ventilation than that which struggled from the kitchen through the door. He was a small, rosy old man from the north of Ireland, and was not in the least discomposed by his accident. "If I'd had the laist dhrop of drink in me, I cud onderstand it; but faith I hadn't tasted," he exclaimed, as the doctor energetically threw his coat and cap on the floor, regardless of the gold lettering and gold buttons, and prepared for business. Two splints were selected, and a roll of cotton bandages taken from a sachel. "Hould on a bit, doctor; me pipe's out," the unfortu-

packing them with oakum before binding them with the cotton ribbon. Once or twice, and only once or twice, the old fellow winced. "Murther, doctor, don't touch me heel; that's where it hurts!" During the rest of the operation he quietly puffed his pipe, soothed his wife, and endeavored to flatter the doctor most outrageously. "Och, doctor, you're the greatest man in the world—mind me heel—be quiet, Mary—that's what ye are, doctor, the greatest man in the world."

"All comfortable, eh?" said the doctor, neatly cutting the last bandage.

"As nice as can be, Sor."

Finding that amputation was not immediately necessary, Mary smiled at last, and tidied her husband's dress before he was lifted by two burly policemen on to the stretcher, which had been brought from the ambulance into the outer room.

The stretcher, like all the appliances of the ambulance, is mercifully ingenious, and devised with the object of giving the sufferer the least possible pain in transportation. It consists simply of a strip of canvas about three feet wide and seven feet long, with a tube at each side, through which the wooden poles for carrying it are slipped. The poles are braced at each end of the canvas by iron cross-bars, which are easily detached; and the beauty of the whole arrangement is that it obviates the necessity of disturbing the patient again on his arrival at the hospital, the stretcher being put upon the bed and the poles being withdrawn. A light mattress and several blankets were spread over the canvas, and the old man was tucked in as snugly as a baby in a crib. "Good-by, Mrs. Murphy," he cried to a neighbor who had come in as the policemen were bearing him to the ambulance. "Good-by, Mr. Sullivan, and it's sorry I am to see ye l'avin' in this way," whereupon the wife burst into fresh tears.

The ambulance had been backed up to the curb, and the tail-board removed. We now discovered that it had two bottoms, and the upper one, which was softly padded, had been drawn off on caster wheels so that it slanted from the end of the vehicle to the sidewalk. The padding was luxuriously yielding, and when the stretcher had been placed upon it, it was pushed into the ambulance, and the tail-board closed upon it. The doctor took his seat behind, and, as we drove off, a voice came from the blankets: "May I ta-ake another draw, doctor?" Assent being given, the blue wreaths of Mr. Sullivan's tobacco rolled upward from the blankets until we trotted under the archway of the hospital and pulled up before the door of the receiving ward, where two orderlies drew the stretcher out and deposited it on a bed in the manner previously described, while Dr. Slaughter reported the case to the house surgeon, who was thence responsible for it.

All cases of casualty are received at the New York Hospital and treated gratuitously if the patient's circumstances require it, although a small sum per week for board is usually expected and paid. The hospital building is probably the most luxurious one in the world, and its administration is as nearly perfect as is possible. It is seven stories high, with a Mansard-roof, and has accommodations for about two hundred patients with their attendants. It has a frontage on Fifteenth Street of 175 feet, and it extends through the block to Sixteenth Street, Sixth Avenue bounding it on the west and Fifth Avenue on the east. Stone, iron, and red brick are prominent materials in the façade, the many windows of which look out upon ornamental balconies. The rear is formed by the old Thorn mansion, one of the largest and handsomest dwelling-houses in the city, which is now used as a residence for the superintendent, a library, and an office, the library containing some 15,000 volumes, besides an important general collection of specimens and a fine pathological cabinet. The water used is partly supplied by Croton pipes and partly by an Artesian well. The heating is done by steam. Near the roof there is a large fan, driven by steam, which compels a draught of fresh air through the building, and, when necessary, the air can be warmed before circulation by passing over hot pipes in the basement. All the kitchens and laundries are in the uppermost stories above the wards, and non-absorbent materials have been used in the walls and floors, with a view to the prevention of the poisons generated by some diseases. The whole structure is as nearly fire-proof as possible; the only wood-work is in the doors and windows; the floors are made of tiles laid in cement on iron girders, and the wainscoting is marble. All parts are connected by the inarticulate speech of electric signal bells, and two elevators run from basement to attic. It is avowed that while no attempt at magnificence has been made, the utmost care has been taken to make every part complete, substantial, and harmonious; but the directors are too modest in this: their establishment *is* magnificent in itself, in its worth, and in its aims.

As we entered the anteroom to the superintendent's office a mournful old Irishwoman was making an application for the admission of her husband, the driver of a coal cart, who had fallen from his seat and been crushed under the wheels. Several other faded and shabby women, all of them Irish, were waiting for an audience, some shedding tears and moaning with the profusion of grief that characterizes their race. Indeed, were it not for the never-ending misfortunes of the Irish, most of the hospitals would have many empty wards, as that nationality contributes a majority of the cases treated.

"There's not wan thing in the building that is not good enough for a church," said the orderly—he, too, was Irish—who became our guide. And as we went along the spacious corridors and through the lofty wards, the disclaimer of magnificence seemed unreasonable. Even such minor details as the designs of the tiles and the gas-fixtures are artistic, and the sunlight streams in every where and carries its golden cheer and revivifying warmth to the pale faces and wasted bodies set in the little cots along

CHILDREN'S WARD, BELLEVUE HOSPITAL.

the wards. Every thing is new, clean, and bright. The brass-work and nickel plate throw back the light in dazzling rays from their burnished surfaces, the white walls are unblemished by speck or crack, and even in the surgical wards the air is fresh and pure. But the humanity and good sense of the design are most conspicuous in the provision made for the floods of sunshine, which is the most potent element usually left out of the *materia medica.* The front of the hospital faces the south, and the sun streams in through big generous windows, wide shafts let more of the shine in from the roof, and on one of the upper stories there is a large solarium, where the radiance of summer is almost perpetual. We ascend by an elevator of more capacity than that of a fashionable hotel—an elevator of varnished maple, which is the wood used throughout the building; and alighting from that vehicle, whose fluency of motion gives one an idea that it may become a mechanical means of getting to heaven, we are conducted into a hall separated from the sky only by a translucent canopy of glass, which so filters the light as it pours through that it seems to become tangible in a golden powder—a shower-bath of disintegrated sunbeams. It is a brilliant, frosty, nipping January day outside; but here there is the balmy mellowness of a temperate summer; plants and flowers are in bloom, and fountains are gurgling, spurting, and bubbling with liquid music. There are fresh and salt water aquariums, in the pale green depths of which strange and beautiful fish disport, and on the tiny islands of cork turtles are airing themselves or luxuriously enjoying the spray of the fountains. The convalescents, sitting on the benches and reclining chairs, feel new blood coursing through them and greater strength in this pleasant atmosphere with the bright surroundings; the wearisome-vibrations of melody transport him through the sky-light, down which the sun comes streaming, to other scenes, which, if we could find them out from the dreaminess of his face, might not be as pleasant as the solarium; but they are home scenes, probably, and it is for home that he longs. A row of old men, all of them showing some deficiency of limb or some scar, lean against one of the walls and stare vacantly and silently across

WRITING HOME ON AN ADJUSTABLE TABLE.

ness of the cot is relieved, and visions arise of the time when their recovery will enable them to bear the friction of the active world again.

The solarium is the cheeriest place about the hospital to the visitors as well as to the patients; it is always pretty and warm, and it is a feature that might be imitated by other institutions, and extended with beneficial results. In a far corner a group of men are sitting, fine-looking fellows most of them, with robust frames; but their pallid faces, just touched by the returning glow of health, their languor of manner, the empty sleeves of some and the crutches of others, record months of suffering and hard-fought battles with death. One is strumming on a Jew's-harp, and the feeble, pinging the floor; and a few children, weazen and pale, limp through a game in the middle of the room, and occasionally give vent to a pitiful little treble of laughter. The women sit apart, some sewing or reading, and others listless and idle, with eyes set upon the invisible space of dreams. It is very quiet in the solarium; the fountains make more noise than the children, who soon grow tired of their play, and sigh wearily; the footsteps are muffled, and the voices are low.

The kitchen and laundry, on the upper floors, are provided with all the modern improvements of a first-class hotel; no fixed dietary scale is adhered to, and both the kind and quantity of food are varied at the discretion of the superintendent. Washing, rinsing, wringing, and mangling are all done by steam machinery, some of which is novel and successful.

We passed from ward to ward, pausing now and then before a case of particular interest, and in each we found exquisite cleanliness and ample space. The cots are of iron, and are provided with adjustable bars by which the occupants can change their positions without help. Each cot is also provided with an electric tube by which the patient can summon the nurse, whose private sitting and sleeping room is at one end of the ward, adjoining the dining-room for convalescents. In one dining-

lights of convalescence. A marble-topped, drop-handled, finely carved walnut bureau, with a half-length mirror, and a wash-stand with unlimited hot and cold water and silver-plated fittings; electric bells communicating with the nurses; a polished walnut study table and an adjustable table—added to the luxurious convenience of the room, the rent of which was fifty dollars per week. But we wonder how many there are in the city, rich or poor, who would not choose the sympathy of a plain home in preference to such formal splendors as these in an institution?

BELLEVUE HOSPITAL.

room that we saw the table was set for dinner with the extreme neatness that one might expect in a popular restaurant, but not in a large public institution. The cloth was snow-white; a clean napkin was folded before each seat, and the service was of a bright silver-plate. At each end of each ward there are lavatories with hot and cold water, and bath-rooms, all patients being required to bathe once a week unless excused by the house surgeon.

On the lower floors of the building there is a theatre for operations and another for autopsies, both provided with every appliance that recent science has devised; and fronting the Fifteenth Street corridor there is a row of rooms for private patients, the rents of which are from fifteen to fifty dollars a week. It occasionally happens that the guest of a hotel or some one who is isolated from friends desires the systematic attention which a hospital can give, and having means, he can occupy one of these rooms, which are handsomely furnished, and equipped in a style particularly adapted for an invalid. Our guide took us into a charming little apartment, with windows facing the south. A beautiful rug was stretched over the middle of the floor; the upholstery was morocco; and besides a lounge, and a wide bed with immaculate linen, there were reclining-chairs, rocking-chairs, *sans-souci* chairs, camp-stools, and foot-stools, that conjured up pictures of the dreamily lazy de-

We have not yet exhausted the resources of the New York Hospital. It has a practically free dispensary, special prison-like compartments for the treatment of sufferers from delirium tremens, and a branch or House of Relief in Chambers Street. Its corporation is enormously wealthy, and received its charter in 1771 from George the Third, through John, the Earl of Dunmore —the original governors, who met at Bolton's Tavern, having been John Watts, Andrew Elliot, Philip Livingston, William M'Adam, Walter Franklin, George Bowne, Abraham Lott, and G. W. Beekman. From 1821 till 1876, 6884 patients were admitted, of whom 908 died, 2940 were discharged well, 1646 in an improved condition, and 1208 unimproved. Not a few animadversions are cast upon the institution, but it is a good thing, and does good work.

To pass from it to the Bellevue Hospital affords a contrast somewhat startling. The one combines in its structure and administration nearly every thing that medical and sanitary science has revealed for the relief of the sick. Most of its patients are poor, but not so poor or alienated from brotherly affection that they are unable to pay the cost of their support; many of them are mechanics or small tradesmen; an impoverished actor or journalist may be found among them; and a few are prosperous and even wealthy. But the other is a hospital for the poorest of the poor, the dregs of society, the semi-criminal, starving, unwelcome class, who suffer and die unrecognized, and to whom charity at the best is cold and mechanical. This is a large and increasing constituency in New York city, where the word pauper is acquiring the dread significance and suggestion of hopeless misery that it has in Great Britain; and the wards are filled with wasted souls drifting through the agonies of disease toward unpitied and unremembered deaths, with no tenderer hand to clasp at the parting than that of the strange nurse, who has grown callous through long familiarity with such experiences. Many of the patients lie for months without receiving one friendly call except from the colporteur, the priest, or the ladies of the Flower Mission—lie and wait with the carelessness of result that makes the days blank and the future a matter of indifference. There is no luxury here; not much gentleness. The building was built for an almshouse or prison some fifty years ago,

Twenty-seventh streets, and covers the whole block between them, First Avenue, and the East River. The river ebbing and flowing, shining and rippling in the sun, and bestirred by traffic, cheers the situation, and a few trees and a patch of grass— all that is left of the wide fields that once swept up to Murray Hill—soften the granite austerity of the eastern front. But Bellevue is still forbidding. A high brick wall isolates it from the thoroughfares. There is one medical college just within the boundaries, and another just outside. The windows of the dissecting-rooms shine until late hours in the night, for there is no scarcity of subjects in colleges which reap the harvest of a charity hospital. And at one end of the dispensary for the out-door poor, which is under the college within the grounds, two downward steps lead into a low-roofed building, over the entrance of which hangs a dingy lamp inscribed with black letters, "The Morgue." The room

A GAME OF DOMINOES, BELLEVUE HOSPITAL.

and its ponderous dull gray mass of granite is sullen-looking and unadapted to its uses. The New York Hospital, with its sunny windows facing the south, and its pleasant surroundings, is less than a mile away; but to reach Bellevue we have to cross a district of tenement-houses, plentifully dotted with shabby little stores and corner groggeries, where the garbage is piled up in the streets, the men are idle, the women slatternly, and the children as nearly nude as the weather permits. It is between Twenty-sixth and

within contains five marble slabs behind a glass partition, with sprays of water falling over them. The dead-house is close by, and several times a week the funereal little steamer bears the unlettered coffins away to Potter's Field. It was a cold November morning when we last saw her leave the wharf, and the fog in which she was soon hidden symbolized the unrecorded lives, the cheerless deaths, and the unattended graves of her load. Suspicious-looking men and untidy women haunt the neighborhood, attracted to it by the morbid curiosity of their diseased minds, and it may occur to them that if they do not die in prison, their death-beds will be here, or in the Charity Hospital on Blackwell's Island, which is visible from the grounds of Bellevue.

The lawn is a favorite resort of the convalescents, who hobble about the paths on crutches in fair weather, or sun themselves on the benches, and even venture to cast a line into the river with the hope of insnaring the fish. Each floor of the main building is traced by a light iron balcony; and here too, when the wind is not bleak nor the atmosphere moist, the better patients gather—the men smoking their pipes, and the women sewing or reading. The movement of the river is soothing and recreative; the sailing vessels trading in Long Island Sound glide to and fro, and the big white passenger steamers plough majestically by like moving palaces.

The activity at Bellevue has no end. The keeper of the lodge at the entrance is continually besought for admission, and so worried by impossible requests that one can pardon his shortness of temper. Young doctors and older professors enter unchallenged; the white ambulances are constantly busy, rolling out on summons, and quickly coming back with new cases; a woman begs to see her sick husband, and has brought some little delicacy with her, but it is after the visiting hour, and because she can not be admitted she goes away weeping, with a dull heart that speaks in her homely face; other visitors, who are more fortunate, are promenading the flags under the gloomy front of the hospital, and supporting the invalids they have come to see—here a pale old man, the human counterpart of a broken reed, is clutching the hand of his little granddaughter, as though life with all its pains is precious to him while that responsive grasp remains; a crippled workman leans heavily on the arm of his wife, who looks anxiously into his face at every step to gauge his suffering; a mother helps her sick daughter along, and a poor fellow who has lost both legs watches them with curiously wistful face, as though he was pining for the day that would bring him his visitors. The picture has many changes, no reverse: it is pain, anguish, or death always. If the spectator is cynical, his morbidity is enlarged; but if, without being an optimist, he can look at it with clear eyes, its gloom and sadness are relieved by a glimpse of the tenderness that blossoms in the hearts of the commonest poor.

Some steps lead to the main entrance, and underneath them is a passage by which the ambulance cases are admitted, a groan telling us that one is at the portals the moment we ascend. The wide hall is flagged and whitened. The warden's office is at one side, with the bright, horribly suggestive surgical instruments stored in glass cases against its walls, and at the other side is the room of the Medical Board, where one of the college classes is assembled. The professor is one of the most eminent surgeons in the world, and is relating some amusing incidents of his early career previous to making the round of the wards. He is a great favorite with the students, and a very prominent member of the faculty. Some thirty-five or forty years ago he came to the metropolis from Kentucky, a rough-and-ready lad, at whom the college authorities looked doubtingly. To-day a small diary carried in his breast pocket is overrun with engagements, and distinguished people travel hundreds of miles to consult him. He works the year round, sparing himself only one week's recreation in the Maine woods at midsummer; but with all his powers of endurance and industry of habits, he can not find time to treat all who would be benefited by his wonderful skill. Prodigious fees are offered to him by the wealthy, and if he worked for gain alone, a little labor would bring him a large income. But he is not regulated by the inhuman supply and demand doctrine. Two cases are presented to him: one, acute, of a charity patient, offering him next to nothing in pecuniary reward, and the other, not dangerous, of a rich man, offering him a splendid fee. If he can not attend to both, he gives his services where they are most required. Physically he is huge of bulk and loud in voice, with a manner striking for its *bonhomie*. Inspiration is carried to the sick-room by his voice, brusque as it is, and his presence is a stimulant to the pining cripple, bringing with it the invigoration of a southern breeze. The most objectionable thing about him is the grip he gives one's hand in greeting, making the fingers, the palm, and the whole length of the arm quiver for half an hour afterward with such agony that whenever a fellow-member of the faculty sees him approaching, he dives his hands into his pockets and imploringly cries, "Oh, don't, doctor, don't!" It would be unreasonable to say of such a man that he is not proud of himself, his work, and his methods; on the contrary, he talks of them freely, and he is never more entertaining than when he is doing so, or uttering fierce denunciations of "old women" in their practice of surgery and therapeutics. The class is in a roar of laughter over some joke when we enter; but the doctor's cigar is almost burned out, and that means more serious matters.

We pass with the class from ward to ward and from cot to cot, the doctor treating the patients with a heartiness that forces an evanescent smile to the saddest faces, and explaining the cases and operations to the class with so much perspicuity and simplicity that the thickest-headed student would have unimaginable difficulty in not understanding. A mite of a boy is sitting in a big chair by himself, a Tiny Tim of a boy, with large, liquid eyes, the whitest of faces, the doctor, whose hands are almost as large as the child's body; he is a sufferer from an obscure disease of a joint, and was brought to the hospital as an incurable case. The doctor's specialty is diseases of the joints,

TAKING AN AIRING, BELLEVUE HOSPITAL.

and the sunkenest of cheeks. "How are you to-day, Sir?" the doctor inquires, in a tremendous tone, that makes the piping answer sound ridiculously small. "Pretty well, thank you, Sir." "Can you walk?" "I guess so, Sir;" and the second answer is in a still shriller key, for the voice has not yet recovered from the exhaustion of the first. Tiny Tim is lifted out of his chair by and by that pre-eminent skill which has cheated death many a time he has saved the child's life. Tim limps across the floor and back again, the longest journey that he has made out of the nurse's arms for some months; a faint flush and a smile of satisfaction lighten his face as he climbs into the chair again. He is out of breath, but when the doctor asks if the exertion hurt him, he readily answers, "Not a bit, Sir." "Now, gentlemen," says the doctor to his class, taking the repaired limb in his hand, " this is a very—" But we are not reporting the doctor's lectures. We stand by the bedside of a woman whose life is ebbing away under the strain of a cancer, and here our good Samaritan speaks more cheering words—the most he can do, for the case is irremediable. One of the white-capped nurses of the training school is watching the patient; she is a fair, wholesome-looking girl, intelligent, neatly dressed, and agreeable in manner. We ask her if there is much extreme suffering in the ward. "That is our worst case," she says, pointing to the woman by whom the doctor and his class are standing; "the poor thing has been here eighteen months without any hope of recovery. No one has been to see her—no relative or friend—in all that time." "Can she last much longer?" "Not more than three months; she is anxious for death, and prays for it." At this moment we feel that the glassy eyes of the sufferer are bearing upon us; her face is colorless, and her lips are pursed as though she desired to hold back the low moan that escapes them. Is not the sight enough to convert one to the doctrine of legalized suicide by proxy, or any scheme of euthanasia? On the next bed a wrinkled and very thin old woman is muttering deliriously and sometimes inaudibly; she is over seventy years of age, and hers too is a fatal case. The nurse is young, pretty, and blooming, and her appearance of health and cheerfulness in the midst of pallid disease seems almost out of place. Is it a consecrated life, the sacrificial impulse of religious fervor? No; her motive is the earning of a livelihood, and she is the pupil of an institution which has opened a new and practicable field of work for American women.

The Training School for Nurses, which now possesses a substantial brick building as a residence in Twenty-sixth Street, opposite the hospital, was opened in May, 1873, to instruct intelligent women in hospital and private nursing. It began with a lady superintendent and a staff of six nurses, whose number has now increased to fifty-six, thirty-eight being actively employed at Bellevue, and three at the Emergency Hospital. Many difficulties were experienced at the start, and though the committee in charge advertised and applied to physicians for aid, four women only were found capable of acting as head nurses, one of whom was soon discharged for inefficiency. Out of seventy-three applicants for admission to the school many were totally unfitted by mental incapacity, others by physical weakness, and a large number withdrew because they would not spend two years in learning the profession. Accepting twenty-nine probationers, the committee was compelled to dismiss three on account of ill health, five on account of inefficiency, and two on account of family claims upon them, leaving nineteen, who succeeded, and proved the advantages of the school to themselves in affording them profitable employment, and to humanity generally in fitting intelligent women to become positive helps in the hospital and sick-room. The requirements of the committee are exacting. Pupils must be from twenty-one to thirty-five years of age, unmarried, obedient, amiable, steadfast in purpose, in good health, having no kind of infirmity, neither deafness nor dimness of vision, and quick in observation. The candidates having assured the committee of their excellence in these virtues, are admitted to the school on probation for one month, being boarded and lodged without expense, but not paid, and at the expiration of that period they engage themselves for a two years' course of instruction and service, with salary, provided they are satisfactory. The course includes lectures on the diseases of children, obstetrics, eruptive fevers, ventilation and bathing, hemorrhages and the circulation of the blood, arteries, respiration and temperature, superficial anatomy and uterine appliances—all of which are given by able physicians and surgeons. Lessons also are given in bandaging, in general ward work, in the management of a sick-room, and in physiology. At the end of the first year an examination of the pupils is held, and at the end of the second year diplomas are issued to those entitled to them. The primary object of the founders was to improve the nursing in public hospitals, and no one can say that improvement was unnecessary, or that it has not been effected. Previous to the opening of the school, Bellevue was a very much mismanaged institution; three patients sometimes slept on two beds, five patients on three beds, and it happened now and then that they slept on the floor. During two weeks of January, 1876, there was no soap in the hospital, and not enough clothing; many patients had neither pillows nor blankets, and forty-eight per cent. of the amputations made proved fatal, owing, no doubt, to the poison in the walls. But the worst feature was the character of the nurses, who were profane, ignorant, careless, heartless, and in most cases utterly unfitted for their positions. We look back with extreme pity to the patients who were immured in the hospital, and dragged through their illness to a long-deferred recovery, or hurried to an avertable death, at that period. The introduction of the young, intelligent, kindly nurses of the training school into the female wards, and a closer supervision of the orderlies in the male wards, have brought about a change for the better, however, and it is now possible to visit the hospital without having our instincts of humanity shocked. Instead of the untidy and often brutal creatures of old, such women as she to whom we spoke, gentle in manner and good to look upon, minister to the sufferers, who, paupers though they are, have claims that are eloquent from their helplessness. The ivy weaving its disks of green around the windows, the illuminated mottoes on the walls, the little odds and ends for diversion and recreation visible where the patients are most loathsome or least interesting, are testimony of the beneficence of the new era.

But the doctor has gone with his class, and we do not find him again until the clinic is over, and he is discussing with the students in a familiar but earnest manner some of the cases that they have seen. Many picturesque incidents appeal to us as we trace him through the wards and the close corridors, which show the unsuitability of the building for hospital purposes, the walls being thick enough for a prison, the roof low, and the ventilation insufficient. The door of the private room of one of the house staff is open, and several young physicians within, stretched out on lounges or easy-chairs, and obscuring themselves in tobacco smoke, are in debate about one of the morning operations; it is a very pleasant little apartment, with plenty of books, pictures, and possibly a skeleton in a closet. Some men with empty sleeves, bandaged heads, and pale faces are playing dominoes at a long table in one of the wards, but even so slight an exertion seems too much for them, and they sigh wearily; and in one of the cots a man whose large frame has lost flesh and strength is propped up with pillows, and is writing a letter home with palsied fingers. Christmas is not yet quite over in the children's ward; toys are lying on the floor, and the evergreen festoons are still hung against the walls. As often as the nurse moves, the children who are up follow her and cling to her skirts, or take her hand with demonstrations of the greatest affection—something that was probably never seen in Bellevue before the training school began to send its pupils there. But the air is not sweet, and we seek the outer space, where the shadows are falling upon the lawn, and the river is shining and tossing in rebellion against the traffic. What we have seen seems like a dream, but it is as great a reality as the granite mass which contains it and looms above us.

Not the least interesting thing about Bellevue is the number which it accommo-

MOUNT SINAI HOSPITAL.

dates. In 1876 the total number of patients admitted was 5165, the total number discharged was 4313, and the total number of deaths was 698. Subdivided by nationality, 2215 patients—the greatest number—were Irish, 1680 Americans, 595 Germans, 256 English, and 56 French. The mortality for 1876 was at the rate of twelve and one-half per cent. The hospital is under the direction of the Commissioners of Charities and Correction, who also control a Reception Hospital at Ninety-ninth Street, with a capacity for 20 beds; the Charity Hospital, on Blackwell's Island, with a capacity for 790 beds; the Fever, Epileptic, and Paralytic Hospital on Blackwell's Island, with 70 beds; the Incurable Hospital, with 180 beds; the Homœopathic Hospital on Ward's Island, with 650 beds; the Hart's Island Hospital for Convalescents, with 326 beds; the Nursery Hospital, with 208 beds; and the Infants' Hospital on Randall's Island, with 450 beds. All of these are free, and their total capacity is for 4986 patients.

The most we can do within the limited space of a magazine article is to select for description those hospitals which are representative; and thus, as the New York is

noteworthy for its magnificence, and Bellevue for its extent, St. Luke's projects itself
as the one having the most home-like qualities. The principle under which it is governed gives it a unique position, the character of a family being maintained as far as is
possible in a public institution. There is
a house father, or superintendent, a house
mother, or matron, and a Protestant sister-

riam of lost relatives, a gift of $5000 endow-
ing a bed in perpetuity, and $3000 endow-
ing one during the life of the donor.

The building is situated in the aristocratic Fifth Avenue, at the northwest corner
of Fifty-fourth Street, in the midst of fashionable dwellings, and within a stone's-
throw of Central Park. The front faces
the south, and is separated from the streets

SHAKING HANDS WITH THE HOUSE FATHER AT ST. LUKE'S HOSPITAL—CHILDREN'S WARD.

hood, the members of which act as nurses,
and are supported by their order independently of the hospital funds, while the relations between physicians, surgeons, and patients are much the same as they would be
in any private household. The founder
of the hospital and the originator of the
scheme was the late Rev. Dr. Muhlenberg,
who, until his death, was the house father
and an untiring *devotee* of the institution,
spreading its reputation by his many kind-
nesses, and making it a great success,
though it began with so small a collection
as thirty dollars, made one Sunday in his
Church of the Holy Communion. In ambulance cases the sufferer is allowed to choose
a hospital, and a large proportion favor St.
Luke's. Seven dollars a week are charged
for board when the beneficiary can afford
it, but of the 1134 cases treated in 1876–77,
891 were gratuitous, 492 were American,
290 Irish, 181 English or Scotch, and 157
Germans or citizens of other countries.
Many of the beds are endowed by church
societies and private individuals *in memo-*

by an inclosed garden, with an ample lawn
and some large shade trees and shrubbery.
The material is brick painted a modest
drab, and the architectural design includes
a central chapel, with wards and corridors
extending longitudinally from it. The
chapel is abundantly lighted and ventilated, and becomes a reservoir of fresh air,
which flows into the corridors, wards, and
stairways, and circulates through the house.
There are six wards—one for boys, one for
men's medical cases, one for men's surgical,
one for women's medical, one for women's
surgical, and one for children. The children's ward is very pretty, and not unpleasant to visit, despite the wan faces of its little occupants, and the history it gives of
pain blighting life in its very infancy. The
sunshine floods the long room; bright green
vines twine lovingly around the windows;
autumn leaves have been combined in tasteful designs on the walls by women's hands,
which have left their dainty impress in all
the wards; the cheering words of the New
Testament are emblazoned in illuminated

letters over the cots, and toys are scattered on the floor in an enviable profusion—toys, "the alphabet of life, through which children learn what poetry, what passion, and what property mean," as a clever anonymous writer has said. The picturesqueness of the effect is heightened by the gay little jackets worn by the patients—the scarlets, blues, and pinks, which must make some of the poor little creatures vain for the first time in their lives. A good sister is reading the marvellous history of "Jack and the Bean-Stalk," illustrated with gorgeous chromo-lithographs, to a tiny cripple, who lies in his cot with his eyes dilating and his hands clutched as his mind intently follows the growth of the bean-stalk and the intrepid mountaineering of the hero who climbed it. A Gothic castle is springing up in the middle of the floor from the industry of two young builders, who are so white and frail

are all white, the bodies all tremulous, and the eyes all pensive. A little carriage is wheeled up to us by a small invalid, who has as much as she can do to propel it; a victim of hip-disease is seated inside, and the disease has left a terrible record of its

The Churchman Cot
Endowed by Children
June 1876.

"THE CHURCHMAN COT," ST. LUKE'S HOSPITAL.

that their structure needs no mortar to be as strong as they are; and there, at the side of another cot, a care-worn man sits and holds the hand of his child and bends over the sad face, which stares vacantly at the ceiling. The ward may be never so sunny, and the effort made to divert and recreate its inmates never so generous, but the faces

ravages in the cadaverous cheeks, the pinched features, and the emaciated frame of the sufferer. The two have come to shake hands with Mr. Baker, the present house father and pastor, who courteously took us through the wards; indeed, the affectionate confidence manifested by the little ones in their guardians at St. Luke's, and at all the other hospitals we visited, bespoke invariable kindness. The chapel has two galleries for the patients of the upper story wards, and is, like the other parts of the building, light, warm, and cheerful. The reading-desk holds a copy of the four Gospels, large quarto in size, each page of which has been written in a legible and handsome style by a former inmate of the institution, and the wide vellum margins are illuminated with original designs, a different one appearing on each page. The oratory of the sisters is near the chapel, and their prayers are heard earliest in the morning and late at night. While St. Luke's is distinctively a Church hospital, however, and was founded by

urday might be instituted, as in London, when collection boxes could be left in public vehicles and resorts, such as dépôts, omnibuses, and street cars, for the reception of the penny of the multitude.

Another distinctive feature of St. Luke's is the privacy allowed to patients, each bed being surrounded by exquisitely clean white cotton curtains. The cleanliness of all the wards and the purity of air are not distinctive, but they are characteristic. The laundry is fitted with the same appliances as that of the New York Hospital, and the weekly wash averages about 6000 pieces. The quiet charm of the children's ward is seen again in the adults', where pictures

THE LAUNDRY AT ST. LUKE'S.

Episcopalians, it is not sectarian in its work, for during the year 1876–77 only 324 of the patients treated were members of that body, and the remainder included 483 other Protestants, 297 Roman Catholics, and 6 Jews. The average cost for each patient during treatment was forty-eight dollars six and a half cents, and the average cost for each person a day was one dollar one and five-eighths of a cent. By the recent introduction of the admirable English custom of having an annual collection made in the churches on a specified Sunday for the benefit of the hospitals, contributions have been gathered for St. Luke's on the last Sundays of December from Episcopal churches, the result last year having been over $5000; and in view of the non-sectarian character of the institution, collections might be made in other churches, and not for this hospital alone, but for hospitals generally; more than that, a Hospital Sat-

and other decorations, the sunny light and the gentle ministrations of the sisters, assuage the weariness of the sufferers' confinement.

The Brooklyn Homœopathic Hospital is even more home-like than St. Luke's—not that the latter is wanting either in endeavor or intention, but because it is very much larger, and because as size increases, the coziness of the domestic circle decreases. Here, also, the nursing is done by a Protestant sisterhood, whose taste and industry have made the wards look very pretty indeed. The building is on Cumberland Street, and is small and unpretentious in its architectural form; it contains some sixty or seventy beds, all of which are free. It has only been open about four years, but in those four years, aside from the fact that it is one of the first homœopathic establishments of the kind in America, it has done splendid work. At the dispensary connected with it over 8000 patients are treated in a year without charge, and over 12,000 prescriptions issued and made up. The medicines, the board, and the nursing are all gratuitous, except to the occupants of a few private rooms, who pay a moderate

her in a boudoir that would charm the greatest ignoramus who ever slept in ignorance of Eastlake, although few of the decorations were costly, and the tasteful effects were mostly the result of home industry, like the book-shelves, which were partly made by

CONVALESCENTS, HOMŒOPATHIC HOSPITAL, BROOKLYN.

sum per week, according to their means; and the government is as mild as that of a well-disciplined family. It is the special aim of the managers, the sisterhood, and the society of ladies in connection with it to have as little red tape and fuss and feathers about it as possible.

Our amiable *cicerone* was Dr. A. E. Sumner, president of the medical and surgical staff, who devotes himself to the work with inexhaustible enthusiasm. "You must let me introduce you to our little sister," he said, as he led us up stairs from the dispensary in the basement to the first floor; and we found her in the prettiest little room conceivable, with a plethora of books, pictures, and knickknacks lying on the tables, covering the walls, and filling *étagères*, brackets, and shelves without number. We found

her own hands; but she was not a little sister at all—that allusion to her was a pleasantry of the doctor's. One of the fullest and most beaming faces that ever left England behind, wreathing itself into constant smiles, shone under the broad white flaps of her cap and above the white lawn collar of her black dress; and her form was such a marvel of rotundity that, with the suggestions of the furniture before us, we could easily imagine her a prioress of mediæval times, and a very good prioress too, without an uncomfortable degree of asceticism in her nature. She took us through the wards, and in every corner we saw the utmost cleanliness and innumerable evidences of the thoughtful care bestowed upon the patients. The wards are scarcely larger than the bedrooms of a big country house, and they are nearly as comfortable. In one we found a pretty young sister amusing some of her charges with a novel instrument of her own construction—an ordinary board with common pins stuck in it in rows, so arranged that a finger-nail run over them gave the sound of a popular air; and another sister sat in the midst of some convalescent women, reading to them while they

material used is principally brick. It has a central administrative department with lateral pavilions, and a large detached barrack ward, which is erected in the garden, and has no communication with the main structure, except by an open corridor. The administrative building contains the various offices; the apartments of the officers and their families; an apothecary's shop and a

THE SOUTH WINDOW, BROOKLYN HOMŒOPATHIC HOSPITAL.

sewed. There are three sisters besides Sister Mildred, the superior, and unless gratitude grows in the hearts of the patients as well as the ivy grows around the windows and covers the dull spaces, they must be ungrateful indeed.

The Roosevelt Hospital, at Fifty-ninth Street and Ninth Avenue, New York, is spoken of by the eminent English surgeon Erichsen as the most complete medical charity he has ever seen. It is near the Central Park and the Hudson River, in a situation both quiet and salubrious. The

laboratory, in which all the drugs used are prepared; a very complete operating theatre; and small wards for patients requiring special accommodations. The barrack ward is devoted solely to the reception of acute surgical cases, and contains thirty-six beds, arranged two by two on each side of the interspaces between the windows. It has an open basement, and a large ventilating space between the ceiling and the roof. Dr. Erichsen also stated, in his address on American surgery before the University College of London, that every appliance which modern science has discovered securing ventilation, cleanliness, and warmth has been introduced into it, and he recommends the adoption of the Roosevelt model in England. The garden contains, besides the

made by atomizing a weak solution, in which his hands, instruments, sponges, are also immersed. The blood-vessels are tied by carbolized cords, the edges of the wound closed by carbolized stitches, and, finally, layers of

THE ROOSEVELT HOSPITAL.

barrack ward, an isolated hut for the reception of erysipelas cases; and in summer, when the flowers and shrubs are blooming, it is much frequented by the convalescent patients. Sixteen hundred and seventeen cases were treated in 1876, 1451 of which were free; 602 were Americans, and 558 were Irish. The death rate of all the cases treated is nine per cent., or more than three per cent. less than that of Bellevue.

The hospital is particularly interesting to the profession from the fact that it was the first in this country to adopt, through the exertions of Dr. Robert F. Wier, the antiseptic method of treating wounds invented by Joseph Lister, a celebrated Scottish surgeon. This method, which has been developed by years of patient research, and has almost revolutionized surgery, is based on the experience that the inflammation which follows a wound, such as an amputation, is due to the decomposition of the discharges that are always formed on any cut surface. The substances formed by the decomposition give rise to erysipelas, hospital gangrene, etc., or they may be absorbed by the system with fatal result. Lister believes he has demonstrated that the cause of the putrefaction is due to the lodgment on the wound-secretions of minute living bodies floating in the air, and he discovered, after trying many other disinfectants, that carbolic acid would kill these germs. The principle, therefore, consists in surrounding a wound from its reception to its cure with an atmosphere charged with the vapor of the acid; and to accomplish this the surgeon operates amid a thin cloud of spray

gauze impregnated with carbolic acid and resin are bound over the wound and a considerable part of the adjoining skin, the resin causing the carbolic acid to be evolved slowly, so that the dressing need not be changed for several days. Dr. Wier considers the success of the method proven, and states that by its use the mortality resulting from serious operations has been noticeably reduced, and that under it the closure of the most serious wounds is truly wonderful.

The Roosevelt Hospital was the last gift of James H. Roosevelt to humanity. He made it the sole legatee of a princely fortune, with the exception of a few bequests to individuals; and as he left no near relatives, the heir-looms of his house are stored in the trustees' room, and his body rests under a plain monument in the garden, with the inscription over it: "Upright in his aims, simple in his habits, and sublime in his benefaction." The hospital is admirably managed by Dr. Horatio Paine, the gentlemanly superintendent; and there is no limit to the charity it dispenses, except in the extent of its funds.

We have not purposed being exhaustive, knowing that to be impossible within our space; and there are many hospitals in the city, such as the Presbyterian and the Mount Sinai, which for their extent and excellence of work deserve attention. The Fruit and Flower missions should also be remembered; but the most we have been able to do has been to describe some of the phases of hospital life by selecting representative institutions.

Rapid Transit in New York City (1910)

THE NEW PENNSYLVANIA RAILROAD STATION IN NEW YORK.

Rapid Transit in New York City

BY HENRY IRVING DODGE

IT is said that William H. Vanderbilt, when asked to subscribe to the building of the elevated railroad in New York, answered, "Nobody will go upstairs to take a train."

With what marked accuracy the prophecy of that far-seeing man—if, indeed, he really made any—is fulfilled, is shown by the fact that more than 800,000 persons mount stairs to take trains in this city every day. And as many more go "down stairs" to take trains. Nor does the subway seem appreciably to have cut into the business of the elevated. To the casual observer, the latter appears to be doing no smaller a traffic than before the existence of its rival. During rush hours the elevated trains are run with such frequency as almost to tread on one another's heels—and packed at that—an endless chain, marked at regular intervals by the colored headlights. The wonder then is how the hordes who habitually take the subway used to travel before that system went into operation. Probably many of the patrons of the elevated

road were diverted from that route, but nowhere near enough to account for the number that travel to and fro on the underground. Nor does the enormous growth of the city adequately explain the vast amount of subway patronage. To be sure, the subway penetrates the remote fastnesses of the Bronx, catching the ebb and flood of daily travel from that quarter. But the people up there used to go back and forth before this route was built. Also the facilities for surface travel have been greatly developed and extended. Be this as it may, the significant fact remains that the underground road is today preparing to extend its platforms to accommodate ten-car instead of eight-car trains.

At first there was much speculation as to the effect of subterranean travel on the health of the passengers. People complained of disagreeable odors, stuffiness, and the like, and even today individual patrons may be found who do not enthusiastically endorse existing conditions. But the New Yorker is adaptable. He had his growl, and then resigned himself to the inevitable. But in all fairness, one must admit that the company did not turn a deaf ear to complaints. Concessions were made in the matter of ventilation. Where available, sidewalks were slatted to let in the air, and rules against carrying lighted cigars, pipes or the unspeakable cigaret were effectively carried out.

To facilitate the loading and unloading of trains and to protect passengers, special policemen, paid by the company and reporting to the Police Commissioner, are assigned for duty at points of greatest congestion. But tho these austere and uniformed personages rarely do more than walk about, there is no question that the moral influence of their presence is effective. Still, a policeman is like a gun, seldom needed, but when needed—needed badly.

When the building of the subway was contemplated, it was estimated that this road would carry some 400,000 passengers per day. But so kindly did the people take to this method of travel, that within a few months after its completion it was running pretty close up to the original estimate of business. In other words, it carried during the year included between January 1 and December 31, 1905, no fewer than 116,209,313 passengers—roughly speaking, 318,000 per day. During the following year 149,-778,370 persons were transported by this route, while in 1907 182,559,990 patrons availed of its services. In 1908, the road carried 220,991,212 passengers, a daily average of 605,455, or 50 per cent. over and above the dreams of the prophets.

On one day, during the Hudson-Fulton celebration, more than a million persons traveled one way or another by this route, but this can hardly be considered a criterion, either of capacity or facility, since conditions were abnormal. One ordinary business day—November 26 of the present year—866,554 passengers traveled by the subway, while those transported under similar conditions for one day on the elevated system numbered 863,921. However, as a rule, the subterranean route carries from 15,000 to 20,000 passengers fewer per day than the elevated; but it is of greatly inferior mileage. The fact that the subway gives its rival so keen a contest and allows it

so small a margin of superiority of absolute business will be appreciated when one considers that the elevated system has altogether over 118 miles of single track.

The subway might be measured thus: The distance from the bridge to Ninety-sixth street being covered by four tracks may be resolved into two double track roads, and so the Broadway and West Farms routes may be considered independently. The distance from the bridge to the Bronx terminal is 13.46 miles, while from the bridge along the west prong of the fork to 242d street is 14.17 miles. The distance from Atlantic avenue, Brooklyn, covered by double track, to Brooklyn Bridge, Manhattan, is 3.25 miles—a total of 30.78 miles of double track. Some three track portions, sidings and turnouts bring the total single track mileage of the subway up to 82 miles. About 16 miles of this is built in the open on a regular elevated structure.

This makes particularly interesting the opinion of Mr. Bion J. Arnold, special consulting engineer of the Public Service Commission. Mr. Arnold says that a subway under New York conditions costs approximately three times as much to build as the present elevated road, and should handle considerably more traffic than one of the latter of corresponding length. It should, therefore, be apparent that subways be constructed only where the traffic be of sufficient density to justify so expensive a type of road.

During the first fiscal year after the beginning of operation the car mileage (by a car mile is meant one car moving one mile) of the subway was 31,931,073. The following year this increased to 37,-184,940, and for the fiscal year ending June 30, 1908, it was 44,005,213. The earnings for the fiscal year of 1906 from transportation and other sources were $7,052,012; for 1907, $8,506,923.61; for 1908, $10,253,337.37. The total operating expenses for these years were $2,-978,109.35, $3,883,369.68, $4,423,313.27, respectively, the net earnings being $4,-073,902.65, $4,623,553.93, $5,830,024.10 for the same years.

It is amazing that a transportation company can carry a passenger seventeen or more miles for five cents. Respecting this, Mr. Arnold claims that each passenger should pay at the rate of a cent a mile in order to make a comprehensive subway system yield a fair return on the

only possible way to offset losses due to passengers riding from ten to fifteen miles for five cents," says Mr. Arnold, "is to furnish a local service which will

THE WAITING ROOM IN THE NEW PENNSYLVANIA STATION.

investment. Passengers carried more than five miles and contributing less than one cent a mile each must be balanced by others traveling less than that distance and thus paying more per mile. "The

attract a greater number of passengers who will ride comparatively short distances on a five cent fare. This short haul business will not be an advantage, however, unless it can be handled in short haul cars, can be accommodated by cars which otherwise would run empty, or can be handled by means of moving platforms at a lower cost per passenger than by train operation. It is a matter of every day observation that there is a large amount of short haul passenger business available in the down town district of Manhattan which is not at present accommodated by the surface or elevated systems, and it is this kind of traffic

twenty-four persons crowded into the two vestibules, and eighteen riding in one vestibule, while uncommon, is not extraordinary. As a matter of fact, a thousand persons to an eight-car train during the busiest hour of the day is no uncommon thing.

Surely there must be some exceptional advantage to outweigh the inconvenience of traveling thru a tube, packed like herring, and with no diverting landscape.

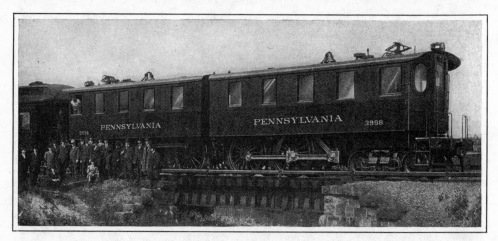

NEW PENNSYLVANIA ELECTRIC ENGINES FOR THE TUNNEL SYSTEM.

which would produce relatively the largest net returns for a subway system."

That unlooked-for business far exceeding the original estimate is coming to the subway is manifested by the action of the company in extending its facilities for handling traffic. The extended platforms will accommodate two more cars. These cars are some fifty-one feet long by eight feet seven inches wide, and seat fifty-two passengers each. It is almost impossible during any hour of the twenty-four to ride from one end of the route to the other without being in a well-filled, if not crowded, car during some period of the journey. So great is the traffic that altho the company runs some thirty-four express and as many local trains per hour during the rush time, it is no uncommon thing to see, besides two lines of strap-hangers, dangling from above and twisting and bobbing and knocking their knees against those of the sitters, and occasionally tumbling into their laps, an interior line from one end of the car to the other. One often sees

The unfortunate thing is, Manhattan Island is so fashioned that people have to live at remote distances from their places of business. And when one considers that persons may travel from Atlantic avenue, Brooklyn, away across Manhattan Island and into the fastnesses of the Bronx—some seventeen or eighteen miles—in fifty minutes and for five cents, he must admit that there is little to growl at. But he does growl, for all of that!

Notwithstanding the strenuous treatment to which passengers are subjected, to the strain of standing for a long time, and to the comparative lack of ventilation, almost no sickness results from traveling in the subway. As a matter of fact, standing up may be beneficial to many persons who have to remain seated during the day, and swinging around and twisting on the strap is the only exercise many of them get.

The engineers of the road are constantly studying up improvements in the handling of passengers. There is no limit to the capacity of the roadbed. But, obviously, trains cannot be run at much shorter intervals. Therefore, the length of the train is to be increased. But with a longer train comes the danger of even greater congestion. To obviate this, side door cars have been introduced to some extent. It is believed by adopting this method of egress, the time devoted to getting a train into and out of the station may be reduced to thirty seconds.

At present the traveling public doesn't quite know how to avail itself of this particular kind of side door, and unfortunately there aren't enough policemen at the congested points to regulate the use of them. It is natural for persons to

The great McAdoo system of tunnels connecting New York and New Jersey is apparently being used by numbers more than sufficient to justify its construction. That portion of the system which runs from Hoboken to Twenty-third street, New York, began operating in February, 1908; the other portion, running from Jersey City to the Hudson-Terminal, July, 1909. About ten miles of tracks are now in use by this system. There are four single tubes under the river. On the Jersey side is a transverse tunnel extending over a mile along shore beneath the tracks of the Pennsylvania, Erie and Lackawanna railroads, with entrances to each station. In Manhattan, the company is pushing its tunnel up

A STATION IN THE NEW YORK SUBWAY.

dash for any opening they see in a subway train, and this they do. Therefore, it is probable that once these doors are applied to all cars, the public will require some little educating before their beneficent efficiency will have been fully attained.

Sixth avenue, and will presently cut under the corner of Bryant Park and connect with the subway at the Grand Central depot. In New Jersey, the system is extending its lines, and within a year will be running trains to and from Newark.

NEW YORK CITY.

In the New York City Subway (1909)

IN THE NEW YORK SUBWAY.

PICTURES BY G. W. PETERS.

Drawn by G. W. Peters.   Half-tone plate engraved by C. W. Chadwick

A TRAIN-DESPATCHER

SWITCH-STATION AT BOWLING GREEN ENTRANCE TO EAST RIVER TUNNEL

The operator at the electric switchboard controls all switches connecting with the tunnel and the Battery Park loop. The illuminated tunnel indicator shows by a red light the exact position of a train after leaving either Brooklyn or New York. In case of an emergency, the operator can stop a train at any point. The telephone in the background connects with a series of others through the tunnel which are used by inspectors and track-walkers.

Drawn by G. W. Peters.   Half-tone plate engraved by H. C. Merrill

A TRACK-WALKER

Drawn by G. W. Peters.   Half-tone plate engraved by H. C. Merrill

A THEATER PARTY WAITING FOR A TRAIN